Claudio confronts Benedick with a sonnet in his handwriting as proof of his love for Beatrice. By permission of the Folger Shakespeare Library.

SEXUALITY IN THE AGE OF SHAKESPEARE

W. Reginald Rampone, Jr.

THE AGE OF SHAKESPEARE

AN IMPRINT OF ABC-CLIO, LLC
Santa Barbara, California • Denver, Colorado • Oxford, England

Library of Congress Cataloging-in-Publication Data

Rampone, W. Reginald.
Sexuality in the age of Shakespeare / W. Reginald Rampone, Jr.
p. cm. — (The age of Shakespeare)
Includes bibliographical references and index.
ISBN 978-0-313-34375-9 (acid-free paper) — ISBN 978-0-313-34376-6 (ebook)
1. Shakespeare, William, 1564–1616—Criticism and interpretation. 2. Sex in literature. 3. Sex role in literature. I. Title.
PR3069.S45R36 2011
822.3'3—dc22 2011008461

ISBN: 978-0-313-34375-9
EISBN: 978-0-313-34376-6

15 14 13 12 11 1 2 3 4 5

This book is also available on the World Wide Web as an eBook.
Visit www.abc-clio.com for details.

Greenwood
An Imprint of ABC-CLIO, LLC

ABC-CLIO, LLC
130 Cremona Drive, P.O. Box 1911
Santa Barbara, California 93116-1911

This book is printed on acid-free paper ∞

Manufactured in the United States of America

CONTENTS

PREFACE

Sexuality in the Age of Shakespeare is intended largely as a reference book whose function is to introduce the topic of sexuality in Shakespeare's plays and poetry to advanced high school students, undergraduates, and a literate general public. *Sexuality in the Age of Shakespeare*'s primary concerns are the theatrical, cinematic, and academic reception and interpretation of Shakespeare's plays and poetry largely within the last 200 years. This text in no way presumes to be exhaustive in its survey of theatrical productions, motion pictures, or literary interpretations of these plays and poetry, but rather its intention is to give college students as well as the general public an overview of English and various European countries' social customs as they relate to marriage and sexuality as a context against which to understand Shakespeare's plays and poems.

In the introduction to the "Background" section, I survey the various reasons historians propose as to why sexuality developed as it did in Greek culture, especially regarding homosexuality, a term which some historians caution us about using because the ancient Greeks that we encounter at the Parthenon understood the issue of sexuality and its inherent power dynamics differently than we do today or even those who lived in medieval and early modern England and Europe for that matter. Therefore, we need to think about sexuality in their terms rather than ours.

Analogously, the ancient Romans too understood sexuality in much the same terms as the Greeks. We learn that the sexual dynamics in Roman sexual relations as in Greek revolved around the dichotomy of passivity and dominance. Freeborn youth were closely watched so that their social status would not be violated by any untoward sexual actions. Therefore, the Lex Scatinia was passed so that the sexual behavior of its citizens would be controlled, particularly same-sex practices. At the same time Rome did allow for female and male prostitution.

With the arrival of Christianity, the Catholic church's clerics changed sexual practices so that there were now prescribed times during which married couples were allowed to engage in sexual relations as these regulations were promulgated through religious manuals. Church councils met throughout the Middle Ages where bishops determined how and when people were permitted to consummate their marriage as well as how to manage their marriages.

In "Sexuality in Shakespeare's World," we survey the extraordinary effect of the Protestant Reformation on Europe and England in terms of marriage and sexuality. Martin Luther for one did not believe in a celibate clergy, for he believed that sexual relations were very important to marriage. Parental support of an upcoming marriage was also very important to Protestants. We also discuss how the Protestant clergy also wanted to control or regulate sexual behavior through a court system that would work in conjunction with civil courts. These kinds of courts emerged all over Europe, and their job was to regulate marital problems such as infidelity, divorce, and even domestic violence. Although adultery can be an embarrassment in today's society as well as a costly legal battle, in early modern Europe adultery, specifically in Germany and Geneva, death could be the penalty for engaging in sexual relations with a man or woman who was not one's spouse. Those who engaged in prostitution, sodomy, and fornication were treated differently depending upon their sex.

We then cross the English Channel to learn of the importance of marriage manuals to ensure a well-governed household. Many marriage manuals were available, and again the writers stressed the need to control one's wife so that she would comport herself in such a way that was in keeping with the behavior of a good Christian woman. Historians suggest that these marriage manuals are representative of the social values of the emergent middle class, but there was disagreement among the divines as to how a husband was to control his wife's actions; one might find corporeal punishment undesirable but unavoidable while another would eschew it altogether. Finally, we discuss the various marriage rituals of early modern England.

In "Sexuality in Shakespeare's Works" we discuss how erotic images or references act to sexualize the setting and the characters in various plays and poems. This chapter provides an overview of a representative number of comedies, a history, tragedies, and a romance in order to indicate the degree to which eroticized classical imagery played a significant role. We consider *The Taming of the Shrew*, which is commonly thought of as a play filled with rambunctious characters, and while that may be true, it also is replete with classical references such as Adonis, Cythera, and Io, among others. In Shakespeare's sonnet sequence of 154 sonnets, the persona critiques the Elizabethan sonnet tradition with his intensely homoerotic relationship with the fair, young man with whom the poet has an amorous relationship and then the intensely eroticized relationship that the poet has with the Dark Lady in the last 27 sonnets.

Romeo and Juliet provides students with the seminal love story of the Western world with its multiple references to Cupid and Diana. *A Midsummer Night's Dream* is also filled with young lovers who face obstacles in the pursuit of love and classical allusions such as Philomela. Unlike *A Midsummer Night's Dream*, *Much Ado about Nothing* has only two sets of lovers, one young and immature and another older and seasoned in the affairs of the heart, but the experienced couple is more skeptical about the nature of love until, of course, they are duped by their friends and family. By contrast, the world of Mistress Quickly's tavern in which Falstaff, Hal, and his cronies exist is far removed from the magical world of mischievous Puck and the four young lovers. Hotspur, Hal's antagonist, and his wife occasion the only space in which serious eroticism enters the action of the play.

In *Hamlet* we move to a tragic world in which we meet the unfortunate prince who must confront his mother Gertrude regarding her extraordinarily hasty marriage to his uncle Claudius after the murder of his father, whom he compares to the sun god Hyperion by way of comparison to Claudius, whom he likens to a satyr. In *Othello* the damned villain Iago convinces his commander Othello that his innocent wife Desdemona is guilty of adultery. Despite the fact the play begins with the marriage of Desdemona to Othello, once Iago makes insinuations of infidelity about Desdemona to Othello, all romance is removed from the drama.

Finally, in *The Tempest* a fairy tale romance comes to fruition with the marriage of Ferdinand and Miranda; not only are allusions to gods and goddesses made by the receptive nuptial couple, they also actually appear at the behest of Miranda's father, the magician Prospero, to bless the marriage while he reclaims his dukedom in Milan.

"Sexuality in Performance" takes up the significance of eroticism concerning the action of the drama in relation to various and sundry stage and film productions of Shakespeare's plays from the time of the earliest productions to the present. The most popular Shakespearean plays of the past are largely the ones which are still the most popular today. In *The Taming of the Shrew* the discussion in theatre histories centered on the issue of performing this play in the 20th century in which a feminist sensibility exists while the play ends with Kate's submission to the male dominated culture of Renaissance Italy represented by Petruchio.

Productions of *Romeo and Juliet* almost beggar description in their multiplicity of interpretations. Each of the productions in the 20th century bespoke the cultural moment of its time as did those in the past. To be sure, Baz Luhrmann's 1996 version mirrors the postmodern moment of the late 20th century with its extravagant costumes and outrély cross-dressed Mercutio, who functions to shock middle-class cultural sensibilities.

Productions of *A Midsummer Night's Dream* run the gamut from the diaphanously winged fairies of Max Reinhardt's 1935 version with its never-never land sensibility with Mickey Rooney as Puck and Victor Jory as Oberon to Peter Brook's 1968 version in which the actors performed in a white cube on trapeze. Inasmuch as Brook's version broke all kinds of aesthetic rules, Michael Hoffman's 1998 production recalled the extravagantly furnished sets of Reinhardt.

Unlike *A Midsummer Night's Dream*, *Much Ado about Nothing* smacks of a reality that most students can easily understand as they do not have to process four levels of experience as they must in *A Midsummer Night's Dream*. Kenneth Branagh's 1993 film version was a cinematic triumph with his portrayal of Benedick and Emma Thompson's portrayal of Beatrice that provided a directness and immediacy to which contemporary audiences could relate.

As You Like It has been hugely popular on stage since the 19th century. It has also enjoyed a cinematic history, first in Paul Czinner's 1936 film version in which

Laurence Olivier starred in his first Shakespearean film role and most recently in Kenneth Branagh's recent attempt to revive interest in *As You Like It,* which is set in 19th-century Japan with the exoticism that is designed to pique present-day culture's concern with colonialism and postcolonialism.

Henry IV, Part 1 will also receive a theatrical overview, but the history of the play will focus on film productions of recent memory such as those involving Orson Welles who performed as Falstaff in *Chimes at Midnight/Falstaff* in 1966 as well as a significant film adaptation titled *My Own Private Idaho* directed by Gus Van Sant, which challenged the traditional interpretation of the role of Falstaff when he was played as an older gay man.

There are untold productions of *Hamlet,* and while we discuss older stage productions, we focus on more recent film versions of the play. Laurence Olivier's brilliant mid-20th-century film version of *Hamlet,* which came under Freudian influence, was perceived as extraordinarily important to Shakespearean film history. Franco Zeffirelli's 1990 film version, which also came under the sway of Freud, starred Mel Gibson and Glenn Close. Finally, to close out the 20th century, Branagh's monumental four-hour version with its hall of mirrors paid tribute to Olivier's own interpretation.

The discussion of *Othello* begins with its first performance at James's Banqueting Hall and its revival immediately after Charles II returned to the throne at the Restoration. Productions became racially charged in 1930 when Paul Robeson, an African American, played the role of Othello opposite Peggy Ashcroft, a British white woman. This racial tension continued into the late 1980s when Janet Suzman produced her rendition of the play in South Africa in 1987 when apartheid was still business as usual. Finally, Trevor Nunn's 1994 version is highly sexualized especially regarding the homoerotic quality of Iago's relations with other characters in the play.

Our discussion of *The Tempest* has its origins in its relation to an actual mishap at sea with the *Sea Venture* in 1609 and time spent by mariners on an island. The play underwent multiple permutations as it was cut and adapted to 18th- and 19th-century cultural sensibilities. The 20th century gave rise to a Freudian interpretation of this text as it did so many others with Caliban and Ariel representing certain aspects of one's psyche. By the end of the 20th century, the punk movement began to make its presence known in productions of *The Tempest* in Ron Daniel's stage version in 1982 and Derek Jarman's far more radical queer punk film version in 1980 in which spiked hair and a great deal of frontal male nudity in addition to Miranda's bared breasts appeared. Audiences in 1991 saw an exquisite film in a high-definition adaptation, *Prospero's Books,* starring John Gielgud as Prospero, with more nudity than earlier film reviewers could ever have imagined.

The next section of the book, "Scholarship and Criticism," treats of the different interpretative approaches that scholars use to make sense of Shakespeare's plays and poems. Teachers and university professors often engage in close readings of the plays, which entail scrutinizing particular lines of verse and even individual words as to how they convey the meaning of that particular play. Around

1980 or so, scholars began to use new critical paradigms to interpret texts of all kinds. Feminist criticism and New Historicism became two of the most frequently used forms of interpretation.

Karen Newman considers *The Taming of the Shrew* in her groundbreaking essay "Renaissance Family Politics and Shakespeare's *The Taming of the Shrew*" using feminist, New Historicist, and psychoanalytic criticism. Newman uses an anecdote that involves a domestic dispute in order to contextualize the tension within the play.

In "'Death-Marked Love': Desire and Presence in *Romeo and Juliet*" Lloyd Davis focuses upon how love and death are inextricably bound together and how ultimately, desire is generated by an absence that can never be fulfilled, while Jonathan Goldberg generates a decidedly provocative interpretation with "*Romeo and Juliet*'s Open R's" in his queer treatment of this play.

In *Romeo and Juliet*'s counterpart, *A Midsummer Night's Dream*, Laura Levine makes the case in "Rape, Repetition, and the Politics of Closure in *A Midsummer Night's Dream*" that Theseus tries to use theatre as a means of metamorphosing sexualized violence, which cannot be accomplished. Throughout the play various characters make subtle and not so subtle intimations of threats of rape and sexual assault.

The Puritans, who did not like theatre for a multitude of reasons, would not have liked *A Midsummer Night's Dream*, but they would have been particularly distressed by *As You Like It*. In *As You Like It*, the character of Rosalind cross-dresses as Ganymede, a figure synonymous with same-sex eroticism in early modern England and Europe. Marjorie Garber argues in her psychoanalytic reading of the play, "The Education of Orlando," that Orlando undergoes three stages of emotional development before he is prepared to have a mature relationship with Rosalind. Here the psychoanalytic aspect of Orlando's changes in personality is the focus of the essay while Valerie Traub, in "The Homoerotics of Shakespearean Comedy," discusses how the transvestism, as she calls it rather than cross-dressing, puts into motion a circulation of homoerotic desire because of Viola and Rosalind's wearing of men's clothing.

From *Twelfth Night* and the realm of gender undecidability, we move to the realm of Messina in *Much Ado about Nothing*. In the significant article "'The Sign and Semblance of Her Honor': Reading Gender and Difference in *Much Ado about Nothing*," Carol Cook discusses how masculine power is enacted throughout the play and at the same time how men manage their fear of female sexuality through jokes regarding cuckoldry, the practice of women engaging in sexual acts with men not their husbands.

Jean E. Howard and Phyllis Rackin's *Engendering a Nation: A Feminist Account of Shakespeare's Histories* makes the argument for women's significant involvement in the formation of England's affairs of state. While critics point to the limited number of female roles in what is known as the Henriad, their presence and impact in them are unmistakable.

In "Looking Well to Linens: Women and Cultural Production in *Othello* and Shakespeare's England," Dympna Callaghan focuses attention upon the production of linens as they reflect women's economic and erotic value to the community at large. Callaghan attributes tremendous sexual value to Desdemona's handkerchief as it is the most ideologically and erotically charged piece of linen in the play.

Janet Adelman, in "Man and Woman Is One Flesh: Hamlet and the Confrontation with the Maternal Body," argues ultimately that female sexuality is corrupting by its very nature and uses feminist psychoanalytic criticism as the lens through which readers and critics can understand Hamlet's relationship with Gertrude, his mother; Old Hamlet, his father; and his uncle and stepfather, Claudius.

Finally, Jyotsna Singh provides a very compelling postcolonial interpretation of *The Tempest* in "Caliban versus Miranda: Race and Gender Conflicts in Postcolonial Rewritings of *The Tempest*" in which she asserts that postcolonial theory does not take into account the difference in power dynamics concerning gender and race.

The last section of *Sexuality in the Age of Shakespeare* includes excerpts from various marriage manuals and their prescriptive advice for creating a successful marriage. I include excerpts from William Whately's *A Bridebush or a Wedding Sermon*, Alexander Niccholes's *A Discourse of Marriage and Wiving, and of the Greatest Mystery therein Contained: How to Choose a Good Wife from a Bad*, Henrie Smith's *A Preparative to Marriage*, and Robert Cleaver's *A Godly Forme of Household Government: For the Ordering of Private Families, According to the Direction of Gods Word*. Secondly, the various bibliographies contain a great number of books and journal articles about Greek, Roman, medieval and early modern English and European sexuality, marriage, and gender relations as well as many books and scholarly articles concerning Shakespeare's plays and poetry. Finally, there is a glossary that defines largely Greek and Roman terms that would be unfamiliar to nonspecialists in those fields.

ACKNOWLEDGMENTS

First and foremost I must acknowledge my undergraduate mentors, Professors Sidney M. B. Coulling, Edwin Craun, and John Evans, at Washington and Lee University, whose exemplary pedagogy and commitment to scholarship profoundly influenced my understanding of who a scholar is. At Harvard University, Professor Marjorie Beth Garber's dazzling intellect and erudition set the standard for which I should strive. At Brown University, it was my good fortune to have Professor Coppélia Kahn and Professor Karen Newman as instructors, whose extraordinary feminist readings reconceptualized my understanding of early modern English texts and changed forever how I read and understand Shakespeare's plays, and it was because of Professor Ellen Rooney's exhilarating literary theory class that I became cognizant of the multiple theoretical paradigms which could be used to make sense of sometimes maddeningly opaque texts. In a later stage of my academic development, I was blessed with meeting Professor Jean Elizabeth Howard of Columbia University, who was an invaluable outside reader on my dissertation and a constant source of encouragement and good will. I must also acknowledge the most expert assistance of librarians Betsy Walsh and Catherine Ziegler at the Folger Shakespeare Library, who were wonderfully helpful and kind to me. Closer to home, I must acknowledge Professor Peter Wiggins, distinguished scholar of English and American literature at the College of William and Mary, who was a never-ending source of sound advice and good humor during the time of this manuscript's completion in Richmond. Most significantly, I must acknowledge my mother, Louise Wilkins Rampone, who has constantly encouraged and supported my academic endeavors all these years through her extraordinary self-sacrifice, love, and concern. I am indebted to her for more gifts than I have paper on which to express my gratitude, but suffice it to say that at the time of this writing I am most thankful for the use of her 52-year-old kitchen table on which this book was written.

1

BACKGROUND

Greek and Roman literature had an extraordinary influence on the production of Shakespeare's plays and poetry. Among the plays with Greek and Roman settings and characters, six of them concern Roman history and six have a Greek context. Shakespeare's first Roman tragedy was *Titus Andronicus*, and it was followed by *Julius Caesar, Antony and Cleopatra*, *Timon of Athens*, and *Coriolanus* while *Troilus and Cressida* especially abounds in conspicuous sexuality set in the ancient period, involving the Greek and the Trojan civilizations. Audiences clearly see the presence of Greek figures in *Troilus and Cressida* in the play's eponymously titled characters of the Trojan War in addition to the homoerotic relationship of Achilles and Patroclus, which is included in the *Iliad*. The Roman plays tend to be more realistic than the Greek ones. The anachronisms are quite amusing, with Hector speaking of Aristotle and Pandarus speaking of Friday and Saturday (Highet 194 and 197).

Shakespeare, however, had greater mastery over Roman than Greek topics. Although Greek drama is certainly more widely celebrated and performed in the 20th and 21st centuries than Roman drama, the English Renaissance writers were far more conversant with Roman plays. They were certainly familiar with Seneca's drama, for his plays had been translated by 1559, and they had been completely translated by 1581 (Highet 198). Finally, eroticized classical references also abound in "Venus and Adonis" and "The Rape of Lucrece," two narrative poems.

The great majority of Shakespeare's plays are set in the late medieval period and early modern Europe (Highet 194). In *As You Like It*, the heroine Rosalind cross-dresses and takes the name of Ganymede, the Greek youth that attracts Zeus, when she escapes into the Forest of Arden, and then at the conclusion of the play, Hymen, the Greek god of marriage, appears to bless her marriage to Orlando. *Much Ado about Nothing*, too, abounds with references to classical figures; when Benedick laments his inability to write sonnets praising Beatrice, he claims that he is not Troilus, Leander, or any other famous lover from ancient Greece or Rome who was quite capable of penning sonnets in honor of his beloved. These classical allusions are constant reminders of the significance of Greek and Roman figures to early modern writers' notions of love, sexuality, and romance. Otherwise, the character of Benedick would never have mentioned them. Finally, in *The Tempest,* the last play of which Shakespeare was the sole author, Prospero conjures up the goddesses Juno, Iris, and Ceres in a masque in order for them to bless Miranda and Ferdinand's upcoming marriage. Shakespeare used Greek and Roman narratives in order to generate engaging and compelling play texts, texts that, while using Greek and Roman characters, reflected the cultural mores of his own day, refashioning them in order to represent early modern England's notions of love, marriage, and sexuality in its time.

Perforce Shakespeare's use of Greek and Roman allusions emerged from his own educational background. One must acknowledge the immense importance of Roman drama by Plautus and Terence on the early modern European curriculum. Jacques Peletier du Mans noted that in 1555 Terence's plays were in everyone's hands. In England Plautus as well as Terence was popular in Latin studies in grammar school. Students were to learn linguistics, morality, and rhetoric from these Roman texts. Despite the social utility of these texts, they were also contested ideologically as these plays have characters who express greed, lust, and duplicity. Nonetheless, Alexander Novall argued at Westminster School in approximately 1545 that prologues to Terence's comedies could be morally enlightening. In fact, Erasmus, who was preeminently knowledgeable of these plays, considered Terence's plays the best texts that instructors could use to teach students Latin style, and even the objectionable sections could prove of educational value to them.

Consequently, Shakespeare availed himself of these texts either in the original Latin or through translations. After all, Shakespeare would have translated some of these Roman dramas as a student at his grammar school in Stratford-upon-Avon. Therefore, Shakespeare used the New Comedy tradition in order to fill his plays with certain types of characters such as the senex, the virgo, the servus, the miles glorious, the parasitus, the matrona, the adulescens, and finally, the meretrix, who translate into the "blocking father, his daughter, her lover, the clever slave and master, the unfortunate lover and worldly courtesan" (Miola 3–5). This study will, therefore, focus upon the eroticized figures of Greek and Roman civilization and how they were integrated within William Shakespeare's early modern English plays and poems at the end of the 16th century and the beginning of the 17th as well as how sexuality functions as a mode of erotic interaction among the characters in his plays and poetry in dramatic productions, films, and literary criticism.

Thus said, one must also remember that the Greeks and the Romans understood sexuality much differently from the Elizabethans and certainly much differently from those living in the early 21st century. Sexuality was defined by one's erotic interactions with another individual in a demonstrable fashion; therefore, the expression "sexual orientation" would have been a meaningless term for anyone living in ancient Greece or Rome or Elizabethan England for that matter. In fact, the word "sexuality" did not even exist; the word first came into existence in the early 19th century. Joseph Bristow cites the first recorded use of the term in

1836 in a collection of poems written by William Cowper (3). Citing the *Oxford English Dictionary*, Merry Wiesner-Hanks asserts, "'Sexuality,' defined as 'the constitution or life of the individual as related to sex' or 'the possession or exercise of sexual functions, desires, etc,' first appears in English only in 1800, and its use signals the beginning of 'modern sexuality.' Because of its recent origin some historians choose to avoid the word 'sexuality' when discussing earlier periods. . . . They point out that ancient Greek and medieval Latin did not even have words for 'sex' or 'sexual'" (3). The etymology of the word "sexuality" provides the cultural history of the word. In other words, Wiesner-Hanks suggests that we cannot impose late 19th- and 20th-century concepts of sexuality onto societies and cultures that did not understand sexual relations in the same way as modern Western society does now.

Terms relating to particular sexualities arrived even later in the English lexicon. Joseph Laurin makes the point that the word "homosexuality" was not even coined until 1869 in German by Karl Maria Kerbeny and in English by Charles Gilbert Chaddock in 1892 (17). The actual citations of the words "homosexuality" and "heterosexuality" that appear in the *OED Supplement* were chosen from a very famous study titled *Psychopathia Sexualis* by the Austrian researcher Richard von Krafft-Ebing. These terms were first used at the turn of the 20th century regarding medical and psychological studies of individuals. Given the fact that these terms entered the English language at such a late date and would be inapplicable to earlier times, David Halperin and Jeffrey Weeks argue that sexuality must be contextualized within its own historical moment in order to be understood as it should (Bristow 5).

In order to understand how Greeks understood their sexuality, one must first know how they understood the concept of gender. According to Charles Freeman, marriage was the most important time in a Greek woman's life. Men married girls between 10 and 15 years younger than they were, and it was at this time that they entered their husbands' homes. Men were to marry between the ages of 28 and 35, which is the age range that Solon, the lawgiver, suggested. People believed that it was better for women to give birth young rather than when they were older. Also it was commonly believed that sexual relations would make life emotionally easier for them. The family of the bride provided the dowry, and one's marital choice was made from within a small group of families (177–78). Eva Cantarella argues that women in Homeric society could walk freely about by themselves, within the city and outside while they were single or married; however, it was from the eighth or seventh century that women could not interact with Greek men (5). Emile Mireaux asserts that women of wealth or position usually had female attendants with them when they walked about the city in the age of Homer. He further suggests that later, however, women were not to leave their home unless they planned to go to a festival, to buy goods, or to attend religious activities (206).

To be sure the spheres of masculinity and femininity were clearly defined within the Athenian home. Mireaux comments upon the division of spheres of influence within the home, for the women's apartments were separate from the men's. For example, Odysseus's wife, Penelope, spent time in her *thalamos*, which was her private chamber, located above the *megaron*, or hall of honor, which was reached by a stairway. Boys no longer slept in their mothers' rooms after the age of seven, and so their rooms were arranged around the court while the girls' rooms were in the center of the house near their mothers' chambers. Those who were affluent had chambermaids to guard their daughters' rooms (206).

By the same token, men had chambers which were designated as their own as well; for example, in Homer's household, the male was clearly in charge of the *megaron* (Garrison 112). Since women ate in their rooms, they were denied the opportunity to interact with male guests in the *megaron* where banquets were held. According to Herodotus at Miletus, women never ate with their husbands even up to the fifth century (Mireaux 207).

These separately gendered spheres of influence were maintained throughout the ancient period. The *andron* was the men's banqueting hall and its adjoining rooms, and the *gynaikon* was the women's apartments. The structure of domestic as well as public life was designed to keep men and women separate from each other, and this practice significantly demarcated the erotic aspect of Greek culture (Garrison 113).

Just as spatial arrangements signaled domesticity as with the *thalamus* versus the *megaron*, where the lord of the manor held sway, so too did clothes function to demarcate the gender differences of men and women. William Harlan Hall describes men and women's attire as essentially one basic piece of clothing, which was held in place and girdled, the chiton or tunic. Sometimes Greek women or men held the lined piece of cloth at the shoulder with a brooch, and it was sewn on one side. For women the garment was gathered at the waist and allowed to hang to their ankles, but men wore it at their knee (Hall 178).

Men enjoyed far greater sexual freedom than women, for they wore no undergarments. Women, however, wore a slip and a breast band or a primitive form of brassiere. They wore sandals and covered their heads with felt hats while walking on dusty roads, and in order to keep warm they wore a light cloak called a himation, and on occasion men would not bother to wear a chiton under their himation, and this would cause embarrassing moments at banquets when the himation would rise above the knee at a banquet in the *andron*. Apparently, men in ancient Greece felt quite comfortable with their bodies exposed, especially at sporting events and baths where they stripped. Thus, the cult of the beautiful male body was born. Yet the Greeks felt quite differently about female nudity as uncovered female bodies were not permitted (Hall 178–79).

Rather than the Greeks' mode of attire or government intriguing modern Western culture, 20th- and 21st-century society is most curious about the ancient Greek civilization's modes of sexual expression, especially their homosexuality and bisexuality, terms which would have had no meaning to the ancient Greeks. As Laurin points out, homosexuality was a prevalent cultural practice, but only male homosexuality influenced its society, not lesbianism; the Greek populace recognized and accepted homosexuality; men generally ignored lesbianism or did not wish to be cognizant of it or simply did not care (59). Some historians have attempted to ferret out the origin of homosexuality in Greek culture. Cultural historians have many theories, but none of them is definitive. Cantarella asserts that homosexuality predates the Homeric period, going back to the tribal past; at this time the organization of society was not yet political but based upon age difference (5–6). In a word, Cantarella thinks that homosexual relations began as a ritual into adulthood. The boy would live with a man during this period of separation while the older male would act as both educator and lover (6).

Cantarella further cites Erich Bethe, who felt that the Greeks thought that the sexual relationship between the man and the boy would transfer masculine virtues from the man to the boy through the seminal fluid of the older man (8). She concludes that regardless of the origin of homosexuality that it is sufficient to know that these erotic encounters between the man and the boy functioned within their culture as a rite of initiation into adulthood. The young man would go on to take his place within society through marriage in which he would give up this formerly passive role with the older man and acquire an active one with his wife, and later he would perpetuate this rite of initiation when he would later take as his lover a young male in whom he would instill the salient characteristics of a responsible Athenian citizen (Cantarella 8).

Pederastic relationships were memorialized and commemorated in verse by Greek poets. One such poet, Theognis, who lived in the sixth or seventh century, wrote 1,400 elegiac poems, most of which praise the attributes of honor and integrity from times' past (Bertman 30). Theognis's poetry concerns both heterosexual and homosexual relationships, but most of his poetry is comprised of erotic elegies that pertain to the pederastic practices of the aristocracy that are shown in "Horses and Boys" in verses 1249–52 and 1267–70 in Bertman's collection. Quite clearly, the persona of this poem bemoans the ingratitude of the youth for whom he has cared and provided physical comfort. The speaker perceives no difference between the attitude of a horse and this young man because both of them will treat whoever is caring for them in the same fashion. It makes no difference who provides for them.

While homosexual relations with youth were supposed to prepare them to become responsible citizens, same-sex relations also provided some form of physical solace for those away from home while they were in the armed services. This was a prevalent means of sexual expression among the men from Sparta, Thebes, and Athens. In fact, Plato actually encourages such activities (Laurin 64). Therefore, the presence of one's lover was perceived as a bonus while in war, for they would fight their best in order to protect each other while in battle.

When we encounter the relationship of Achilles and Patroclus, who are known for their military prowess, within the *Iliad*, one immediately notices an intense affection between them. After Patroclus's death at the hands of Hector, Achilles becomes inconsolable; as Marilyn Skinner points out, "The hero's subsequent hysterical reaction to the news of his friend's death, his fanatical thirst for revenge, and his persistent grief and sleeplessness even after Patroclus is buried seemed no less excessive to ancient critics. Modern readers are also struck by the constant embracing and touching of the corpse, his self-confessed longing (pothos, 19.32021, a word often found in erotic contexts) for the dead man, his stern refusal of food and drink and his mother Thetis' consoling advice," who suggests that it would be good for him to love a woman (*Sexuality in Greek and Roman Culture* 43).

Garrison, too, opines about the relationship of Patroclus and Achilles and its relation to the warrior culture of the ancient Greeks. The Greeks tended to represent Achilles and Patroclus and the assemblage as an army in Thebes of an entire corps of male lovers, which was referred to as the Sacred Band of Thebes. After all, this culture produced its earliest epic which comprised an elite warrior class that revolved around male companions (61). What is very intriguing about their relationship is that Achilles, while younger than Patroclus, was certainly the dominant partner in the relationship, which Halperin believes would have mystified their own contemporaries (Skinner *Sexuality in Greek and Roman Culture* 44). At the same time this reversal of roles may have been perceived as a subversion of the power dynamics within the relationship.

Interestingly, there is no reference to pederasty in Homer's *Iliad* and *Odyssey*. According to Marilyn Skinner, pederasty defines "the social custom whereby adult male Greeks courted citizen youths as sexual objects" (10). The Greeks used the terms "erastes ('lover') for the adult male and eromenos ('beloved') for the youth" (*Sexuality in Greek and Roman Culture* 10). Skinner makes the point of clarifying the highly ambiguous term of youth. She suggests that Greek men became interested in other males from the time "of [their] secondary sexual characteristics at puberty until the growth of the full beard, an approximate age range of fifteen or sixteen to eighteen. Younger boys, though, were not off-limits" (*Sexuality in Greek and Roman Culture* 11). Laurin's critique of pederasty is consonant with Skinner's in that he, too, asserts that the Greeks believed that it was best for pederastic relationships to begin at the age of 15 and end at the age of 18 when the youth had a full beard, but that it was "reprehensible" for the boy to be younger than the age of 12 (Laurin 76).

Laurin also approves of Cantarella's critique of the educational system of young women because she clearly differentiated between the role of the lover in the homosexual relationships of boys and girls. Male youth had adult lovers for the purpose of furthering their education into manhood (125). The *thiasoi*, however, were women who lived in groups, and these groups were not limited to only those on Lesbos, which is the apparent origination of the word "lesbian" (Cantarella 79). On the island of Lesbos the figure of Sappho, a poet, emerged in the sixth century. She was the head of these women's associations, which provided young women with the skills and experiences that would prepare them for adulthood, which was somewhat analogous to the experiences that men had in male groups. These young women were taught how to sing, dance, and play a musical instrument so that they would be cultivated, but they were also taught how to use their beauty and seduction in order to become erotic objects of desire, but perhaps more importantly they would become desirable women whom men would wish to marry (79).

Although some of the Greeks' sexual practices may be unacceptable to many individuals living today, there were some, in fact, which disturbed Greek culture as well. Generally speaking, first, Greek culture was condemnatory of only the passive member of the same-sex male relationship because Greek culture disapproved of passivity in men. The role of the passive male caused contestation, tension, and hypocrisy (Cantarella 46). Secondly, prostitutes were held in contempt as might be expected by members of Greek culture, and there were two kinds of prostitutes. Skinner asserts, "Women who provided sex for money were designated by one of two nouns: pornai ('whores') and hetairai (literally 'companions')" (98). The men who frequented the *pornai* were largely those from the lower classes, but the *hetairai* might have two or three men with whom they met on a regular basis (98). While the *pornai* may have stood in a doorway presenting themselves for sale, the *hetairai* went to the symposium or were hired to entertain (Skinner 98). Analogously, there were two kinds of male prostitutes as well, also called the *hetairai* and the *pornai*. The *pornai* met for impromptu erotic encounters and received disapproval by the populace, and, therefore, they had to meet a particular legal regulation. Only the *pornos* was placed on special lists and was required to pay a tax called the *pornikon telos* (Cantarella 49). Apparently, the Greeks had a hierarchy of prostitutes analogous to their hierarchy of governmental offices.

Just as Greeks engaged in homosexual relations so too did the Romans, but the Romans did not wish to take responsibility for its introduction into Italy. Therefore, the Romans referred to pederasty as the "Greek vice," but of course, Roman adult males pursued youth just as the Greeks did (Cantarella 97). Skinner argues that in Latin literature the paradigm of sexual relations seems very much like the sexual relations prevailing in Greek art and literature from the Archaic to the Hellenistic period, which revolved around the polarity of dominance and passivity in relationships (195). Cantarella supports this thesis in that Roman power was directed toward dominance in relations with others (*Sexuality in Greek and Roman Culture* 98). At the same time Cantarella proposes that the pederasty which the Greeks practiced would never have been tolerated by the Romans because of the amount of time, energy, and effort required on the part of the adult lover in order to nurture the youth into a mature, responsible citizen. According to Cantarella, the practice of pederasty necessitated that the older male lover spend a great deal of time developing the youth's character and martial ability. This process would be unacceptable to an older male Roman because it would demonstrate a deficiency in his own masculinity (98). Therefore, the kind of mentoring in which Greek men engaged with Greek youth would be antithetical to the Romans' attitude toward freeborn Roman youth. Cantarella hastens to mention that this erotic relationship between the adult male and the youth was just as it was in Greece with the exception that it lacked an educational component, and this relationship with the older man would end as soon as he entered the state of marriage at which time this male was fully integrated into Roman society (125).

Moreover, one must keep in mind that in the Greek city-state known as the polis, the number of men was fairly small, and it was important that they maintained control over women, children, and slaves. Unlike Greek culture, Roman culture had greater nuances in its social hierarchy, and therefore, social status was more important in determining power relations than one's actual manhood (Skinner 195). Social class was simply of much greater significance to the Romans than to the Greeks, and so a Roman's sexual power in a relationship was largely determined by his or her place in the social hierarchy.

At the same time one does not wish to diminish the significance of the adult male body in Roman society and culture. First of all, the term *vir* did not simply define a biological male, but a male of a certain social and gender status, and this is a highly significant distinction from a *kinaidos*, a man who permitted himself to be penetrated anally (Skinner *Sexuality in Greek and Roman Culture* 212). According to Jonathan Walters, "*Vir*, therefore, did not denote an adult male; it refers specifically to those adult males who are freeborn Roman citizens at the top of the Roman social hierarchy. A term that at first appears to refer to biological sex in fact is a description of gender-as-social-status, and the gender term itself is intimately interwoven with other factors of social status (birth and citizenship status, and respectability in general) that to us might not seem relevant to gender" (*Roman Sexualities* 32). The inviolability of the freeborn Roman male's body was of the greatest concern to his identity.

Since the physiological integrity of the freeborn male body was so important, young freeborn youths were closely guarded. A freeborn youth was known as a *praetextatus* because he was not an adult male, and therefore, he held a liminal position in society. Moreover, this male youth would have attendants just as women of his social class did (Walters 35). Plutarch relates how Roman fathers protected their sons from unwanted advances by having them wear gold bullas around their necks. This bulla functioned as an index of one's social status. Apparently, it was not uncommon for sexual advances to be made toward youth, and so the urban praetor determined the regulation for the protection of the *pudicitia* (modesty or honor) not only of women but also of *praetextati*—that is, those boys who had not reached puberty (Cantarella 100).

Because Roman society was concerned about its members' sexual conduct and safety, the Lex Scatinia was enacted to control the sexual practices of its citizenry, especially homosexual behavior (Cantarella 107). Skinner argues that this law was passed so that those who transgressed sexual codes could be punished; however, there is discrepancy regarding all that the law entails. Nonetheless, it is very clear that unmarried women and boys were treated in the same fashion concerning sexual violations in that sexual relations with them was determined a sexual offense, referred to as a *stuprum*, and by the third century, authorities were calling for a "capital punishment" for those who seduced unmarried women and boys (Cantarella 199–200).

By and large, Romans thought highly of the social institution of marriage, and so it is not surprising that the Romans would have the Lex Scatinia in place. In fact, Romans, in general, felt that by having children and educating them that they were fulfilling their civic responsibilities. The *pater familias*, the Roman father, had much power and authority over his own children. He had the authority to determine whether the child would be accepted into the family at birth, who the child would marry, and even if he or she could divorce. In as much as marriage was encouraged in Republican Rome, in some instances, marriages could not take place; for example, a freeman could not marry a prostitute, an actress, a slave or freed slave, or a woman over 50 years of age despite the fact that Roman law acknowledged concubinage as an agreement in those situations or in situations in which the people concerned did not want to be married (Wiesner-Hanks 26).

The Romans provided its citizens two kinds of marriage. The power of the Roman father was known as *patria potestas*, which allowed fathers to have permanent control over their children, included having the "rights of life and death over them" (Skinner *Sexuality in Greek and Roman Culture* 202). At the time of a woman's marriage to a man, the man could take control of her with much the same authority as her father. The property that the woman possessed became the dowry that she brought to the marriage.

She became a member of the family on much the same basis as would his daughter; if the woman's husband were to die without a will, his property would be divided among all of them equally. In the second form of marriage, the young woman and her possessions stayed within the power of her father while he remained alive. If the wife died intestate, then her father's family and all its members would inherit her property (Skinner 202). Apparently, Roman women had several options as to how they wished to negotiate their married lives.

Just as Roman free males could marry and become integrated into the fabric of society, so too could they just as easily engage in sexual relations with prostitutes, and there was no social shame incurred in doing so. Citing an example from Livy in which the Roman Lucius Flaminius had a man killed at a gladiatorial gathering in order to please Philip, a male prostitute, referred to as a *scortum*, Cantarella concludes that Romans thought that it was perfectly acceptable to engage in sexual relations with such an individual. In fact, there was even a feast day in the Roman calendar for female prostitutes (April 26) and one for male prostitutes (April 25) (Skinner 102).

From a legal standpoint, prostitutes were clearly disenfranchised as they were not allowed to speak for others in a court of law; moreover, they were generally not allowed to accuse others of wrongdoing, and they were certainly not allowed to be elected to the position of magistrate (Edwards 66). The praetor's edict concerning prostitutes encouraged judges and juries in particular not to pay attention to the testimony of an individual whose livelihood was made through disgraceful ways. One judge advised jurors that the testimony of gladiators and persons of that ilk was to be trusted or believed only if they were tortured (73). Finally, despite the fact that actors, gladiators, and prostitutes were highly visible figures and stigmatized for their professions, the Roman public was powerfully drawn to these individuals (69).

By the second century, adult males were openly pursuing freeborn boys. Juventius happened to be one of the freeborn boys who was pursued by Catullus, a Roman poet, known for his verse addressed to both men and women. Catullus was born into a wealthy family in Verona. Although he lived to be only 30 years old, he left behind a short collection of poetry that is witty, engaging, and at times very risqué. In poem No. 99 Catullus laments the indifferent response with which his kiss is met by Juventius (Cantarella 123). Cantarella notes that here we find the motif of kisses, and that Juventius pretends to be repulsed by Catullus's kiss.

In a word, Juventius behaves coyly so that he makes Catullus apologize and weep. He also makes the poet comport himself in a mode of behavior that is contrary to what would be perceived as masculine and what would fit the Greek fashion of pederastic love (123). Yet what is more compelling is Catullus's juxtaposition between his idealized kiss and a prostitute's. Quite clearly this juxtaposition serves to contrast the difference of feeling that Catullus would have for a prostitute and the feeling that he has for this exalted boy. As Cantarella suggests in contradistinction to his forebears, Catullus takes his position as someone who violates men as a form of punishment, an enemy, someone whom he hates, and someone who has treated him wrongly. The beloved receives only kisses and caresses, which are the pleasures that come with romantic relationships (Cantarella 125).

Although Catullus expresses pederastic affection for Juventius, he would never wish for any anyone to perceive him as effeminate because his verse has a feminine quality, for he renounces two of his friends in a sexually graphic poem when they suggest he is effeminate. Aurelius and Furius anger Catullus when they laugh about his relationship with Juventius, and he in turn suggests that he will force them to perform oral sex on him as a way of reinforcing his masculinity. This sexual act would be the most humiliating for any Roman male to perform. By Catullus's responding in this fashion, he is unequivocally asserting his masculinity and his dominant sexual identity (Cantarella 123–24).

Catullus also adores Lesbia in poem 72, "Revelation," but to no avail (Bertman 73–74). Skinner argues Catullus "expresses a corollary social alienation by inverting standard gender arrangements in both his narrative compositions and his erotic verse" ("Ego Mulier" 131). Throughout poem 76, the narrator articulates a profound sadness at being incapable of pleasing Lesbia. The speaker is certainly frustrated by Lesbia's indifference to all that he has done for her, and he realizes the futility of pursuing this relationship any longer. Skinner argues that the speaker evinces feminine weakness of will as he develops a more fixated lust on her ("Ego Mulier" 131). Both of these love affairs are equally intense, but the love affair with Lesbia is on a more elevated level of feeling and emotion (Cantarella 128).

Much like Catullus, Tibullus was a bisexual male from a wealthy Roman family, and like Catullus's love affairs, his, too, were conflicted. He wrote poetry to both Delia, Nemesis, and Marathus, and the ones that he wrote to Marathus are less mannered than the poems that he wrote for Delia (Cantarella 129). In "Cursed" the speaker bemoans the fact that the woman he loves is absent from his life, and all that he uses as substitutes are inadequate to her presence. In this poem the speaker attempts to assuage the emotional pain of his beloved's absence with alcohol, but in this instance the alcohol is transformed to tears. Even the woman with whom he is intimate cannot replace his true love, and she, of course, realizes that he is not really interested in her but another woman, but Tibullus, too, loved boys as well.

Just as Catullus loved Juventius, Tibullus loved Marathus. Marathus was also unfaithful to Tibullus just as Juventius was unfaithful to Catullus except Marathus was unfaithful with a woman. In "Elegy 8" the speaker once again laments the disdainful attitude that the youth has toward him after all of the kindness that he has shown him (Cantarella 130). This boy is indifferent to the kindness of his lovers and their emotional suffering. Cantarella notes that the speaker soon comes to the realization that he no longer has Marathus, for he is sexually involved with a woman, a woman to whom the speaker introduced him. Moreover, the boy has received gifts from a man, and now he is not only his lover, but that of this man's wife as well.

As shown in the late Republic, bisexuality was prevalent in Roman culture, and while engaging in sexual relations with boys was legally punishable under the Lex Scatinia, this same-sex erotic practice had become socially permissible (Cantarella 155). During the Empire Period, a change in Roman society's attitude toward sexual practices began to take place. Moreover, Roman society perceived sexual relations between adult males in which one was passive as quite disturbing for lawmakers, and they, in turn, began to pass legislation in an attempt to repress such activities. To be sure, the influence of the spread of Christianity functioned to curtail same-sex erotic practices among men (Cantarella 155). Finally, one must remember that there were other mitigating factors that affected sexual practices among the Romans of the Empire Period and early Christianity.

Michel Foucault argues that during the time of Rome's greatest power the men of the aristocracy became more concerned about their physical and spiritual well-being. Therefore, these attitudes that the Romans espouse regarding sexual relations are not identical to those of the early Christians in which the sexual act itself is deemed spiritually toxic; moreover, the practice of pederasty was condemned as against natural law (Skinner, *Sexuality in Greek and Roman Culture* 243). According to Skinner, Foucault asserts that the Romans began to place greater value on the institution of marriage. Marriage, according to Foucault, had functioned as a contractual agreement which involved political, economic, and social matters in which there was property and real estate to be transferred between families. Again, one's marriage in Rome had been more of a socioeconomic concern than one of romance and affection. As a consequence of the change in the aristocracy's attitude toward marriage, the urban underclass followed suit, and so marriage became significant because of its value as a source of emotional and psychological support, and so Roman culture, in turn, began to embrace it as well (Skinner *Sexuality in Greek and Roman Culture* 243).

One must also remember that the transition in Roman society's attitude regarding sexuality had occurred before the early Christian church placed its own stamp on it. In fact, Cantarella cites Veyne as arguing that Roman sexual morality was no longer based on bisexuality or a mode of aggressive heterosexuality, which was focused upon procreation and its possibilities through marriage (188). With the advent of Christianity, members of the Catholic faith were enjoined to restrain their erotic urges and wait until marriage to explore their sexuality but only for reproductive purposes.

With the intervention and implementation of canon law, which is church law, the early Christian church began to enforce its prescriptions regarding marriage and sexual practices. As early as the second century, manuals such as *Didache* or

Doctrine of the Twelve Apostles began to appear. Christians were persecuted by the Roman Empire, and then church authorities penalized those who violated the church rules that it set forth, and by the time of Emperor Constantine I (311–337), the authorities of the Christian church began to receive help from the Roman authorities in order to enforce its own rules and regulations regarding sexual behavior (Brundage, "Sex and Canon Law" in *Handbook of Medieval Sexuality* 33–34).

By the fourth century Emperor Constantine had legalized Christianity and later embraced it himself, and so with the acceptance of Christianity as the official religion, Christianity became part and parcel of the empire's legal system. Therefore, the early church fathers gained increasing power and authority in their dioceses, and at the same time the church fathers began to be advocates of asceticism; in other words, priests and prelates began to encourage strict self-control over one's sexual urges. St. Jerome (ca. 347–419/420) was an especially ardent advocate of virginity. Jerome compared virginity to gold and marriage to silver, and so he strongly encouraged women to follow the path of virginity in order to advance their social standing as women were clearly perceived as subordinate within the church's spiritual hierarchy (Wiesner-Hanks 30).

In as much as the Christian church's belief system was different from that of the Romans, the Middle Ages held two perspectives of women's sexuality which it acquired from the world of ancient medicine. First, the Galenic model argued that both men and women generated seed, and therefore, women were supposed to experience pleasure in sexual relations in order to release the seed. On the other hand, the Aristotelian model asserted that women did not create seed and that their pleasure in the sex act was not essential for the reproductive process. As a consequence of these theories, the early Christian world perceived male and female sexuality as very different, and although the church fathers may have changed Greco-Roman perspectives concerning sexuality, they maintained a gender-specific focus (Salisbury 84–85).

Secondly, just as the ancient world divided the population according to gender, so did the early Christian church. The church fathers defined men by their mental capacity and physical strength. Hence, men by nature would have dominion over women. Analogously, the early Christian church, according to Paul Verne, maintained the belief of the Romans that in order to be male one must be active and to be the recipient of an action was degrading. Finally, the early Christian church was not as accepting of same-sex eroticism as the Romans were (Salisbury 85).

It was during the period from the fifth through the ninth centuries, which historians refer to as the early Middle Ages, that people occupying central and north Europe were converted to Roman Catholicism, and so the Catholic church tried to combine German beliefs and traditions and orthodox church doctrine. The Catholic church's teachings were reinforced by letters that the pope sent about various issues of concern, referred to as decretals, and they became part of determinations reached by church councils and in effect became a part of canon law. Some of these letters were generated by actual situations that he was to adjudicate, and so the pope functioned as a member of the judiciary would in the secular realm (Wiesner-Hanks 34–35).

In addition to the decretals, the Catholic church developed a guidebook of penance called the penitentials which became very influential from the 6th to the beginning of the 11th century, and they focused upon issues related to sexuality, regulating even sexual relations in marriage. Even newly married couples were to refrain from engaging in sexual relations immediately after marriage. Archbishop Theodore's *Penitential* instructed newly married couples to refrain from being in the church for 30 days after being married. After that period spent engaging in sexual relations, they were to spend 40 days in penitence. Again, these prescriptive injunctions regarding sexual relations underscore the belief that sexual relations, even within marriage, were less than irreproachable and maybe even sinful (Brundage, *Law, Sex, and Christian Society* 152 and 159).

Regulations concerning sexual practices extended not only to when a married couple was to engage in sexual relations but how they were to do so. Ruth Mazo Karras informs her readers that couples were to abstain from sexual relations during the woman's menstrual period, or between the time they made a confession and the time they received the Eucharist at Mass. The penitentials of the early Middle Ages were very prescriptive concerning the time during which couples could legitimately have sexual relations. For example, couples could engage in sexual intercourse on fewer than half the days in the year. The dates and times during which couples could not engage in sexual relations were Sundays, Wednesdays, Fridays, and many holidays, and all of Advent and Lent were days of abstention. Periods of women's menstruation, pregnancy, and lactation were also off limits (Karras, *Sexuality in Medieval Europe* 75). Again, one must wonder how seriously early Catholics followed this prescriptive behavior that the church fathers mandated.

Inasmuch as the clergy attempted to control both married and unmarried members of their church, they worked to reform married clergy as well. With the reform movements of the late 11th century concerning clerical chastity, the church began to delineate much more carefully the lives of the laity and clergy (Karras, *Sexuality in Medieval Europe* 44). Wiesner-Hanks provides a great deal of information demonstrating how the church was in the process of changing how the clergy were to live their lives. The church issued a degree in 1059 ordering all clergy to be celibate but stopping short of insisting on disturbing the families of those who were already priests. In the next century clerical authorities were less reluctant, and two church councils, the First and Second Lateran Councils, in 1123 and 1139 stated in no uncertain terms that priests were not allowed to marry and any currently existing marriage was invalid (Wiesner-Hanks 38). The First Lateran Council asserted that "marriage of any one in the higher orders was forbidden. This was a major step, since as Frazee points out, 'church leaders now presumed to say, for the first time, that the clerical order was an impediment to marriage.' At the Second Lateran Council this legislation was brought to its logical conclusion when the ordination of married men was prohibited" (McGlynn and Moll 107). Moreover, later in 1179, at the Third Lateran Council the church promulgated that clergy who were incapable of stopping their homosexual activities were to be stripped of their positions as priests and that members of the laity were to be excommunicated. From 1250 or so onward civil courts increased the severity of the punishments for those convicted of sodomitical activities, which were defined as "crimes against nature." Lesbianism was rarely mentioned by church fathers because they had a difficult time conceptualizing sexual relations between two women. The Roman Catholic church found sexual relations without the penetration of a penis difficult to imagine (Wiesner-Hanks 38).

So important was the concept of chastity to the Middle Ages that chaste marriages emerged among some married couples. Atkinson avers that the politics of virginity was less determined by St. Jerome's fear of sexuality but more so by St. Augustine's more humane perspective. Women in chaste marriages who were not virgins were permitted an honorary virginity (McGlynn and Moll 110). Karras, too, cites Atkinson regarding the issue of chaste marriages, who discovered a difference in attitude from the 13th century forward concerning virginity as a psychic or religious mode of being rather than one determined by one's physical state (*Sexuality in Medieval Europe* 53). Margery Kempe is one of the most famous examples of a woman who wrote an autobiography in which she recounts her decision to live a chaste marriage. McGlynn and Moll assert that she is rarely thought unusual, but she is seldom taken seriously (115). Karras cites one of Margery's visions of Christ in which she perceives him as her spiritual husband, but clearly, erotic overtones abound in her accounts of her visions of Christ (*Sexuality in Medieval Europe* 56).

The first real crackdown concerning homosexual practices came in 1051 with the publication of St. Peter Damian's *Liber Gomorrhiamus* in which he denounced sodomites, especially those within the clergy, among whom the practice of homosexuality was thought to be widespread. St. Peter Damian argued that homosexual practices within the church were extremely destructive to the spiritual purity of the church (Johansson and Perry 167). Apparently, priests were associated with same-sex eroticism throughout the Middle Ages.

When the news of St. Damian's book reached Pope Leo IV (1049–1054), he acknowledged the existence of same-sex erotic activity, but he did not make any sweeping change in ecclesiastical policy regarding priests who were caught in homosexual acts. Maybe Leo IV thought expelling homosexual priests from the priesthood would cause more harm than good, but Hildebrand (Gregory VII, 1073–1085) made sweeping changes by requiring that priests be celibate. This concern with celibacy by extension generated the impetus for the eradication of heretics and homosexuals, and so the Third Lateran Council of 1179 declared that clergy who were guilty of sodomy, also referred to as "crimes against nature," were to leave the priesthood or remain in perpetuity in monasteries (Karras, *Sexuality in Medieval Europe* 167–68). To be sure, the ecclesiastical trend toward more repressive measures against sexual infractions became the norm in the Middle Ages.

Fines against sodomy varied from castration, exile, and even death under secular law courts from the 13th century. Historians know of the first documented execution upon the conviction of sodomy in Western Europe in 1277 (Karras, *Sexuality in Medieval Europe* 175). Sodomy could even be the cause of finding oneself in a literary hell. Sodomy has been a great concern of the city fathers of Florence since the late Middle Ages. One of the most famous sodomites of late Medieval Italian literature is Brunetto Latini, Dante's teacher, with whom he speaks at length when Dante meets him in Canto 15 of the *Inferno*. Here in the seventh circle Brunetto Latini suffers with the others who committed sodomy, but when Dante sees his former teacher, he responds very warmly to him despite his place in hell. Dante perceives Brunetto Latini as a fatherly figure, who is profoundly concerned about Dante's future. Michael Rocke points that Dante evinces a great deal of respect and affection for Brunetto Latini, and that there is a literary history of references to homosexuals. Accounts of same-sex eroticism between men abound in tales, anecdotes, and poems that vary from satire to elegies; in fact, it was against the law of the land to write or even sing songs about same-sex acts (4).

The earliest records in Florence regulating sodomy date to 1284 in which those convicted were exiled. By 1325 there were more statutes concerning same-sex relations, and men convicted of sodomizing boys were to be castrated; boys between the ages of 14 and 18 years of age who willingly engaged in sodomy were to pay a fine of 100 lire, and boys under the age of 14 years of age were to pay a fine of 50 lire or be flogged nude through the streets of the city (Rocke 21).

In response to the outcry regarding sodomy, the Office of the Night on April 17, 1432, was "instituted to appoint a special magistracy to pursue and prosecute sodomy" (Rocke 45). Reprising Rocke's research, Karras asserts, "This body set up boxes in which people could deposit anonymous accusations of sodomy. Those accused would be interrogated and invited to implicate others. The penalty was remitted if a man denounced himself and named his partners, and about forty men on average did so every year" (*Sexuality in Medieval Europe* 139). There was a spate of regulations between 1432 and 1542. The councils within the city of Florence passed 17 significant reforms concerning the penalties to be meted out for sodomitical offenses. However, by the middle of the 16th century, the Venetian and Florentine citizenry's concern regarding sodomy had lessened a great deal. The law which was passed in 1542 signaled the end of the fixation on same-sex eroticism (Rocke 66). What is truly extraordinary is the number of accusations and convictions in a city of approximately 40,000 people.

From the court proceedings dating from 1478 to November 1502, historians know that 4,062 people were involved in homosexual sodomy more than once. The Office of the Night garnered 638 convictions, which comprised an average of 37 or 38 convictions per year. Given the data that are available, on the average 50 males were convicted annually for homosexual sodomy, excluding heterosexual offences (Rocke 66). Perhaps one of the most enigmatic events to occur at a sodomite's execution took place in Avignon in 1320 when a 13-year-old boy was to be burned for having been the passive partner while his active partner was condemned and burned to death as scheduled. In the case of the youth, the Blessed Virgin Mary saved him from death just at the moment that the pile of wood on which he was situated was to be ignited. As a consequence of this preternatural event, the pope at the time declared this event a miracle and saw that a chapel was built there in honor of the appearance of Mary (Karras, *Sexuality in Medieval Europe* 140).

Unlike same-sex relations between men, lesbianism did not generate the same level of fear and hostility as governmental bodies did not perceive it as subversive of the societal status quo. St. Augustine wrote a letter to a number of nuns in 423 C.E. addressing the issue of female same-sex relations (Murray 195).

Not only did Augustine warn against the same-sex female eroticism, but so did Donatus of Besançon in his seventh-century text *Regula ad Virginea* in which he cautioned nuns about having overly affectionate relationships. He even went so far as to advise nuns as to how they were to sleep so as to avoid the occasion of sin by sleeping apart from each other (Murray 196). Here, too, the religious hierarchy was fearful that same-sex erotic activities would occur among women who were living closely in a communal fashion.

Just as there were laws prohibiting same-sex eroticism among men, so too was there some legislation regarding same-sex eroticism among women, but there was little. The French *Li Livres de jostice et de plet,* which was drawn up in 1260, addressed homoeroticism among both men and women. This law stated that men convicted of sodomy for the first two times should be sentenced to mutilation and castration and to be burned for the third offence (Murray 201).

Perhaps what offended the secular and religious sectors of society more than same-sex eroticism was the use of artificial devices in order to stimulate themselves sexually, for the Carolingian writer, Hincmar of Reims, castigated those who engaged in these practices in his *De divortio Lotharii et Tethbergae* (Murray 198). These "certain devices" were perceived as very subversive of cultural orthodoxy because the women's use of them appropriated male privilege by mimicking the phallus.

The only other woman who caused as much social unrest in medieval Europe and England was the prostitute, yet Germany, France, Italy, and England had city-owned brothels, which were founded in the late 14th and 15th centuries because prostitution fulfilled a necessary evil as St. Thomas Aquinas thought. It was hoped that brothels would prevent the following problems: there was the fear on the public's part that prostitutes soliciting customers on the street would stir up a scandal, and so prostitution was to be contained in a house. If they were allowed to walk the streets, some men might mistake law-abiding women as prostitutes. Prostitutes also were thought to obviate the practice of homosexuality for lack of available women as in the city of Florence in which the town fathers actually opened a brothel so that the young men would have sexual relations with prostitutes so as not to take up the practice of same-sex eroticism permanently and diminish the population of the city. Lastly, the city fathers were concerned that chaste women might be corrupted (Karras, "Prostitution in Medieval Europe" 244–45).

Although there were laws prohibiting prostitution, they were never a successful deterrent. As early as 1277, there was a law prohibiting the "whore of a brothel" from being within the walls of the City of London. Later in 1310, Edward II required the mayor and the sheriff of London to "abolish brothels, which were harboring thieves and murderers, and to be sure, there were severe penalties for those found guilty of prostitution" (Karras, *Common Women* 14). Authorities meted out increasingly severe penalties for those who were convicted for the second and third times: "A common whore was 'taken from the prison to Aldgate, with a striped hood, and a white rod in her hand, and from there taken with minstreley to the thew [a pillory for women], and there the cause is proclaimed, and from there through Cheap and Newgate, then to Cock's Lane to remain there.' A second offense required the whore to remain on the thew, and a third required the cutting of her hair and banishment from the city" (*Common Women* 15). Apparently, the white rod was the symbol of prostitution.

Karras provides narratives of several prostitutes because of London's wonderful judicial records. Isabella Wakefield began her life as a prostitute and later became a brothel keeper at the beginning of the 15th century; she was accused of fornicating with a priest and of being a bawd in 1404 (66). Another prostitute, Alice Dymmok, in Great Yarmouth, was charged with being a bawd and a brothel owner and maybe a prostitute. In spite of being fined for her various infractions of the legal code, she continued to break the law (68). Finally, the prostitute about whom historians have the greatest amount of information happened to be a male transvestite by the name of John/Eleanor Rykener, whose customers apparently believed him to be a woman. Once he was apprehended, he told the authorities that he had spent five weeks in Oxford as an embroideress and engaged in sexual relations with students and then another six weeks in Burford where he worked as a tapster at an inn and engaged in sexual relations for money with foreign merchants and friars. What is interesting about his case is that he was not described as being attired as a prostitute but dressed as a woman. John/Eleanor Rykener was apparently quite adept at his or her trade (*Common Women* 70–71).

The end of the medieval period ushered in a time of extraordinary change in culture and society because of the Protestant Reformation in Europe and England. It was tantamount to the change from the bisexual cultures of ancient Greece and Rome to the heterosexual one that has dominated Western civilization since the second century. With the Reformation, no longer would the pope be the head of the ecclesiastical realm for Christians in England and in parts of Germany and Switzerland, but more than ever before Christians would look to their newly translated Bible in English for answers to questions concerning faith and morality.

WORKS CITED

Alighieri, Dante. *The Divine Comedy of Dante Alighieri: Inferno*. Trans. Allen Mandelbaum. New York and London: Bantam, 1982. Print.

Bertman, Stephen. *Erotic Love Poems of Greece and Rome: A Collection of New Translations*. New York: New American Library, 2005. Print.

Bristow, Joseph. *Sexuality*. London and New York: Routledge, 1997. Print.

Brundage, James A. *Law, Sex, and Christian Society in Medieval Europe*. Chicago: New York and London: U of Chicago P, 1987. Print.

Brundage, James A. "Sex and Canon Law." *Handbook of Medieval Sexuality*. Ed. Vern Bullough and James A. Brundage. New York: Garland, 1996. 33–50. Print.

Cantarella, Eva. *Bisexuality in the Ancient World*. Trans. Cormac O'Cuilleanain. New Haven, CT, and London: Yale UP, 2002. Print.

Edwards, Catherine. "Unspeakable Professions: Public Performance and Prostitution and Ancient Rome." *Roman Sexualities*. Ed. Judith Hallett and Marilyn B. Skinner. Princeton, NJ: Princeton UP, 1997. 66–95. Print.

Finley, M. I. *The Ancient Greeks: An Introduction to Their Life and Thought*. New York: Viking Press, 1963. Print.

Freeman, Charles. *Egypt, Greece and Rome: Civilizations of the Ancient Mediterranean*. New York and Oxford: Oxford UP, 1996. Rept. 1999. Print.

Garrison, Daniel H. *Sexual Culture in Ancient Athens*. Norman: U of Oklahoma P, 2000. Print.

Hall, William Harlan. *Ancient Greece*. New York: American Heritage Press, 1970. Print.

Highet, Gilbert. *The Classical Tradition: Greek and Roman Influences on Western Literature*. Oxford: Oxford UP, 1985. Print.

Johansson, Warren, and William A. Percy. "Homosexuality." *Handbook for Medieval Sexuality*. Ed. Vern Bullough and James A. Brundage. New York: Garland, 1999. 155–89. Print.

Karras, Ruth Mazo. *Common Women: Prostitution and Sexuality in Medieval England*. New York and London: Oxford UP, 1992. Print.

Karras, Ruth Mazo. "Prostitution in Medieval Europe." *Handbook for Medieval Sexuality*. Ed. Vern Bullough and James A. Brundage. New York: Garland, 1996. 243–60. Print.

Karras, Ruth Mazo. *Sexuality in Medieval Europe: Doing unto Others*. New York and London: Routledge, 2005. Print.

Laurin, Joseph R. *Homosexuality in Ancient Athens*. Victoria, BC, Canada: Trafford, 2005. Print.

McGlynn, Margaret, and Richard J. Moll. "Chaste Marriage in the Middle Ages: 'It Were to Hire a Great Merite.'" Ed. Vern Bullough and James A. Brundage. *Handbook for Medieval Sexuality*. New York: Garland, 1996. 103–22. Print.

Miola, Robert S. *Shakespeare and Classical Comedy: The Influence of Plautus and Terrence*. Oxford: Clarendon Press, 1994. Print.

Mireaux, Emile. *Daily Life in the Time of Homer*. New York: Macmillan, 1959. Print.

Murray, Jacqueline. "Twice Marginal and Twice Invisible: Lesbians in the Middle Ages." *Handbook for Medieval Sexuality*. Ed. Vern Bullough and James A. Brundage. New York: Garland, 1999. 191–222. Print.

Rocke, Michael. *Forbidden Friendships: Homosexuality and Male Culture in Renaissance Florence*. New York and London: Cornell UP, 1996. Print.

Salisbury, Joyce. "Gendered Sexuality." *Handbook for Medieval Sexuality*. Ed. Vern Bullough and James A. Brundage. New York: Garland, 1996. 81–102. Print.

Skinner, Marilyn B. "Ego Mulier: The Construction of Male Sexuality in Catullus." *Roman Sexualities*. Ed. Judith Hallett and Marilyn B. Skinner. Princeton, NJ: Princeton UP, 1997. 129–50. Print.

Skinner, Marilyn B. *Sexuality in Greek and Roman Culture*. Oxford: Blackwell Press, 2005. Print.

Walters, Jonathan. "Invading the Roman Body: Manliness and Impenetrability in Roman Thought." *Roman Sexualities*. Ed. Judith Hallett and Marilyn Skinner. Princeton, NJ: Princeton UP, 1997. 29–43. Print.

Wiesner-Hanks, Merry E. *Christianity and Sexuality in the Early Modern World: Regulating Desire, Reforming Practice*. New York and London: Routledge, 1999. Print.

2

SEXUALITY IN SHAKESPEARE'S WORLD

The Protestant Revolution was certainly one of the most significant events in the history of the Western world. With the advent of Martin Luther's 95 Theses, the theological and social landscape of England and Europe was forever changed. Luther along with Ulrich Zwingli disavowed many of the major tenets of the Catholic church such as the value of good deeds, the doctrinal power of the pope, and the significance of custom. By the 1530s the ideas of the Protestant Revolution had extended beyond Germany to England and Scandinavian countries. John Calvin's Protestant ideas began to spread from Geneva to France, Hungary, and Poland. Calvin's ideas in turn influenced John Knox in Scotland in the 1550s (Wiesner-Hanks 60–61).

The issue of sexuality figured significantly in changes that Luther proposed. In one of his first treatises, Luther sharply critiqued the idea of priestly celibacy. Luther believed that marriage was good for one's Christian life, and so he married Katharine von Bora in 1525 after she had left the convent in which she had lived. So as far as Luther was concerned, the pursuit of celibacy was futile. Moreover, Luther did not consider marriage a sacrament and did not believe that marriage bestowed grace upon the couple involved. Luther believed that sexuality was extremely important to marriage, and he felt that couples should be granted divorces in cases of adultery, incompatibility, impotence, and desertion (Wiesner-Hanks 61–63).

Unlike Catholics, most Protestant theologians believed that the consent of the couple's parents and a public ceremony were necessary in order for a marriage to occur. Festivities following the wedding ceremony were to be conducted with due respect and dignity for the occasion. The celebrants were not to engage in drunken revelry and jokes, which mocked the sexual aspects of marriage. Although Luther himself had blessed bridal beds, Protestant thinkers generally frowned upon such practices because of the superstitious overtones that such rituals called to mind. Common folk beliefs entailed untying knots and throwing grain in order to increase the male's fertility. Rather than drinking a final toast before the couple retired to bed, they were to engage in prayer. After the consummation of the marriage, the couple was supposed to take up residence in a peaceful fashion and contribute to the life of the community (Wiesner-Hanks 64).

Although Protestant thinkers recognized the importance of sexuality to marriage, Calvin was stricter regarding sexual practices within marriage than Luther. Calvin thought that married couples should practice "matrimonial chastity." Robert Cleaver, a Puritan writer, clearly articulated these beliefs in *A Godly Forme of Household Government* (1603). Cleaver felt that married couples should engage in sexual relations for the purpose of the procreation of the species in order to increase those in Christ's church, and if couples simply pursued their lustful desires that their offspring would be monsters or fools or wicked individuals. As far as Cleaver was concerned, neither partner should engage in contraception. To do so is to risk the wrath of God and the consequent birth defects that one's child may incur (Wiesner-Hanks 65).

In as much as the Protestants sought freedom from the authority of Rome, the religious reformers also wanted to regulate sexuality through a court system in which they would work with secular courts, and so the first Protestant court was a marriage court founded in Zurich in 1525 by Zwingli. The judges on these courts in Zurich and other cities were not only clergy but also members of the city council. These courts came to be called "marriage courts" because marital matters concerned these courts of their time, but they, like the Catholic courts before them, began to address other sexual offenses such as prostitution and fornication while also addressing absenteeism from church, blasphemy, and gambling. Rulers in Saxony and Württemberg created church tribunals composed of clergy and laity, some of whom were lawyers. In the city of Strasbourg, the city fathers refused to allow clergy on these marriage courts (Wiesner-Hanks 67–68).

These consistory courts sprang up elsewhere in France, Germany, Scotland, the Low Countries, and even northern Ireland, as Calvinism spread throughout Europe. For example, in many parts of Germany, the ruler would delegate a consistory while in France, and in some of the Low Countries, pastors and other members of the laity would compose the consistory. Outside of Geneva, these courts were organized hierarchically, and they, too, would preside over a number of cases, but generally 30 to 80 percent of the cases were of a sexual nature. Those who had committed a sexual transgression were required to confess their guilt before the court, and even before the congregation which they attended on a regular basis. Only rarely did those who were accused of a sexual crime claim to be innocent, and those who did so were forced to take complicated vows of compurgation, which was a process by which the accused were required to find members of the community who could under oath attest to their upstanding characters (Wiesner-Hanks 69).

Certainly, courts were called to intervene in the matter of divorce, but in most instances courts did not become involved unless the situation was unavoidable as in the case in which the argumentative couple caused a public uproar and disturbed their neighbors. Generally speaking, the aggrieved party was the wife who alleged that her husband had assaulted her with various articles of furniture. In most instances, the husband was reprimanded, and the couple was sent home. Only when the parties in question returned a third or fourth time was a stricter punishment meted out to the offending spouse. Again it is important to remember that domestic violence was viewed much differently in the early modern period than it is in the 21st century. Husbands were allowed to correct their wives by physical punishment if they needed to do so, and courts apparently felt that this form of correction was socially if not legally acceptable as long as the husband did not draw blood or strike his wife with a stick wider in diameter than his thumb, hence the term "rule of thumb." In some situations in which the courts did not intervene in order to protect the wife from a violent husband, it resulted in her death (Wiesner-Hanks 76).

Although Swiss, German, Scottish, Scandinavian, and French Protestant courts allowed divorce for any number of reasons, startling changes in the rate of divorce in these countries did not occur. For example, the cathedral court of Stavanger in Norway, which covered a great deal of territory, granted only 18 divorces between 1571 and 1596. It seems almost unbelievable, but the city of Geneva had only three divorces between 1559 and 1569. Because of the foundation on which early modern society was built, the disillusion of a union was the most desperate measure that a couple could take in order to resolve an incompatible relationship. For example, in what was considered at the time the open-minded city of Basel between 1550 and 1592, only one half of all the petitions for divorce were granted. The most compelling reasons for which a divorce would have been allowed would have been because of adultery or desertion. Even in cases of impotence or desertion, the couple would have been sent home to attempt sexual relations once again, or in the case of desertion, the aggrieved party would have been required to search for the missing spouse once again in order to be certain that the spouse could not be found (Wiesner-Hanks 79).

Punishments for the crime of adultery, however, would be treated very seriously because it undermined the social order. The legal code of the Holy Roman Empire, the Carolina Constitutio Criminalis in 1532, made adultery a capital offense, and in a few instances those found guilty of adultery were executed. There were some extreme penalties meted out in Germany. One woman was burned alive in 1508 for adultery. Another woman in 1527 in Zittau was drowned for adultery. Punishment for men could be equally severe. Despite the fact that there was no provision in the city charter for the death penalty in Geneva, two men were beheaded in addition to several others who were executed that day, and to be sure, one's punishment was influenced by one's gender and social status within the community. In Geneva in 1566, an adultery law was passed that made double adultery of equivalent value in which the sentence of death was delivered for both parties (Wiesner-Hanks 77).

Sexual offenses such as fornication, prostitution, and sodomy were handled in a variety of fashions in early modern Europe. Theoretically, men and women who were guilty of fornication were to be treated equally, but in point of fact, men who were found guilty of this transgression were given a slight fine and required to take a vow not to engage in this behavior again and sent on their way while unmarried women, on the other hand, were incarcerated, faced bodily punishment, and were sometimes sent away from the town in which they lived even if they were pregnant, as if their pregnancy should determine their treatment by the community. Some religious reformers thought that these women should be treated more kindly (Wiesner-Hanks 77).

Prostitution was also taken quite seriously in early modern Europe. In Protestant Germany from 1520 to 1590, almost all cities, initially Protestant and then Catholic, closed their houses of prostitution. With the crackdown on prostitution, religious and secular figures increasingly perceived prostitution as a far worse crime because the prostitute not only undermined the sexual integrity of herself, but she also undermined that of her customer. The closing of brothels, of course, did not end the practice of prostitution. Women continued to be investigated by civic authorities. Of course, the delineation between prostitution and fornication was a very thin one, and in addition to working as a laundress or selling fruits and vegetables in the public square, some women would continue to engage in sexual relations in exchange for money (Wiesner-Hanks 86).

Perhaps the most heinous transgression in the criminal code with the exclusion of murder was sodomy. Sodomy became a capital crime in England and the Holy Roman Empire in the 1530s; in the Holy Roman Empire bestiality was included within the meaning of the term, and while the Scots Parliament refused to placate the leaders of the Scottish church to make illegal the transgressions enumerated in the book of Leviticus, the fact of the matter was that the legal system executed those found guilty of sodomy and bestiality as a matter of course. In fact, one German judge said that the crime was considered monstrous, and the culprit was punished by fire (Wiesner-Hanks 87).

In spite of the draconian denunciations of religious and civil authorities concerning sodomy, few cases regarding sodomy were actually tried in the 16th and 17th centuries. The legal record indicates that regions of Europe practicing Calvinism were more inclined to prosecute people for practicing sodomy than those of the Anglican or Lutheran faith. For example, in Geneva legal authorities prosecuted 62 cases for sodomy and obtained convictions in 30 cases between 1555 and 1678; in the Calvinist city of Emden in Germany, the cases regarding sodomitical relations constituted a mere 1 percent of all cases involving sexual transgressions which came before the church tribunal from 1558 to 1745. Finally, while the Puritans may be perceived today as the early modern counterpart to the Moral Majority, the Puritans were much more concerned about cases of illegitimacy and blasphemy than sodomy (Wiesner-Hanks 87–88).

Just as the Protestant church continued to reform its religious tenets, in many ways, the Catholic church's early modern notions of sexuality were entangled with earlier pre-Reformation ideas. It is important to remember that Martin Luther concurred with St. Augustine's association that erotic desire and humanity's original sin were incurred in the fall from grace in the Garden of Eden (Wiesner-Hanks 105). Luther asserted in his Commentary on Genesis that the sin of lust was because of the fall. Therefore, erotic desire had to be regulated. At the same time that Luther disagreed with Augustine concerning the most effective means of maintaining control of sexual desire, many of Augustine's ideas regarding sexuality influenced Protestant thinkers' ideas (Crawford 75).

Catholic thinkers along with Protestant ones questioned the value of clerical celibacy. Desiderius Erasmus lauded married life in his *The Institution of Christian Matrimony*, and Martin Le Maistre (1464–1536) and John Major (1470–1550), who were religious thinkers at the University of Paris, believed that sexual pleasure experienced in marriage was in no way sinful. In fact, Major suggested that the sin involved in sexual relations in marriage was comparable to eating a beautiful apple for the pleasure of it; in effect, there was no sin committed. In fact, at the Council of Trent, the representative for Duke Albrecht of Bavaria proposed that compulsory clerical celibacy come to an end in the strongest of terms. Despite the fact that clerical celibacy was hotly debated, the Council of Trent decided to insist upon mandatory celibacy by having more closely monitored observation and a more exacting selection process of candidates for the priesthood (Wiesner-Hanks 105).

The Council of Trent decided to have greater restrictions on houses of female religious by placing them under threat of excommunication or civic punishment. Women were to be decisively removed from the carnal delights of the world according to Pope Boniface VIII's extremely severe restrictions (Wiesner-Hanks 106). The Catholic church continued to express its concern regarding the power of female sexuality at the same time as it sang the praises of female virginity; Italy saw an outpouring of chapels dedicated to female martyrs (106). Venice alone had some 50 convents within its environs (Laven frontispiece). Not only did the Council of Trent enforce the enclosure of nunneries, but the council's decision was confirmed through Pope Pius V's bull *Circa pastoralis* in 1566. Ironically, the city of Venice, which was famous for being disobedient to the Vatican's dictates, actually was in agreement with the Catholic church (Laven xxvi).

Ironically, a woman's commitment to a religious life was conceptualized as a marriage to none other than Christ. Just as brides who would marry men would wear white, so too would young women who would become brides of Christ. At the most important moment in this ceremony in which a woman would become a full-fledged member of the convent, the patriarch of the Venetian church, who presided over the ceremony, would place a "wedding ring" of sorts upon the woman's finger (Laven 24). Women were to make their religious vows just as freely as women were supposed to marry men of their free will. This, of course, was not always the case as Sir Henry Wotton, the English ambassador, made known in a letter in 1608, when he asserted that some women were compelled to enter convents against their will by their parents "who to spare so much marriage money, impose commonly that life upon three daughters at least if they have five, and so in proportion" (Laven 25).

One of the most famous early modern Italian women writers to be sent by her family to a nunnery was Elena Cassandra Tarabotti, who thought she had a "forced vocation." It was her unhappy fate to be the oldest of six daughters as well as lame. Her parents decided that they would spend their time and energy trying to find husbands for their younger daughters who did not suffer any deformities so that they could concentrate on their dowries. Needless to say, her frustration at being penned up in a convent did not go without notice as she decided to publish a description of her plight in an autobiographical work called *Inferno monocale* (*The Nun's Hell*) in which she recounted in vivid detail the events that she experienced. Tarabotti recounts in dramatic detail the horror of entering a nunnery against one's will (Laven 24). Not only parents but aunts and uncles tried to convince their nieces that their entering a nunnery was in the best interest of their families so that the young women would feel guilty if they disappointed them. Writing to his niece, Giovanni Loredan encouraged Laura Pasqualigo to enter the convent as instructed for the good of her family's reputation because marriage partners from different social classes were strongly discouraged for financial reasons (Laven 44). Apparently, thousands of young women were at once cajoled and coerced into taking vows of chastity, poverty, and obedience regardless of their personal feelings or inclinations.

In as much as some women such as Elena Tarabotti perceived convents as prisons for young women, they were also thought of as places of piety and peace, where women had an opportunity to receive an education and exercise a degree of autonomy over their own lives that would be denied to other women. At the Council of Trent in 1563, the Catholic church definitively declared the superiority of the single state over the married one in contradistinction to the beliefs of the professing Protestants. The Catholic church was so concerned over the preservation of the virginity of the young nuns in their convents that the Council of Trent declared that nuns were not to leave the convent for any reason without receiving the bishop's approval, and no man was to enter the convent for any reason (Laven 86). Not only did the Catholic church fear for the sexual safety of its nuns, it also feared that nuns themselves might be overcome by erotic desire for sexual relations with men. It was widely believed during the early modern period that women were more lustful than men, and for this reason nuns had to be watched as closely as any other women.

By literally walling women within the convent, the church fathers felt that they were best safeguarding the virginity of its nuns, yet in the convent at Sant' Andrea, the enemy infiltrated its walls in the most cunning of fashions. Sant' Andrea had become known for its gossiping nuns. It was here that a woman by the name of Felicita brought news and gossip from outside the convent walls. In addition to bringing the nuns news who waited at the convent's gates on a regular basis, she also coyly bantered with them in a provocative fashion. One sister, Zorzi, recounted how Felicita could be seen consorting with nuns of this convent in a most licentious way. Apparently, she put her hand on Suor Gabriela's breast, and they kissed each other (Laven 133). In fact, some times the same-sex eroticism was generated between two nuns, and it was for this reason that nuns' sleeping arrangements were regulated, but attempts to control the nuns' sexuality met with futility at Santa Maria in 1594 when "significant love affairs" came to light between nuns and some young girls who were boarded there. The next year in 1595 at Santa Croce della Giudecca more same-sex affairs became known. At San Iseppo in 1626, Suor Fiorenza became a person of interest, for the church fathers requested that she be closely observed when she went to the parlor and that note be taken with whom she went; apparently, she had been seen in the parlor with Suor Elena and Suor Chiara and with her skirts lifted and their hands in her undergarments. To be sure, same-sex eroticism occurred among nuns in convents despite all attempts on the part of the clergy to control their sexuality (Laven 192–93).

Perhaps one of the most sensational of scandals involved nuns at the convent of San Zaccaria, which was regarded as one of the most aristocratic of convents. Laura Querini and a friend of hers, a *conversa,* Zaccaria, made a hole in one of the nunnery walls so that two men could enter the nunnery for the purpose of engaging in sexual intercourse with them. When the Venetian patriarch himself questioned Querini, she told him that she came there when she was very young and later took her vow at the age of 15 when she did not really want to become a nun (Laven 186). Querini's description of her experience was not unlike many other young women who literally grew up in convents with little experience of the outside world, and once they had a taste of freedom, they certainly wanted more. It is quite clear that these young women had made decisions about their lives for which they were really unprepared.

Moreover, Querini went on to confess that she had met the man under the alias Zuanne Cocco six years before through Donna Cipriana. While at first she was content to meet this man 20 years her junior, her interest soon escalated into full-blown sexual relations, as she passionately pursued this man; she recounted in graphic description how she went about entangling him in her desires having fallen in love with him, and she even used prayers and spells to cause this man to fall in love with her (Laven 187). Not only did she break her vow of chastity, but she also transgressed gender norms by pursuing this younger man and even violated religious law by using sorcery in order to gain sexual access to him. All of Querini's behavior is indicative of the degree to which she was desperate for erotic experience with men and how unfit a candidate she was for the sisterhood.

Just as some Venetian women wanted to extricate themselves from convents in which they did not wish to remain, so too did some other Venetian woman wish to extricate themselves from marriages in which they did not wish to remain. Joanne Ferraro reminds her readers that in late Renaissance Venice it is important to note that women in troubled marriages would have a good chance of having their marriages annulled (13). This reality was made manifest by the number of annulments granted. Twenty-nine years were selected by chance from 1565 and 1624. During these 29 years, women initiated 75 percent of all annulments, and 118 annulments were granted between 1565 and 1624; there were approximately 4 of them per year. In most cases the determination of the annulment is unknown, but records indicate that of the 43 decisions that are known, 39 were decided in the wives' favor (Ferraro 29).

At the same time that women obtained annulments, the Catholic church tried to enforce its religious authority by emphasizing the sacramental quality of marriage as opposed to the contractual quality of it. Even as the church was attempting to exercise greater control over marriage, so too was the Venetian state. According to the Catholic church, the wishes of the couple were of greater importance than those of the parents. Most significantly, the church fathers stressed the fact that marriages were not to be dissolved. The only instances in which the Catholic church allowed a couple to live separately from each other were in cases of the individuals' desire to join the priesthood or sisterhood, adultery on the part of either spouse, or when either party was in grave danger (Ferraro 4).

Women and men sought annulments in early modern Venice for a variety of reasons. One of the most frequently given by women was forcible marriages. In 1617 Camilla Belloto made a request for an annulment in the Patriarch's Court from her husband Angelo de Bollis. Angelo had failed to care for her as he had promised; in fact, he attempted to prostitute her to a man he knew. Six months later they were separated from each other; Camilla had returned to her father's house. At the time of the annulment, Camilla claimed that her father had forced her to marry de Bollis. Moreover, she claimed that her father had committed adultery, assaulted her mother, and threatened to kill her if she refused to marry de Bollis. Perhaps the most compelling evidence that she offered the church court was her nightgown which she wore on her wedding night. Camilla's sister offered a cogent account of what occurred on the night of Camilla's wedding; she never engaged in sexual relations with her husband and was resistant to go to bed with him (Ferraro 37). Given the fact that Camilla never consented to the marriage, the court ruled in favor of an annulment.

In the even more dramatic case of Vittoria Cesana's marriage to Giovanni Battista Barbaro, Antonio Cesana actually put a knife to his daughter's throat in order to force her to marry Barbaro. To be sure, Vittoria could generate compelling narrative. When she was asked how her father threatened her, she informed her interlocutor that he put a knife to her throat and said he would kill her (Ferraro 42). Women frequently claimed that they had agreed with their voices but not with their hearts as was previously seen in the cases of forced vocations to the sisterhood. In an effort to strengthen her case, Vittoria also argued that it was well known to the general public that she was unhappy with this marriage. Vittoria claimed that she had been forced to spend three days and nights with him and that as far as she was concerned the marriage was invalid (Ferraro 37). Vittoria even went so far as to secure two witnesses who avouched that they had seen her father threaten her through a keyhole. Perhaps this overly graphic account was fiction, but again this was the case of a forced marriage, and so the court annulled it (Ferraro 45).

Thus far, only fathers of young women have been blamed as the cause of forced marriages, but mothers, too, exercised a great deal of influence and power over their daughters. In a case in which one young woman was threatened with disinheritance, Helena Corner was forced to marry Giovanni Badoer because of her mother's power over her. When her lawyer made Helena Corner's case for an annulment, he emphasized the significant age difference between them; for example, Helena was 15 years old while her spouse Giovanni was 40 years old (Ferraro 55). (At this time the average age for a bride was 15 years of age while that of a groom was more than 30 years of age [Ferraro 62].) Her attorney asserted that Helena would have never married Giovanni had it not been because of her mother's control of her finances. She left Giovanni, and she took up residence in a oasis of sorts for women of the nobility, but her mother made her return to her husband, and she pursued an annulment from Giovanni only after her mother's death. Because of the evidence of impotence, the ecclesiastical court annulled Helena's marriage. Ferraro avers that in Helena's situation and others' that mothers with strong personalities were frequently mentioned when women petitioned for annulments. The fact that mothers were mentioned in these documents provides historians today with an understanding of mothers' influence in Venice in their families and their immediate social groups (Ferraro 55).

While the ecclesiastical court seemed to have had an easy decision to make in the case involving Helena Corner, the one involving Camilla Benzoni, who was from a wealthy family, was much more complex and knotty. Camilla decided to end her marriage in the fall of 1590 on the grounds that the marriage had never been consummated. She did not argue that this was a forced marriage but one in which her husband, Gasparo, was incapable of functioning sexually with her. She provided the court with an explicit account of her sexual experiences with her husband immediately after the wedding. After an initially unsuccessful attempt at sexual intercourse on their wedding night, they continued to try to engage in sexual relations. Camilla shrewdly included all of the needed items in her story that would convince the court of the validity of her claim that her marriage to Gasparo was never consummated. At the same time Camilla maintained what was more than likely a pretended naïveté; in spite of the fact that they did not engage in sexual relations on their wedding night, Gasparo informed Camilla that the wedding bedclothes were laundered in order to maintain the pretense that they had been stained with her hymenal blood (Ferraro 73).

When Gasparo was questioned about his sexual capacity, he claimed to have penetrated her hymen. In fact, he even went so far as to describe the proportions of his penis in admirable terms, for according to Gasparo, it was neither too long nor too short or for that matter neither too wide nor too narrow (Ferraro 81). Finally, in September 1591, Giovanni Mocenigo, the Auditore Generale, decided that they would not receive an annulment because they had been legally married; nonetheless, the marriage had remained unconsummated, and so they were required to return to their home and attempt to engage in sexual intercourse again before she could make another request for an annulment (Ferraro 84).

As indicated at the outset of this discussion of love and divorce early modern Italian style, women were quite adept at initiating these annulment proceedings, but occasionally a husband would enact one when he felt sufficiently compelled to do so as Zuane Bonifacio Facini, a wine merchant, did when he claimed that his wife Zuana was an adulteress. One witness on the part of Zuane claimed that Messer Palao arrived with a boatman to take them to a theatre while they engaged in erotic dalliance. Other women came forward to undermine Zuana's reputation. Donna Maria claimed that Zuana beat her husband, and Dona Marina asserted that Zuana was a courtesan who accommodated men in the public sphere. Zuana counterclaimed that her husband sent men to her with whom to engage in sexual relations (Ferraro 112). Apparently, Zuane had tried to use his wife as a prostitute. Finally, when Zuana did secure permission to live separately from her husband, she took up residence with a merchant. In an attempt to defend her behavior, she claimed that she had no choice but to leave her husband and live with another man who would provide her with a living (Ferraro 113). Perhaps there was a question of who was actually guilty in this case. Although Zuana was hardly a paragon of virtue, the legal system decided the case in favor of her, and so the Signori di Notte exonerated her on October 30, 1579 (Ferraro 115).

In Spain as well as in Italy, the vexing question of what was the more appropriate place for women was vetted, and Seville, like Venice, was a major European entrepôt that experienced growth and development in the late 16th and 17th centuries. The expansion of Seville's population had made it the fourth largest city in Europe by the end of the 16th century; it contained a population of more than 100,000 people. Seville's population doubled between 1520 and 1580 (Perry 5–6). Because the Catholic church's beliefs about the gender of women influenced how they were perceived by the general public, there was a great concern on the part of the Catholic church as to how to maintain these women free from sins of the flesh.

Either the convent or marriage could provide an appropriately safe shelter for women, according to the thinking of the day. It was believed that marriage would be the solution to the problem of sexually unruly women. Unfortunately, the number of widows, abandoned wives, single mothers, and bigamists grew immensely in early modern Seville during periods of famine and plague, especially from 1580 to 1582 and 1599 to 1600. Nonetheless, marriage was believed to be absolutely necessary in order for society to have a workforce composed of unpaid women, and emergent capitalism was perceived as a threat to this unpaid labor force. If marriage was not available for some women for whatever financial or personal reasons, maybe the nunnery would function as an adequate enclosure for them. Instead of becoming brides of men, these women could become brides of Christ. Historians of the early modern European period will forever debate the question of whether convents were places of freedom or restriction for women; they were sources of education for women in spite of the fact that their actions were overseen by priests, but these women known as *beatas,* while venerated for their religiosity, lived outside the walls of convents and their rules and regulations, but others were prosecuted by the Inquisition for their heretical ideas, visions, and miracles thought to be false, and "spiritual arrogance" (Perry 12–13).

Of all Spanish humanists of the early modern period to provide religious instruction to women, Juan Luis Vives is the most famous for his *The Instruction of a Christian Woman.* His main concern was that women should be trained to be helpful and hardworking housewives. In a word, they were to conform to the prescriptive description of chaste, silent, and obedient wives. They were to eschew dancing, reading romances, indolence, applying cosmetics, and speaking in public; after all, loquacity in a woman was interpreted as an index of sexual promiscuity (Perry 53).

Vives was particularly concerned that a young woman would become enamored of a young man and allow her erotic feelings to overcome her sense of moral probity. He strongly suggested that women not involve themselves in romantic relationships because they were prone to becoming enamored of men and would allow the experience to consume them. They were to be devoid of erotic desire, but they were to love God, Christ, the Virgin Mary, and her mother, St. Anne, all the saints, and of course, their own parents (Perry 54).

Vives wanted young women to avoid eroticism at all turns, and it is for this reason that women were not even allowed to read courtly romances filled with knightly adventures such as *Amadis de Gaula* and *Florisande* because he was fearful that they would be aroused with erotic desire for the knight in the romance. Needless to say, these texts were very popular, especially *Amadis*, for seven separate editions of it were published between 1520 and 1547. Finally, Fernando de Roja's *Tragicomedia de Calisto y Melibea*, which was referred to most often as *La Celestina*, most enraged the righteous indignation of Christian humanists and clergy, for it was an unabashed depiction of unbridled erotic love and the use of love magic by an old woman for her own financial advancement (Perry 56).

Not all Christian humanists and religious teachers felt the same way about female sexuality and marriage as Vives did. Erasmus was known as one of the most significant proponents of the Italian Renaissance, but Vicente Mexia and Luis de Leon had different ideas about sexuality and its relation to marriage. Erasmus believed that there was a spiritual component to marriage and that marriage was the best way to preserve chastity in the faithful. Chastity, for Erasmus, was the epitome of human existence, but his doctrines' influence decreased with the advent of the Inquisition. Mexia took a companionate notion of the wife's relationship to the husband (Perry 60). Mexia believed that reason must govern eroticism in sexual relations, and he also thought that a wife could deny sexual relations to a husband who wanted to engage in sexual relations solely for the purpose of eroticism and not for the purpose of procreation, which according to the Catholic church was the primary purpose of sexual relations. Finally, Luis de Leon in his treatise *La perfecta casada* asserted that marriage was a physiological and political need. He felt that it was the means of continuing humanity, creating new servants for God, honoring the land, and giving glory to Heaven. For Luis de Leon the primary concern of marriage was an economic matter by which the financial advancement of the family was the family's paramount issue (Perry 65).

Of course, convents always provided an alternative from marriage for women. Given society's concern for the safety of young women in convents, one is surprised that young men, called *devotos*, made nuns objects of devotion. These men could have been either religious or lay who communicated with these nuns during Mass and later sent them gifts. Church authorities were not amused by such behavior, and so they attempted to keep these men from these nuns in order to protect their reputations as well as that of their order. For example, church authorities received in 1613 news that prebendaries pursued nuns in the Convent of Santa Paula in Seville (Perry 80).

Certainly, the church authorities were most concerned that these nuns' virginity remain intact, and to be sure, the Inquisition did prosecute those individuals guilty of fornication. The Inquisition pursued 174 people between 1559 and 1648 because of "simple fornication," which was actually heterosexual relations between two unmarried people. In these cases the individuals in question were punished because they argued that simple fornication was not a mortal sin, not because they engaged in sexual relations. In fact, 87 percent of those prosecuted for simple fornication were men while the women who were prosecuted were widows or unmarried women. Contrary to what one may expect, few prostitutes were prosecuted (Perry 120).

Some authorities thought that prostitution was necessary because it generated an index by which sexually inappropriate behavior was defined. Legalized prostitution had been tolerated because it was believed to prevent much more serious sexual transgressions, namely, adultery, incest, the propositioning of sexually chaste women, and perhaps worst of all, the heinous crime of sodomy. Yet with the outbreak of syphilis in 1568, the brothels within Seville saw a significant scrutiny of its prostitutes. City officials agreed to examine the prostitutes much more frequently and to send those who were sick to the city hospitals. Beginning in 1570, new ordinances required doctors to examine prostitutes every eight days and inform city officials of any prostitutes who were ill. With the increased regulation of the brothels, the padre in charge of the brothel became a municipal position. Secondly, the city official was not permitted to rent clothes to the women in the brothel, nor was he permitted to make them loans. While these women were still perceived as sinners, they were still required to attend Mass on Sundays and holy days and to abstain from prostitution on these days as well. Finally, for women who wished to give up working in the sex trade, they had the option of entering the Convent of the Most Sweet Name of Jesus, which had been created in the middle of the 16th century for prostitutes who were repentant, and they were required to adhere to a severe schedule of prayer and work in order to repent of their past transgressions for the rest of their lives (Perry 137, 139, and 141).

The most egregious sexual violation was clearly sodomy. *Las Siete Partidas* demanded the execution of those convicted of the crime of sodomy as it was a crime "against nature" with the exception of those who had been made to engage in such acts against their will and for those who were younger than 14 years of age. Interestingly, civic officials were not worried about lesbianism. Homosexual relations caused such ado that those accused of such an offense were segregated from other prisoners in the Royal Prison in Seville lest they be contaminated. In Hapsburg Spain both secular and ecclesiastical courts prosecuted cases involving sodomy. Most civic authorities in Castile, however, adjudicated these cases. In most instances, those found guilty were burned at the stake. Between 1567 and 1616 71 men met this horrific fate in Seville. Lastly, while information regarding an early modern sodomitical subculture may seem bizarre or unusual, there was one such instance in which one could be led to believe that such a subculture may have existed, for in 1585 Pedro de Leon described a group of eight men led by Diego Maldonado, who were burned; they had met outside the city walls in an area called Huerta del Rey among fig trees in an attempt to prevent their illegal sexual acts from becoming known, but unfortunately, they were unsuccessful in this endeavor. Later in 1600 15 more sodomites were prosecuted and burned. These groupings of men suggest that a homosexual subculture may have existed, but because court records are incomplete, it is impossible for historians to make that determination without further information (Perry 123–24, and 126).

Like Spain, early modern France also shared many of the same concerns regarding sexuality and its relation to marriage as its other European neighbors. French parents were also quite concerned with the independence that some of their children exhibited in their marital choices. Parents began to exert pressure in the French courts in the late 15th century as they were very worried about clandestine marriages, and so by the 16th century even the Catholic church expressed worry about clandestine marriages. For example, in 1544 and 1553 the bishops of Autun, Jacques Hurault de Cheverny and Philibert Dugny de Courgengouch, would not allow priests to marry couples who were not from their own parishes. So concerned was the French representation at the Council of Trent that the French king wanted the Catholic church to make it mandatory that the parents' consent take on so much doctrinal significance that the couple's marriage would be invalid without it. The French monarch's desire was in vain, and the "Tametsi" decree reinforced the importance of the consenting couple to the marriage's legitimacy (Farr 92).

Since parental approval, especially that of the father, was so important to a legitimate marriage, it is necessary to consider clandestine marriages and *rapt*. These violations of the criminal code must not be conflated with the act of rape, which was forced sexual relations without the desire of marriage, whereas *rapt* was "forceful abduction or seduction with the intention to marry without parental approval" (Farr 90). One must note that there was a noticeable difference between what the Catholic church required for a legitimate marriage and what the kings of France did. While the Council of Trent simply needed the consent of the couple in order for the marriage to be legitimate, the royalty of France insisted upon the approval of parents, especially that of the couple's fathers. Farr asserts that this imbroglio involving ecclesiastical authorities and the country's royalty was settled by a fictitious legalism, *rape de seduction* (91).

The French royalty wanted to use the clergy to control marriages, particularly those of the respectable social classes. In 1579 Henri III in the ordinance of Blois encouraged members of the clergy to investigate the character of those who wished to be married, and he forbade them from getting married if their parents or guardians were not approving of their marriages, and the clergy were to enforce this policy unless they wanted to be accused of aiding and abetting those who had committed *rapt* (Farr 94). Finally, Henri III's linkage of clandestine marriage with *rapt* was a highly significant change in the laws of the land. Unlike the edict of 1556, which was created in order to prevent clandestine marriages and required the transgressive party to be disinherited, the individual who was convicted of *rapt* was sentenced to death. Since capital crimes were to be tried in secular courts, the link that Henri III forged between *rapt* and clandestine marriage seriously called into question the authority of the church in these matters of marriage. As demonstrated in these issues of *rapt* and clandestine marriage, ecclesiastical and secular issues were inextricably bound up together until the 18th century (Farr 94–95).

Just as prostitution was permitted in Spain, so too was it permitted in France. Prostitution as elsewhere had been viewed as a necessary social evil, and while there were licensed brothels, prostitutes were not permitted on the streets as they were unlicensed, nor were procuresses allowed to practice their trade. Prostitution was legalized in France before 1561 given that the brothels had licenses. The French crown decided to end the operation of brothels in 1560 at the behest of the Third Estate at the Estates General; this is the only truly important act directed against prostitution before Louis XIV promulgated three statutes specifically regarding prostitution in Paris in 1684 (Farr 139).

Not only prostitution was prosecuted, but procuring was as well; in a good number of cases involving prostitution and procuring that were appealed to Parlement between 1571 and 1726, there were 76 cases in lower courts; of the 79 individuals who were prosecuted for procuring, 61 were women and 18 were men. When one looks more closely at the decisions made by the Burgundian judges, one will see that they were not as the legal theorists would have liked. Only four death sentences were handed down out of the 76 cases mentioned, and each of them had additional charges against them. In most instances judges meted out less harsh punishments. In the case of the widow Jeanne Le Bon, who was found guilty of procuring, she was sentenced to the pillory where she was to wear in the middle of the day a miter upon which was indicated her crime and lack of value to the community in which she lived. After undergoing this humiliation, a rope was placed around her neck, and she was led to the town square where she was flogged until she was bleeding, and at this point she was banished from the town's city limits. As time passed, the judiciary became increasingly progressive, and so the last time that corporal punishment was implemented was in the case of prostitution and procuring in 1644, but the public ritual of having a miter placed on the procuress and the banishing of the procuress remained in place. Punishment by branding and mutilation was overturned by the Parlement when the lower courts advocated such treatment of prostitutes and others (Farr 142–43).

Across the English Channel change was underway in ecclesiastical and secular circles, but even before the publication of *The Book of Common Prayer* in 1559, Heinrich Bullinger's *Der Christlich Eestand* (1540) was circulated in Zurich. It was the most popular marriage manual by a significant Protestant thinker and the most often printed Protestant European work in England during the reigns of Henry VIII and Edward VI. Carrie Euler reminds historians of this book's tremendous significance, "A translation by Miles Coverdale, titled *The Christen state of Matrimonye* went through no less than eight editions, seven of which were reissued between 1541 and 1552. . . . Puritan writers like William Gouge, John Dod, and Robert Cleaver extracted many of Bullinger's ideas on marriage and the family and used them in their own books" (367–68). The translation of Bullinger's book shows that connections existed among translators, publishers, and evangelical preachers in England and Europe.

Significantly, Euler argues, "Ironically, one reason for the book's popularity was its close resemblance to pre-Reformation domestic conduct books. Finally, evidence from correspondence and English evangelical literature demonstrates the reliance of the English evangelicals on Bullinger's marital theology and the influence of *Der Christlich Eestand* on the Edwardian Reformation, particularly on Archbishop Cramner's project to revise England's ecclesiastical laws in 1552" (370). Therefore, it is extremely important to remember that many of the English marriage manual writers were recipients of much of Bullinger's Continental thought concerning marriage.

One must also remember that society thought that women had to be controlled by the patriarchy both before and after the Reformation. *The Book of Common Prayer* of 1559, which contained the Protestant marriage service, strongly encouraged women to listen to the "teachings of St. Paul and to 'submit yourselves unto your own husbands, as unto the Lord, for the husband is the wives head, even as Christ is the head of the Church.' These prescriptions were amplified in the Elizabethan *Homilies* first published in 1563 and ordered to be read at church services when there was no sermon" (Eales 24).

The marriage manual, the *Homily of the State of Matrimony*, promulgated that the state of marriage was created by God in order that women and men would be able to live in amity, produce children, and avoid the sin of fornication. In a way marriage functioned so that men and women could eschew sexual transgressions. Again, these manuals made plentiful use of biblical quotations. Here St. Peter encourages husbands to "treat their wives as 'the weaker vessel'" (Eales 24). Wives were to be obedient to their husbands while children and household servants were to heed the command of the mistress of the house. At the same time husbands and wives were enjoined to be patient with each other, and husbands were not to strike their wives under any circumstances even if she were angry, inebriated, or abusive (Eales 25).

These conduct books were some of the most influential texts printed in the early modern period. The majority of them were purchased between the late 16th century and the Civil War. One scholar by the name of Kathleen Davies asserts that these books were widely read because they are indicative of what constituted the values of the "urban bourgeoisie" (Eales 25). Many Protestant clergy wrote these books, and they enthusiastically defended and defined marriage because it was the means by which they separated themselves from the Catholic church, and the paradigm of a married clergy was much more significant to them than it had been earlier (Eales 25).

There are many clerical writers who provided Protestants with advice books regarding how and why one should marry and what one's duties to one's spouse were once one had entered the state of matrimony. Today the texts of Nicholas Alexander, Richard Baxter, Thomas Becon, Edmund Bunny, Robert Cleaver, John Dod, Thomas Gataker, William Gouge, Henry Smith, and William Whately give historians of early modern English marriage a sense of how the early modern English conceptualized the responsibilities and obligations incurred upon the state of matrimony. These writers emphasized the teachings of Saints Paul and Peter in that women were to be submissive to their wives, and their subservient state was a product of humanity's fall from grace in the Garden of Eden (Eales 25).

William Gouge was once the Puritan rector of Blackfriars in London. His most celebrated text, *Of Domesticall Duties*, is a compilation of homilies that he gave and dedicated to his parishioners. His comments concerning a wife's subservience to her husband garnered him disapproval. He felt obligated to explain why he believed as he did. Therefore, he explained his beliefs regarding husband-wife relations. Gouge believed that the wife should share in the governance of the household. He asserts that husbands are not to abuse their authority, and as a consequence wives should not have any reason to complain about her subservient position to her husband (Amussen 44–45). Although Gouge felt that he had to make this apologetic statement, his attitude regarding the role of the husband in the family structure was made clear when he compared the position of the husband to a king in a castle and also compared the family to a commonwealth that the husband is to govern as a state (Amussen 37).

What is extremely important to keep in mind is that all of these marriage manuals interpreted early modern families through the lens of biblical texts as did Gouge's *Of Domesticall Duties*. Gouge's marriage manual was divided into eight sections. The first section of the book focuses on the Pauline Ephesians 5:22–6:9. The second section of the book stresses the reciprocal duties of wives and husbands to each other. There are also sections concerning the duties that children have to their parents and the duties that parents have to their children; lastly, there is a section defining the duties that servants have to their master and the duties that masters have toward their servants (Amussen 38).

Most of these conduct manuals have two significant points. Amussen argues that women and children were obedient to husbands and fathers because of particular responsibilities that they fulfilled for their spouses and offspring. All of these relationships had their own interpersonal dynamics. Gouge did, in fact, deal with the sexual relationship in marriages. He perceived the conjugal relationship as necessary to the functioning of the marriage, and therefore, for this reason he was in favor of permitting divorces if the husband was impotent but not in the case of infertility. Finally, just as all relationships were reciprocal, so too were both husband and wife responsible for the financial well-being of the family (Amussen 38–39 and 41).

Not all of these writers always agreed with each other as to how husbands were to treat wives. William Whately in *A Bride-Bush; or, A Direction for Married Persons* (1619) clearly differed from Gouge in his opinion as to how one should treat one's wife. He admonished at one point that if a woman thought that she was her husband's equal or superior, she would be unable to reach a status of grace or salvation. Although Whately knew that a man's wife may hold a socially higher position, she would still be required to be subservient to him. Whately also placed great emphasis on a wife's silence in the presence of her husband and other men. A woman's silence was, after all, one of the three qualities that was prized as a wifely attribute (Eales 25–26). Whately clearly broke ranks with William Gouge's attitude toward the practice of wife-beating. Whately averred that a husband really should not assault his wife because it was a sign of arrogance on the part of the husband and abjection on the part of the wife (Amussen 42).

William Gouge was even more opposed to corporeal punishment than Whately, for he apparently believed that his striking his wife was equivalent to his striking himself, and he encouraged husbands to refer the matter to the appropriate magistrate. Not especially enlightened by today's standards, he opined that men's beating their wives was not a particularly efficient way of correcting them (Amussen 43).

Protestant thinkers believed that women should be educated so that they could read the Bible and other devotional texts in order that they could lead morally upright and chaste lives and later teach their own children to read after they married. Vives, while not a Protestant divine, was a Spanish thinker whose enormously influential book, *The Instruction of a Christian Woman*, was translated and had gone through nine English editions by the end of the 16th century. Eales argues that Vives perceived connections between chastity and learning; godly learning was thought to elevate the mind to an understanding of goodness. Hence, the intellect could repel impure thoughts and so lift it. Vives suggests very strongly that girls eschew romances and study the Bible and read the great church fathers, Jerome, Cyprian, Augustine, and Gregory, as well as classical writers such as Seneca, Cicero, and Plato (36). Vives, in *The Office and Duties of a Husband*, elaborated upon the advice book which he had written in English in the 1550s. He believed that women should not be allowed to read frivolous books, and at the same time he did not wish women to engage with serious books that dealt with profound theological concerns, but they should read books that inculcated virtue and holiness. Conversely, he thought that men should have knowledge of politics, history, grammar, logic, and mathematics. Moreover, women should not have skill in oratory for fear of women gaining confidence in public speech, which would be a violation of their injunction to silence (Eales 37).

There were, however, a few women who wrote books concerning youth's coming of age and marriage for their daughters. Dorothy Leigh's manual for mothers, *The Mother's Blessing* (1616), provided advice to young mothers and their children. She said that she wanted men to hold the major place of importance in marriage, but a man's wife was not to be his servant (Eales 29). Amussen asserts, "Wives were joined with their husbands in the management and supervision of the household. The household manuals expected women to make an important economic contribution to the household: they emphasized the wife's role in provisioning the household, and the importance of her thrift" (41). To be sure, Leigh thought that women should be an integral part of the household.

Leigh, like other mothers during her time and like mothers today, was quite concerned about her children making the right choices in marriage, and, of course, making the right spousal choice was as difficult then as it is today. Although there was no ritualized process which one followed per se in order to find a spouse, certain patterns existed by which one became integrated into the large early modern English community. Those who were wealthy and possessed a great deal of property have the most information recorded about their lives and apparently engaged in the largest number of activities prior to their marriages while those of lesser financial status seem to have acted with less formality, but each couple's courtship experience differed for any number of reasons. It is sufficient to deduce that when women and men from as far-flung regions as Kent, Derbyshire, East Anglia, and North Country, both rural and urban areas, act in a similar fashion, a common culture is at work (Cressy 234).

Because of the importance of economic stability in early modern marriage, complex security systems provided for the financial well-being of the bride. Sometimes the success of the match would depend upon the marriage dowry (the money or property that the wife contributes to the marriage); then there were portions which were the share of an estate that one could inherit which had been brought to the marriage; and finally, the jointure was the estate, which was kept for the wife at the time of her husband's death. There was certainly a struggle for power between the patriarchal power of the family and the desire for personal happiness on the part of the young couple (Cressy 234–35).

If one is to judge from autobiographical accounts that have survived of men receiving matrimonial proposals, it would appear that young men did not have any lack of them. In 1590, the Elizabethan magician Simon Forman claimed that he had been offered several women as wives between Easter and Whitsuntide. Sir William Ashcombe received several marriage proposals beginning at the time that he was a student at the Inns of Court. His account provided the important moments in his courtship of women from initial meetings with women to considering the quality of the woman in question, and finally, whether to continue to pay court to the woman or stop doing so (Cressy 239).

Certainly, one of the rituals by which men paid court to young women was through the process of gift giving. Gifts of ribbons, gloves, coins, even girdles were exchanged. Usually, these gifts indicated an intensity of the feelings between the man and woman. The financial value was of far less significance than their symbolic implications. Moreover, a ring was exchanged when the couple became betrothed to each other. A young man might give a gift of a 10-shilling piece of gold or a ring of that value. One church lawyer by the name of Henry Swinburne said that men gave bracelets, chains, and jewels. The ring was the embodiment of the marital promise. These exchanges could also be perceived as an imposition; they could be interpreted from a number of positions. The fashion in which a gift was given and received indicated its significance (Cressy 263–64).

When Rosa Clarke of Burton, Leicestershire, removed a ring from Thomas Wawton's finger and accepted a pair of gloves, religious bodies would consider these transactions as signs that this couple was progressing toward matrimony (Cressy 264). These actions were, in effect, contracts, and couples could make them in two ways. First, there was the contract that could be articulated in *verba de presenti*, which was an "immediate and indissoluble commitment expressed by the words 'I do'; *Verba de futuro*, a promise of future action expressed by the words 'I will'; or conditionally, such as 'when I inherit my land' or 'if your mother will provide us a house'" (Cressy 267). These formulaic statements were designed in order to avoid confusion and embarrassment concerning the initial marital matter under consideration.

Henry Smith, best known for his *Preparative for Marriage*, believed that the couple should take time to reflect upon the decision they were making between the contract and the actual marriage ceremony. He, too, believed that there should be some kind of ritual, which confirmed the marital agreement (Cressy 267). In an illustration from *The Roxburghe Ballads* titled *A Pleasant New Ballad of Tobias*, one sees a couple having their hands held by a member of the clergy as they celebrate their betrothal ceremony with witnesses in order to give greater dignity and significance to this occasion (Cressy 267–68).

William Gouge thought that some kind of formal agreement should be made when the couple "manifested a mutual liking each to other" in the presence of witnesses. For Gouge, this was to be a rather ritualized ceremony in which the woman and man took each other's hands and repeated the formula to each other. As far as Gouge was concerned, this contract was the initiation into marriage. Gouge also believed that this action should be transacted in front of witnesses as he clearly thought of this transaction in legal terms. This verbal contract made the couple into an "espoused man and wife in the time present" and so they were bound to marry each other in *per verba de futuro*. Given there was no impediment to their marriage because of an earlier marriage agreement, or impediment because of closeness of blood relation and mental competence, no one had the legal power to separate them. Gouge wanted the couple to reflect upon the importance of this decision in their lives, and he also took note of the fact that some families celebrated the espousals with greater merriment than the actual wedding (Cressy 270–71).

Apparently, many couples thought they could live together as husband and wife after the espousals, but this was not the case. There was a great deal of social pressure for the couple to be married in a church in order for the process of marriage to be complete. Nonetheless, historians know that some couples engaged in sexual intercourse before marriage because the parish registries indicate that "some 20 to 30 percent of all brides [bore] children within the first eight months of marriage" (Cressy 277). The actual rate of infants born out of wedlock was very low, hovering between 2 and 4 percent, and these pregnancies were associated with espousals that had been broken. Under the reign of Charles I, the number of infants born out of wedlock dropped, which demonstrates a change in the culture's sense of morality or greater sexual restraint (Cressy 277).

The historical record indicates that of those who reached adulthood in the 16th century, some 90 percent would marry while 80 percent would marry in the 17th century. The mean age of marrying for the first time was 27 or 28 years of age for men and 25 or 26 years of age for women. This demographic account explains to some extent the growth of population in the 17th century (Cressy 285). Initially, some historians may comment on the late date of marriage for many of these individuals, but again, many couples may have been cautionary for fear of marrying without sufficient income to support a family. In fact, some ministers and parish officers actively tried to prevent marriages of very poor community members regardless of their age because they believed that they would become a financial burden to the community and thereby increase the poor rates (Ingram 131).

Inasmuch marriage was encouraged by the ministers of the community, there were times during which marriage was prohibited. The principal times during which marriages were not performed were Lent in order to prepare for the feast of Easter, Rogationtide and Trinity in late spring, the Ascension, and Advent in preparation for Christmas. The church calendar was complex and confusing because the date of Easter changed on a yearly basis. Fortunately, almanacs provided parishioners the change of the church holidays. The Church of England had some 144 days during the year that were designated as inappropriate for marriages, which was almost 40 percent of the calendar (Cressy 298–99).

The publication of the banns of marriage was an extremely important part of the marriage process. It was required that the banns be published three times during the regular church year. This requirement was found in the *Book of Common Prayer* and reiterated in the canons of 1604. The publication informed neighbors of the upcoming wedding and also informed the community in which the couple lived of the impending marriage. The ringing of bells occurred in some regions of England at the publication of the first banns, which was called a "spurring peal." These announcements gave the neighbors and townspeople time to consider whether there was any reason for which this couple should not be joined in matrimony. William Gouge realized the importance of the banns of marriage because it provided sufficient time between the creation of the contract for the marriage ceremony not only for the couple to reflect upon their decision but also for the banns to be read three times so that the couple could prepare everything that they needed to live as husband and wife (Cressy 305–6).

Most of the marriages took place during times of abundance. In farming country there was a noticeable increase in marriages after harvest, specifically September in southern England and closer to Martinmas, which was November 11 in the north. In pastoral regions of England, there was a significant increase in marriages after lambing and calving occurred. Moreover, the timing of servants' contracts also affected the marriage rates, especially with the increase in rural specialization as the 17th century progressed. Urban areas such as London experienced a leveling off of marriages because the growing season had less and less of an impact on it, and so an even distribution of marriages appeared. Still marriages were prohibited during Lent, Advent, and Rogationtide unless the couple obtained a special license (Cressy 301).

Certainly, one of the greatest concerns among the clergy and civil authorities was the business of clandestine marriages. Despite the fact that couples may have fulfilled the least requirements of the law for marriage by only their consent outside of a church, they were far from meeting their social and cultural obligations by marrying in this fashion. The fact of the matter was that the great majority of the marriages were solemnized in a ceremony by a minister. Even clandestine marriages took place in a church with an ordained minister performing the ceremony. It is important to note that the period from 1560 until 1640 was a time of social regularity and conformity in marital matters. With the creation of parish registers in 1538, ecclesiastical and secular courts created a textual record of all marriages (Cressy 316).

Only the most radical reformers advocated civil marriages, for the majority of the Puritans and Church of England clergy were in agreement that a marriage was to take place in a church and that it should take place in an open and public fashion. Theoretically, marriages were to occur between the hours of 8 and 12 in the morning in the presence of the bride and groom's parents, family, friends, and neighbors. John Angier, a Presbyterian, was married publicly in a Manchester church in 1643 at which time two sermons were delivered (Cressy 319–20).

Marriages in pre-Reformation England began at the church porch rather than at the church altar. This interstitial space indicated the place where the sacred and the secular met. However, according to a Tudor etiquette book, the son of an earl could be married at the choir door below the chancel. By contrast, the Protestants put marriage inside the church making it the center of activity. Nonetheless, the ritual of the family paying the bride's dowry at the door of the church continued through the 17th century regardless of the fact that the marriage took place at the altar (Cressy 336).

Certainly today the giving away of the bride in marriage by her father is perceived of as a residual ritual from earlier times in which women functioned as chattel that was passed from father to husband. Richard Hooker, a defender of the Church of England, approved of the father's giving away the bride. He argued, "It putteth women in a mind of duty whereunto the very imbecility of their nature and sex doth bind them, namely to be always directed, guided and ordered by others" (Cressy 339).

Next came the "handfastening, the taking and loosening of hands, and the plighting of troths," a ceremony that was very much like the Catholic pre-Reformation one except at the end of it, the ceremony was concluded with the words, "according to God's holy ordinance" rather than "if holy church will ordain it" (Cressy 340). Significantly, the woman said much the same as the man in the marriage ceremony with the exception "to obey." Finally, came the ring. To be sure, rings, then as now, were laden with many meanings and associations. The minister was to take the ring from the book on which it had been placed and give it to the man who was instructed to place it on the fourth finger of the woman's left hand, and the man was to say, "With this ring I thee wed; with my body I thee worship; and with all my worldly goods I thee endow" (Cressy 340). Some English did not like the inclusion of the ring in the ceremony because it reminded them too much of the rituals associated with the Catholic church, nor did some of the Puritans appreciate the reference to the man worshipping his wife's body as a distant allusion to pagan worship (Cressy 340).

The celebrations that accompanied weddings were a source of trouble for Puritan ministers. To be sure, more cultural energy went into wedding celebrations than the formality of the marriage service. Reformers in the 16th century inveighed against these wedding celebrations largely because of ideological reasons. These celebrations began with overindulgent eating and drinking. According to Miles Coverdale, members of the wedding party would attend the service somewhat inebriated. Coverdale provides an especially vivid description of a wedding celebration that outraged him because of the frenetic dancing and leaping about and then the lifting of women's dresses in a risqué fashion that bordered on vulgarity (Cressy 352).

In addition to revelry, gift giving was a significant component within the marriage festivities. Elizabethan and Stuart weddings were marked by the giving of gloves, brideknots, and favors that the bride and groom gave to each other and were also given to guests to be worn on their wedding clothes as expressions of their affection and reminders of the wedding. Guests of wealthy brides and grooms became accustomed to receiving a pair of gloves, and even those who may not have attended the ceremony might expect to receive a pair (Cressy 362).

Flowers, too, were an important aspect of the wedding celebration, and they, of course, held a multiplicity of meanings. Garlands of flowers indicated "the gladness and the dignity of the sacrament" (Cressy 363). At bride-ales, celebratory gatherings in honor of the couple, the house would be filled with sweet herbs in order to indicate that all discord and strife were to be put aside and replaced with peace, happiness, and mildness. Moreover, the church also included references to different kinds of flowers as indexes of different virtues. Roger Hacket of North Crawley, Buckingham, gave a homily as a present and referred to the flowers in the wedding bouquet— primroses, maiden's blush, violets, and rosemary—as indicative of particular attributes such as obedience, mild patience, and faithfulness to the wife, and wisdom, love, and loyalty to the husband, which were qualities that society highly prized in spouses (Cressy 365). Even the flora of the garden could be co-opted to control the behavior of the wife by the husband.

In early modern England as today, not all weddings ended happily ever after, but unlike today, marriages were usually not annulled because they were forced marriages or unconsummated. Bigamy involved far more cases; between 1572 and 1640, 44 witnesses testified in cases of bigamy. The typical story involved one spouse thinking the other was dead and the later reappearance of the missing spouse. The laws of the land stated that one could only remarry after the disappearance of one's spouse for seven years. The most significant part of legal proceedings involved the separation of spouses for two reasons, adultery or extreme cruelty. Almost always men sued for separation because of adultery, and women sued for separation on the grounds of their husbands' violence (Gowing 182–83).

Early modern narratives about adultery almost always involved the wife. A husband's adultery rarely constituted grounds for separation. While wives sued for separation because of adultery, it was most likely within the context of either cruelty or desertion and the creation of another household with another woman. On the other hand, tales of a wife's adultery emphasized either a single event or the repetition of events which focused on the wife's refusal to adhere to the socially acceptable standards of an early modern English wife (Gowing 188–89).

These cases concerning adultery hinged on testimony from witnesses attesting to the behavior of the wife or husband in question. Suspicion of a woman's infidelity might be construed through seeing the woman at unusual places that one would not be inclined to see such a person. Early modern courts heard much testimony from neighbors, servants, and apprentices regarding the woman of the house in which they observed suspicious behavior; it was not out of the ordinary for them to peer through windows, stand in dark out-of-the-way corners, and create a hole in a wall by which to watch adulterous behavior. One such case involved George Mathew, who testified in the case involving George Marr against his wife Margaret in 1573. He testified that he saw Margaret Marr with Edmund Allen in bed partially unclothed through a hole in the wall. Apparently, the early modern household provided little secure privacy with the prevalence of large keyholes, thin walls, and cloth partitions which allowed inquisitive servants and apprentices to learn of their masters and mistresses' activities, legal or otherwise (Gowing 190).

The question often arose as to what the husband was to do once he had learned of his wife's infidelity. The fact that his wife slept with another man made him a cuckold, which was associated with the betrayed husband with proverbial horns on his head, but if the man learned of his wife's infidelity and did nothing to stop it, then he was a wittold, a husband who in effect overlooked his wife's adulterous behavior. Maybe husbands expressed shock and horror in an effort to mitigate the ridicule that would accompany the exposure of the wife's adultery. After William Loder found out his wife Elizabeth was unfaithful in 1625, he informed his friends of what she had done and played up the shocking nature of her actions, and took his friends to the room in which the adultery actually occurred (Gowing 192).

Just as William Loder was very much concerned with his reputation, so too were women, especially those who were slandered. Four times as many women as men brought slander cases of a sexual nature before 1600; it was closer to six times as many between 1600 and 1640 (Gowing 65). In the 17th century, 130 men and women came to church courts testifying in cases involving slander concerning sexual issues. Secular courts also experienced a rise in the number of defamation cases, which they attempted to limit. Seventy-five percent of all cases involving slander were brought by women. Slander of women was also a crime usually committed by women. The majority of both the defendants and the plaintiffs were married women, and most of these women were from the middling sort, who were the wives and daughters of merchants and artisans and were their husbands' partners in their businesses (Gowing 61).

While women did call each other slanderous names such as prostitute, whore, or quean, the defamers rarely believed that these women in question had engaged in illicit sexual relations with other men. Rather this was a form of verbal abuse, but some women in fact did engage in prostitution. Those women who did engage in prostitution were known for their use of cosmetics. Sara Wood told Martha Rowe that she had a box of cosmetics and was a "painted gille" (Gowing 80). Prostitutes were most known for their noses, and their noses functioned as a metaphor for the tails that they were to represent. In other words, the face was to act as an index of the sexual practices of the woman.

Unlike women's genitalia, men's sexual organs were not objects of shame. Men's genitals were described quite precisely. In 1620 one woman told another that her husband's penis had never been disfigured with small pox and cut in half.

On another occasion John Ashenden told a court about a conversation he had concerning the drawing of a penis on the wall of a tavern. He was asked by one interlocutor as to whether his sexual organ was of that length, and he said not yet. On the other hand, women's genitals did not appear on tavern walls. Rather "tail" is the only reference that was made to women's genitals on a regular basis. References to women as "tails" were a source of contempt. Finally, men's genitals are described as intriguing or fascinating while women's are described as repellent or disgusting (Gowing 81–82).

Clothes also functioned as an index of the sexual behavior of a woman. Those who made degrading comments about prostitutes' attire focused upon their violation of sumptuary laws which regulated individuals wearing certain kinds of clothes based on the quality of the garment's material, cut, color, or texture. These sumptuary laws were in effect until 1604. Women were advised to wear clothing that reflected their husbands' social station. Silk, satin, and taffeta were luxurious fabrics that women of the nobility wore. The wearing of sumptuous clothes by prostitutes and the abject nature of their livelihood created a stark juxtaposition. Again, clothes functioned as significant sartorial markers that allowed all members of society to know one's social status by sight on any early modern street (Gowing 82–83).

One's clothes were to signal not only one's social status but also one's gender. King James expressed cultural anxiety about women wearing men's clothes, especially wide hats, doublets, and short hair. There was little chance of these women being taken for men, but the concern was rather that their cross-dressed appearance indicated sexual availability. The primary concern was the breeches, which signaled the patriarchy. The popular literature and ballads of the day focused on the pants as the center of male power. In fact, the accusation of wearing the breeches was enough for some to consider it slander when someone had posted a paper stating that Alice Baker wore the pants in her family (Gowing 84).

By far the most outrageous sexual offense was sodomy. The Puritan writer John Rainolds argued that homosexuality "was a sin to which men's natural corruption and viciousness is prone" (Bray 17). Inasmuch as this sexual transgression was inveighed against, there were surprisingly few cases brought to court. Research regarding the Essex Quarter Sessions between 1556 and 1680 indicate not one single case involving homosexual behavior, and research of the Essex Assize between 1560 and 1680 found only one case. In a study of the Somerset Quarter Sessions, the same results were found for 1601–1660; only two cases were found. For a 66-year period from 1559 to 1625, all the counties of Kent, Sussex, Hertfordshire, and Essex had only four indictments concerning homosexuality (Bray 71).

Finally, there was the occasional high-profile case involving someone of prominence within the country as in the case of John Atherton, the bishop of Waterford and Lismore, who was executed by hanging in 1640 after he was found guilty of incest, rape, adultery, and, finally, sodomy (Bray 14). If scandals were incorporated into popular verse, certainly knowledge of these sexual activities was available to the woman or man on the street of early modern London or another large urban area as evidenced by a black letter ballad, which was printed as a broadsheet circa 1570 and titled "Of the Horrible and Wolful Destruction of, Sodome and Gomorra" that is housed in the British Library (Bray 19). Not surprisingly, scandals of a sexual nature spread through both word of mouth and the printed text, which circulated within large, metropolitan circles.

WORKS CITED

Amussen, Susan Dwyer. *An Ordered Society: Gender and Class in Early Modern England.* New York: Columbia UP, 1988. Print.

Bray, Alan. *Homosexuality in the English Renaissance.* Boston: Gay Men's Press, 1982. Print.

Crawford, Katherine. *European Sexualities, 1400–1800.* Cambridge: Cambridge UP, 2007. Print.

Cressy, David. *Birth, Marriage, and Death: Ritual, Religion, and the Life-Cycle in Tudor and Stuart England.* New York and Oxford: Oxford UP, 1999. Print.

Eales, Jacqueline. *Women in Early Modern England, 1500–1700.* London: UCI Press, 1998. Print.

Euler, Carrie. "Heinrich Bullinger, Marriage, and the English Reformation: *The Christen state of matrimonye in England,* 1540–53." *Sixteenth Century Journal* 34.2 (2003): 367–93. Print.

Farr, James R. *Authority and Sexuality in Early Modern Burgundy (1550–1730).* New York and Oxford: Oxford UP, 1985. Print.

Ferraro, Joanne M. *Marriage Wars in Late Renaissance Venice.* New York and Oxford: Oxford UP, 2001. Print.

Gowing, Laura. *Domestic Dangers: Women, Words, and Sex in Early Modern London.* Oxford: Clarendon Press, 1998. Print.

Ingram, Martin. *Church Courts, Sex, and Marriage in England, 1570–1640.* Cambridge and New York: Cambridge UP, 1990. Print.

Laven, Mary, *Virgins of Venice: Broken Vows and Cloistered Lives in the Renaissance Convent.* New York: Viking, 2003. Print.

Perry, Mary Elizabeth. *Gender and Disorder in Early Modern Seville.* Princeton, NJ: Princeton UP, 1990. Print.

Wiesner-Hanks, Merry E. *Christianity and Sexuality in the Early Modern World: Regulating Desire, Reforming Practice.* London and New York: Routledge, 2000. Print.

3

SEXUALITY IN SHAKESPEARE'S WORKS

Sexuality plays a highly significant role in many of Shakespeare's plays and poems because it structures gender and power relations among characters. The following plays and poems indicate the importance of sexuality between men and women and how sexuality affects their relationships. The first play to be considered is *The Taming of the Shrew,* which is celebrated for its robust physicality of Katherina and Petruchio's relationship, and can too easily border on farce if its slapstick humor is overplayed. The *Sonnets* recount ambivalent and unresolved conflicts among the persona, the young man, and the powerfully erotic woman, whom the persona vehemently denounces on occasion.

Then in *Romeo and Juliet* one finds the archetypal play of young love that has become for Western civilization the epitome of heterosexual relations while *A Midsummer Night's Dream,* which is often thought of as a comedy of young love that eventuates in marriage, at the same time reminds its audience of the dark underside of human sexuality in which danger and violation lurk. *Much Ado about Nothing* is once again another comedy in which young love is celebrated in the relationship of Hero and Claudio, but at the same time a more mature love that has become seasoned is also depicted between Beatrice and Benedick who love each other but feel compelled to engage in verbal dueling not completely unlike that of Petruchio and Katherina. *Henry IV, Part 1,* a history play, focuses largely upon the coming of age of young Prince Hal and his need to demonstrate his ability to rule responsibly after the death of his father Henry IV, but this play also concerns the sexual relationships of Falstaff and Mistress Quickly and Hotspur, Hal's rival, and his wife.

Sexual relations take a decided turn for the worse in Shakespeare's tragedies, for in *Hamlet,* the supreme drama of Western theatre, tragedy ensues after Hamlet's mother, Gertrude, marries his uncle, Claudius, soon after his father's death/murder; and consequently, a sexually conflicted relationship occurs between Hamlet and Ophelia in which Hamlet finally exhorts her to join a nunnery where she will be safe from the temptations of the flesh because he himself is repulsed by female sexuality. Sexuality becomes the means by which humanity can be degraded as well as elevated. In yet another tragedy, female sexuality takes center stage, for *Othello* presents sexuality, especially Moorish sexuality, as rapacious and violent in its relationship to white female sexuality in the husband and wife relationship of Othello and Desdemona. Finally, Shakespeare takes his audience to the fanciful world of *The Tempest* in which Prospero's daughter, Miranda, whose name means one who is wondered at, meets her prince charming, Ferdinand, but at the same time there is the ominous reference to Sycorax, Caliban's mother, who was a sorceress and engaged in sexual relations with the devil in order to produce Caliban, who is sexually attracted to Miranda. Caliban, however, is sequestered from her by Prospero so she may be able to marry Ferdinand in order to build a powerful dynasty between himself and the King of Naples.

Our discussion of Shakespeare's plays does not, however, begin in the realm of magic and romance; rather it begins with a play often associated with the school of hard knocks more so than fancy and whim. *The Taming of the Shrew* opens with the induction, a framing scene, in which the character of Christopher Sly, a beggar, is convinced by a lord that he is of noble birth in order to play an elaborate trick on him. He is literally picked from the gutter having been expelled from a tavern by the hostess for refusing to pay for glasses that he has broken. The lord commands his servant to have him taken to his best room which should be decorated with "wanton pictures" (44); the chamber should be aromatic, and pleasant music should be played. Bartholomew, the lord's page, dresses as a woman so Sly can have some female companionship, and the lord is very amused at how his page will respond to the sexual advances of Sly. The lord's hoped-for desire is fulfilled when the cross-dressed page comes to Sly, and Sly commands, "Servants, leave me and her alone. / Madam, undress you and come now to bed" (Induction II.114–15). The page boy fends off Sly's unwanted sexual advances by reminding him that engaging sexual relations too soon after his illness would not be in the best interest of his health.

A potentially erotic disaster is circumvented by the quick-thinking page unlike the scenarios of sexual violation from the classical past that adorn the walls of the lord's finest chamber. In these dire situations clever responses do not save young women from rape and death, for the first serving man asks Sly if he likes the pictures in this chamber as he describes the images of Adonis and Cytherea on the tapestry. The lord tells Sly of Io, who was "beguiled and surprised / As lively painted as the deed was done" (52–53). Finally, the third serving man tells of Apollo's mad pursuit of Daphne, which eventuates in her transformation into a laurel tree. Whether these images are individual or combined on one tapestry, they are all standard fare from Ovid's *Metamorphoses* (Oliver 100). Significantly, they are all scenes of sexual violence. Cytherea otherwise known as Venus objectifies Adonis as many men have done so to women, and she pursues him to his detriment by his being gored by a boar, which functions as his symbolic castration and death. (Shakespeare's narrative poem, "Venus and Adonis," recounts this series of sad events in exacting detail.) Io is raped by Jupiter (Zeus), who had concealed himself by a cloud. Finally, Daphne, who does not desire the sexual advances of Apollo, prays to the gods for an escape, and they in turn transform her into a laurel tree (Oliver 101). All of these classical figures meet certain death and destruction trying to avoid rape or sexual advances of one kind or another.

When the first scene opens, Baptista, Katherina's father, remonstrates with Hortensio, a suitor and Gremio, an old man and a figure of fun, who want to marry Bianca, and he informs them that Bianca cannot marry until Katherina does because Katherina is older. Baptista says that he may "court her at [his] pleasure" (I.i.54) to which Gremio responds by saying "[t]o cart her rather" (55). Carting was a punitive practice by which prostitutes were punished. They were driven through the streets of the city to the appointed place of punishment. Katherina immediately responds by asking her father if her marriage to Gremio was "to make a stale" (58) of her. Because of her father's treatment of her, she implies that he is treating her as a bawd would a prostitute.

Juxtaposed to Katherina is Bianca, who attracts Lucentio. He looks on this scene of family strife and realizes that Bianca should be his wife because she displays sweet maiden modesty and obedience to her father by agreeing to learn Latin and music. Lucentio sounds like the lover who places his beloved on a pedestal when he tells Tranio, his servant, "Hark, Tranio, thou mayst hear Minerva speak" (I.i.84). Minerva was the goddess of wisdom, and some say she was the inventor of the flute (Oliver 110). Bianca has been transformed into a goddess, and he has never even spoken to her. Lucentio functions as a kind of stereotype, for he exclaims, "Tranio, I burn, I pine, I perish, Tranio, / If I achieve not this young modest girl" (I.i.152–53). Lucentio is representative of a Petrarchan and New Comedy lover (Mikesell 111). Lucentio suffers as do all of the young lovers who experience love at first sight in early modern English plays, and so he decides to impersonate a schoolmaster who teaches Latin in order to gain access to Bianca while his servant pretends to be Lucentio in order to negotiate a marriage settlement for his master, for Lucentio is so insistent upon meeting Bianca privately that he would abase himself in the most abject fashion in order to have her love.

When Petruchio comes to Padua, the dynamics of the wooing change considerably because he is, after all, a fortune hunter of sorts. He states his position to Hortensio whom he knows, "I come to wive it wealthily in Padua; / If wealthily, then happily in Padua" (I.ii.74–75). Petruchio looks at marriage as a financial transaction, and therefore, he does not care how loudly the woman shouts, as Petruchio says, "For I will board her though she chide as loud / As thunder when the clouds in autumn crack" (I.ii.94–95). This statement clearly has sexual overtones, for Beatrice in *Much Ado about Nothing* tells the masked Benedick that she wishes he had boarded her.

Hortensio explains to Petruchio that Bianca cannot marry until Katherina has, but no one is interested in her because she is a shrew and therefore known for her "scolding tongue" (I.ii.99). Apparently, the meaning of the word "shrew" underwent changes in its meanings during the early modern period, and Marjorie Beth Garber cites them:

> a wicked, evil-disposed, or malignant man; a mischievous or vexatious person; a rascal; a villain

the Devil;
a thing of evil nature or influence;
a person, especially (now only) a woman given to railing or scolding or other perverse or malignant behavior; frequently, a scolding or turbulent wife

Garber points out that the word "shrew" increasingly came to refer to a woman who is unruly, especially a wife (66).

Of course, Petruchio is undeterred in his pursuit of Katherina, and once he is assured by Baptista of what her dowry will be, he is ready to meet her alone. When Petruchio does engage with her, he does so in a playful, even teasing fashion in order to gauge her disposition to him. Appropriately, he plays upon her name by referring to her as "Kate of Kate Hall" and his "super dainty Kate." Katherina is not amused by his witty wordplay, for he largely describes her in opposition to how others perceive her. Kates are delicacies or fine meat (Oliver 143). Moreover, she wishes to define herself through her independence of thought and action. The witty wordplay quickly gets out of hand and ends up in a risqué bandying of words. Maurice Charney argues that the dialogue between Petruchio and Kate is a battle of wits. Petruchio is not as powerful as he thinks, for Kate is as sharp-tongued as he; moreover, the conversation is also of a sexual nature (Charney 51). In fact, the banter gets out of hand with Petruchio going so far as to suggest that she says that he has his tongue in her vagina or anus (Partridge 255). At this point Katherina becomes irate and strikes Petruchio. It is important to note that in the early modern English period "scolding = active use of the female tongue = female sexuality = female penis" (Jardine 121).

At the same time that Petruchio can express risqué banter, he can also make elegant classical allusions with which he compares Katherina to Diana, who is the goddess of chastity. In fact, he tells Baptista that he believes Katherina will be a second Griselda for patience as well as a Lucrece, a Roman woman known for her chastity because she committed suicide out of shame after she was raped by her brother-in-law, Tarquin. While Baptista is dumbstruck by the turn of events culminating in the upcoming wedding of Katherina and Petruchio, he really is unconcerned as to why they are marrying each other. He simply wants Katherina to marry so he can marry Bianca, and he even admits to acting as a merchant in his negotiation of Katherina's marriage to Petruchio. Tranio, pretending to be Lucentio, extends the metaphor by referring to Katherina as a commodity that was before him awaiting its destination on the perilous sea. It is because of these kinds of mercantile metaphors that feminist scholars argue that Baptista uses Katherina as a means of exchange "on a desperate mart" (II.i.229) as Baptista admits.

The real taming of Katherina occurs after Petruchio gets her home to Pisa where he starves her and keeps her awake by arguing all night. Petruchio knows very well what he is doing, for by exhausting Katherina physically and psychologically, he believes that he can gain mastery over her. Petruchio envisions himself as lord and master of his household. Coppélia Kahn strongly believes that Petruchio's comparison of Katherina to a falcon very much surprises the 20th-century audience as well as Shakespeare's audience regardless of the fact that the early modern English audience would have a great deal of respect for falconry as an aristocratic pastime (111–12).

Katherina's speech concerning wifely obedience at the end of Act V functions as the summation of how a wife should perceive her relationship to her husband according to early modern English mores. She instructs Bianca and the Widow in their duties and allegiance to their husbands, for they are their lords and sovereigns and owe them complete obedience. Katherina implicitly compares a husband to a prince, a sovereign, or other governmental figure to whom the wife must owe all allegiance and obedience. Although Katherina speaks the orthodoxy of the day, one wonders whether this is a performance for those at this family gathering. Kahn suggests that this verbal performance is like the one on the road to Padua in which Katherina agrees to whatever Petruchio says is in the sky whether it be sun or moon. Moreover, this speech is a demonstration of her obedience to her husband before someone in a public sphere. Secondly, while the speech argues for the subordination of women, it allows Katherina to overpower her listeners. Finally, this complete change of character is largely reflective of farce (Kahn 116).

At the end of the play, we are left with Lucentio and Hortensio and their respective wives, Bianca and the Widow, who refuse to come when called, but Katherina does come much to their surprise. One may wonder who in fact is married to the shrew or shrews. The fact of the matter is that Petruchio is now able to have Katherina at least perform outwardly as she should according to the social conventions of the time. Kahn makes an extremely astute remark regarding gender and power relations when she argues,

> It is Kate's submission to him that makes Petruchio a man, finally and indisputably. This is the action toward which the whole plot drives, and if we consider its significance for Petruchio and his fellows, we realize that the myth of feminine weakness, which prescribes that women ought to or must inevitably submit to man's superior authority, masks a contrary myth: that only a woman has the power to authenticate a man by acknowledging him *her* master. (117)

Whether Katherina truly believes what she says at the play's end, audience members may never know, but surely Katherina and Petruchio do love each other, for Petruchio says, "Why, there's a wench! Come on, and kiss me, Kate" (V.ii.180). At the end of Act V, Petruchio gives the command, "Come, Kate, we'll to bed" (V.ii.184).

Despite the popularity of narrative poems such as "Venus and Adonis" whose provenance is Ovid's *Metamorphoses* (Williams 119), sonnets were all the rage at the end of the 16th century in England, but they took their place of origin in Italy. The Italian influence in English verse began with Thomas Wyatt's and the Earl of Surrey's imitations of Petrarch's poetry, which was printed in Tottel's *Miscellany* (1557). The sonnet, which means "little song, is usually 14 lines but not always. It originated in the thirteenth century with the poet Giacomo da Lentini. Italian sonnets most often took the form of an eight line octave (abbaabba) and a six line sestet (cdecde); the English sonnet was modified because of a deficiency of words ending in rhyming vowels; consequently, the English poets developed three quatrains and a final couplet of two rhymed words (abab cdcd efef gg). The purpose of the rhyming couplet was to provide some kind of closure, even a commentary of sorts on the preceding three quatrains. The interest in sonnets reached its peak in the 1590's" (Miola 33).

We know that Shakespeare's sonnets were printed in 1609 and that some of them had been written 10 years earlier; they even appeared to conform to the literary expectations of his time (Wells 39). Shakespeare's *Sonnets*, which contain some of the most heartfelt expressions of love and are certainly some of the most enthusiastically discussed and debated poems in English literature, do not directly concern death, but rather the sonnet sequence or cycle begins with exhortations from the poet or narrator to the beautiful young man whom he advises in the first 17 sonnets to marry in order to have an heir so that his beauty and lineage will be propagated. Needless to say, Shakespeare's *Sonnets* are the most psychologically complex and nuanced of any written in the early modern English period or any time for that matter.

The first 126 sonnets ostensibly address a beautiful young man whom the poet initially strongly urges to marry in the first 17 sonnets; the relationship between the poet and the young man has its erratic and erotic emotional vicissitudes varying from sonnets of high praise for the young man's beauty and importunities to beget an offspring to denunciation and a sense of betrayal for perceived slights on the part of the young man toward the older poet. The structure of the sonnet sequence is such that the poet discontinues his relationship with the young man at the end of "Sonnet 126" in order to pursue a tempestuous relationship with the famous Dark Lady in "Sonnet 127" about whom more ink has been expended than the endeavor has been worth because no woman has ever been conclusively identified as the Dark Lady.

Moreover, these first 126 sonnets are thought to have been carefully arranged, and Shakespeare wrote them over a long period of time. Burrow opines that they were composed between 1591 and 1604 (105). Suffice it to say that by 1609, Shakespeare had decided that he wanted to have others recognize his authorship of these sonnets. In any event this 154 sonnet sequence does appear to narrate the emotional vicissitudes of a relationship between an older patron and a young man in sonnets 1 through 126 in whom he has a romantic interest, and then later the patron has a torrid relationship with a woman about whom he speaks with great anger and frustration from sonnet 127 through 154, and finally, Wells does remind us that the poet does refer indirectly to the young man in "Sonnet 144" when he speaks of the "two loves he has" (53).

Despite the number of sonnets in this sequence or cycle, the poet speaks with an incandescent intensity. There is a sense of urgency as the inexorable passage of time diminishes the opportunities for the young man to marry and procreate in the first 17 sonnets. In "Sonnet 12" the repetition of the word "when" sets up a powerful response to the series of events that occur in the sonnet. The first reference to time that the narrator makes is to a clock which indicates the passage of time, and then he immediately juxtaposes the image of the end of a beautiful day to "hideous night" (2). The narrator places images of light and dark and beauty and ugliness in juxtaposition in order to create a very powerful contrast. In lines three and four, he does much the same again with the juxtaposition of light and dark in the image of the young man's once "sable curls all silvered o'er with white" (4). Then the poet moves from the young man to elements of the natural world: a tree which is barren of its leaves because of the onset of cold weather in fall; here, too, the poet speaks of the image of a leafless tree in relation to the vitality of summer's verdure now "all girded up in sheaves" (7). The beauty of summer will be placed on a bier in much the same way that the deceased "with white and bristly beard" (8) would be.

After the two quatrains, there is a turn in the poem or a reconsideration of the poet's attitude concerning the young man's beauty, for the poet states, "Then of thy beauty do I question make" (9). Burrow glosses this line to mean "speculate about" (404), for the poet imagines that the beauty of the young man will terminate "in the wastes of time" (10). In other words, his beauty will come to nothing because he refuses to marry and produce an heir. Consequently, he, too, like other wonderful products of this world such as "sweets and beauties," will be wasted and thrown away because they have spoiled (Burrow 404). Therefore, the poet concludes with the couplet at the end of the sonnet, "And nothing 'gainst Time's scythe can make defense / Save breed to brave him when he takes thee hence" (13–14). A scythe was a metal device with a blade used to harvest crops, especially grain. Here Time's scythe is an image of death and destruction as it will ultimately cut down the young man once he becomes old and has no offspring to perpetuate his lineage, and so the poet argues that the only defense against death is to procreate children. Perhaps this is too harsh of a reading. Rather there is a sense of beauty being overwhelmed by the far more powerful force of death, and so this sonnet ends on a note of resignation. The young man has one option: procreation.

Unlike "Sonnet 12" which is spoken in absolute terms, "Sonnet 20" is a study in ambiguity and complexity. The narrator of "Sonnet 20" begins by asserting that the young man has a face comparable to a young woman's "with nature's own hand painted" (1). The narrator implies that the young man's face has makeup on it. The most enigmatic phrase in this sonnet, or for that matter, perhaps in all of the sonnets, is the narrator's reference to the young man as "the master mistress of his passion" (2). Many scholars have consumed much ink trying to ferret out the meaning of this expression. Some feel that this allusion is indicative of a homoerotic relationship or a feminine quality about the young man in question or maybe has the place of importance in this sonnet sequence that a woman would otherwise have (Burrow 420). He then describes the young man as he would otherwise a woman, but despite the fact that he has a "woman's gentle heart" (2), it is not like a woman's heart in that it is not subject to "shifting change as is false woman's fashion" (3). The implication is that the man would be more steadfast in his love and loyalty to him than a woman would be. Not only is he more faithful, he has an "eye more bright than theirs, less false with rolling" (5); for the second time the word "false" is used in association with women. Moreover, the power of the man's gaze is so enthralling that it gilds whatever it views. The knotty line "A man in hue, all hues in his controlling" (7) has been variously glossed; perhaps his beauty mesmerizes all who look on him, or he is a man who can take on any complexion and therefore, make everyone submissive to his wishes (Burrow 420).

Once again, the poem takes a new direction after the two quatrains. Now the poet suggests that the young man was originally supposed to be a woman until "Nature as she wrought thee fell a-doting" (10), and consequently, the addition of the male sex organ added "one thing to my purpose nothing" (12). The words "one" and "nothing" both refer to the penis (Burrow 421). The couplet once again at the end of the sonnet functions to comment upon the preceding 12 lines: "But since she pricked thee out for women's pleasure, / Mine be thy love, and thy love's use their treasure" (13–14). First of all, these two lines are fraught with bawdy puns, for the word "prick" was slang for the penis in the 1590s (Burrow 421). These lines have been interpreted in a number of ways. The most common reading of the couplet asserts that nature created this person as a male, and consequently, the young man was to please women sexually while the poet is to have the love of the young man. Stephen Orgel, however, using the Quarto edition of this text with its original spelling, which does not have apostrophes, makes the case that instead of giving sexual pleasure to women, that the young man, on the contrary, is to receive sexual pleasure as women do (Wells 64). Whether the poet and the young man ever had a sexual relationship is impossible to determine; the fact of the matter is that this subtly ambiguous language adds all the more to the complexity and nuance of the sonnet sequence.

"Sonnet 55" shifts from exhortations to marry and allusions to sexual ambiguity as "Sonnet 12" and "Sonnet 20" do respectively to the poet's argument that this sonnet sequence will allow the young man's beauty to live in perpetuity long after he has died. The poet makes an extraordinary claim: "Not marble, nor the gilded monuments / Of princes shall outlive this pow'rful rhyme" (1–2). Despite the physical qualities of marble and "gilded monuments" (1), these sonnets will still be read many years in the future, and consequently the memory of the beautiful young man will be maintained; moreover, his memory will "shine more bright in these contents / Than unswept stone besmeared with sluttish time" (3–4). Burrow suggests that monuments with their inscriptions become dirty over the passage of time, but this will not happen to the memory of the young man because the memory of his life is preserved through these magnificent poems (490).

The poet implies that unlike "gilded monuments" (1) and marble, which "wasteful war" (5) and "Mars his sword" (7) can destroy, these poems will allow his memory to be preserved in spite of "war's quick fire" (7). The speaker becomes especially impassioned in the second quatrain when the poet articulates a very audacious assertion that men and women will remember him in spite of death and "all oblivious enmity" (9). It is almost as though the poet feels compelled to make such a grandiose assertion in order to believe in the immortality that these lines can provide the young man after his death. Once again, the poet ends the sonnet with a straightforward yet very compressed and vigorous statement: "So, till the judgement that yourself arise, / You live in this, and dwell in lovers' eyes" (13–14). In a word, until the Last Judgment at the end of world when Christ is to return to judge the living and the dead, the memory of the young man's life will remain in the memory or consciousness of all those who read these sonnets, for he will "live in this" (14), and the "this," of course, refers to the sonnet sequence.

The poet shifts thematic gears in "Sonnet 73," for he contemplates his own mortality rather than that of the young man as he does in "Sonnet 55." In this most autumnal of sonnets, the narrator compares his life to fall when the young man may perceive in the older poet a time "When yellow leaves, or none, or few, do hang / Upon those boughs which shake against the cold" (1–3). A sense of austerity pervades this sonnet from its opening lines. This image of the harsh onset of winter is reinforced by the allusion to "bare ruined choirs" (4). Here the barren trees can be compared to the ruined choirs of a church. A sense of profound desolation envelopes the tone of this sonnet. As Burrow points out, the trees are reminiscent of Gothic tracery (526), a beautifully elegiac image. The poet senses his own mortality by comparing his death to the setting of the sun—that is, "the twilight of such day" (5).

The poet uses powerful visual allusions in order to concretize the imminence of his own death. In this instance the fading glory of the sunset is juxtaposed to "black night" (7). It is at this time that "death's second self," which is a metaphor for sleep, causes everyone to go to bed in order to prepare for the next day. The poet begins the third quatrain with the anaphora "In me thou seest," with which he begins the second one, which reinforces the visual elements in the sonnet. In this instance the poet compares his life to a dying fire, which rests upon the ashes of the wood that provided its fuel. It is important that these are the "ashes of his youth" (10); once again, the poet juxtaposes the "ashes of his youth" (10) and his "death-bed" (11). Here again as in previously discussed sonnets, the final couplet ends on a note of resignation and acceptance of the inevitability of the poet's own demise: "This thou perceiv'st, which makes thy love more strong, / To love that which thou must leave ere long" (13–14). The poet exhorts the young man to love those with whom he associates because they will one day die, and he will be unable to love them as he may wish. Implicitly, the poet makes reference to himself in this statement reminding the young man to love him despite the vicissitudes within their friendship.

"Sonnet 116" continues the theme of difficulties within the relationship between the poet and the young man implying they have "a marriage of true minds" (1), and that no impediments or obstacles should be allowed to intrude upon it. Therefore, the poet begins to define love through the process of opposition using the same words by which to conceptualize the definition of love: "love is not love / Which alters when it alteration finds, / Or bends with the remover to remove" (2–4). Having defined what does not constitute love, the poet now defines it: "it is an ever-fixed mark" (5). Invoking the rhetoric of Petrarchan imagery, the poet alludes to "tempests" (6) which do not intimidate the power of love. Rather love is a force that guides the "wandering barque" (7) through tempests so that it can emerge unscathed. Without love this boat which functions as a metaphor for the couple's relationship will be drifting aimlessly across the sea of erotic human experience.

In the third stanza the poet shifts his tone from celebrating the power of love to the fact that Love is not a delusional, romantic young man, but rather he is acutely aware of the force or influence of Time on human affairs. After all, as the poet asserts, "Love's not Time's fool, though rosy lips and cheeks / Within his bending sickle's compass come" (9–10). The poet is cognizant of the devastating effect of time on beautiful "rosy lips and cheeks" (9). Once again the nearly ubiquitous image of the sickle appears in the sonnet ever ready to mow down young life. The fact of the matter is that rosy lips and cheeks coexist with the reality of death always ready to bring human existence to an end. Ending this quatrain, the poet reiterates that love is ever steadfast like the north star by which mariners guide their ships, for "Love alters not with his brief hours and weeks, / But bears it out even to the edge of doom" (11–12). The poet suggests that true love will endure until the Last Judgment in much the same way as the life of the young man will be remembered in his poetry as the poet has asserted in "Sonnet 55." Finally, the poet articulates a condition contrary to fact when he avers, "If this be error and upon me proved, / I never writ, nor no man ever loved" (13–14). This sonnet sequence is textual proof of his love for the young man.

"Sonnet 126" acts as the terminus of the young man and poet's relationship. He addresses the young man in the most affectionate and admiring of terms: "O thou my lovely boy" (1). This term of address has generated a great deal of discussion concerning the nature of the relationship that these two men enjoyed. Burrow cites this as the only occasion on which this term appears in this sonnet sequence. Apparently, this term of affection was used in Phileon Holland's translation of Plutarch's *Moralia* in which the speaker refers to a "smooth and lovely boy" (Burrow 632). In this particular situation of the young man in "Sonnet 126," he is shown holding "Time's fickle glass, his sickle hour" (2). The narrator asserts that Time holds a "fickle glass," which is an hourglass that tells time as well as his "sickle hour," which in turn will cut down the young man in much the same way it would crops or grass. Both of these images foretell the destruction of human life and the futility of human desire for immortality. The poet paradoxically opines that the young man has grown while his contemporaries have withered. In fact, the narrator uses the word "grow" twice to describe the young man's physical state. The first quatrain breaks off with a dash, and the second quatrain begins in the subjunctive mood, expressing a wish or a desire or a condition contrary to fact. The poet suggests that if Nature is the monarch over human and natural ruin, then she can retard the exactions of Time by "pluck[ing]" him back; ultimately, Time will prove the victor over Nature in the struggle to possess the young man. The narrator avers that Nature does have the capacity to "disgrace" (8) Time, but Time is the more powerful force. The third quatrain begins with the narrator's warning to fear Nature.

Despite the fact that the young man may be Nature's "minion" (9) or darling, she cannot protect him from the ravages of time: "She may detain, but not keep her treasure!" (10). The narrator is emphatic about the limit of Nature's capacities to restrain a transhistorical force. The last two lines of the sonnet function in the same way as the couplet has in earlier sonnets in that this couplet concludes the action previously delineated: "Her audit (though delayed) answered must be, / And her quietus is to render thee" (11–12). The poet uses the language of accounting in order to make sense of Nature's attempt to restrain the young man from Time by including the words "audit" (11) and "quietus" (12). Burrow says that the word "quietus" is used to indicate the "settling of a debt" (633) while the word "audit" refers to an examination of one's financial records. The *OED* indicates that an audit was "originally listened to as an oral presentation" (635). By the end of the poem, the transfer of the young man to Time from Nature becomes almost a financial transaction.

After "Sonnet 126" the poet almost exclusively addresses the Dark Lady whose identity has never been determined despite the exhaustive efforts that scholars have made to obtain it. Needless to say, the poet's relationship with the Dark Lady is always fraught with turmoil; in an effort to critique the Petrarchan commonplaces of the sonnet sequence's praise of feminine beauty, the narrator articulates a devastating indictment of the sonnet's literary tradition in "Sonnet 130." The narrator begins by informing the reader that his lover's eyes are unlike those of the sun; the point, of course, is that stereotypically the poet of a sonnet sequence would usually claim that his mistress's eyes were brighter than the sun's rays, but the poet claims the contrary. Throughout sonnet sequences the woman's beauty is often compared to an object in nature, and without a doubt they always excel it in its attractiveness. Red coral was apparently used by poets as a stock comparison to a woman's lips (Burrow 640), but in this instance the coral is redder than the woman's lips and therefore, more appealing. Then the poet sets up a series of if . . . then statements in which the antithesis of the expected response is given. In the first instance the poet asserts, "If snow be white, why then her breasts are dun" (3). Dun is a rarely used word meaning "dingy brown" (Burrow 640). Then the poet shifts to the texture of his mistress's hair in which he claims that wires grow on her head, an assertion that sounds comic, when one attempts to visualize such a spectacle. Moving from the texture of her hair to the color of her skin, he disparages its complexion by suggesting that it does not possess the combination of red and white in order to produce the complexion that was then desirable in young women. Having surveyed the aesthetic appeal of the woman, he then takes up the aromatic quality of the woman's breath in which the lover asserts that perfume smells better than her breath. Lastly, he comments upon the auditory quality of her voice in which he determines that the sound of music is euphonically of a higher aesthetic quality than the sound of her voice.

The statements that the poet makes appear more as insults than a realistic description of her, but finally, at the end of the third quatrain, he asserts with absolute sincerity: "I grant I never saw a goddess go: / My mistress when she walks treads on the ground" (12–13). The honesty with which he speaks of this woman best represents his feelings about her as there is a sense of integrity in his comments. As for the couplet, he opines quite forthrightly, "And yet, by heaven, I think my love as rare / As any she belied with false compare" (13–14). So in essence, the poet argues that despite the fact that he does not praise this woman in an extravagant fashion, his love is as precious and valuable as the love that a man would have for any other woman, who is praised extravagantly. In many ways the poet attempts to bring a sense of honesty to the complex dynamic of erotic relationships.

The last sonnet under consideration treats of the poet's relationship with both the fair young man and the Dark Lady. He makes his relationship clear about them in the first two lines of the sonnet: "Two loves I have, of comfort and despair, / Which like two spirits do suggest me still" (1–2). He soon clarifies which of the two individuals provides "comfort" (1) and which provides "despair" (1). He refers to the young man as "the better angel" (3) and the Dark Lady as "the worser spirit a woman colored ill" (4). Rather than her complexion, the reference to her being "colored ill" (4) is an allusion to her evil nature (Burrow 668). The poet suggests that she will "win" (5) him "soon to hell" (5); "hell" was a contemporary reference to the vagina in the early modern period (Burrow 668). He is fearful that the young man may come under the deleterious influence of the Dark Lady, worrying that his "purity" (8) will be contaminated by her "foul pride" (8). Once again the poet juxtaposes antithetical qualities of "purity" (8) and "foul pride" (8) in order to concretize how unlike these two figures are.

Ultimately, the poet is fearful of her polluting him sexually as he surmises: "I guess one angel in another's hell" (12). The poet uses the word "hell" literally and metaphorically, for the poet suggests that the young man's relationship with the Dark Lady can place him in an emotional "hell." Moreover, he opines that if he is engaging in sexual relations with her, then he literally is in her "hell" given the slang of the early modern period. He concludes that he will remain in a state of epistemological uncertainty concerning the relationship between the young man and the Dark Lady, "Yet this shall I ne'er know, but live in doubt, / Till my bad angel fire my good one out" (13–14). Burrow suggests that this couplet may mean that the Dark Lady may later reject him, give him a venereal disease, or literally expel his friend's penis from her vagina (668). Fittingly, this sonnet ends ambiguously as do many of the sonnets in this sonnet sequence because the sonnets depict relationships which are fraught with the all too human trials and tribulations of our daily experiences and could never terminate with the definitude that would be a welcome relief to the tumultuous representations of erotic interaction delineated in these sonnets.

Romeo and Juliet is the archetypal story of young love that ends tragically because of interfering parents and various authority figures, but it is also one filled with passionate desires and brutal violence because of the feud between the Capulets and the Montagues. Although one thinks of *Romeo and Juliet* as a play filled with high-flown poetry in which the hero and heroine express tender feelings of heartfelt desire, it is also a play that is filled with the bawdy language of the Nurse and Mercutio who ground erotic desire in bodily physicality.

In the opening scene of the play, two of Capulet's servants, Gregory and Sampson, engage in risqué banter regarding cutting off the heads of the maids when in fact they are referring to penetrating their hymen. Here they associate sexuality with violence; in fact, they perceive the two experiences as almost interchangeable. Sampson asserts: "I will push Montague's men from the wall, and thrust his maids to the wall" (I.i.15–16). Quite clearly, Sampson celebrates sexual violence in this passage, even as he compliments his own fleshly appearance as he opines, "I am a pretty piece of flesh" (I.i.28). He even finds himself attractive, expressing a degree of self-congratulatory auto-eroticism. Coppélia Kahn notes the many puns on the word "stand" as a reference to an erection and comments on how fighting in this feud is indicative of masculinity in addition to bravery (88).

Weaponry and sexuality are interchangeable in *Romeo and Juliet,* for Sampson says, "My naked weapon is out" (I.i.32). When old Capulet asks for his "long sword," Lady Capulet comically responds, "A crutch, a crutch—why call you for a sword?" (I.i.72). Garber argues, "Lady Capulet is clearly casting on her husband's martial—and perhaps his marital swordsmanship. In this play as in so many others of the period a capacity to handle one's sword is—hundreds of years before Freud—seen as a sign of manliness" (191).

From the violent streets of Verona, the play shifts to a quiet conversation between Romeo and Benvolio concerning the nature of love. Romeo is the stereotypical Petrarchan lover who rhapsodizes about love in the most extravagant fashion (Garber 192). Benvolio surmises that Romeo is in love because Romeo expresses frustration in gaining his beloved Rosaline's favor. He suggests that she is inaccessible, for she is like Diana, the goddess of chastity and the hunt. Rosaline is the archetypal lady on a pedestal who is unapproachable as she is the living embodiment of chastity who is unmoved by the allure of eroticism from Cupid's arrows as she possesses the qualities of Diana.

Mercutio, unlike Benvolio, has no patience with lovers' sighs and moans. When Romeo complains to Mercutio about the brutality of love, he responds: "If love be rough with you, be rough with love; / Prick love for pricking, and you beat love down" (I.iv.25–26). Maurice Charney opines, "Between Mercutio and the Nurse, *Romeo and Juliet* has one of the largest sexual vocabularies in Shakespeare" (120). This discourse harkens back to that of Samson's "pretty piece of flesh" (I.i.28).

If Mercutio's vocabulary were not sexualized enough earlier, surely it breaches the grounds of decorum in his conversation after the masked ball when he and Benvolio search for Romeo. Mercutio's discourse is filled with bawdy puns and references to male and female sexuality as he describes Romeo's purported relationship to Rosaline, but of course, Mercutio does not realize that Romeo is no longer interested in her:

> 'Twould anger him
> To raise a spirit in his mistress' circle
> Of some strange nature, letting it there stand
> Till she had laid it and conjured it down:
> There were some spite. My invocation
> Is fair and honest, in his mistress' name;
> I conjure only but to raise up him. (II.i.24–30)

As Jill Levenson asserts, this passage is replete with bawdy double entendres to male sexuality; for example, the allusion to "spirit," according to Levenson, refers to both "incorporeal being" and "penis" (205). In fact, Mercutio's sexual comments become increasingly lewd, for he compares Rosaline to a medlar, a fruit that looks like a small apple with brown skin that has a large eye.

The medlar tree produces a fruit that can only be eaten when it is too ripe, which is similar to the loquat or the persimmon, and it looks like the female genitals (Charney 121). Here the visual representation becomes sexually graphic:

> Now will he sit under a medlar tree
> And wish his mistress were that kind of fruit
> As maids call medlars when they laugh alone.
> O Romeo, that she were, O that she were
> An open-arse, or thou a popp'rin' pear. (II.i.35–39)

The "popp'rin' pear," which was named after the Flemish town of Poperinghe, and resembles male genitals, provides Mercutio with more double entendres concerning sexual intercourse and a man's body, with the pun on "pop her in." Even the references to the Os in this passage can be interpreted as images of female sexuality (Levenson 206). Male and female sexuality are ubiquitous in this passage.

Romeo and Juliet, indeed, contains passages that range from the sexually graphic to the sublime depending upon who is speaking to whom. When Romeo addresses Juliet in the famous garden scene, he sounds as if he is addressing an ethereal goddess having descended from the empyrean. Romeo suggests that Cupid's wings enable him to leap over the garden walls of the Capulets' home. In fact, as Garber asserts, "The walled garden, like the biblical enclosed garden, the *hortus conclusus*, was emblematic of virginity in art and poetry" (199). Romeo would be killed by the Capulets because they would assume he is a thief and an agent of sexual transgression so his presence in the Capulets' garden is doubly dangerous.

Intriguingly, death and eroticism are inextricably linked throughout this play. For example, as Garber makes clear at the outset, when Romeo and Juliet first meet, Juliet declares, "If he be married, / My grave is like to be my wedding bed" (I.iv.247–248). Later Lady Capulet in a moment of frustration with Juliet at her refusal to marry Count Paris exclaims, "I would the fool were married to her grave" (III.v.139). In the same scene Juliet begs her father not to make her marry Paris:

> Delay this marriage for a month, a week;
> Or if you do not, make the bridal bed
> In that dim monument where Tybalt lies. (199–201)

Here again eroticism is bound up in death. The two experiences are inseparable in *Romeo and Juliet*.

In the tomb scene in which Romeo and Juliet take their lives, the imagery is powerfully eroticized. When Romeo sees Juliet in her coma-like sleep, he queries:

> Shall I believe
> That unsubstantial death is amorous,

And that the lean abhorred monster keeps
Thee here in dark to be his paramour? (V.iii.102–5)

Romeo perceives death as the monstrous lover of Juliet. Moments later he imbibes the poison that he has purchased from the apothecary, and utters his final words, "Thus with a kiss I die" (120). The word "die" was a slang term indicating orgasm. It was commonly believed that each orgasm lessened one's life by one day, hence the term *la petite morte*, or little death.

Later in the same scene, Juliet commits suicide, uttering equally erotic language, "O happy dagger, / This is thy sheath. There rust, and let me die" (169–70). Appropriately, the etymological derivation of the word "vagina" is sheath. Garber argues that these might be what one would call "erotic suicides" given the iconography of the imagery that is associated with their deaths. The cup from which Romeo drinks his poison has been always associated with female sexuality, and the dagger with which Juliet commits suicide is surely phallic (Garber 201). Kahn very cogently makes a case for the gory entrance to the Capulets' tomb functioning symbolically as a "defloration or initiation into sexuality, and a birth" (101). Moreover, Juliet has premonitions that her wedding bed will be her grave, and three young men who participated in the feud are also buried there with her (Kahn 101). In the final analysis, one cannot think of Romeo and Juliet without thinking of sex and death being inextricably bound up.

Unlike *Romeo and Juliet*, *A Midsummer Night's Dream*, also written in 1595, is known as a beautiful play celebrating young love and marriage when in point of fact it, too, comes perilously close to tragedy at the beginning of the play when Egeus, Hermia's father, demands that she marry Demetrius against her will just as Lord Capulet demands that Juliet marry Paris. Once again patriarchal pressure to marry is applied to a daughter by a father. Throughout the play characters allude to sexual violence and death in much the same way as they do in *Romeo and Juliet*. Even in the opening scene Duke Theseus of Athens tells Hippolyta, the former Amazon queen, whom he has defeated in battle: "Hippolyta, I wooed thee with my sword, / And won thy love doing thee injuries (I.i.16–17). Theseus returns to Athens victorious in battle, and with him he has in his possession Hippolyta as a captive bride. The sword functions here as it does in *Romeo and Juliet* as a metaphor for phallic power and might.

The idea of forced marriage is immediately reinforced with the frustrated figure of Egeus, who complains that his daughter Hermia refuses to marry Demetrius, the man that he has chosen to be her husband. The concept of death and desire quickly becomes of great importance as soon as Hermia impulsively demands to know what is the worst punishment that she can receive for disobedience to her father's will, and Theseus lets her know that she has few choices in this marital matter: marriage to Demetrius, entering a convent, or death. Louis Adrian Montrose argues, "Theseus's rhetoric concisely stages a Reformation debate on the relative virtues of virginity and marriage. He concedes praise to the former, as being exemplary of self-mastery, but nevertheless concludes that the latter more fully satisfies the imperatives of earthly existence" (127). Theseus speaks in absolute terms regarding Hermia's choices, and the decision to live in a nunnery is equivalent to certain extinction with no possibility of procreation. The vivid allusion to the "cold fruitless moon" (73) immediately calls up an association of Diana, goddess of the hunt and chastity. To be sure, Theseus represents chastity negatively which denies any possibility of erotic pleasure and happiness in this life. Therefore, he advises Hermia to think carefully about the decision that she is about to make.

Just as there are problems involving romantic love in the Athenian court of Theseus, so too in Fairyland is the marital conflict between Oberon, King of the Fairies, and Titania, Queen of the Fairies, that escalates from accusations of infidelity against each other regarding their extramarital relations to their arguing over the little Indian boy, who has been raised by Titania because of the death of his mother in childbirth. Therefore, Oberon vows to humiliate Titania by having her fall in love with a grotesque beast after he sprinkles the juice from a particular flower called love-in-idleness, which is a pansy, into her eyes. This passage is highly eroticized with its phallic reference to Cupid's "fiery shaft" (II.i.161). Oberon juxtaposes the chaste moon to the intense sexuality of Cupid's eroticism. Of course, "love's wound" (167) is a result of phallic penetration, and the accompanying hymenal blood changes the color of the flower from white to purple. Maurice Charney thinks that the allusion to the "imperial vot'ress" (163) may be actually a "gracious compliment to Elizabeth, the Virgin Queen" (10). Consequently, when Titania awakens, she will dote upon the next creature that she sees regardless of its beauty or intelligence. The act of doting is much decried in Shakespeare's plays because it is an excess of affection, and the lover makes a fool of himself or herself in the process.

Helena, too, dotes upon Demetrius even after he tells her that he does not love her, and she exclaims, "And even for that I love you the more" (II.i.202). The dark underside of *A Midsummer Night's Dream* becomes quite visible when Demetrius becomes so angry with Helena that he threatens sexual violence, for he tells, "You do impeach your modesty too much, / To leave the city" (II.i.214–15). Helena certainly puts herself in harm's way by pursuing Demetrius despite the fact that he has made professions of love to her before the play begins but clearly no longer cares about her. While this play may be perceived by some as a play about young love and marriage, it surely makes manifest the potential danger of male sexuality to a woman when the male is angry and hostile toward his former beloved.

The danger of male sexuality is made all the more manifest in the next scene in which Titania plans to sleep, but before doing so, her fairies sing her a lullaby in which they invoke Philomel, a classical figure invoked to protect women from sexual violation, as protection for Titania from snakes and reptiles. The figure of the snake is certainly one of sexual transgression in Western civilization. The phallic threat looms even as Titania sleeps, but the sexual danger is reinforced by this allusion to Philomel. It is significant to note that Philomel is a "nightingale, named after Philomela, [who was] raped by her brother-in-law Tereus who also cut out her tongue" (Holland 170). As beautiful as the fairies' lullaby may sound as they sing it, its message reminds one of the possibility of sexual danger and violation in the Athenian woods.

At the same time in another part of the Athenian woods, Lysander becomes amorous with Hermia, and he complies with her request to sleep some distance from her as befitting behavior that "[b]ecomes a virtuous bachelor and a maid" (II.ii.65). No sooner asleep, Puck arrives upon the scene and places the love juice upon Lysander's eyes thinking that he must be Demetrius because he sleeps so far from Hermia, and thereupon when Helena wakes Lysander, he regales her with a litany of Petrarchan platitudes regarding her female beauty and follows her as she runs away from him thinking that he is mocking her. Awaking from her nightmare, Hermia is alarmed by Lysander's absence:

> Help me, Lysander, help me! Do thy best
> To pluck this crawling serpent from my breast!
> Ay me, for pity. What a dream was here?
> Lysander, look how I do quake with fear.
> Methought a serpent ate my heart away,
> And you sat smiling at his cruel prey. (II.i.151–56)

To be sure, this is yet another example of a phallic violation. Norman N. Holland suggests that we should move beyond the simplistic symbolic system of early psychoanalysis. He argues, "At the deepest level of the dream, that desire for possession becomes eating and thus fusing with and taking away a person's essence. . . . Phallic intrusion and possession become a hostile, consuming, oral possession. The dominant image to me seems to be the mouth: the serpent's eating and Lysander's smiling" (81). At the same time Hermia is certainly a very frightened woman who feels abandoned by her lover in the middle of the woods.

Despite the fact that all of the romantic entanglements are untied for the young lovers by the end of the play, the fear of sexuality and death is reinforced by the playlet, "Pyramus and Thisby," performed by the rude mechanicals after the wedding ceremonies as the evening's entertainment. In many ways this scene duplicates the tomb scene in *Romeo and Juliet* in which Bottom playing Pyramus comes upon Thisby's bloody cloak which was accidentally dropped by her when she heard the lion roar, and Pyramus immediately assumes that Thisby has been sexually violated and killed by a lion. Pyramus's reference to defloration certainly indicates some kind of sexual violation on the part of the lion on Thisby. Garber suggests, "[H]e seems to think it means something more like 'ravaged' or 'destroyed,' but the sexual overtones are clear, whether or not Pyramus can hear them. . . . Violation by a 'monster' whether the serpent of Hermia's dream or the ass-headed hybrid of Bottom's has been a constant theme" (234). Thisby, in turn, much like Juliet, also kills herself after she returns to where Pyramus found her bloody cloak where he later killed himself thinking that Thisby is dead.

As Garber aptly remarks upon this play, "A *Midsummer Night's Dream* is *Romeo and Juliet* turned inside out, *Romeo and Juliet* transformed into a comedy" (213); nonetheless, the possibility of sexual violation is always just beneath the surface of this play despite the widely held belief that this play is about young love and marriage, but this play comes perilously close to the edge of tragedy at certain moments; after all, Egeus is much like Lord Capulet, for he insists that his daughter Hermia marry Demetrius, the man of his choice, under pain of death. Happily, the play concludes with Titania and Oberon blessing the wedding beds within Theseus's manor so that none of the offspring from the unions of that night are afflicted with any facial disfigurement or birth defect which precedes the final request by Puck for the audience's forgiveness if this play has offended any member of it.

Sexuality in *Much Ado about Nothing*, too, is a powerfully divisive issue as it comes precipitously close to causing disaster within the community of Messina because Hero, one of the play's heroines, is scandalized by the charge of sexual infidelity. The drama opens propitiously enough with the arrival of Don Pedro and his men, Benedick, Claudio, Conrad, Borachio, and Don Pedro's formerly estranged brother Don John, who plays the role of the malcontent. Love and eroticism are at the forefront of the drama as Benedick and Beatrice exchange insults regarding their appeal to members of the opposite sex. Erotic sparks fly from the initial salvo between the two, for both are former lovers. Benedick calls Beatrice Lady Disdain, but Beatrice retorts that she would prefer to hear a dog bark at a crow than hear a man say that he loves her. Both Beatrice and Benedick display a sense of anger and resentment because of some past relationship. When the witty banter abruptly ends at Benedick's scoring the last point in the repartee, Beatrice utters under her breath, "You always end with a jade's trick. I know you of old" (I.i.140). While Benedick can engage in satirical banter with Beatrice, it is all too obvious that she was deeply hurt in this relationship with him.

On the other hand, Hero and Claudio are the epitome of young, innocent lovers who have the blessings of their community and most importantly, Leonato, Hero's father, the governor of Messina. To be sure, Claudio is dumbstruck by Hero's beauty, having returned from martial activity with Don Pedro. Claudio spews the rhetoric of the Petrarchan lover for whom Benedick has contempt, but Don Pedro indulges him and says that he will disguise himself and woo her in his place and negotiate the marriage settlement for him with Leonato. Don Pedro is accustomed to being in charge and enjoys negotiating this marital arrangement. Sheldon Zitner insightfully notes that Don Pedro appears to be excited about arranging this match, but it was not unusual for one to have an arranged marriage if one were of Claudio's and Hero's social status. Moreover, Hero functions as a "prize" (Zitner 108). That said, Don Pedro sincerely wishes his friend to be happy, and there is a sense of joy in his desire to do this for Claudio's happiness in marriage.

Unfortunately, Don John, Don Pedro's malcontent brother, decides to collude with Borachio and Conrad, his henchmen, to undermine the marriage of Hero to Claudio by having Borachio appear with Margaret, one of Hero's ladies-in-waiting, at the window of Hero's room on the night before the wedding. Overcome with outrage, Claudio decides to denounce Hero at the wedding after seeing Margaret, whom he believes to be Hero, late at night. Therefore, Claudio renounces her using the language of a betrayed lover, referring to her as "the sign and semblance of her honour" (IV.i.33). He feels an intense sense of betrayal as he exclaims, "Out on thy seeming! I will write against it. / You seem to me to be Dian in her orb" (IV.i.56–57). Claudio juxtaposes the chaste figure of Diana to the highly erotic figure of Venus as a point of contrast in order to indicate how he perceived Hero before he saw the purported infidelity between Hero and the "ruffian." Again Venus and Diana are prominent figures around which notions of sexuality and purity circulate. The theme of appearance versus reality is a prevalent one throughout this play beginning at the masked ball at which Don Pedro pretended to be Claudio. In this instance, appearance is far from the truth of reality.

While Claudio writes an epitaph to hang upon his beloved's tomb, Benedick attempts to write sonnets to give to Beatrice, but Benedick is completely inadequate to the task. The practice of writing sonnets is at once absurd and futile for Benedick because they do not speak to his experience as a lover to Beatrice of all women. Benedick asserts that he lives in the here and now, not in the mythological past as some of the figures are invoked by poets for inspiration such as Leander who pursued Hero to his detriment and Troilus who pursued Cressida futilely. Claire McEachern notes Hero's name "was notorious from Christopher Marlowe's poem, 'Hero and Leander' (1598), where it belongs to a priestess of Venus who forsakes her vestal duties for her lover" (147). Benedick avers that his love for Beatrice is genuine rather than a performative set piece written to demonstrate a particular kind of literary tradition.

Claudio, like Benedick, must accept his marital responsibilities seriously and not as a callow youth. When Claudio appears at the marriage altar for the second time supposedly to marry the niece of Leonato, he wants to lift the veil of the masked bride he is to marry, but he is forced to marry this woman sight unseen as a test of his loyalty and faith in Leonato's word, for Leonato tells him: "No, that you shall not till you take her hand / Before this Friar and swear to marry her" (V.iv.56–57). To Claudio's wonderment, the purported niece is none other than Hero, whom he is overwhelmed to see, exclaiming, "Another Hero!" (62). Hero is certain to validate her virtue, "One Hero died defiled, but I do live, / And surely as I live, I am a maid" (63–64), yet clearly, Leonato gets the last word on this matter by reminding Claudio of the reason for which she was "dead": "She died, my lord, but whiles her slander lived" (66).

Slander was extremely damaging to the sexual reputation of women in early modern England, and one can see how seriously women took slanderous words by the number of lawsuits that women brought against women and men, and so Hero's reputation is happily resuscitated along with herself. At the same time, Charney feels that it is very unfortunate that Hero and Claudio's characters are never developed as Beatrice and Benedick's are (47).

Even Benedick and Beatrice are brought to a union after they are forced to acknowledge their love for each other by their peers, Claudio and Hero. When Benedick claims not to love Beatrice, Claudio produces "[a] halting sonnet of his own pure brain, / Fashioned to Beatrice" (V.iv.87–88). In turn, Hero also produces one written by Beatrice, "And here's another, / Writ in my cousin's hand, stol'n from her pocket, / Containing her affection unto Benedick" (88–90). One is reminded at this time of Leonato's earlier assertion in the orchard that Beatrice would stay up late at night writing love poems for Benedick. Eroticism is textualized through the production of sonnets, that most mannered of romantic poems. The irony is that Benedick and Beatrice are not the storybook lovers who engage in the highly romanticized rhetoric of the other young lovers, but yet they are the ones who are ultimately entrapped by it, and so the play ends with Benedick's encouragement to Don Pedro to get himself a wife, for "There is no staff more reverend than one tipped with horn" (123–24), reminding Don Pedro of the possibility of cuckoldry, a risk that all men take in marrying women.

Shifting genres from comedy to history, one sees that the playwright, William Shakespeare, places increased emphasis upon affairs of state at the same time domestic concerns are also made manifest in comedic moments in *Henry IV, Part 1* with Prince Hal and his surrogate father figure, Falstaff, who replaces his own father King Henry IV. Here the competing affairs of state are set against those of the home and, indeed, they tend to dominate the play. In the first instance, the old Vice figure of Falstaff is known for his proclivity for gluttony, inebriation, and sexual promiscuity. Hal, heir apparent to the throne of England, has no patience with Falstaff when he asks him the time. Hal sardonically responds, "Unless hours were cups of sack and minutes capons, and clocks the tongues, and dials the signs of leaping houses, and the blessed sun himself a fair hot wench in flame-coloured taffeta, I should see no reason why thou shouldst be so superfluous to demand the time of the day" (I.ii.6–10). Falstaff, however, is in a questioning mood, and then he asks Hal, "And is not my hostess of the tavern a most sweet wench?" (I.ii.38–39). Hal replies with yet another question which focuses upon female sexuality, "And is not a buff jerkin a most sweet robe of durance?" (41–42). Falstaff wants to know what does he have to do with a "buff jerkin" (41), and Hal again answers a question with a question, "Why, what the pox do I have to do with my hostess of the tavern?" (46–47). Again, the exchange of lewd innuendo continues as Falstaff asserts, "Well, thou hast called her to a reckoning many a time and oft" (I.ii.48–49). David Bevington glosses "reckoning" as meaning "account of behavior," "settle of tavern bill," or "rendezvous in which a tavern wench is to show her worth" (137).

While King Henry and many members of his court may believe Hal to epitomize the prodigal son by consorting with the likes of Falstaff, Peto, and Bardolf, Hal is actually preparing himself to rule after his father's death because he, in effect, will know who his subjects are and their cultural sensibilities; in effect, he will be able to speak their language because of his acquaintance with them, but this association is, in fact, a kind of performance, much like Petruchio's in *The Taming of the Shrew*, for Hal, in his very famous soliloquy in I.ii, very vividly describes how his "loose behavior" is like a garment, not unlike an actor's costume, that he will "throw off" (196) at the appropriate time. At the same time he describes his unsavory friends as "foul and ugly mists of vapours" (186) and "contagious clouds" (190) who "strangle" (191) him. Hal informs the audience that his activities with Falstaff and his cronies are largely performative. In other words, as soon as he comes into his kingship, he will cast aside individuals such as Falstaff and Peto, who obscure his regal glory. After all, Hal compares himself the to the sun whose beams are diminished because of clouds, and, indeed, when he sees fit, he will transform himself into one whom his father will respect and admire, but for the time being he is on holiday. Leisure, too, grows wearisome when that is all one does, as Hal opines in this speech: "If all the year were playing holidays, / To sport would be as tedious as to work" (191–92), for King Henry IV is extremely concerned about the rule of England after his death under the reign of his purportedly prodigal son who evinces no sense of responsibility to the kingdom.

By contrast to King Henry's son, Hal, Sir Henry Percy, better known as Hotspur, is the antithesis of Hal. Hotspur is a valiant warrior who prizes honor above everything in life. In fact, at the beginning of the play, King Henry wishes that Hotspur were his son, and fancifully opines that a fairy exchanged Hotspur for Hal in his cradle, but such is not the case, and King Henry comes to accept his son after the son defended him against Douglas on the battlefield. Hotspur is also a married man, and one is inclined to think that based upon the representation of him in this play that he is actually married to martial concerns rather than marital ones. Hotspur is absorbed in the affairs of state concerning meeting Mortimer, Glendover, and Douglas on the ninth of the next month when Lady Percy, his wife, asks him about his lack of attention to her. To be sure, Lady Percy is despondent because of Hotspur's lack of amorous attention. She implies that they are no longer engaged in sexual relations as she has been banished from her husband's bed. She wonders aloud what could take him from their intimate erotic life. Hotspur's only response is a taciturn, "What ho!" (II.iii.62). Upon receiving news of state, he asks for his horse. When Lady queries him as to what carries him from her, he humorously replies, "Why, my horse, my love, my horse" (73). Having been answered in such an indifferent fashion, she playfully asserts, "I'll know your business, Harry, that I will" (77).

Nonetheless, Hotspur assures her, "So far afoot I shall be weary, love" (81). When Hotspur refuses to answer her question directly, Lady Percy playfully tells him, "In faith, I'll break thy little finger, Harry, / An if thou wilt not tell me all things true" (84–85). Bevington suggests that the "little finger" to which Lady Percy refers is a "lover's pinch or wringing" (176), but Eric Partridge glosses the word as "penis" (179). Hotspur jokingly says that he does not love her, but it is clear to the audience that he does. To be sure, the conversation indicates that Hotspur and Lady Percy care about each other, but they exist in two very different realms, and the sphere of realpolitik takes precedence over that of the domestic, and for this reason Hotspur refuses to tell her the matter of state affairs that takes him from their bed, and so Hotspur keeps the two domains separate as he tells her, "Thou wilt not utter what thou dost not know" (107).

While the marital relationship of Hotspur and Lady Percy may appear peculiar because of the lack of communication, the one of Mortimer and his wife may appear absurd, for Mortimer speaks no Welsh, and his wife speaks no English, and so Glendower, his father-in-law, must interpret for him. There is a none too subtle eroticism about this scene. Glendower must inform his son-in-law, Mortimer, that his wife wants him to lie down on the "wanton rushes" (III.i.208). This moment is reminiscent of the scene in which Hamlet places his head in the lap of Ophelia when they watch *The Mousetrap*.

It is clear that Glendower enjoys the world of the imagination and magic while Hotspur does not. Jean E. Howard even goes so far as to describe their relationship as antagonistic, for she asserts, "Hotspur calls Glendower a liar and denounces magic as the work of the devil" (173). Hotspur declares that "mincing poetry" (III.i.129) unnerves him more so than any other noise, but he does become amorous on occasion despite the whimsical world that Glendower endorses, "Come, Kate, thou art perfect in lying down. / Come quick, quick, that I may lay my head in thy lap" (222–23). The sexual overtones here are quite patent. When Hotspur refuses to stop moving his head about in Lady Percy's lap as Mortimer's wife begins to sing in Welsh, Lady Percy tells him that she will break his head if he refuses to do so, and so she says, "Then be still" (234). Earlier she told him that she would break his "little finger," with its subtly erotic overtones. He replies, "No, 'tis a woman's fault" (235). Here again, Bevington suggests that Hotspur makes a "bawdy quibble on *still* in the sense of 'sexually passive' [which] asserts a masculine aggressiveness that is apparent in the next line about the Welsh lady's bed" (220). The relaxed eroticism in which Hotspur and Lady Percy engage in this scene is set against the harsh reality of war in which Hotspur will soon engage in the remainder of this play.

This domestic idyll functions as a respite from the brutality of war as Hotspur reminded Kate in the previous scene. In as much as the marital relations may appear tenuous and fragile in *Henry IV, Part 1*, they are strengthened by the marriage of Henry V to Katherine in an attempt to bring peace between England and France. In the tragedies that we will soon consider, the erotic bonds between men and women are irreparably destroyed in all but the rarest instances.

In *Hamlet*, arguably Shakespeare's greatest and most enigmatic play, the issues of sexuality and gender take the audience's attention and have taken scholars' and critics' for literally centuries. Scholars and critics have spent reams of paper discussing and arguing why Hamlet responds as he does to the marriage of his mother Gertrude by his uncle Claudius after such a short period of time following his father's death, or more precisely, murder, and why Hamlet shows such reluctance to take revenge against his uncle once he learns from his father's ghost of his murder in the palace garden while he was asleep.

Hamlet is emotionally overwhelmed by the death of his father and his mother's "o'erhasty marriage" (II.ii.57) to his uncle, Claudius, and so love, sexuality, and marriage are deeply contested concerns for Hamlet. He simply does not know what to make of his family's situation. He refuses to throw off his "inky cloak" (I.ii.77), his mourning garments, and reenter the daily life of the court as he is expected to do. Gertrude has already taken a second husband. He is encouraged by both his mother and his uncle to end his mourning and take up the work of the living, but Hamlet is incapable of accepting his mother's marriage to his uncle to which he compares to an "unweeded garden" (I.ii.135). The state of marriage and, for that matter, the state of Denmark are compared to a garden that has not been managed as it should have been; therefore, it has become "rank" (136) and "gross" (136). Much more significantly, Hamlet clearly obsesses about his mother's marriage to his uncle within two months of the death of his father. He compares his father to Hyperion, the god of the sun, and Claudius to a satyr, which was half man and half goat, an image of unbridled lust. Charney notes that even in the first scenes one can discern that Hamlet has lost his faith in women. References to incest are frequent, mainly in the scenes when the play begins. Hamlet thinks that his mother was very sexually driven even when she was married to his father (75–76). Hamlet is simply obsessed with the fear that female sexual infidelity engenders. He concludes, "Frailty thy name is woman" (146), which sums up his attitude that women are easily led astray by erotic desires. Again, it was widely believed in the medieval and Renaissance periods that women were far more sexual than men, and therefore, they were more subject to sinful, erotic activity.

Because of his mother's marriage to Claudius, Hamlet's relationship to Ophelia is ruined, and even she is counseled by her brother Laertes not to take so seriously the amorous protestations of Hamlet, for he advises her to guard against whatever tokens of affections that he offers her. Laertes is principally concerned with Ophelia's keeping her virginity intact in order to be marketable at the time of her marriage. Her virginity is her "chaste treasure," which she cannot open to Hamlet's or her erotic desires. Charney argues, "'Chaste treasure' is vulgar, the direct representation of sexuality in monetary terms" (76). Laertes attempts to make her frightened of sexuality so that she will be disinclined to accept Hamlet's affection. Ophelia is reminded that Hamlet is the heir apparent who will invariably marry a member of royalty, and so she need not waste her time with him, but she is disheartened by his advice, for she sadly opines, "Do not, as some ungracious pastors do, / Show me the steep and thorny way to heaven" (I.iii.47–48). As if Laertes's admonitions regarding sexuality are insufficient, Polonius tells her: "You speak like a green girl / Unsifted in such perilous circumstance. Do you believe his tenders as you call them?" (I.iii.101–3). When Ophelia tells him that she does not know what to think, he informs her that he will tell her what to think. "Do not believe his vows, for they are brokers, . . . But mere implorators of unholy suits / Breathing like sanctified and pious bawds / The better to beguile" (127 and 129–31). Therefore, Ophelia sadly acquiesces to Polonius's demands. Clearly, she feels as though she cannot influence Polonius's attitude toward her sexuality in any way.

The issue of sexuality becomes further complicated by the ghost of old Hamlet's father to his son. While he is very perturbed by the marriage of his mother Gertrude to his uncle Claudius, he becomes emotionally unhinged when he learns that his father has been murdered. Old Hamlet tells Hamlet: "[S]leeping in the orchard, / A serpent stung me" (I.v.34–35). Here Claudius appears as a serpent in the royal orchard not unlike the serpent who appears in the Garden of Eden in order to spoil the earthly happiness of Adam and Eve. This is a moment of primordial transgression. It should come as no surprise that Janet Adelman in her powerful essay, "Man and Wife Is One Flesh: *Hamlet* and the Confrontation with the Maternal Body" argues, "The poisoning of Old Hamlet is ostentatiously modeled on Cain's killing of Abel" (*Suffocating Mothers* 24). The ghost of Hamlet's father calls Claudius an "incestuous, . . . adulterate beast" (I.v.43) who was able to seduce Gertrude with his "wicked wit" (45) and "gifts" (45). The ghost itself becomes so enraged at the actions of Gertrude that he must calm himself in order to tell Hamlet exactly what happened in the royal orchard because sunrise will come soon, and since he was murdered without the benefit of confession, he, therefore, went to his eternal judgment without having been absolved of his earthly transgressions.

Hence, he is in Purgatory where he must atone for his wrongdoings. Although the approach of dawn comes quickly, the ghost returns to the theme of incest and adultery, reminding Hamlet of his obligation to cleanse the court of immorality and sexual infidelity, for he tells Hamlet, "Let not the royal bed of Denmark be / A couch for luxury and damned incest" (I.v.82–83). Luxury, of course, means lust, which was the deadly sin of Luxuria that is found in the Middle Ages (Hibbard 190). In addition to avenging his murder, the ghost of Hamlet's father urges Hamlet to "leave [Gertrude] to heaven" (86).

While Hamlet attempts to make sense of this horrific information provided by his ghostly father, Polonius presents Gertrude and Claudius part of a sonnet and a letter that Hamlet has given to Ophelia in addition to the report of Hamlet's having come to Ophelia in a distracted, disheveled state, which Polonius immediately takes to be a condition of madness brought on by Ophelia's refusal to accept his protestations of affection. In a prolix discourse, which is Polonius's wont, he informs Hamlet's mother and uncle that Hamlet "fell into a madness" (II.ii.145). As far as Polonius is concerned, Hamlet's behavior is the "very ecstasy of love" (II.i.103). Earlier Gertrude had correctly deduced the reasons for Hamlet's unusual behavior: "His father's death and our o'erhasty marriage" (II.ii.57). Now having heard Polonius's long-winded explanation concerning Hamlet's peculiar behavior with Ophelia, Gertrude changes her mind, concurring with Polonius, "It may be—very likely" (152). In fact, Gertrude tells Ophelia that she hopes that it is because of her "good beauties" (III.i.40) that Hamlet acts so erratically.

Claudius is determined to find out why Hamlet behaves so strangely, and so he and Polonius decide to hide behind an arras while Ophelia talks to Hamlet. Hamlet becomes extremely vitriolic toward women in this dialogue with Ophelia. It is quite obvious that he no longer believes that women can be chaste. In one of the most memorable questions in *Hamlet*, he asks Ophelia, "Are you honest?" (III.i.104). Hamlet, of course, wants to know if she is chaste. Earlier in II.ii, Hamlet told Polonius that he is a fishmonger, whose tertiary meaning is "one whose womenfolk are likely to be beautiful, wanton, and prolific" (Hibbard 212), and Polonius replies, "Not I, my lord." (II.ii.175), and Hamlet's rejoinder is, "Then I would you were so honest a man" (II.ii.176). Hamlet has no faith in the honesty of men or women regardless of the sense in which the word is used.

In fact, Hamlet tells Ophelia that she should never have believed him when he told her that he loved her. Finally, in a fit of anger, Hamlet importunes Ophelia, "Get thee to a nunnery. Why, wouldst thou be a breeder of sinners?" (III.i.122–23). This line has been variously interpreted. Charney suggests, "'Nunnery' was used ironically in Shakespeare's time to mean a brothel. The scene is full of misogyny that connects with earlier scenes in the play" (77). Philip Armstrong uses a Lacanian psychoanalytic paradigm to interpret this line. He suggests that this scene between Hamlet and Ophelia, during this symbolic encounter, takes place while

Polonius watches her, and this vacillation between overevaluation and detestation of the flesh shows Ophelia as an object of desire. Hamlet's attitude is summed up in the word "nunnery" which could refer to either a religious house. such as a convent, or to a brothel. Hamlet begins to separate himself from Ophelia as his fantasized object of erotic desire, and consequently, he starts to feel revulsion for his formerly overevaluated object of desire (83). Finally, Hibbard avers that Hamlet means exactly what he says. The only way that Ophelia will not be a "breeder of sinners" is to enter a nunnery. Moreover, he is convinced that Hamlet's order to go to a nunnery is not remotely ironic (243). Given the punster that Hamlet is, it should be no wonder that he wants her to be mindful of both meanings of the word, and she has the choice of choosing whichever one she feels is more applicable to her desire or condition. Working himself into a frenzy, Hamlet exclaims, "For wise men know what monsters you make of them" (141–43). He alludes to the imaginary horns on the head of the man whose wife is unfaithful to him. Bolting from the stage shouting, "To a nunnery, go" (150). Hamlet's dramatic departure certainly convinces Ophelia of his insanity.

Perhaps in one of the play's most celebrated scenes, Hamlet confronts his mother, Gertrude, concerning her infidelity to his father after he has killed Polonius hiding behind the arras. Many psychoanalytic critics have interpreted this scene as the one in which Hamlet most clearly exhibits his erotic desire for his mother. Some critics have even gone so far as to argue that he attempts to rape her as he pushes her onto the bed. To this reader's mind the most powerful moments in this scene are those in which Hamlet forces his mother to acknowledge her complicity in her husband's murder. Using a mirror as a metaphor of her inner being, Hamlet insists, "You go not till I set you up a glass / Where you see the inmost part of you" (III.iv.20–21). Once he kills Polonius, Gertrude exclaims, "O, what a rash and bloody deed is this!" (28). Hamlet, however, rebuts her statement with "A bloody—almost as bad, good mother, / As kill a king and marry his brother" (29–30). Gertrude responds quizzically, "As kill a king?" (31). Still unconvinced of her role in her husband's murder, Hamlet continues his accusations by once again comparing his father to Hyperion, while comparing Claudius to a "mildewed ear / Blasting his wholesome brother" (65–66).

By the end of this passage in which Hamlet asks his mother no less than four questions concerning how she could possibly be involved sexually with Claudius, she admits her indirect involvement in her husband's downfall and death. This is the moment at which Gertrude realizes the degree to which she has transgressed familial and cultural boundaries by her marriage to Claudius, but Gertrude never specifies what these "black and grained spots" (82) are. Moreover, metaphorically, Hamlet is not satisfied with Gertrude's admission of guilt, for he continues to rant and rave, comparing the parental bed to one which possesses the "rank sweat of an enseamed bed, / Stewed in corruption, honeying and making love / Over the nasty sty" (85–87). The reference to "stewed" is in association to brothels (Hibbard 282), and a "sty" is the habitation of pigs, which reinforces the bestial quality of the relationship between Claudius and Gertrude. When Gertrude can no longer endure the devastating indictments that Hamlet makes against her, she, finally, implores Hamlet, "O speak to me no more. / These words like daggers enter in my ears" (85–86). Hamlet's words do, indeed, cut like a knife. In the next play, *Othello*, marital bonds are irrevocably destroyed when Othello kills Desdemona in a fit of jealousy having been convinced of her infidelity.

The issue of jealousy in *Othello* is deeply bound up with those of race and sexuality. Othello, a Moor, who has risen to the rank of general of the Venetian forces, marries Desdemona, the daughter of Brabantio, one of the city's senators. As Ania Loomba so eloquently articulates, "*Othello* is both a fantasy of interracial love and social tolerance, and a nightmare of racial hatred and male violence" (91). Just as this play may be a "fantasy of interracial love and social tolerance," it is also one in which cultural fears of the exotic other are played out with devastating consequences, resulting in the deaths of several of the play's main characters.

The play opens with Iago, whom Othello has passed over for promotion, shouting incendiary words outside Brabantio's chamber's window concerning the loss of Brabantio's money and his daughter, Desdemona, who has married Othello. Desdemona is equated with monetary worth as Iago screams, "Thieves, thieves, thieves! / Look to your house, your daughter, and your bags!" (I.i.79–80). Iago quickly escalates the intensity and graphic sexual nature of his commentary regarding her elopement with Othello. He and Desdemona are equated to an "old black ram" and a "white ewe" respectively. The ram is associated with erotic strength and power, and its blackness as well as its horns are representative of the devil. The reference to animals is indicative of miscegenation as a transgression of the established order; hence, miscegenation is associated with that which is monstrous as the progeny of unorthodox sexual relations taking place between various animals not of the same species. Illustrations of devils depicted them as having monstrous proportions (Neill 203). Here Iago attempts to create a vivid image in Brabantio's mind's eye of sexual relations between Desdemona and Othello, when he definitively asserts, "I am one, sir, that comes to tell you your daughter and the Moor are now making the beast with two backs" (115–16). Roderigo in less provocative language tells Brabantio that Desdemona has been "transported . . . [t]o the gross clasps of a lascivious Moor" (123 and 125). After Roderigo makes reference to the law of the land and the possible penalty for his attempting to delude him concerning his daughter's behavior, only then does Brabantio believe the horrifying news that Iago and Roderigo tell him.

Once Brabantio confronts Othello, he remains incredulous that his daughter, who has the greatest number of marital choices, would select Othello over one of the "curled darlings of the nation" (I.ii.68). In fact, he claims that if it were not for the power of magic, she would never have expressed any affection for him by "[r]unning from her guardage to the sooty bosom / Of such a thing as [Othello] art" (70–71). (This is the same accusation that Egeus makes against Lysander when his daughter Hermia refuses to marry the man he has chosen for her.) Apparently, the belief in the power of magic was still held in early modern England. Even after the Duke arrives to adjudicate the case against Othello, Brabantio continues to argue that Desdemona's desire for Othello is "For nature to so preposterously to err" (I.iii.62). The word "preposterously" takes the meaning of "monstrously, perversely, contrary to the order of nature" (Neill 219). For Desdemona to fall in love with Othello is, as Brabantio asserts, "[a]gainst all rules of nature" (102). Othello is given an opportunity to defend himself against accusations of witchcraft, which in England was a capital offense, and having given a lengthy account of how and why he knew the family and the stories that he told Desdemona, he told of how Desdemona would "come again, and with a greedy ear / Devour up [his] discourse" (149–50). Here Desdemona is represented as an active agent in this account rather than a passive victim of Othello's tales of travel and adventure.

When Desdemona is called upon by her father to give a reason for her marriage to the Moor, she argues quite cleverly that she realizes that she must respect him because he is her father and because of the life that he has given her, yet at the same time she, in an equally eloquent manner, argues the case that she should be able to choose her own husband because just as she is leaving him for Othello so did her mother leave her father for him, and so Brabantio abruptly ends his plea to the Duke with "Goodbye, I've done! / Please it your grace, on to the state affairs" (188–89). Desdemona's desire to marry Othello confounds Brabantio's understanding of female sexuality. As Loomba powerfully asserts in *Gender, Race, Renaissance Drama*, "Active female sexuality is disruptive of patriarchal control, not just because it is an emblem for, or analogous to, other sorts of rebellion, but because it threatens the power base of patriarchy which is dependent upon its regulation and control" (56). Moreover, by speaking publicly, Desdemona transgresses early modern social decorum as women were to be silent, but here she is given an audience, and she speaks articulately and persuasively.

At the same time that Iago attempts to foment tension between Brabantio and Othello via Desdemona, he pretends to be his heartfelt confidant. He then turns his attention to Cassio, who succeeded him in the position of Othello's lieutenant, in order to use Cassio as a means of destroying Desdemona and Othello's marriage. What is perhaps most peculiar is Iago's claim that Othello and Emilia, Iago's wife, have engaged in sexual relations, for Iago states,

> And it is thought abroad that 'twixt my sheets
> He's done my office. I know not if 't be true,
> But I, for mere suspicion in that kind,
> Will do as if for surety. (I.iii.376–79)

Neill believes that Iago links the usurpation of his bed with the usurpation of his lieutenancy by Cassio (239). Not only does the issue of female sexuality concern Desdemona, but here according to Iago, it concerns his wife Emilia. Moreover, Iago makes his sexual jealousy known yet again in a soliloquy in which he asserts, "I do assert the lusty Moor / Hapt leapt into my seat" (II.i.286–87) (Neill 239). Finally, Iago is so sexually insecure that he thinks Cassio may have slept with his wife too, "(For I fear Cassio with my nightcap too)" (298). Earlier in his conversation with Roderigo, Iago described Cassio as "handsome, young, / and hath all those requisites that in him that folly and green minds look after" (238–40). Many critics wonder if Iago is attracted to either Othello or Cassio because he appears extremely concerned about their sexual prowess regarding women, especially his wife. Moreover, one wonders if Iago feels deficient in his capacity as Emilia's husband.

Throughout this play Iago possesses a voyeuristic interest in others' sexual relations. While Cassio relaxes with Iago before he is to begin his night watch, Iago tries vainly to engage him in bawdy repartee as to how Desdemona and Othello will spend their wedding night. Iago initiates the dialogue with the risqué comment, "[H]e hath / not yet made wanton the night with her, and she is sport / for Jove" (II.iii.15–17), but Cassio still thinks of her in a chivalric fashion by replying, "She's a most exquisite lady" (18). Iago insists upon using provocative language, but Cassio, who is usually thought to be a better educated and refined character than Iago, refuses to engage in inappropriate, off-color banter concerning the wife of his commanding officer.

Failing to make Cassio engage in risqué banter about Othello and Desdemona's wedding night, Iago decides to go one better by cajoling Cassio into drinking a stoup of wine with him against his better judgment. Once inebriated, Cassio goes offstage where he is insulted by Roderigo, and they in turn begin to fight with their swords at which point they return to the stage, and Montano, the governor of Cyprus, attempts to calm Cassio, who foolishly wounds Montano. Othello is called from his bridal bed, and he adjudicates what has occurred by demoting Cassio and leaving Iago to oversee the guard of the town and to "silence those whom this vile brawl distracted" (II.iii.247). This is yet the first part of Iago's insidious plot to undermine Othello and Desdemona's marriage, for he advises Cassio that he should ask Desdemona if she would importune Othello to reinstate his lieutenancy. Meanwhile he plans to convince Othello of Desdemona's infidelity. Iago uses the imagery of poison. This allusion to pouring pestilence or poison into someone's ear is curiously reminiscent of the murder of Hamlet's father in the royal garden by Claudius, Hamlet's nefarious uncle (Neill 277). In both instances the insidious quality of the villains' intent predominates one's conception of their actions; moreover, Claudius's dastardly, nefarious murder of Hamlet's father seems almost clumsy by comparison to these underhanded actions of Iago, who throughout the play has the complete confidence of Othello and others around him even as he does everything within his power to undermine their lives.

Iago begins his subversion of Othello's belief in Desdemona's fidelity by pretending to withhold information regarding his wife's interaction with Cassio. Hesitating to answer Othello's question concerning Cassio's honesty, Iago engenders doubts in Othello's mind and forces him to exclaim, "By heaven, thou echo'st me, / As if there were some monster in thy thought / Too hideous to be shown" (III.iii.109–111). Honesty in men in the early modern period was generally thought to concern their truthfulness while honesty in women concerned their chastity. Here again is this emphasis on visuality and unnaturalness. Having piqued Othello's curiosity as to Cassio's honesty, Iago warns Othello about the effect of jealousy on one's psyche, and he refers to it as a "green-eyed monster" (III.iii.169). Apparently, jealousy was thought to be caused by bile that gave one a green complexion;

hence, Othello is "green-eyed" because of the obsessive observation which eventuates in Othello's desire for "ocular proof" (Neill 292).

Othello's obsession with "ocular proof" is presaged early in this discussion with Iago when he asserts, "I'll see before I doubt" (III.iii.193). Iago continues to focus on the visible representation of unfaithful wives, "In Venice they do let God see the pranks / They dare not show their husbands" (III.iii.205–6). First, Venice was well known throughout the early modern world for having a very licentious citizenry who engaged in decadent sexual practices on a regular basis, for Venice was especially known for its prostitutes; moreover, later in the play Othello denounces his wife by telling her that he "took her for that cunning whore of Venice" (IV.ii.90). Iago refers to "pranks" as sexual escapades in which women engage behind their husbands' backs and thereby turn them into cuckolds. After all, Othello moments earlier told Iago, "Exchange me for a goat / When I shall the business of my soul / To such exsufflicate and blown surmises" (III.iii.183–85). Goats are particularly associated with unbridled lust, and the horns of the goat in turn are associated with cuckoldry (Neill 293). Othello leaves Iago profoundly disturbed by his report of women's infidelity.

When Othello sees Desdemona immediately after his conversation with Iago, he informs her of his headache, and immediately she offers him her napkin, which is the all-important handkerchief that Othello had passed on to her from his mother as a sign of their marital fidelity. He responds that it is too small because horns are growing from his forehead. Already Othello has reservations about his wife's fidelity. One must wonder why a man of Othello's standing in Venice who has just married the beautiful, young daughter of a Venetian senator should possess such doubts. Charney believes that beneath the bravado of Othello's military accomplishments he seriously doubts his worthiness to be Desdemona's spouse (102).

In the next scene the import of this handkerchief comes to the fore when Emilia apprises Iago that she has found it. Emilia knows the value that Desdemona places on the handkerchief, and then she shows it to Iago who has asked her to steal it. Surely he, too, knows the value of this handkerchief to Desdemona and Othello's marital stability. Emilia gleefully tells Iago: "I have a thing for you" (III.iii.304), to which he retorts, "You have a thing for me? It is a common thing—" (305). (Iago puns on the word "thing" which is a slang term for female genitalia as used in the title *Much Ado about Nothing*.) When Emilia reminds Iago of the much sought-after handkerchief, he immediately is overjoyed, and he refuses to return it to her and sends Emilia away so he may use it to whatever untoward practice that he can devise. He is well aware how suggestible Othello is, and in a very famous passage, Iago states, "Trifles light as air / Are to the jealous confirmations strong / As proofs of holy writ" (III.iii.324–26). Iago realizes that this is the one piece of evidence to convince Othello of Desdemona's infidelity with Cassio.

When Cassio sees Othello again, Othello demands "ocular proof" (III.iii.362) of Desdemona's unfaithfulness, and Iago's "proof" convinces Othello, but first Iago recounts or better yet constructs a fanciful account of what sounds as much like a homoerotic fantasy as evidence of heterosexual spousal infidelity. In early modern England and Europe the practice of more than one person sleeping in one bed at a time was not uncommon, and so it is for this reason Iago may tell Othello of his sleeping in bed with Cassio and his experience with Cassio that night:

> In sleep I heard him say "Sweet Desdemona,
> Let us be wary, let us hide our loves";
> And then, sir, would he gripe and wring my hand,
> Cry, "O, sweet creature!", and then kiss me hard,
> As if he plucked up kisses by the roots
> That grew upon my lips, then laid his leg
> Over my thigh, and sigh, and kissed, and then
> Cried "Cursed fate that gave thee to the Moor!" (III.iii.420–27)

Obviously, according to this fanciful account, Iago acts as proxy for Desdemona while Cassio kissed and placed his leg over Iago's thigh. This powerfully erotic image is more reflective of Iago's conflicted sexuality than anything else. Iago's omission of what he said or did to Cassio after he made this sexual advance is unusual to say the least. Othello's response to Iago's imaginative homoerotic fantasy is simply, "O monstrous! Monstrous!" (428). The image of monstrosity is prevalent in *Othello* as Karen Newman has noted in her essay "'And wash the Ethiop white': Femininity and the Monstrous in *Othello*" and will be discussed in a later chapter.

While this erotically charged account strongly riles Othello, Iago's allusion to the talisman-like handkerchief forces Othello to the brink of madness when he queries Othello as to seeing the handkerchief with the strawberries on it. The handkerchief acts as proxy for the "ocular proof" that Othello insists upon in order to be convinced of Desdemona's infidelity. Neill argues quite cogently regarding the place of the handkerchief in the sexual scheme of the play. The handkerchief is representative of the winding sheets that were stained with hymenal blood, which was symbolic of Elizabethan marriage (155). Traditionally, strawberries were thought of as a kind of aphrodisiac, but Neill gives their multiple significances, "[I]n Christian iconography, by contrast, the plant's habit of simultaneous flowering and fruiting had made it an emblem for the chastity and fertility of the Virgin Mary" (155). Suffice it to say that Othello is convinced of Desdemona's guilt and now wants Iago to kill Cassio as he attempts to find an appropriate way to kill Desdemona. Therefore, the scene ends with Othello elevating Iago to the rank of lieutenant and Iago metaphorically pledging his loyalty and devotion to Othello as he very emotionally declares, "I am your own for ever" (III.iii.479).

Tellingly, Iago had moments earlier told Othello, "Let him command, / And to obey shall be in me remorse, / What bloody business ever" (III.iii.467–68), to which Othello replies, "I greet thy love, / Not with vain thanks, but with acceptance bounteous" (469–70). Neill again provides insightful commentary on this scene by suggesting that this language is akin to that of master and servant, but also that which a husband and wife would exchange with each other (312), which reinforces the homoerotic overtones of this scene with Othello and Iago.

At this junction Iago has effectively undermined the marital integrity of Othello and Desdemona's relationship. Tragically, the end of the play eventuates in the murder of both Desdemona and Emilia by their respective husbands, the murder of Roderigo by Iago, and finally, the suicide of Othello after he learns from Emilia that Iago has duped him. Throughout this play sexual jealousy has been the dominant concern, but at the same time the Venetians' fixation upon the exotic quality of Othello's ethnicity because of the fact that he is a Moor, a cultural outsider, worsened his social situation; since Othello was a Moor and thought to be sexually powerful and lustful, the court culture of Venice certainly must have viewed Othello differently from other generals from the Veneto in the past. The collision of sexual jealousy and cultural difference generates a heady brew of political and erotic tension in this early modern European city in the Levant that leads ineluctably to civic and social unrest and, ultimately, spousal homicides.

In the romances which came at the end of Shakespeare's dramatic career, there is a shift in the sexual sensibility of the young men and women who fall in love and marry. The romances hold out the possibility of hope and redemption after the characters' trials and tribulations. In *The Tempest* (Orgel), the last play to which Shakespeare can claim complete authorship, the hero and heroine, Ferdinand and Miranda, are brought together by Prospero, Miranda's father and the island's resident magus, who is capable of creating a storm at sea that shipwrecks Prospero's evil brother Antonio, and his two partners in crime, Sebastian and his brother, Alonso, the King of Naples. Because of this stormy sea that Prospero engenders, Ferdinand and Miranda find themselves a wife and a husband respectively but only through the power of magic. From the moment that Ferdinand and Miranda meet, they fall instantly in love in the same way that a young couple would in a fairy tale with all of the requisite magic and music. After Ferdinand is tossed upon the shore, Miranda spies him lying upon the beach, as Miranda exclaims, "I might call him / A Thing divine, for nothing natural / I ever saw so noble" (I.ii.416–18). Ferdinand also mistakes her for an otherworldly being by referring to her as a "goddess" (424). Both of them are initially incapable of realizing the mortality of the other. Ferdinand asserts she is a "wonder," and ironically, her name means one who is wondered at or admired, but she quickly disabuses Ferdinand of that delusion. Prospero notices that they have "changed eyes" (442). The implication is that their eye beams have interlocked, and it is quite apparent that they are already in love, but Prospero is well aware that their easily gained affection may quickly lead to premarital sexual relations, for Prospero believes that Ferdinand may not value the love that Miranda has for him if he gained it too easily, and this possibility concerns Prospero immensely. Therefore, when he accuses Ferdinand of usurpation of the island, which ironically is exactly what Antonio in conjunction with Sebastian and Alonso have done in Milan, Miranda strongly objects to Prospero's accusations because of Ferdinand's physical attractiveness.

Miranda subscribes to the Platonic notion that outer beauty is indicative of inner goodness, but Stephen Orgel opines, "Miranda's speech expresses more naivete than Platonism" (126). By the end of this scene, Prospero fears that Miranda may dote upon Ferdinand and not really understand the nature of men's erotic desires as she is only 16 years of age and very much an ingénue in the ways of human sexuality. Hence, she should not fawn upon him; after all, Prospero rebukes her because he wants Miranda to mature into a responsible young woman and to see men for who they are, not through rose-colored glasses which will surely cause her pain and anguish in years ahead if she does not develop a greater understanding of male sexuality.

As a form of test in order to determine Ferdinand's loyalty to Miranda, Prospero manacles him and forces him to chop logs, a most degrading act for any member of royalty. So moved upon seeing Ferdinand cut this wood, Miranda insists upon helping him. Of course, Ferdinand is horrified at the very idea of his beloved chopping wood while he stood idly, for this would be the antithesis of the Petrarchan ideal of courtly conduct. Yet Miranda asserts that she is no better to engage in physical labor than he; moreover, she wishes to cut this wood out of love for him because it would alleviate his pain, and that would give her pleasure. In many ways Ferdinand is the perfect prince of fairy tales because his description of Miranda betokens an idealization of female beauty and perfection that is unrealistic. He refers to her as "Admired Miranda, / Indeed the top of admiration" (III.i.37–38). While the blandishments of the Petrarchan lover may be extraordinarily flattering, the woman to whom the compliment is made needs to know whether the man sincerely loves her, or whether this mannered discourse is simply a rhetorical game, and so Miranda asks Ferdinand directly if he loves her, and his reply is as passionate as hers is to the point, "I, / Beyond all limit of what else i' th' world, / Do love, prize, honour you" (71–73). Prospero, of course, looks on this scene of young love, and he is truly pleased, for his plan to have them meet and fall in love is preeminently successful, and so the scene ends with a marriage proposal in which Ferdinand kneels before Miranda as a sign of his honor and devotion to her. At the end of this betrothal, there is a hand clasping, an outward and visible sign of their future union as husband and wife; they must now await marriage at the door of the church once they return to Naples.

Given the conventionality of this play, one can only expect the transfer of the daughter to the future husband by the father of the bride in a transaction in which she functions as a "gift" (IV.i.14) which has been "worthily purchased" (15). Nonetheless, Prospero warns Ferdinand of the danger of "break[ing] her virgin-knot" (16) and the ensuing consequences, which will be marital discord. Moreover, he abjures Ferdinand that he must "not give the dalliance / Too much the rein. The strongest oaths are straw / To th' fire i' th' blood" (51–53). Be that as it as it may, Prospero presents them an absolutely splendid wedding gift in the form of a masque, an elaborate courtly entertainment involving singing, dancing, music, beautiful costumes, and sometimes a god or goddess descending to earth on a cloud, which he conjures up for the pleasure of his daughter Miranda and Ferdinand, his future son-in-law. Three great goddesses—Ceres, Iris, and Juno—celebrate and bless the marriage of this couple while Juno sings this triumphant song of joy to celebrate the future marriage of this young couple. Not only will Miranda and Ferdinand be prosperous, happy, and blessed with children, but they will be beneficiaries of the bounty of the earth. Without a doubt the goddesses' song has a celebratory, even jubilant quality about it:

Earth's increase, foison plenty,
Barns and garners never empty,
Vines and clust'ring bunches bowing;
Spring come to you at the farthest,
In the very end of harvest! (IV.i.110–15)

As Virginia Vaughan notes, eroticism is conspicuously absent from this scenario. Moreover, she argues that Prospero exiles Venus and Cupid from the masque. On the contrary, the goddesses Ceres and Juno represent love based on chastity and moderate passion (71). Ferdinand wishes that he could remain forever in this magical world, but Prospero must address the "foul conspiracy / Of the beast Caliban and his confederates" (139–40), and so he does.

Once Prospero regains control of all the individuals on the island, he can, finally, introduce Alonso, the King of Naples, to Miranda, who is betrothed to his son Ferdinand. Even this scene is filled with a quasi-theatrical quality, for Prospero ironically commiserates with Alonso because of the supposed loss of his son in this tempest only to pull back a curtain so that he can see Ferdinand and Miranda playing a game of chess. Miranda exclaims, "Sweet lord, you play me false" to which Ferdinand replies, "No, my dearest love, I would not for the world." (V.i.172–73). Orgel argues that this game has significant political overtones, "The territorial ambitions of their elders are transformed by Ferdinand and Miranda into the stratagems of chess. . . . The game was an aristocratic pastime associated especially with lovers, often with illicit sexual overtones, and also served as a frequent allegory of politics" (197). Happily, Ferdinand and Miranda's "political" conflict is resolved just as their fathers' is so that Prospero, the ultimate stage manager, may achieve the ends that he set out to accomplish at the beginning of the play, and so for Miranda, it is, indeed, a "brave new world" (84) in which she and Ferdinand may go forth and live their lives in mutual trust and happiness.

WORKS CITED

Adelman, Janet. *Suffocating Mothers: Fantasies of Maternal Origin in Shakespeare's Plays, Hamlet to The Tempest*. New York and London: Routledge, 1992. Print.

Armstrong, Philip. *Shakespeare in Psychoanalysis*. London and New York: Routledge, 2001. Print.

Bevington, David, ed. *Henry IV, Part I*. By William Shakespeare. The Oxford Shakespeare. Oxford: Oxford UP, 1998. Print.

Burrow, Colin, ed. *The Complete Poems and Sonnets*. By William Shakespeare. The Oxford Shakespeare. Oxford: Oxford UP, 2002. Print.

Charney, Maurice, *Shakespeare on Love and Sex*. New York: Columbia UP, 2000. Print.

Coenen, Dorothea. *The Chiron Dictionary of Greek and Roman Mythology: Gods and Goddesses, Heroes, Places, and Events of Antiquity*. Trans. Elizabeth Burr. Wilmette, IL: Chiron, 1998. Print.

Garber, Marjorie Beth. *Shakespeare after All*. New York: Anchor, 2005. Print.

Hibbard, R. G., ed. *Hamlet*. By William Shakespeare. The Oxford Shakespeare. Oxford: Oxford UP, 1998. Print.

Holland, Norman N. "Hermia's Dream." *Annual of Psychoanalysis* 7 (1979): 369–89. Rpt. in *Shakespeare's Comedies*. Ed. and Intro. Gary Waller. London and New York: Longman, 1991. 75–92. Print.

Holland, Peter, ed. *A Midsummer Night's Dream*. By William Shakespeare. The Oxford Shakespeare. Oxford: Oxford UP, 1998. Print.

Howard, Jean E. *Engendering a Nation: A Feminist Account of Shakespeare's English Histories*. London and New York: Routledge, 1997. Print.

Jardine, Lisa. *Still Harping on Daughters: Women and Drama in the Age of Shakespeare*. New York: Columbia UP, 1989. Print.

Kahn, Coppélia. *Man's Estate: Masculine Identity in Shakespeare*. Berkeley and London: U of California P, 1981. Print.

Klett, Elizabeth. "*The Taming of the Shrew*." *Shakespeare Bulletin*. 23.1 (2005): 149–51. Print.

Levenson, Jill. Ed. *Romeo and Juliet*. By William Shakespeare. The Oxford Shakespeare. Oxford: Oxford: UP, 2001. Print.

Loomba, Ania. *Gender, Race, Renaissance Drama*. Manchester, UK: Manchester UP, 1989. Print.

McEachern, Claire, ed. *Much Ado about Nothing*. By William Shakespeare. The Arden Shakespeare. London: Thompson, 2006. Print.

Mikesell, Margaret Lael. "'Love Wrought These Miracles': Marriage and Genre in *The Taming of the Shrew*." *The Taming of the Shrew: Critical Essays*. Ed. Dana E. Aspinall. New York and London: Routledge, 2002. 106–29. Print.

Miola, Robert. *Shakespeare's Reading*. Oxford: Oxford UP, 2000. Print.

Montrose, Louis Adrian. *The Purpose of Playing: Shakespeare and the Cultural Politics of Elizabethan Theatre*. Chicago: U of Chicago P, 1996. Print.

Neill, Michael, ed. *Othello, the Moor of Venice*. By William Shakespeare. The Oxford Shakespeare. Oxford: Oxford UP, 1998. Print.

Newman, Karen. "'And wash the Ethiop white': Femininity and the Monstrous in *Othello*." *Fashioning Femininity in English Renaissance Drama*. Chicago: U of Chicago P, 1991. 71–93. Print.

Oliver, H. J., ed. *The Taming of the Shrew*. By William Shakespeare. The Oxford Shakespeare. Oxford: Oxford UP, 1998. Print.

Orgel, Stephen, ed. *The Tempest*. By William Shakespeare. The Oxford Shakespeare. Oxford: Oxford UP, 1998. Print.

Partridge, Eric. *Shakespeare's Bawdy*. London and New York: Routledge, 1968. Print.

Vaughan, Virginia Mason, and Alden T. Vaughan, eds. *The Tempest*. By William Shakespeare. The Arden Shakespeare. London and New York: Thompson, 2000. Print.

Wells, Stanley. *Looking for Sex in Shakespeare*. Cambridge: Cambridge UP, 2004. Print.

Williams, Gordon. *Shakespeare, Sex, and the Print Revolution*. London and Atlantic Highlands, NJ: Athlone, 1996. Print.

Zitner, Sheldon, ed. *Much Ado about Nothing*. By William Shakespeare. The Oxford Shakespeare. Oxford: Oxford UP, 1998. Print.

4

SEXUALITY IN PERFORMANCE

Shakespeare's plays have been staged and filmed in a myriad of settings and scenarios. We know that Shakespeare's plays were staged in the Globe Theatre in the afternoons while there was still plenty of natural sunlight with its groundlings open to the elements as they stood in what today would be considered the best viewing area in the theatre. However, if one could afford to attend Blackfriars Theatre, one would experience the plays within an enclosed space with illumination provided by chandeliers hanging over head.

Since we have considered the topic of sexuality in the previous plays, we will continue to do so regarding the stage and film versions of largely the same plays so they may be viewed from a performative lens of interpretation rather than only a textual one. As noted earlier, *The Taming of the Shrew* has always been a popular play on the stage because of the boisterous, knockabout slapstick of its principals, Petruchio and Katherina. The historical record indicates that *The Taming of the Shrew* was performed at both the Globe and the Blackfriars as well as before the court of Charles I and Henrietta Maria on November 26, 1633. Then just two days later John Fletcher's sequel was performed; it was intriguingly titled *The Woman's Prize; or, The Tamer Tamed,* and in this sequel Petruchio takes a second wife after Kate dies. Here the scenario is reversed, for the new wife decided that she would announce her plan to tame Petruchio in the second scene. Now Petruchio must meet the demands of this new wife by giving her what she wants (Oliver 65).

The 18th century saw a more conventional representation of the play with David Garrick's Catherine and Petruchio, albeit in three acts. Apparently, Petruchio appreciates her ability to act on her own behalf having smashed a lute over the head of Hortensio, and in the final scene Kate delivers her lecture to Bianca concerning a wife's duties to her husband without any wager being made by Petruchio and the other men. This version of the play remained on the stage for 100 years in America and England (Oliver 68–69).

Finally, in 1844, *The Taming of the Shrew* was performed in its entirety, including the Induction at the Haymarket Theatre in London with only two sets. The character of Christopher Sly became quite important, but the return of

Mrs. Nisbett to the stage signaled a significant presence, for now the issue of how to make Kate's inferior status palatable to London theatregoers had to be confronted. Samuel Phelps, playing Sly, decided to cut the final scene of Kate's submissive speech, which resulted in a mixed response (Oliver 70).

The 1920s ushered in modern-dress productions replete with automobiles. H.K. Ayliff's 1927 production with Mary Ellias as Katherina and Basil Sydney as Petruchio was quite successful. In 1928 the Birmingham Repertory Theatre's production ran for 175 performances, and it was set among the metropolis's social elite so when the production was moved to London, the focus on modern-day dress offended some theatregoers and critics because this change of costume brought to the fore some of the current gender issues, specifically women's newly granted right to vote and the inclusion of the infinitive "to obey" in the marriage vows. Nonetheless, the role of Katherina, a flapper, played by Eileen Beldon, was brought under control by the end of the first scene of the second act. Although she fought courageously with Petruchio, she finally broke down in tears. Some reviewers of the play thought that the ideological implications of Katherina's mistreatment would be overlooked by their female audience members because of the heavy emphasis placed upon high fashion in this production of the play (Schafer 29).

The first Shakespearean play that was a feature-length film with sound happened to be *The Taming of the Shrew* starring Mary Pickford and Douglas Fairbanks who were directed by Sam Taylor in 1929. In this film version, slapstick was still the dominant mode of interaction between the characters. Fairbanks and Pickford are both wielding whips like animal trainers at a circus. In one scene the camera pans up the stairs which shows the detritus of Kate's last angry fit. Finally, the camera shows the shrew herself holding a whip (Rothwell 30–31).

At the end of the play, Kate does engage in a subversive wink to her sister Bianca when she makes her speech concerning a wife's duties, for when she is to utter the phrase, "to obey," she looks at her sister as if to indicate that this is all part of Petruchio's bet (Rothwell 34). In the newspapers a number of reviewers responded to that subversive little wink. E.A. Baughan believed that Kate's counsel to Bianca and the Widow is contradicted when she winks at the audience. Hence, the independence of women in the United States has been pacified because no American woman would allow her husband to be the head and ruler of the family (Jones, *Shakespeare's Culture in Modern Performance* 28). Some film critics thought the film was entertaining as far as farce was concerned, but one reviewer for the *Observer* was not so kind when he opined that the Mickey Mouse cartoon was the finest example of cinematography shown on that occasion (Haring-Smith 126). Again, the critical reception was mixed, but nonetheless, this film demonstrated that Shakespeare's plays could be made available to audiences of an immensely greater scope.

Lynn Fontanne and Alfred Lunt were the most famous theatrical married couple in the 1930s, and their performances of Kate and Petruchio in the 1930s in Harry Wagstaff Gribble's 1935 production of the play were interpreted as a representation of their marital relationship. Their production later inspired Cole

Porter's 1948 musical, *Kiss Me Kate*, which was made into a film in 1953, starring Howard Keel and Kathryn Grayson. In the Fontanne/Lunt production while Kate battled Petruchio fiercely, she was thought to be in love with him, and therefore, her acquiescence was also thought to be "tongue-in-cheek," according to one reviewer (Schafer 32; Rothwell 302).

Perhaps the most celebrated husband-wife team of the second half of the 20th century was Elizabeth Taylor and Richard Burton, who starred in Franco Zeffirelli's film version of *The Taming of the Shrew* in 1967. Taylor is like all of the Kates before her, fiery and boisterous. Given the hot-tempered personality of a shrew, everyone, especially Burton, was surprised when Taylor gave the famous speech on submitting to one's husband without irony. However, Kate's bolting from Petruchio when he asked her for a kiss made the scene problematic (Rothwell 132–33).

Perhaps one of the finest productions of *The Taming of the Shrew* took place in 1976 by the American Conservatory Theatre in San Francisco with the principals Fredi Olster and Marc Singer as Kate and Petruchio respectively, whose performances are very much in the commedia dell'arte fashion, as Hal Holbrook tells the audience at the beginning of the film. Much of the time, Petruchio is shirtless, displaying his perfectly tanned muscular chest which oozes eroticism. In fact, when Gremio, a doddering suitor of Bianca, first meets Petruchio, he pokes at his strongly built legs and makes sounds that indicate that he is impressed, if not pleased, with their muscularity. Kate displays a noticeable interest in Petruchio

Elizabeth Taylor and husband Richard Burton star as Kate and Petruchio in Franco Zeffirelli's *The Taming of the Shrew*. AP Photo.

when she first sees him as she walks around him, smiling as she looks down at his buttocks and then immediately looking back up when she comes to face him. Kate certainly knows a fine specimen of a man when she sees one, but Kate, too, evinces an unmistakable eroticism and sensuality, and all of the bawdy innuendo of a tongue in Kate's tail is presented with relish and bravo. William Ball and Kirk Browning's version of *The Taming of the Shrew* was nothing short of a virtuoso performance, which was brilliantly executed by all members of the acting company.

The Taming of the Shrew continues to be immensely popular today. Recent productions have taken Kate and Petruchio to the American West of the 1880s. At the Stratford Festival of Canada at the Festival Theatre in Stratford, Ontario, in 2003, Miles Potter as Petruchio, according to Justin Shaltz, excitedly performs his role, but he also makes ancillary characters into cartoonish figures (Shaltz 63). Kate is as wild and wooly as ever in this production, prompting Petruchio to draw his revolver at one point for his own protection. Kate, of course, has a great deal of wit, and apparently, her anger functions as a defensive mechanism against aging (64), which Shaltz continues to mention in his review, but indeed, she has a reason to be angry when Petruchio throws her across his shoulders and carries her off on their wedding day as she kicks and screams. Yet when Kate kneels and places her hand on Petruchio's boot, he, too, kneels, and after they kiss each other, they stand up together, signaling their mutual equality (65).

Sidney Berger's production of *The Taming of the Shrew,* also set in the 1880s, tended to gloss over the gender issues, according to Elizabeth Klett, so that differences are reconciled. First, the play focused on "broad comic humor" (150) with Bianca playing the role of a coy young woman who is the apple of her father's eye and who drops many handkerchiefs for Lucentio to retrieve for her. In fact, much of the sexual innuendo concerns Bianca, for the actors emphasized words such as "instruments" and "fingering" in III.i and later in IV.i. Bianca actually climbed on top of him and rode him as if he were a horse at a rodeo while she waved his hat over her head, and to be sure the comic scene between Kate and Petruchio in II.i was also quite risqué as Petruchio pulled Kate onto his lap and attempted to lift her off the floor. At one moment, she pointed to his groin and said derisively, "You are withered," which embarrassed Petruchio. It is only after Kate and Petruchio engaged in the moon-sun debate that Petruchio showed affection toward Kate, and she was at once surprised and pleased. At the end of the play, when Kate is supposed to demonstrate submission, Petruchio grabbed Kate's hand when she attempted to place it under his foot, kneeled, and kissed it. Klett argues that this gesture indicated Petruchio's desire for equality in the marriage, and most intriguingly, she points out that the epilogue from John Fletcher's play *The Women's Prize; or, The Tamer Tamed* was added to the dialogue in the last scene and was not identified as such in either the performance or the program notes, and seemed to function as a commentary on the action in *The Taming of the Shrew* (150–51).

Just as Petruchio can be played with a soft, romantic quality about him, he can also be played with an extraordinary masculine quality as Ryan Shively did in David H. Bell's production at the Chicago Shakespeare Theatre on the Navy

Pier in 2003. Elizabeth Charlebois described Bianca's suitors as feminine by comparison. Hortensio was an effete academic, and Tranio was a dandy. Petruchio, on the other hand, arrived without a shirt. Appearing as an extra from *Rebel without a Cause*, he came to the wedding on a motorcycle wearing biker gear with a large leather codpiece, orange boxer shorts, and torn jeans, which Klett described as a "colorful caricature of masculinity" (108); he sounded extremely attractive despite what Klett asserts.

According to Charlebois, Bell added greater "psychological realism to Katherina and Bianca than he [did] to the male characters in the play" (109). Nonetheless, the physicality of the fighting took on an unnerving quality when Petruchio stripped her to her slip, at which point she ripped the shirt off his back, but they both eventually found themselves in a pool of water. Surprisingly, they finally kissed each other, but when Kate's father, Baptista, arrived with the newspaper people, she became her shrewish self again and violently grabbed his groin, and Petruchio actually fainted.

At the wedding Petruchio was his typically unruly self, and when he took her to his home, "it seem[ed] more like seduction than romance" (114). Moreover, instead of a wildly erotic honeymoon, Petruchio appeared sexually uninterested in her. Nonetheless, in the final scene again, as in several others, when Kate offered to place her hand beneath his foot, Petruchio jumped from his chair and keeled beside her and kissed her hand. Charlebois provides a fine feminist reading of this last scene in which she argues that paradoxically Petruchio can behave this way because in the final analysis he held all of the power in this relationship and that it is rather Petruchio's taking her hand in this dramatic fashion that was the real performance, not her act of submission to Petruchio (114).

As far as recent film adaptations of *The Taming of the Shrew* are concerned, we have *10 Things I Hate about You*, directed by Gil Junger based on a screenplay by Kristen Smith and Karen McCullah. This particular adaptation is set at Padua High School in Portland, Oregon. Michael Friedman, in his article, "The Feminist as Shrew in *10 Things I Hate about You*," argues that cliques in high school are similar to "class divisions within society at large, particularly those explored by Shakespeare" (47). The character of Katherina is played by her 20th-century counterpart, Kat, whose feminist tendencies have similarities with Kate in that she speaks her mind to men in a forthright fashion. Interestingly, in the course of the film, both sisters become more like each other regarding feminist ideals (59). Finally, Friedman argues, "Kat and Bianca stand for two different audiences for teen comedy: adults who grew up during the second wave of the feminist movement of the 1970s and that generation's teenage children, who shrink from the feminist label while sharing its values" (62). To be sure, *10 Things I Hate about You* is a wonderfully amusing and engaging take on *The Taming of the Shrew*.

Moving from *The Taming of the Shrew* to *Romeo and Juliet*, one of the most beloved tragedies of Western civilization, is no easy leap, but the plays function as powerful contrasts of how tragedy and comedy are closely aligned at times because a father's approval or disapproval of one's spousal choice could spell joy or sadness for a young woman or man in the early modern period. Despite the fact that *Romeo and Juliet* have mesmerized seemingly countless generations of audiences, sadly, no record remains of its initial performances. Jill Levenson points out that no date of any performance exists before the Restoration. Shakespeare may have written the play during a time of confusion in the theatre caused by the plague or the vagaries of royal support; after all, the theatres were closed in London from 1592 to 1593. Levenson opines that the Chamberlain's Men may likely have performed the play in The Theatre and then later at the Curtain (61). Although the stage history of *Romeo and Juliet* is murky before the Restoration, there is an abundance of theatre later. *Romeo and Juliet* was immensely popular in the 18th century; for example, thanks to the archival work of Charles Beecher Hogan, we know that 399 performances were staged between 1751 and 1800; another stage historian, Felicia Hardison Londre determined that 352 revivals of the play were performed in less than four decades after World War II. Only in the 20th century has *Hamlet* been staged more frequently than *Romeo and Juliet*, but adaptations that were less than textually accurate were the reasons for its popularity (Levenson 70).

With the return of Charles II to the throne in 1660, *Romeo and Juliet* also returned to the stage, appearing on March 1, 1662, at a small theatre that was a remodeled tennis court in Lincoln's Inn Fields (Levenson 71). For the next 100 years or so, *Romeo and Juliet* saw more than its share of deletions and additions, including scenes, characters, endings, and words that did not appear in the original text. Thomas Otway's *History and Fall of Caius Marius* in 1679 at the Duke's Playhouse is the first version to demonstrate these kinds of changes. In this stage version of *Romeo and Juliet*, the eroticism of the romance was subsumed within the political turmoil of Rome (Levenson 73).

In 1744 Colley Cibber readjusted the focus of the play from political turmoil to domestic disputes between the anger of the mothers of the Capulet and Montague families; in this scenario the wives of Capulet and Montague are against the proposal that Romeo and Juliet should marry. Although Cibber and Thomas Sheridan's productions had short runs, David Garrick's production, which began on November 29, 1748, had over 329 performances of the play at Drury Lane and Covent Garden between 1748 and 1776. This stage version was the dominant interpretation for the next 97 years, and it was on the stage until the late 19th century (Levenson 75).

By the beginning of the 19th century, Garrick's script of *Romeo and Juliet* began to change with John Philip Kemble, another important director of his age, in 1803 with the advent of realistic pictorialism, which focused on realistic stage properties. Moreover there was an increased concern about historical accuracy in the production of the play, and so it was during the 1845–1846 theatre season that Charlotte Cushman came to the stage, and fortunately, she reinstituted the play's text in its entirety while performing Romeo. This treatment of the play displaced Garrick's hold on it, and consequently, it was the dominant stage interpretation of the play for the next 23 years. While Garrick made both of the lovers of equal importance and "uniformly pathetic," Cushman concentrated upon Romeo (Levenson 82–83).

William Poel was yet another director who heralded another trend, and he was concerned about the staging of historically accurate productions of Shakespeare's plays, and so finally, in John Gielgud's 1935 production Laurence Olivier and Gielgud exchanged the roles of Romeo and Mercutio while Peggy Ashcroft played the role of Juliet in which the entire text was used, and the play was continuously acted on a permanent set with a central tower with spaces on each side of the tower to perform (Levenson 85). Following Gielgud's production in London at the New Theatre, Irving Thalberg and George Cukor's exquisite film version of *Romeo and Juliet* in 1936 set new standards of cinematic excellence. The entire film embodied the Renaissance concept of symmetry and balance with the Capulets and Montagues' procession side by side to the cathedral in the piazza. Rothwell takes exception to the elegance and high-toned quality of the film, for he asserts that despite all of the film's polish, the acting becomes mannered and overly conventional (Rothwell 40–42). The dignified procession to the church as well as the framing of each character under which his or her name appears at the beginning of the film smacks of cinematic self-consciousness that attempts to call attention to its own perceived significance, but perhaps this kind of pomp and circumstance was expected by audiences when they attended a production of this ilk.

Unfortunately, however, Rothwell fails to note the foolery and fun in the ballroom scene in which dancers playfully joust while wearing about them the frame of a horse, and Mercutio comically inserts a faux sword into one of the rumps of the horses and withdraws it mangled. Moments later he himself has one of the faux swords placed between his legs as he scampers from the ballroom, an action recalling Jonathan Goldberg's sodomitical assertions concerning Mercutio's sexual interests. Romeo and Juliet speak clearly and convincingly, but they lack the passion which the text indelibly inscribed in the audience's heart (Rothwell 44). Given the Hays Code in effect, one wonders how erotic Romeo and Juliet could have been in 1936.

Franco Zeffirelli's *Romeo and Juliet* (1968) was the embodiment of a youth culture celebrating sexuality, peace, and freedom, but Garber reminds us that at one time the play was perceived quite differently by its audience, for she asserts, "Given *Romeo and Juliet*'s almost automatic modern association with youth culture, and the by-now- proverbial identification with its title characters, it is of some interest to remind ourselves that for many years the star parts were those of Mercutio and the Nurse" (390); moreover, only a short time earlier, Romeo was played by 43-year-old Leslie Howard and Juliet was played by 35-year-old Norma Shearer in Irving Thalberg and George Cukor's film version; in Zeffirelli's film version, teenagers played the roles of Romeo and Juliet. Romeo was played by 17-year-old Leonard Whiting, and Juliet was played by 16-year-old Olivia Hussey.

In many ways Zeffirelli's version was the most audacious of its time because he brought to the fore the nudity of the hero and heroine as well as the homoerotic elements that inhere in *Romeo and Juliet* in the relationship between Romeo and Mercutio, which are located at the margins of the play. Romeo and Juliet's

The 16-year-old British actress Olivia Hussey and 17-year-old British actor Leonard Whiting, who play the leading roles in Franco Zeffirelli's film version of Shakespeare's *Romeo and Juliet*. AP Photo/Dear.

bedroom scene could even be shown in 1968 with images of nudity, but homosexual desire could not be shown directly (Donaldson 146). Donaldson points out that Zeffirelli "locates the tragedy of Romeo and Juliet in the patriarchal values and pressures of Shakespeare's 'Verona,' and especially in the destructive workings of misogyny and its corollary, male fear of intimacy with other men" (153).

Furthermore, one of the main components of this sex-gender system is the importance given to the phallus. Here in early modern Verona the sword is the metaphoric equivalent of the penis, which Donaldson astutely underscores; he believes that the emphasis placed on the codpieces of the Capulets, especially on that of Tybalt, highlights the social significance of the phallus to this early modern Italian culture. Moreover, the anatomization of male bodies causes the viewer to perceive that this treatment of the male body gives pleasure to the audience, even as they engage in street violence (Donaldson 154).

The film culminates in the final scene in which Romeo and Juliet take their lives. Deborah Cartmell argues that the womb-like tomb with its pillars indicates the scene's eroticism. Both are seen embracing in this last scene. Cartmell suggests that Zeffirelli amplifies what Garber describes as an "allusively sexual act," (45) in which Juliet wields the dagger and enacts her phallic penetration. The scene ends with the lovers smiling in each other's arms as an expression of their victorious erotic violation (45).

The third great film version of *Romeo and Juliet* came at the end of the 20th century in Baz Luhrmann's *William Shakespeare's Romeo + Juliet* (1996) starring Leonardo DiCaprio as Romeo and Claire Danes as Juliet. Set in Verona Beach, this is a scenario that is scarred by gang wars and political graft; in a Miami-like city, gangs roam the streets, and the Capulets and the Montagues become crime families. In this film version Romeo and Juliet function more as "loners than passion-blinded, parent-controlled innocents. They identify, moreover, with other alienated teenagers who have created and thrive in their own, marginalized world" (Wilson 183). The character of Romeo is represented by DiCaprio's androgynous appeal, a kind of Greek godlike youth who has a polymorphous sexual quality in which both men—gay and straight— and young women are drawn. At the same time that Romeo can become tearful during the last half of the film, he can also kill Tybalt, thereby conforming to the outward and visible image of masculinity. Because DiCaprio participates in the violence, he is perceived as part of multiple masculinities (Hodgdon 135).

Finally, the character of Mercutio greatly problematizes masculinity, for he is played by Harold Perrineau, who delivers an excellent speech concerning Queen Mab, and whose friendship with Romeo suggests a hint of same-sex eroticism, as he cross-dresses in a miniskirt when he attends the Capulets' masquerade ball while Romeo wears the armor of a chivalric knight. In many ways Mercutio continues the theatre's tradition of representing Mercutio as a cultural outsider (Rothwell 243).

One of the most provocative staged interpretations of *Romeo and Juliet* is Joe Calarco's *Shakespeare's R & J*, which is set in an all-male prep school with a cast of four students. The play, which opened in January 1998 on Theatre Row, garnered positive reviews, and when it had completed its 162nd performance, this production earned the title of the longest-running *Romeo and Juliet* on or off Broadway. Critics have praised the actors' "energy and kineticism," which made the play seem as if it were being performed for the first time (Shteir 6). To be sure, the all-male cast reconceptualized the play in a fashion that was perceived by most theatregoers as unusual. Calarco states very emphatically what this play concerns as he clearly does not want playgoers confused as to his intentions regarding issues of gender or sexual orientation: "This play is about men. It is about how they interact with other men. Thus, it deals with how men view women, sex, sexuality, and violence. This play is not *nor should any production of it* be strictly about homoeroticism. Nor should it be strictly about homophobia" (Calarco 5–6). Thus said, one can approach the play-text with a better understanding of what Calarco wishes to accomplish in this production of the play.

In the production that was performed at Theatre Row, the only props were a footlocker that functioned as bed, horse, and altar and a piece of red cloth that served as a veil, a shroud, and a pool of blood in a production with no set changes or costume changes (Shteir 6). Regardless of who directs this play, the scenery will be minimal because Calarco thinks that this play is exciting as it represents the epitome of drama in that only four actors without costumes or props—with the exception of composition books, the play, and a piece of three-foot red fabric—were used in the production (Calarco 6).

The play opens with the students dressed in slacks, ties, and sweaters, or blazers, and they march in a military fashion into the space, having brought with them their composition books, at which point they kneel as if in church. Student 1 recites "Sonnet 147" of Shakespeare's sonnet sequence while Students 2, 3, and 4 make the act of contrition. The recitation of this sonnet is very appropriate commentary on the action of the drama in *Romeo and Juliet*. The school bell rings, and the students march off to their next class where they learn the rudiments of the Latin conjugation of the verb "to love," which nicely corresponds to the first line of "Sonnet 147," "My love is as a fever, longing still." Then they move to their geometry class where they learn that the square of the hypotenuse is equal to the sum of the squares of the remaining sides. Next they go to religion class where they learn the Ten Commandments. Finally, they attend a sociology class in which they learn about the differences between men and women and their attendant responsibilities to each other. Student 4 reads from a book, "It is a woman's responsibility to maintain the comfort and the decency of the family. It is she who makes etiquette, and it is she who preserves the order and the decency of society. Without women, men soon resume the savage state, and the comforts of home are exchanged for the misery of the mining camp" (12). Student 2 also reads from a book that upholds the orthodoxy regarding gender roles in society, "A bold man may disregard and disobey the most sacred laws and customs, but he cannot, he dare not disregard a woman's influence, for the amiable woman rules the haughty man. Hence the business of the man is to govern the world, and the destiny of a woman is to charm and influence it" (13). At this point more bells ring, and class is dismissed. The students are now left to their own devices, and Student 1 takes a copy of *Romeo and Juliet* with a red scarf, but before they commence their reading of the play, Student 1, played by Greg Shamie, casts the spell by reciting the speech that Puck tells the fairies when he first appears in *A Midsummer Night's Dream*, and he takes the role of Romeo while Daniel Shore takes the role of Juliet quite seriously. Shewey notes, "The most poignant moment of *R & J* is the final scene, an all-too-familiar tableau of queer adolescent angst . . . even for Shore as his Juliet— this passion play was just for fun, a schoolboy crush. He alone was playing for real" (Shewey 53).

At the same time in Manhattan, a more conventional production of *Romeo and Juliet* was directed by James Bundy at the New Victory Theatre and set in the late 19th century, but Juliet's wardrobe could have come from the Renaissance. Hamish Linklater, who performed the role of Romeo, appears "as a Byronic poet and behaves like early Robby Benson, falling in love with goofy adolescent rashness" (Gates, "In the 19th Century" E6). Although Anita Gates thinks Linklater and Heather Robison are wonderful actors, she has reservations about the quality of their acting regarding Romeo's banishment. She, however, does concede that the love scenes make up for that shortcoming. As far as the character of Mercutio is concerned, Daniel Pearce plays the role ambivalently, for Mercutio sometimes appears as a heterosexual who criticizes campy femininity, but on other occasions he may be sincere in his representation of this gay character (E6). Overall this was a very engaging performance by all those involved.

In as much as *Romeo and Juliet* has been the object of immense theatrical and academic study, so too has *A Midsummer Night's Dream* rivaled it for critical attention in both the theatre and the academy. Although *A Midsummer Night's Dream* was written in 1595 or 1596, the exact date of its performance cannot be established. Like many of Shakespeare's plays, *A Midsummer Night's Dream* also underwent textual changes. Between 1661 and 1816 *A Midsummer Night's Dream* underwent a number of truncations and abbreviations. In 1662 Samuel Pepys, an inveterate playgoer, attended a performance of *A Midsummer Night's Dream*, and he later wrote in his diary that it was the most absurd play that he had ever seen (Holland 99).

Not only did directors and actors significantly change the play by shortening it in order to suit their own dramatic needs, but they were also bothered by its plot. When Francis Gentleman edited the text in 1774 for Bell's Shakespeare, he was concerned about its childish plot with a miscellany of events and contrived arrangements of different styles (Holland 101). Edward Malone, another very important editor of the period, was infuriated to find the "fable thus meager and uninteresting" (Holland 101).

By 1816, the theatre manager Madame Lucia Elizabeth Vestris and an Italian contralto began to restore Shakespeare's text to the play in Vestris's production of it in Covent Garden in 1840. Actually, James Robinson Planche deserves a great deal of the credit for restoring Shakespeare's language to the play; he was also responsible for the costumes and the beautiful last scene, which was extraordinary with more than 50 fairies flying or dancing around the galleries and stairs. In fact, Vestris played the queen of the fairies, Titania, and sang nine songs while a girl played the role of Puck (Halio 25–26).

The next great shift in *A Midsummer Night's Dream* occurred on October 15, 1856, in Charles Kean's production in which he deleted 800 lines in order for the performance to last less than three hours in spite of all of the dancing and Mendelssohn's music. By the end of the 19th century, Augustin Daly had gone to even greater lengths in his creation of spectacles and pantomimes in 1873, and later in 1888 he staged the play with John Drew, Otis Skinner, and Ada Rehan while Isadora Duncan went so far as to wear papier-mâché wings. By 1895 Daly had placed electrical lights on his fairies, and Lilian Swain played the role of Puck and Ada Rehan played the role of Oberon, receiving high praise from George Bernard Shaw (Halio 30).

Increasingly, spectacle was touted over historical and textual accuracy by Herbert Beerbohm Tree, whose 1900 production of *A Midsummer Night's Dream* was a vision of pictorial splendor with thyme and wild flowers and thickets and a background of trees replete with rabbits running across the stage as Julia

Neilson played Oberon. Other directors who lacked the financial resources of Tree, such as William Poel, Gordon Craig, and Harley Granville Barker, had other ideas regarding the staging of Shakespeare's plays by reducing the amount of scenery and thereby reducing the visual distractions. While some 220,000 people saw Tree's production of *A Midsummer Night's Dream*, the advent of film would increase a director's audience to an unprecedented number of viewers (Halio 31–32).

Max Reinhardt also celebrated the magnificence of pictorialism. He had begun directing *A Midsummer Night's Dream* in 1905 at Neues Theatre in Berlin and continued to direct it all over Europe eventually reaching Los Angeles's Hollywood Bowl in 1934, and finally, it culminated in his celebrated film version of 1935 with American actors Mickey Rooney as Puck, James Cagney as Bottom, Anita Louise as Titania, Victor Jory as Oberon, Olivia de Havilland as Hermia, and Dick Powell as Lysander, all of whom were big-name Hollywood stars. This magnificent production cost Warner Brothers $1.5 million and used a sound stage of over 38,000 feet. Erich Wolfgang Korngold arranged the music according to Mendelssohn's *Overture to a Midsummer Night's Dream* in addition to incidental music (Halio 37; Rothwell 35).

Despite the joy of young love and marriage, there is clearly an undercurrent of evil in the Dieterle-Reinhardt version of this film. Rothwell rightly remarks upon this film's "darker gothic subtext, embodying in its varied strings and horns the contradictory motifs to come—nuptials and feasting, and high hopes, yet poised on the edge of a dark wood harboring acts of unspeakable bestiality" (Rothwell 35). Others have noted the untoward edginess that lurks beneath the surface of the filmic text; Philip McGuire notes Hippolyta's silence at the beginning of the film. He suggests that she is angry at the rape of the Amazons, and so she may have a feminist agenda (Rothwell 36). Halio believes that it is best that Titania and Bottom's erotic encounter not be discussed because it is so absurd, but it is heartfelt and emotionally engaging. When Oberon sees his Fairy Queen, he begins to have pity on her and, finally, removes the spell. Meanwhile, the gnome orchestra performs Mendelssohn's "Nocturne" (Halio 93).

The next version of *A Midsummer Night's Dream* of import is Peter Hall's 1968 film version in which Derek Godfrey played Theseus, Ian Holm played Puck, Judi Dench played Titania, and Helen Mirren played Hermia (95). This film version, like Max Reinhardt's, presents the dark side of human existence. Rothwell suggests that Hall "stabs at the darker side of the dream, the dream that turns into a nightmare in a dark wood" (147). The eroticism in this film is quite palpable as Titania and Oberon are virtually nude. Titania wears what looks like a bikini bottom and nothing covering her breasts; Oberon appears as a satyr with pointed ears and a green complexion, and Oberon's behavior is completely in keeping with his appearance, yet despite the sinister quality about Reinhardt's Oberon, Hall decided to focus upon the sensuality of their sexual relations and not its brutality (Halio 101); after all, the spell under which Oberon places Titania allows her to fall in love with any wild animal, and it could prove to be physically and emotionally devastating to her. When Titania does become enamored of Bottom, she does not allow him to escape her, but he reluctantly agrees to go to her bower. Then she lowers him to the ground in order to engage in sexual intercourse (Halio 102).

Rehearsals for Peter Brook's groundbreaking version of *A Midsummer Night's Dream* began in the summer of 1970 and continued for eight weeks until the production began. Brook was concerned with the actors conforming to his concept of the production. The set was to resemble a white squash court which had two small stage doors in the rear wall with ladders on the downstage edges which would lead to catwalks. From these galleries the actors could watch the play when they were not onstage. Titania's bower was a hammock made of red ostrich feathers, and the fairies had trapezes to use as needed, and the actors wore oversized pants that were loose and baggy, made of satin and tie-dyed blouses, and the women wore dresses that were like tunics. The fairies wore plain tunics, except for Oberon, Titania, and Puck, who wore bright colors that were fluorescent, which created a strong contrast against the white walls of the set. Oberon and Titania wore silk gowns while Puck had an oversized jumpsuit. Brook also decided to double the actors' roles by having Theseus and Hippolyta play the roles of

British actress Judi Dench, in costume for her role as Titania, in Shakespeare's *A Midsummer Night's Dream*, at the Royal Shakespeare Theatre, in Stratford-upon-Avon, England, April 17, 1962. AP Photo.

Oberon and Titania respectively. Brook may well have implied that Oberon and Titania were the alter egos of Theseus and Hippolyta by having them double up these roles. Finally, the set was extremely well lighted as Brook believed that it was necessary to dispel any sense of illusion about the play (Halio 50–51, 56, and 59). As provocative as this production was scenically, the actors' amorphous costumes certainly did not eroticize the characters' bodies

By dispelling any sense of illusion, Brook could address issues of sexuality. He very much wanted to emphasize the relationship of love and sexuality or rather love in its relation to sexuality. It was at this time that Brook had formed a significant friendship with Jan Kott, who was an important Polish scholar and critic, and whose book *Shakespeare Our Contemporary* was very influential to Brook in his understanding of both *King Lear* and *A Midsummer Night's Dream*. Kott argued that much criticism and performances of this play failed to recognize the play's very powerful sense of sexuality and violence. Halio in the same vein argues that the fact that Theseus wooed Hippolyta with violence presages the violation that Oberon enacts when he places the love juice on Titania's eyes later in the play in addition to the rancor that ensues once the lovers enter the woods (57). The fact that Titania wooed an ass is of particular significance. Kott says that all of the animals that Oberon mentions while conjuring his spell are those of great sexual potency, but of all the animals that he mentions, the ass is the one that has the greatest sexual power and the largest and hardest penis. Moreover, Titania engages with the unsavory sphere of sexuality with much greater intensity than any other character in the play. The interaction between them continues to intrigue audience members (Kott 227–28).

The sexual intensity between the young lovers is also made manifest when Demetrius kisses Helena and then she faints, and he runs away; moments later, she gets up and follows him while the fairies leave the gallery. Puck returns to his trapeze and passes the love-in-idleness to Oberon as he swings along the side of him. Titania also makes great use of her bower, which is nothing more than a hammock with its ostrich feathers which can be lowered. This most unusual of bowers is the site of much erotic activity (Halio 64).

The next scene is also one filled with eroticism. Lysander sings "Fair Love" to the accompaniment of a guitarist. While Hermia lets Lysander know that he should lie at a greater distance from her out of a sense of modesty, Lysander comes closer to her and pulls her to the stage floor and kisses her. She at this point decides to make him stop his amorous advances. The music of the guitarist continues until they fall asleep (Halio 64).

After the singing of the assified Bottom awakens Titania, she begins to woo Bottom with great intensity. In order to emphasize the vulgar intensity of this scene, an actor places his arm between Bottom's legs in order to signify his virility. Halio quotes David Selbourne who writes, "The arm is moved in phallic pride" between Bottom's legs while paper plates and streamers come down from the gallery. Bottom makes a neighing sound and raises his arms as one would do after enacting a heroic feat. Oberon and Puck swing on trapeze during this unbridled expression of eroticism to the accompaniment of Mendelssohn's "Wedding March," which functions as a biting bit of satire of 19th-century traditions. Brook obviously wants to challenge theatregoers' conventional understanding of this play through his subversive reading of *A Midsummer Night's Dream*, but the most significant point to remember is the celebratory quality of the actor's actions (Halio 66). One really cannot underestimate the theatrical influence of Brook's production of this play because of its radically transgressive reading of this text.

Perhaps the next really significant theatrical production of *A Midsummer Night's Dream* was Robert Lepage's 1992 version at the Royal National Theatre. Lepage wished to have *A Midsummer Night's Dream* take his audience back to the origins of existence and to form links between the uncivilized world and the civilized one; therefore, Lepage creates a violent sexual union between a sexually ambivalent Puck and a fairy with a blue face at the beginning of the second act in what amounts to group sex in the mud and the loud noise of Bottom and Titania engaging in sexual relations. As Halio points out, with so much physical interaction between characters, both audience members and actors found it difficult to focus on what was said and done by the actors and what was the connection between the two. This issue constituted a significant difference between Lepage's and Brook's production of this play, for when the actors in Brook's production did not perform, they looked over the parapet of the white box and listened carefully to their fellow actors, and finally, while Lepage's production appeared to be quite unconventional by most 20th-century theatrical standards, he did try to maintain the primacy of the play's text (Halio 123–24 and 127).

Adrian Noble directed the last groundbreaking production of *A Midsummer Night's Dream* with the Royal Shakespeare Company. In this production the dominant concept of the play concerned a descent into one's unconscious. The significance of the unconscious seemed to have been represented powerfully in Puck's interactions with Oberon, for no sooner had Oberon and Puck planned how to punish Titania for not relinquishing the Indian boy, Puck kissed Oberon on the lips, which was clearly a homoerotic overture that was not developed in the course of the play. Moreover, the disorientation of the young lovers in the woods corresponded to the forest symbolically as the unconscious. When Jane Edwards reviewed this play in *Time Out*, she believed that Robert Lepage at the National as Noble grounded his production in the dreams of the characters' supposed sexual desires and covert fears. However, while Lepage's dreamworld had mud and water, Noble and Antony Ward's dreamworld consisted of entrances and appearances and disappearances, which led provocatively into the realm of the characters' unconsciousness. In the final analysis, this production concerned Hippolyta's dream (Halio 134, 136–37, and 142). Whatever one makes of Lepage's dream of *A Midsummer Night's Dream*, one can be sure that it would be a psychoanalyst's delight.

The next really significant film version of *A Midsummer Night's Dream* arrived in 1999 with Michael Hoffman's star-studded cast which included the likes of Michelle Pfeiffer as Titania, Kevin Kline as Bottom, Rupert Everett as Oberon, and Christian Bale as Demetrius among others. This particular version, set in Italy at Monte Athena in the 1890s, is lushly appointed with all of the accoutrements of a magnificent manor with exquisitely manicured lawns and gushing fountains.

When Egeus appears with Hermia, Lysander, and Demetrius before Theseus, the lawgiver of Monte Athena, in order to have the marriage of Hermia to Demetrius adjudicated, Theseus opens a legal text in order to consult it; despite the juridical importance of this meeting, even here Lysander played by Dominic West and Demetrius played by Christian Bale engage in a shoving match when Demetrius tells Lysander that he should marry Egeus. Given the gravity of the situation, Egeus gives Hermia time to consult her feelings. Stephen Buhler asserts, "Theseus is portrayed as empathetic and solicitous, expressing deep concern about Hermia's suitability for the veil and deciding to remonstrate privately with Demetrius and Egeus in response to Hermia's clear displeasure" (52–53).

Soon thereafter the young lovers are in the Athenian woods, and Lysander and Hermia are tired from walking and decide to sleep, but Lysander quickly becomes amorous removing all of his clothes and even sporting an unseen erection, causing Hermia to give him a petticoat with which to cover himself. Buhler believes that Lysander appears defenseless in his makeshift loincloth or his diaper that is too big for him, which was made of one of Hermia's slips (Buhler 55). This viewer thought that Lysander is never vulnerable in the least; rather he functions as a gorgeous piece of eye candy for women and gay men who would watch the film. Despite the fact that the play is set within the late Victorian period, once the lovers are in the woods, often thought of as a metaphor for the characters' unconscious or libido, they become less inhibited. As evidenced by the fight in the mud pond between Helena and Hermia, Buhler argues that Hoffman reduces Hermia and Helena's relationship to "merely mud-wrestling over men" (54) by his deleting Helena's lines (III.ii.203–214) in which she recounts their long youth's friendship during which they spent time working on their samplers. For a moment eroticism becomes a parody of itself, for the men almost fall into the pond, no longer voyeurs but participants in the muddy melee as Lysander approaches its edge to pull Helena from the mess.

Happily, Oberon is concerned about Helena, and, ironically, it is because of her unhappiness that Oberon instructs Puck to place the love-juice on the man who does not love her. Buhler opines that as an openly gay man, Rupert Everett, in both his film roles and in his personal life, can make decisions about heterosexual relationships with an emotional detachment, and while there is no overt homoeroticism in this particular film version, there is a certain homosociality among the rude mechanicals as Bottom's marriage is surely a loveless one, and it is only through his camaraderie with his fellow friends that he has any sense of community. Reinhardt's and Dieterle's 1935 film version originally planned to include a disapproving Mrs. Bottom, but perhaps having James Cagney, star of gangster films from the 1930s, take the role of Bottom obviated that possibility (Buhler 57).

The character of Bottom surely satisfies Titania in Hoffman's film version. His erection admirably impresses Titania and her train of fairies. When Titania and Bottom engage in sexual relations, she climbs on top of him. Here Bottom quits himself well. Buhler implies that Titania is unaccustomed to intense erotic pleasure, perhaps suggesting that the Fairy King may be less than adequate in the lovemaking department (Buhler 58).

Finally, the issue of gender identity is addressed in the performance of *Pyramus and Thisbe* in which Flute plays the role of the young woman. Hoffman stresses the anxiety with which Flute (Sam Rockwell) experiences performing the role of Thisbe. Flute tries to speak in a falsetto voice despite the audience's laughter, and he mangles his lines as he talks about "kissing the wall's stones," a slang term for testicles. It is also interesting to point out that Snout looks concerned when Flute has his sword pointed at his groin area, but the rude mechanicals make it through the playlet in spite of themselves (Buhler 59).

In the performance of Shakespeare's plays, everything old is new again with the all-male version of *A Midsummer Night's Dream* that Edward Hall, no relation to Peter, produced at the Watermill Theatre and Propeller at the Brooklyn Academy in March 2004. All objects on the stage are either black or white and illuminated by a dingy blue light. The center of the stage is bare except for a wooden box with a mirror on top of it. The costumes of the actors reflect this black-and-white contrast of the set. All of the actors wear white union suits with black shoes; some, however, wear black corsets attached to them over their union suits, and each of the actors has a harmonica that he wears around his neck. Jane Collins asserts that Hall made casting choices that had nothing to do with the actors' physical characteristics which would diminish the differences between their being perceived as either male or female (118).

While the sex of the actor is of no significance in this version of *A Midsummer Night's Dream*, Collins argues, "The fairy world is marked by campy song and dance numbers that defy the pejorative use of 'fairy' to describe gay men by enacting those cultural stereotypes. These fairies really do act like 'fairies'" (119). At the same time these actors are quite adept in using body language in order to indicate their femininity. As interest in early modern theatrical practices becomes more popular, more and more of all-male or even all-female versions of early modern dramatic texts will inevitably occur.

Much Ado about Nothing contains some of the wittiest repartee in English literature. Because of Beatrice and Benedick's initially sardonic asides in the first scene, one cannot help but wonder how this most verbally scintillating battle of the sexes will conclude. *Much Ado about Nothing* was a popular play, which was performed until the playhouses were closed by Parliament in 1642. The prominence of Beatrice and Benedick was shown by one of two allusions to the play when it was referred to as *Benedicte and Betteris* in an account of the Lord Treasurer in 1613; even Charles I referred to it as *Benedik and Betrice* in his copy of the Second Folio (Cox 3).

When Charles I returned to the throne in 1660 ushering in the Restoration, William Davenant came to the forefront with his adaptation of *Much Ado about Nothing*. He decided to alter the original play by including characters from *Measure for Measure*. Benedick, changed into a rake, decided to lead a revolt against the social strictures of Angelo in which he attempted to rescue Claudio and

Julietta from jail. In Davenant's adaptation of *Much Ado about Nothing*, Benedick is Angelo's brother, Beatrice is Angelo's ward, and Julietta is Beatrice's cousin. Davenant took a little more than 100 lines from *Much Ado about Nothing*, and he provided more risqué dialogue between Beatrice and Benedick, which was in keeping with the banter of characters in *The Way of the World* and other Restoration drama than audiences of the early modern period preferred (Cox 9).

The first actual performance of *Much Ado about Nothing* took place after the Restoration in 1721 in Lincoln's Inn Fields, and the play was later performed in 1737, 1739, and 1746. Between the Restoration and 1737 a shift occurred in the sensibility of audiences because of the increased influence of the middle class in which a greater emphasis was placed on the function of drama to edify and enlighten and, therefore, there was a reduction in the inclusion of risqué or off-color dialogue and a greater interest in romantic comedy and the importance of marriage (Cox 10–11).

By midcentury *Much Ado about Nothing* was the most frequently performed Shakespearean comedy. David Garrick's operation of Drury Lane engendered this renewed enthusiasm for this play from 1747 to 1776. Garrick was responsible for this resurgence of interest in Benedick, whom he performed in a lively, somewhat eccentric fashion. Hannah Pritchard played the role of Beatrice from 1748 to 1756, and she engaged in a robust exchange of witticisms; when her daughter took over the role in 1756, it was thought that the part lost quite a bit of its worth, and in the final season of Garrick's career in 1776, he gave the role to Frances Abington after which she performed the role at Covent Garden from 1783 until 1789. Garrick was not really concerned with probing the psyche of the characters in the play. The accounts that remain of his productions of this play indicate that there is not much in the way of attraction between Benedick and Beatrice (Cox 11–12, 14).

Elizabeth Younge and Elizabeth Ferren's acting styles reflected the 18th century's last couple of decades' concern with sensibility, and therefore, they lacked the trenchant quality with which Abington approached the character. Yet from 1798 until 1808, Dorothy Jordan was the most significant actress to play the role of Beatrice, and while she did not possess the elegant manners of Abington and Ferren, she had an enthusiastic sense of joy, which mitigated Beatrice's sharp-tongued dialogue (16). The changes in acting style also extended to changes in the text itself in which Charles Kemble deleted about 20 percent of the play (17).

Representations of Beatrice varied on the Victorian stage, but the dominant representation of her performance was mitigating her sharp tongue in order that she conform to the social expectations of 19th-century women. The three most important actresses who played the role of Beatrice in early Victorian England were Helena Faucit, Louisa Nisbett, and Ellen Tree-Kean. Faucit epitomized the 19th-century woman of a profound depth of emotion who was able to be sensitive and serious. Nisbett, on the other hand, played the role with enthusiasm and joy, but Faucit was more admired because she performed the role with greater nobility. Ellen Tree-Kean was able to combine the qualities of both Faucit and Nisbett; she garnered the approval of her audiences in America in 1837–1839 and continued to do so after marriage to Charles Kean (Cox 35–36).

Apparently, not all of the actresses who performed the role of Beatrice adhered to this Victorian vision of sweetness and light to which the era subscribed. Fanny Stirling, Charlotte Cushman, and Mary Warner were among those whose performances did not satisfy the critics' cultural expectations of womanhood. Stirling seemed to possess a shrewish quality in the delivery of her lines; Cushman came off as a boisterous woman lacking the refinement of a woman of her social position and upbringing; and Warner was deficient of sufficient femininity (39), but Ellen Terry, unlike Stirling, Cushman, and Warner, was one of the most admired actresses of her day and was able to remake the role of Beatrice. In her earlier performances, the role was one of a lighthearted woman, and so when she makes her request to Benedick to kill Claudio, the audience is taken aback, but in her later performances she evinced greater passion, and she more than likely presented Beatrice with less sharpness than Kean. In a word, Terry had the ability to combine the qualities that the Victorian sensibility prized at the same time that she possessed a joy that her audiences found very pleasing (Cox 40 and 42).

Over this period in which sets become simpler because of William Poel and Edward Gordon Craig, there was an absence of productions of *Much Ado about Nothing* beginning in 1905 until about 1925, but touring companies performed the play, and it was performed at Stratford, where there were 35 productions of it while *Twelfth Night* had 39 productions and *As You Like It*, the most popular play of all, had 43 productions (Cox 47; Zitner 64). In fact, one of the best productions before World War II was Harcourt Williams's at the Old Vic in 1931 with its simplified set which focused on the actors' speech. The great John Gielgud played Benedick while Dorothy Green performed Beatrice with elegance and sensitivity (Fox 53).

The performances of John Gielgud from 1949 to 1959 and Douglas Seale in 1958 were beautiful and harmonious. Given the depressed economic condition of Britain after World War II, one can easily understand why such productions of *Much Ado about Nothing* were so popular. Gielgud's production in particular garnered a great deal of attention and praise (57), and it achieved the cultural importance of Irving's productions. The productions were especially elegant and sumptuous, and Mariano Andreu created rich settings, and the costumes were designed to remind the audience of the fact that they were in a theatre as the sets were particularly clever (Cox 60–61).

The sixties saw a significant shift in the performances of *Much Ado about Nothing* in which Franco Zeffirelli ascribed carnivalesque qualities to them such that they exuded anarchic energy and vitality set in a small town in Sicily around 1900. The costumes were based upon the sugar dolls of Sicilian folk art. Leonato was comparable to the mayor of a town in the provinces while Don Pedro was a caricature of a Latin American petty dictator. Apparently, some 300 lines were changed to standard modern English. Therefore, this production caused quite a bit of controversy, both praise and criticism; Zeffirelli's production raised the question as to the degree to which the director should be allowed to alter the original play. This issue would become increasingly important in 20th-century productions of Shakespeare's plays (Cox 69).

Joseph Papp's and A. J. Antoon's productions of Shakespeare in Manhattan's Central Park engendered a great deal of enthusiasm; their Delacorte Theatre production in 1972 was quickly followed by the CBS television production in 1973, which was set in small-town America in 1910. As Fox sensibly points out, the production veered between farce and romantic comedy while the more serious, more untoward sections of the play were not addressed. Fox opines that Beatrice demonstrates her independence by having a cigarette with some of her female friends, an act that would have been considered inappropriate for a refined young lady at that time, but perhaps more subversively, she also puts down her glass of lemonade and drinks from Benedick's glass of beer after he and the other members of the army return to Messina. Sam Waterson, playing Benedick, lacks the robust exuberance that 20th-century audiences have come to expect from Benedick. Borachio and Conrad don clothes appropriate to Chicago gangsters, and the police force, the Watch, is more reminiscent of the Keystone Kops than any remotely competent law enforcement officers (Cox 69–70).

At the same time some critics thought that the play's ambience was too lighthearted to accommodate some of the drama of the play's serious concerns such as the slander of Hero and the deception of Don Pedro. For example, the figure of Dogberry appears as an incompetent older man who is more concerned with the position and title that he holds than the effective operation of the Watch. Dogberry reacts as though he is so personally hurt by the insulting comments made by Conrad that he looks like he is about to cry at the end of the scene, which reinforces the absurdity of the conversation among Dogberry and Borachio and Conrad, and yet at the same time Leonato is a powerful, older man who continually pushes Claudio hither and fro as he confronts him, slapping him about his head and shoulders after he has slandered his daughter at the altar. Leonato does not appear as a pathetic old man chasing Don Pedro down the street as Don Pedro and Claudio hasten to leave Messina in Kenneth Branagh's 1993 film version of *Much Ado about Nothing*.

All in all, this production has all the markings of a made-for-television film with the many close-up rather than long-distance shots. Nonetheless, Altoon provides a frisson to the scene in which Claudio hangs an epitaph upon Hero's tomb asking for forgiveness as he penitently stands in the pouring rain without the protection of an umbrella. Finally, while some applauded Altoon's production of *Much Ado about Nothing* because he made the play so accessible to the American public, others criticized it because the setting's numerous artifacts of early 20th-century Americana such as the Victrola that Benedick plays when Beatrice visits him and the carousel from which Beatrice and Hero descend at the second wedding ceremony overpower the characters' witty dialogue. In other words, the highly detailed sets with all of their turn-of-the-century bric-a-brac distract the audience from the dialogue (Cox 70).

Trevor Nunn's earlier 1968 stage production was much edgier in its depiction of sexuality. Sexuality was a significant component in the production of this drama in both positive and negative ways. Margaret, who is mistaken as Hero, is represented as having a great deal of erotic energy. Benedick and Beatrice are represented as a rather offbeat couple of the 1960s while Don Pedro, who is typically played as a dignified gentleman, is represented as at once "benevolent" and at the same time as possessing "an undercurrent of malignity" (71). Fox astutely asserts that this production balances the tension between the comic and the evil forces that lurk beneath the surface of this otherwise lighthearted romantic comedy (71).

By contrast to the BBC/TimeLife production, Kenneth Branagh's film version of *Much Ado about Nothing* is truly a joyful and exuberant interpretation. In the opening moments of the film, Beatrice, played by the incomparable Emma Thompson, reads a ballad from a book concerning the deception and duplicity of men. The ballad appears in white on a black screen as a way of preparing us for Elizabethan verse (Buchanan 202). An extremely cute messenger with whom Beatrice playfully banters appears in great haste in order to inform Leonato of the immediate arrival of Don Pedro, who has recently returned from war with Benedick, Claudio, and the rest of his army. The men gallop up to Leonato's villa filmed in the slow motion of parodic martial grandeur reminiscent of *The Magnificent Seven*. The villa at which the action of the drama occurs is the 14th-century Villa Vignamaggio, which is located in Tuscany's Chianti wine region where the Mona Lisa whom Leonardo da Vinci painted once lived (Rothwell 250–51).

The audience is immediately made aware of the sensuousness of Beatrice as she playfully pulls grapes from their stem and places them into her mouth and that of the messenger after they finish their exchange of one-liners. The stripping off of clothes as the men and women begin their baths concretizes the physicality of the actors' bodies. There is quite a bit of female and male nudity, even a flash of male genitalia. Conrad delightfully pushes Don John under water as they bathe. After all of the members of the household repair to their rooms to prepare for the masked ball, perhaps a bit of homoerotic interaction occurs between Conrad and Don John, for Conrad is shown massaging Don John's well-oiled back while he sullenly stews over how he can cause harm and embarrassment to Don Pedro and those with whom he associates. This scene clearly smacks of an unmistakably lubricious quality. Deborah Cartmell asserts, "The homoeroticism of the film, if it exists at all, is in the figure of the bad guy, Don John (Keanu Reeves); his evil nature is discovered in the darkened and steamy atmosphere of his dressing room while he is being massaged by Conrade: stripped to the waist, with glistening torso and in tight leather trousers, he evokes a dazzling and sinister sex symbol. The good guys—the heterosexuals—win in the end; and this is a representation of sexuality, validated by the impartial language of Shakespeare, which the British can be proud to export" (49).

While there is a joyous celebration of life's physicality in this film version of *Much Ado about Nothing*, the male characters evince a deep-seated misogyny. The intensity of anger and violence that Claudio and Leonato express is very disturbing. At the wedding Claudio denounces Hero because he believes that he has seen her with another man at her bedroom window on the night before they are to marry. The physicality of the violence is unmistakable as Claudio throws Hero to the ground at which point she is slapped by her father, Leonato. Buchanan astutely notes that male characters demonstrate a great deal of anxiety about women's sexual practices because they seem to be incapable of treating them other than as marketable goods (204).

Rather than address their culture's pandemic misogyny, this film production would like to use Don John as the scapegoat onto whom Claudio, Don Pedro, and Leonato can place the blame for their virulent denunciation of Hero. As Buchanan argues, "The effectiveness of his villainous scheme is wholly dependent upon an inherently prejudiced attitude in the others that makes them so suggestible and subsequently so violent in response. . . . Branagh's interest is not in the ways in which this play can point to the more mixed tone of the endings of Shakespeare's late plays (particularly *The Winter's Tale*, with which it shares narrative elements)" (205). Kenneth Rothwell makes the same argument regarding how Branagh does not want to ask troubling questions that would undermine the play's rather pat ending. Rothwell, however, does not hesitate to ask highly provocative questions that may upend this play's heterosexual matrix of desire: "Is the wit of Beatrice and Bendick really a cover-up for closeted lesbianism and homosexuality? 'Middlebrow' filmgoers with 'upwardly mobile tastes' out for popcorn and a good time at the mall do not want to hear about such destabilizing matters, which are best left to the seminar room" (252). Crowl sums up Branagh's intent to combine the cultural sensibility of Shakespeare's and Hollywood's romantic comedies reminiscent of the screwball comedies from the 1930s to the 1950s. Concluding his consideration of this film version of *Much Ado about Nothing* with a rhetorical triumph of sorts, Branagh provides his audience the best version of a Shakespearean comedy on film despite the fact that he has a foot in the worlds of both film and theatre (Crowl 78).

Since Branagh's 1993 film version of *Much Ado about Nothing*, there have been many intriguing and engaging staged productions. Rebecca Patterson's 2003 all-female casting is one of the most provocative and inviting in recent history. In this particular version, Messina is placed in a tropical setting with a great deal of brightly colored fruit and very erotic choreography in a very feminine world that exudes fertility. Oranges appear quite frequently on stage because of a number of jokes about them in which they are either carried or consumed (Pollard 115). After all, Beatrice, played by Zainab Jah, compares Claudio to a Seville orange whose color is associated with jealousy when he thinks that Don Pedro has wooed Hero for himself, and ironically, Claudio refers to Hero as a rotten orange, and he tells Leonato not to give her to him, for he suspects her of being unfaithful on the previous night

Eroticism is at the core of this play's production, for the play begins on a highly sexualized note with a veiled woman tossing rose petals around her. Moments later when the military arrives, one of the men who is in the troop approaches her, and they begin to tango while the men commence in dance-like duels. This is to represent the collision of male and female worlds in which one engages the senses while the other is grounded in order and exactitude. Intriguingly, this dance recurs throughout the play like a refrain (Pollard 116). Finally, the physicality in the production is to be found in other situations with Benedick, played by DeeAnn Weir, going into the audience to hide while Dogberry and Verges also go into the audience searching for malefactors; at another time Beatrice pushes Benedick to the wall for a kiss after he had done the same to her. Pollard argues that there was an equality of the sexes in Beatrice's doing this to Benedick. Moreover, cross-gender acting is not a theatrical curiosity, but rather these kinds of productions initiate an enthusiastic coyness concerning gender roles (115). Overall, one could surmise that this was quite a successful performance of *Much Ado about Nothing*.

Like many of Shakespeare's plays, *As You Like It*, too, has no surviving records of its first performance despite the fact that literary historians know that Shakespeare wrote the play in the middle of 1600. It would not be performed for another 140 years (Brissenden 1). The play was revived on December 20, 1740, at Drury Lane, having been performed 28 times that season. From that time, *As You Like It* became very popular on the London stage (Marshall 10).

The revival of interest in *As You Like It* also saw the emergence of actresses such as Hannah Pritchard and Kitty Clive, who played the roles of Rosalind and Celia respectively. While some may have welcomed Pritchard's acting as versatile and her voice as pleasant, Samuel Johnson, one of the great arbiters of 18th-century literary aesthetics, considered her vulgar and stupid. Pritchard was soon to have a rival in Margaret Woffington when she performed at Drury Lane in 1741. She was known for her beauty, her sensational love life, and her "breeches" roles. Moreover, she was known for her erotic allure as she exposed her ankles and calves which would attract male members of the audience. Surely, this added attraction of erotic visual pleasure increased the play's popularity (Marshall 11–13).

In 1785, Dora Jordan arrived on the stage to play Rosalind. She was known as the mistress of the Duke of Clarence, who later became King William IV, and had 10 children by him. At the same time, she was quite admired and apparently inappropriate sexual advances were made to her in the form of propositions. In fact, she was pregnant when she first performed the role of Rosalind. Moreover, Jordan was so famous that she had her portrait painted by Gavin Hamilton (1723–1798) (Dusinberre 16).

Jordan was admired for her svelte physique and beautiful legs and well-fitted male costumes. Brissenden believes that her presence at Drury Lane was the reason for which *As You Like It* was performed more frequently than any other Shakespeare play from 1777 until 1817. Known for her vivacity, Jordan performed the role of Rosalind until she was over 50 years of age at Covent Garden in 1813 and 1814 (Marshall 15–17). Apparently, male members of 18th-century audiences were titillated by seeing a woman impersonate a man, but again the actresses' actual sex was readily discernible, but what most concerned some theatregoers was the risqué quality of the "cuckoo's song" (Marshall 18).

Drury Lane remained a center of theatrical importance with the presence of Charles Macready as stage manager in 1842. Macready also brought in Louisa Nisbett for the famous 1842 production (Marshall 24). She was known for enthusiastic acting in the tradition of the hoyden. She was described by Samuel Phelps in exaggerated terms; his account sounds more akin to a description of a Greek goddess than a mortal woman with her eyes like crystals and her voice compared to liquid music, but another critic was more concerned with her acting ability, claiming that she did not plumb the depths of the character of Rosalind (Marshall 26).

Yet there was a sea change afoot. Helena Faucit was to become the new essence of femininity for Rosalind. George Fletcher believed that the character of Rosalind had to be rescued from the crude representation as she presently appeared on the stage. Julie Henkey has argued that Faucit came by many of her ideas about Shakespeare from the Romantics, for she had a very ethereal notion of what constituted femininity for the stage. This notion of femininity was vividly realized in her description of it when she effused sentimentally (Marshall 27). Twenty-six years after playing the role of Rosalind, she was described as an intelligent and graceful actress with an enchanting voice who performed the role of Ganymede (Brissenden 57).

At mid-century, there was a spate of very fine Rosalinds on both sides of the Atlantic. In 1851, the year of the great Crystal Palace, Charles Kean's wife, formerly Ellen Tree, performed the role with liveliness and pleasantness. Richard White stated many years later that she was the only Rosalind capable of indicating what we would think Rosalind would experience emotionally at seeing the bloody handkerchief (Marshall 29). At the same time on the other side of the Atlantic, Charlotte Cushman was regarded as the finest actress of her time; moreover, she was the only actress who was successful in Europe who did not perform the role of Rosalind in the same way as Helena Faucit did. When Cushman dressed as Ganymede, she acquired the same mind-set as a conventional male of her time. She not only looked like a man, but her voice and movements resembled a man as well. Some critics thought she was superior to Faucit's Rosalind. Mary Anderson was also lauded for the same reasons as Helena Faucit. As extraordinary as Anderson was, there was yet another new star rising on the horizon in 1889.

On December 17, 1889, Ada Rehan gave her first performance as Rosalind at Augustin Daly's theatre in New York. Daly made alterations in the play so that he could showcase his new star with her enthusiasm and energy. On August 26, 1897, the play was performed as the first open air production at Stratford, but unfortunately, it rained and so it was moved to the Memorial Theatre. George Bernard Shaw expressed his contempt for the production that Daly directed, but he thought very highly of Rehan's performance. Perhaps the critic writing in August 28, 1897, for the *Leamington Courier* paid Rehan the highest possible compliment when the reviewer averred that there has never been a more engaging Rosalind (Lynch 134).

By 1919 Nigel Playfair broke new theatrical ground with his production of *As You Like It* at the Stratford Theatre which had been closed from 1916 to 1919 because of World War I. Playfair hired Charles Lovat Fraser to design the sets, but instead of attempting to create sets that had long been familiar, Lovat created an appearance based on medieval tapestries and missals. The costumes looked medieval and were quite vividly colored pink, lime-green, scarlet, and saffron

(Marshall 56). The foliage in the forest of Arden was in light and darker tones of blue-green, and the costumes for Orlando and Adam were in ochre and brown while the colors in the court were bright colors such as cobalt, lemon, vermillion, and emerald. Furthermore, the text was performed virtually in its entirety (Brissenden 62). Apparently, this new theatrical aesthetic was not well received by the public (Marshall 56). Happily, Athene Seyler, who played Rosalind, was praised for her humor, tenderness, and pleasantness, and even Herbert Marshall's performance of Jacques was praised as a powerful performance, which was an individualistic and interesting examination of a cynic (Brissenden 63).

While Playfield attempted to introduce innovations in staging to the general public, William Poel attempted an introduction of a more academic nature at Maddermarket Theatre on September 23, 1921, with the complete version of the text which was performed in Elizabethan costumes. The director, Nugent Monck, referred to the staging of *As You Like It* as the first example of a 16th-century stage production since the time of William Shakespeare (Brissenden 63).

In 1932 Harcourt Williams staged a rather severe version of *As You Like It* at the Old Vic, and this did not garner him the kudos that he would have liked. This was the first significant modern staging of this play in Elizabethan costumes (Brissenden 64). The reviewers in the *Times* were not particularly pleased as they said they desired "more grace of scene and less geometry" (Brissenden 61). Peggy Ashcroft, one of the finest actresses of the 20th century, was criticized for lacking style and speaking her lines inarticulately. Only four years later, in Esme Church's production, which was costumed in a Watteauesque fashion, Edith Evans, then 48 years of age, performed the role of Rosalind (Brissenden 63). Rather than allowing Evans's age to work as a disadvantage, Church had Evans behave as an insolent Rosalind instead of a sentimental one (Marshall 62).

No productions of *As You Like It* were staged between 1937 and 1955 in the theatres in London despite a fainthearted attempt at Stratford in April 1944 only two months before the Normandy Landing. Glen Byam Shaw in 1952 produced a staging of the play, and Margaret Leighton acted in a tomboyish fashion. With the coming of the 1950s, a new woman was about to emerge. Leighton's Rosalind was out of keeping with traditional images of Rosalind. This Rosalind was more androgynous and even intellectual (Dusinberre 19). While Shaw's production was chic in its cosmopolitanism, Robert Helpmann produced at the Old Vic in 1955 what was tantamount to a return to the pictorialism of the past with his background of trees that appeared to have come from one of Hans Breughel's paintings. Rosalind, played by Virginia McKenna, came off as a sensible young woman who would have been disinclined to have listened to all of Orlando's talk concerning love (Marshall 62–64).

Happily, in 1957, once again Peggy Ashcroft took to the stage as Rosalind, and whatever she lacked as Rosalind in 1932, she made up for her deficiency at Stratford then, but more importantly, by the middle of the 20th century, gender was of great significance, for *As You Like It* is very much about issues of gender and sexuality. Eighteenth-century productions presented Rosalind as tomboyish, and the 19th century was preoccupied with feminine expressions of emotion, but by the middle of the 20th century, theatregoers were no longer entertained by these attempts at verisimilitude. With increased examination of gender roles, playgoers became aware of the transgressive possibilities of these cross-dressed roles (Marshall 64).

The next really significant production came in 1961 with Vanessa Redgrave, Michael Redgrave's daughter, playing the role of Rosalind. Vanessa Redgrave established the gold standard by which future actresses playing Rosalind would be measured (Marshall 70). Redgrave possessed three advantages with which to perform Rosalind: beauty, height, and youth. She performed the role in a tomboyish fashion clad in a short-sleeve shirt, denim pants, and a worker's cap, and by doing so she appeared as a harbinger of the freedom-loving 1960s. Dusinberre opines that Redgrave's tomboyish interpretation of Rosalind was a success in the early swinging 1960s (19).

This production of *As You Like It* seemed to have something for everyone. Redgrave, wearing a smock, pants that fit closely called pedal pushers, and a cap under which she pushed her hair, appealed to many members of the audience for multiple reasons. Perhaps the women were taken by the slender-looking young man while the men saw the slim young woman dressed as a man. Tony Church, who performed the role of Duke Frederick, believed that Ian Bannen, who played Orlando, made his performance more difficult than he needed by responding to the role of Ganymede as opposed to the young woman playing Rosalind

British actress Vanessa Redgrave stars as Rosalind, with actor Ian Bannen as Orlando, in a scene from Shakespeare's *As You Like It,* during a dress rehearsal at the Royal Shakespeare Theatre, Stratford-upon-Avon, July 4, 1961. AP Photo.

(Brissenden 65). The next innovation in staging Shakespeare's *As You Like It* was Clifford Williams's all-male cast. Williams argued that the point of this production was to show how love transcended sex and gender (Marshall 72). This was a curious time for the production of *As You Like It* at the Old Vic in 1967 because the legalization of gay relations between consenting adults occurred one year after this production of *As You Like It* was staged (Dusinberre 19). Williams made a rather high-flown statement regarding his reason for an all-male production of this play. He asserted that he included an all-male cast because he wanted to achieve a spirited purity which transcended sensuality in pursuit of a poetic sexuality (Marshall 72).

The central role of Rosalind was played by Ronald Pickup who was described as wearing a white suit and behaving awkwardly; nonetheless, Pickup was praised for his ability to transcend gender (Marshall 73). Suffice it to say the other cross-dressed members of the cast received no such praise. In fact, some members of the cast played their roles in a campy and risqué fashion which seemed to be at odds with Williams's goals (Lynch 148). For example, the role of Phoebe, performed by Anthony Hopkins, was a struggle, and at one point Hopkins wanted to leave the production (Marshall 74–75). To be sure, this was a signal theatrical achievement.

The next production of importance was Buzz Goodbody's in 1973; she was the first woman to direct a play on the main stage at the Royal Shakespeare Theatre at Stratford. She decided to have the actors wear modern dress. Rosalind, played by Eileen Atkins, wore a tightly fitted jacket and jeans (Brissenden 68). Rosalind was played by a 39-year-old woman, and so she was a mature woman who was not given to romantic fancy as she would perhaps be otherwise played. Ganymede wore little in the way of disguise. The court scenes were indicated through the use of gilt chairs, a candelabra, and suspended metallic tubes (Lynch 149).

Twelve years later Adrian Noble and his set designer Bob Crowley decided to remove the ambiance of a pastoral idyll that was a cliché regarding *As You Like It*. Noble wanted to explore the psychological qualities of the play, specifically "a liberal feminist notion of gender fluidity" (Marshall 83). This particular production was replete with Jungian symbolism as the program notes included excerpts from Jung's works. The characters of Rosalind and Orlando became "Jungian images of the animus (the masculine in the feminine) and the anima (the feminine in the masculine)" (Lynch 155).

Not only do Rosalind and Orlando function as the anima and animus of Jungian symbols, but there were also several Jungian symbols on stage such as the clock that did not tick until the end of the performance, a moon which became larger as the characters neared the Forest of Arden, and a large mirror. The mirror functioned to indicate the various antitheses in the play such as country and court, female and male, nature and art (Lynch 155–56). All in all, Juliet Stevenson found this play to be at once "dangerous" and "subversive" and called into question categories of gender (Marshall 85).

If Adrian Noble's 1985 production did not challenge gender norms, surely Declan Donnellan's production in 1991 at Cheek by Jowl did in that all of the actors were male. In this particular version of the play, Rosalind was played by Adrian Lester, a black actor, who was described as "graceful, sensuous, and funny" (Marshall 88). To be sure, this production of *As You Like It* called into question the boundaries of gender and sexuality. Since the production was willing to ask questions about one's desire and identity, the play produced a kind of sexual energy. What is most interesting about the play is the complexity and subtlety of the gender and sexuality of the characters; after all, the relationship between Orlando and Rosalind was much more complex than strictly gay as the erotic desire of each character was ambiguous (Marshall 89).

Some critics were not as kind as Jonathan Bate who praised this production because of its use of stage props, which was representative of the Globe Theatre (Lynch 159–60). Michael Hattaway asserted that the play was used to meet a gay agenda and another thought of Jaques as "a would be sugar-daddy" to Orlando and Ganymede, but Adrian Lester had the best comeback when he opined, "What could be more heterosexual than four weddings at the end of a play?" (Marshall 89–91). While some critics did not wish to engage with the political overtones of Donnellan's production, James C. Bulman certainly realizes the significance of them. He asserts that such reviewers are equivalent to critics' refusal to deal with the ideology of the play's sexuality in a homophobic society, which was the reason for that production's interpretation (34). Dusinberre says that Bulman believes that the Cheek by Jowl production attended to important forces that engaged people in the last 25 years of the 20th century, and some of the critics appeared to deny the ideological concerns at the core of the production (20). Bulman, on the contrary, perceives this production of *As You Like It* as profoundly political in nature, concluding his essay with a powerful statement, "In 1991, I would argue, when AIDS was still regarded as God's revenge on homosexuals and homophobic violence was commonplace, it would have been impossible for a production as daring as this *not* to ground itself in gay political discourse" (41).

Regrettably, directors have made few film versions of *As You Like It*. The first sound version was Paul Czinner's in 1936 (Marshall 66). The casting of Elisabeth Bergner, Czinner's wife, as Rosalind has yielded mixed responses from critics. Lynch asserts that she was miscast as Rosalind, and she was even outdone by Sophie Stewart, who performed the role of Celia, and that for all of Laurence Olivier's brilliance as an actor, he could not compensate for Bergner's lackluster performance (164). At the same time, Kenneth Rothwell argues that Bergner saved the film from wreck and ruin with her sprightly performance. Apparently, Roger Manvell thought little of her performance, believing that she possessed a "self-destructive femininity" and expressing contempt for her "habit of turning somersaults" (Rothwell 49). Marshall believed that the process of courtship allowed Rosalind's personality to be expressed as she runs about joyfully in the Forest of Arden (Marshall 66). Most significantly, this film version of *As You Like It* demonstrates that Shakespeare's plays can be conveyed realistically on film.

The BBC television version of *As You Like* was sadly uninspired despite the fact that it was filmed on location at Glamis Castle in May and June 1978 (Lynch 165). Most regrettably, Rosalind and Orlando lacked the chemistry that is needed to make this a successful production; this was also true for the relationship between Rosalind and Celia. Touchstone, the court's clown, too, lacked the energy and vitality in his relationship with Audrey. This production was yet another insipid film version of a Shakespearean play (Marshall 80).

The most recent version of *As You Like It* was produced by HBO in 2006 and directed by Kenneth Branagh. This is an extremely engaging film set in 19th-century Japan with the principal characters functioning as displaced Englishmen who have colonized the country, and so the film begins with a Japanese mime performing for Duke Senior (Brian Blessed) and his retinue while Duke Frederick (also Brian Blessed) and his henchmen are outside at night in an adjacent waterway; Duke Frederick's men are also on the roof of Duke Senior's home where they are in the process of cutting a hole into it so they may drop into his home when the moment for the attack is given. In a flash Duke Frederick attacks Duke Senior's home and holds him and his retinue captive. The fact that Brian Blessed plays the roles of both dukes illustrates the use of the doubling of actors on the early modern stage and at the same time the psychological doubling of characters.

Rosalind realizes that she must flee her evil uncle Frederick's court after being threatened with death if she remains there so she decides to cross-dress as Ganymede while Celia dresses as Aliena with Touchstone in tow; they soon find themselves in the Forest of Arden. Rosalind wears the least disguise, a brown hat and a brown coat. Only a blind and deaf Orlando would be incapable of recognizing Rosalind. Touchstone rudely approaches Corin regarding a place for them to spend the night and to eat. In this scene Rosalind/Ganymede takes charge and secures a cottage in which they can sleep as well as buy sheep to raise in an adjacent pasture. Celia as the exhausted young lady from the court foolishly falls off the branch of a tree as she enthusiastically expresses her desire to live in the Forest of Arden. Corin, much like Adam, becomes another provider of sorts for this group of ill-prepared urbanites.

Rosalind as Ganymede teaches Orlando to be a good lover because he has fallen in love with Rosalind, and of course, Orlando writes sonnets in Rosalind's honor. Moreover, Celia has gained access to them and is reading them too, and teases Rosalind about them. Ironically, Rosalind makes no attempt to maintain her disguise. Rosalind asks Celia many questions regarding Orlando, and she replies in a very dramatic, exaggerated fashion. There is a self-theatricality about this conversation, for Rosalind is very expressive when she is with Celia. Jaques, however, does not share Orlando's passion for writing sonnets and chides him for marring the barks of the trees as they stand under what resembles a bamboo arch with extensions on each side of it with window-like structures, as Celia looks on expectantly. S/he is referred to as a "fair youth" by Orlando after s/he promises Orlando that she will cure him of being in love by giving him good counsel, for s/he claims to know the marks of love, and s/he initially thinks that he lacks those particular qualities, as s/he tells Orlando in a rather affected fashion, "You are rather point-device in your accoutrements, as loving yourself than seeming the lover of any other" (Brissenden III.ii.367–69).

Once again in order to demonstrate a contrast between high-flown Petrarchan ideals of female beauty and devotion and the gross physicality of earthy eroticism, Audrey, the serving woman from Duke Senior's court, and Touchstone, the jester with a penchant for risqué repartee, provided a contrast to the courtly rhetoric of Orlando and Ganymede. In fact, Audrey slaps him no less than three times within a minute when he makes references to her sluttishness, which she interprets as allusions to her, but he allays her fears regarding her chastity when he proposes to marry her.

Phoebe and Silvius, whose very name means woods, constitute the third couple, but their relationship parodies that of Petrarchan lovers with Silvius's doting devotion to Phoebe, who disdains him. When Rosalind meets Phoebe and Silvius, she immediately rebukes her for her contempt for him. Phoebe then begins to twist her hair in a schoolgirl fashion in order to indicate her awkwardness around Ganymede, falling in love with her/him. Rosalind/Ganymede speaks in a stentorian fashion to Phoebe, commanding her to kneel, and she tells her that she is essentially a commodity to be sold on the marriage market and that it will not always hold its value, "For I must tell you friendly in your ear: / Sell when you can, you are not for all markets. / Cry the man mercy, love him, take his offer" (III.v.60–62). Phoebe is a caricature of a Petrarchan lady who does not value the love that a man has for her. Phoebe puts her hands on Silvius's face, and then she hugs him when she is upset.

In yet another absurd romantic situation, the clownish figure of William is infatuated with Audrey. When Touchstone meets him with Audrey, Touchstone asks him a series of questions pertaining to his identity and whom he loves. Referring to him as a clown, Touchstone shakes hands with him, crushing his hand as a means of intimidating him so that he will stay away from Audrey despite the fact that she has no interest in him, cruelly using him as a figure of fun. This treatment seems especially problematic as William is a sweet-natured Asian man who means no harm to anyone. Both Touchstone and Audrey take unfair advantage of him, which reminds the audience that beneath the play's lighthearted comic fun is a dark underside.

One comedic moment becomes quasi-serious as Rosalind asks Celia to marry her and Orlando. Celia expresses significant reluctance in enacting the marital rite. Orlando and Rosalind knee and look over a ridge in the offing. Rosalind actually becomes teary-eyed when Celia enacts the marriage rite. Rosalind seems incredulous that Celia has actually enacted the marriage rite as a priest. At this point, it is Rosalind's turn to act like a Petrarchan lover, saying, "I'll go find a shadow and sigh till he come" (IV.i.205).

In this film version of *As You Like It*, Kenneth Branagh sees fit to include the lion attack on Orlando, who is badly wounded, despite the fact that Oliver fended the lion off by striking it with a large rock, and Oliver reports this unfortunate event. Through this near miraculous turn of events, Oliver encounters Celia in whom he instantly falls in love in true Petrarchan fashion. Oliver appears transformed, a different kind of person after this near-death experience with the lion. Putting Celia down, Oliver produces a bloody handkerchief, which promptly causes Rosalind/Ganymede to faint. He says that he is and is not himself as he has undergone a spiritual transformation because his brother saved his life, and then he bound up his brother's wound after he was attacked by the lioness. The issue of identity comes to the fore in this scene as Oliver undergoes an identity change in the same way that Rosalind/Ganymede's real identity is revealed. Oliver's telling Rosalind/Ganymede to "counterfeit to be a man" (IV.iii.172) is a powerful example of verbal irony as she has pretended to be a man ever since she entered the Forest of Arden.

Branagh tries to add a bit of comic eroticism by having Orlando come upon Rosalind/Ganymede when she is bathing, and her breasts are obscured by the branch of a tree. Only in the Forest of Arden would a hero not recognize his nude heroine. The next time they meet, Orlando says that he realizes that he can no longer pretend that Ganymede is Rosalind. He reaches a crisis junction from which there is no turning back, for he runs away from Rosalind/Ganymede and leans against a tree while he cries in desperation. Now Rosalind knows that Orlando loves her, for he exclaims, "I can live no longer by thinking" (V.ii.49).

In the concluding scene, domestic order is finally achieved through the right pairing of couples. Celia appears in a white kimono with dogwood and flowers in her hair, and Rosalind appears in a white dress with a bright red jacket with bright red flowers in her hair. Here the paternal recognition between Rosalind and Duke Senior occurs without the aid of Hymen, the Greek god of marriage, for Corin plays Hymen's role by his pairing of lovers, which acts to ground the experience of the lovers in an empiricism that all of them can understand; after all, he originally came to Japan as a missionary to convert the Japanese to Christianity. Once the lovers have been paired, they dance in a circle, celebratory of unity and harmony, and run back to Duke Senior's home while they joyfully dance as Branagh's ubiquitous white confetti falls, covering everything.

The epilogue is one of the most inventive dramatic moments in the play as the actor playing the role of Rosalind divests herself of her gendered theatrical identity, for she walks from the set into the area where there are camera crew members. This breaking of the fourth wall calls the film viewers' attention to the fact that they are, in fact, watching a film. Walking to her trailer, the actor opens its door and enters it, and it is at this point that the audience hears Kenneth Branagh say, "And cut," calling attention to the fact that the film is complete, for the audience does not need to suspend its willing disbelief any longer.

Unlike many of the comedies that are populated with young couples in pursuit of love and marriage, *Henry IV, Part 1* has been a long-time favorite on the English stage, despite having few speaking roles for women. Nonetheless, this was a very popular play (Bevington 69). In fact, *Henry IV, Part 1* was in such demand that it was performed at the Red Bull immediately after, if not before, the Restoration, by a troupe of actors who may have constituted Thomas Killigrew's King's Company in 1660, the year of Charles II's restoration to the throne of England, having returned from his exile in France (Bevington 70).

Apparently, theatre managers such as Thomas Betterton in the late 17th century made few cuts in *Henry IV, Part 1*. Stage managers consulted the folio concerning issues of profanity and vulgarity. In spite of the fact that theatre managers significantly altered *King Lear* and *The Tempest, Henry IV, Part 1* suffered minimal cuts despite the excisions of Lady Percy's major speeches in II.iii., part of the "play extempore" in II.iv., and Glendower's speech with his wife and daughter (Bevington 71).

While some women were offended by the character of Falstaff because of his vulgarity in the 18th century, others were offended by the lack of female roles (Kastan 73). The histories include few roles and lines for women, and *Henry IV, Part 1* includes the least dialogue for women; women speak fewer than 3.5 percent of the dialogue in this play. It should come as little surprise that so few lines are spoken by women given the importance placed upon military endeavors. As Kastan sardonically opines, the women in this play are the Hostess and Hotspur and Mortimer's wives, and Mortimer's wife can converse in only Welsh (74).

Interestingly, the second half of the 19th century had fewer memorable productions of *Henry IV, Part 1* because the play was not conducive to elaborate settings despite the work of Herbert Beerbohm Tree, who staged an elaborate production in 1896, but attitudes were changing regarding the Henriad by the early 20th century (Kastan 90 and 92). By the beginning of the 20th century, at least one director of Shakespeare's history plays, Frank Benson, thought that these history plays should be viewed in relation to each other, and so he began to stage "cycles" of these history plays at Stratford between 1901 and 1906, and so the trend continued with Barry Jackson's pairing *Henry IV, Part 1* and *Henry IV, Part 2* with the performance of the first part in the afternoon and the second part in the evening on Shakespeare's birthday in honor of the opening of the New Memorial Theatre, which was attended by Edward, the Prince of Wales. Sadly, Orson Welles less successfully attempted to combine *Henry IV, Part 1*; *Henry IV, Part 2*; and *Henry V* in a work titled *Five Kings* in Philadelphia in 1939 (Bevington 78–79).

During World War II there was a need for an increased sense of nationalism in England, and so there was a revival of these most patriotic of Shakespearean plays at the Old Vic in 1945, in particular *Henry IV, Part 1*, which was directed by John Burrell and starred Ralph Richardson and Laurence Olivier as Falstaff and Hotspur respectively. Olivier's performance of Hotspur was at once one of soldier and lover. His first scene was with Margaret Leighton as Lady Percy, and Scott McMillin describes it as "romantic, sexy, and charged with the impatience of a man who might rather be on horseback. His scenes with the other rebels, especially in the 'pluck up drowned honor by the locks' speech to Northumberland and Worcester (I.iii.201–208), seemed more romantic than politically astute as though this kind of imagination should be devoted to Margaret Leighton" (24). Leighton garnered attention in this play because of her ability to stand up to Olivier's decision to represent their relationship in a romantic fashion. Sybil Thorndike's role as Mistress Quickly seemed too small for her, and she received scant attention for her role in the play. As McMillin remarks, there are few opportunities for women in *Henry IV, Part 1* despite Burrell's attempt to indicate the sympathetic relationship between Lady Percy and Lady Mortimer in Act III (30–31).

Under the direction of Anthony Quayle in the 1951 production at the Shakespeare Memorial Theatre at Stratford-upon-Avon (McMillin 36), Richard Burton performed the role of Prince Hal. In this production Hal's renunciation of Falstaff (played by Quayle) is initiated early in the tavern scene. Richard Burton as Hal stresses the dignity and resolve of the young man who would be crowned King Henry V, but he does not try to instill a sense of real joy (Bevington 81). Hotspur, played by Michael Redgrave, by comparison to Hal, is rambunctious, especially in his interaction with Lady Percy, played by Margaret Jeffords; the initial scene between Hotspur and Lady Percy has an undertone of sexual playfulness. Hotspur sits on a table, and then Lady Percy sits on his lap with the scene culminating in Hotspur dropping her onto the floor at the conclusion of their conversation. Apparently, audiences in the early 1950s were unaccustomed to such roustabout behavior by such characters of aristocratic status, but this treatment of this scene became standard in the future (McMillin 45).

One of the most significant film versions involving Prince Hal, Falstaff, Hotspur, and Henry IV came in 1966 with Orson Welles's extraordinary *Falstaff*. In this prodigious production Welles starred as none other than Falstaff, Keith Baxter as Prince Hal, the incomparable John Gielgud as Henry IV, and Norman Rodway as Hotspur. Anthony Davies emphasizes the great differences between the realm of Henry IV's court and Falstaff's Boar's Head Tavern. Davies presents the distinctions in absolute terms as nothing can reduce the emotional indifference that stone walls resonate. The castle represents the frigid stolidity of medieval rule, which Bolingbroke epitomizes (125).

By comparison to Henry's palace, the world of the tavern is one made of wood, but it is also a sexualized space (Davies 126). There is also a relaxed sexual ambiance about the tavern, for Falstaff makes bawdy comments to Mistress Quickly even as she berates him about the money that he owes her for all of the food and drink that his massive frame has consumed there. At one point in the repartee, Falstaff jocularly declares of Mistress Quickly, "Why? She's neither fish nor flesh; a man knows not where to have her" to which she unwittingly undermines her chastity even more by asserting, "Thou art an unjust man in saying so. Thou or any man knows where to have me, thou knave, thou" (Bevington III.iii.122–25).

Even in the interaction between Hotspur and Kate, a playful romanticism makes itself known in opposition to the seemingly loveless castle of Henry. Even Hotspur, who in Henry IV's words is the theme of honor's tongue, appears ridiculous when he becomes so concerned about the upcoming battle with Henry IV's forces that he goes outside the room in which he has been bathing in no more than a large bath towel which promptly falls off him revealing his buttocks, a position that constitutes the antithesis of irreproachable chivalry. Davies puts it best when he points out the humor of the blatant nudity in contrast to the suit of armor on the castle walls (131).

Davies makes an extremely perceptive comment concerning the displacement of eroticism onto militarism in this play. Moreover, he believes unfulfilled sexuality subtends all of the relationships in this motion picture. This issue becomes apparent in the sexual looseness of Doll Tearsheet, in the frigid masculinity of the king's court, in the hints of same-sex eroticism between Poins and Hal, and the lack of any maternal figure (131). The fact of the matter is that Hal is quite friendly with many of the young women in the Boar's Head Tavern; for example, when the chief justice comes for Falstaff, Hal jumps into bed with a young woman, not Poins! As intriguing and provocative as some of Davies's and also Sylvan Barnet's assertions may be, especially the one concerning the relationship between Hal and Poins, one must look closely at what actually happens in this film. Barnet makes similar remarks about Poins and Hal's relationship. Barnet laments Welles's representation of both Hal and Poins which the splicing of these films or plays together distorts in addition to presenting Hal as Poins's feminine, bisexual lover (242).

To be sure, the most subversive recent treatment of Prince Hal and Falstaff is embodied in Gus Van Sant's film adaptation of *Henry IV, Part 1* titled *My Own Private Idaho* (1991), a title derived from a song by the musical group, the B-52s, which is called "Private Idaho" (Kastan 105). In much the same vein as Falstaff, *My Own Private Idaho* shares many of the same concerns. For example, in Van Sant's film version of *Henry IV, Part 1* Scott, the prodigal son of the major of Portland, who functions as the figure of Hal, is played by Keanu Reeves, and Bob, played by William Richert, functions as the figure of Falstaff, who in this instance is an older gay man with a cocaine addiction who enjoys the presence of adolescent boys, and like Falstaff, he awaits Hal's coming into his own as king, for Bob is eager for Scott to celebrate his 21st birthday so that he can inherit his father's estate. The characters spend much of their time in a dilapidated hotel which acts as a substitute for the world of the tavern in *Henry IV, Part 1*. Barnet notes a similarity of borrowed lines from *Henry IV, Part 1* in I.ii.; for example, in the first speech that Hal addresses to Falstaff, he states, " 'Unless hours were cups of sack, dials the signs of leaping houses, and the blessed sun himself a fair hot wench in flame-colored taffeta' is transformed into 'Unless hours were lines of coke, dials looked like the signs of gay bars, or time itself were a fair hustler in black leather' " (Barnet 244). At the end of the film, Scott gives up his life of drug use and same-sex relationships in order to conform to social expectations by taking a wife after he travels to Italy (Kastan 105). Yet ultimately, one feels compelled to ask just how closely related *My Own Private Idaho* is to *Henry IV, Part 1*. Barnet is almost resigned to assert, "*My Own Private Idaho* is what it is, but it does derive partly from the relatively new, darker interpretations of the Henry plays," and so Barnet concludes, "In the context of the film, Scott decided to conform to the heterosexual middle-class world of his father, renouncing the beliefs of the cultural outsider" (245).

In "Hal's Desire, Shakespeare's Idaho," Jonathan Goldberg takes a much more academically aggressive line of approach regarding the issue of sexuality. When he confronts the nature of Hal's relationship with Falstaff, or more precisely the question of whether Hal engages in sexual relations with Falstaff, Goldberg responds that one cannot answer this question with incontrovertible definitude, because the play does not provide evidence that will conform to the 20th-century's concepts of heterosexuality and homosexuality. Audiences cannot determine if Hal engages in sexual relations with Falstaff (57). Goldberg argues that sexuality was understood differently during the early modern period than it is understood today in the early 21st century and that it is futile to attempt to answer this question. He emphasizes that sexual relations were a transitional period in Shakespeare's psychological growth, which he left behind as he grew older; at the same time, same-sex erotic relations were not a marginal part of the Elizabethan world (59). Goldberg makes his argument that sexual desire or eroticism is a product of a specific historical moment, and to use such terms as homosexual and heterosexual is an anachronistic practice as the early modern English and Europeans did not conceptualize of their sexual identities through a set of sexual or ontological orientations. Rather men and women engaged in specific sexual practices, which were judged or regarded as moral or immoral or legal or illegal largely because of the imprimatur or disapprobation of the ecclesiastical and civil authorities of their day.

While *Henry IV, Part 1* may be viewed for its rambunctious joie de vivre, *Hamlet* has been forever known as a drama concerning high seriousness and purpose which addressed issues of profound epistemological and ontological significance. Whole books have been devoted to the meaning or significance of *Hamlet*. Critics and theatregoers alike have been perplexed by the manifold subtleties and nuances within the three different editions to which scholars refer as *Hamlet*. More scholarship has been produced pertaining to *Hamlet* than any other work of literature. There are in excess of 400 articles per year written about *Hamlet* according to the *Shakespeare Quarterly Annual Bibliography* (Taylor and Thompson 2).

Hamlet was, of course, first known for its production on the stage. The first recorded performance did not occur on a London stage but rather upon the *Consent*, a ship that was headed toward Bantam and the Moluccas. The *Consent* had been sponsored by the East India Company which had charted a course to the East Indies in March 1607. Captain Keeling anchored off the coast of Sierra Leone, and Keeling's journal indicates how he allowed the crew members to assuage the tedium of their time by performing *Hamlet*. Needless to say, some scholars have argued that this is a fictitious account; in 1898 Sidney Lee argued this account was a forgery in his *Life of Shakespeare*, and furthermore, this fraud was created by John Payne Collier and others; later in 1950 Sydney Race in *Notes and Queries* made a similar claim, asserting that pertinent pages from Keeling's journal were missing and that the sailors on board the *Consent* would have been incapable of learning both *Hamlet* and *Richard II*. Rather than arguing for or against the authenticity of the claim that *Hamlet* was performed, Taylor and Thompson are more intrigued by "what the terms of the debate tell us about attitudes to Shakespeare's status in relation to class, race and national culture" (55).

Scholars, however, can say with complete certitude that the first performance of *Hamlet* occurred in London at Court in 1619 with Joseph Taylor, who more than likely played the role of Hamlet despite the fact that the 1603 Quarto claims that the play had been performed "diuerse times . . . in the Cittie of London" (Taylor and Thompson 97). Literary historians know that by 1637 when *Hamlet* was performed at Hampton Court, the play had eight printed editions published in 1603, 1604, 1611, c.1621, 1623, 1632, and 1637. This attests to the popularity of the play on stage, if not in print (Taylor and Thompson 97). Needless to say, the Civil War brought productions of even the ever popular *Hamlet* to a standstill for all intents and purposes.

By the time *Hamlet* had reopened after Charles II returned to the throne in 1660, the license to perform *Hamlet* had changed hands from the King's Company to the Duke's Company. William Davenant received credit for training Thomas Betterton to perform Hamlet and Betterton's wife to perform Ophelia. Davenant altered the play significantly by removing Voltemand, Polonius's advice to Laertes, Hamlet's advice to the players when they visit the court, and Fortinbras's initial appearance. Only Hamlet's world-renowned "To be or not to be" speech survived unscathed by Davenant's excisions. In all, Davenant had cut the play by 2,800 lines which was approximately 25 percent of the play from Quarto 2 (Dawson 31).

Unlike Betterton, Garrick was known for his speed and vitality as well as his range of emotion; apparently, his eyes were able to shift from one emotional state to another, and this theatrical ability was extremely important to Garrick as an actor, but his greatest asset was his attention to detail concerning psychological nuance. There was a great deal of importance placed upon one's individual experience (Dawson 32). A German scientist by the name of Georg Lichtenberg described the performance of Garrick while performing the "ghost scene" in 1774 in which Garrick demonstrated a psychological complexity in his performance of the role of Hamlet. His performances were known for their very complex psychological states of being; in fact, it was the hallmark of his acting style. This spectral visitation for some members of the audience was the most important moment in the play (Dawson 33–34).

Perhaps the most radical innovation that Garrick made was his alteration in the text itself when in 1772 he cut the gravediggers' scene and the entire fifth act. In this particular version, the play ends suddenly after Laertes comes back to Elsinore at which time Hamlet fights him in the graveyard. In this scene when Hamlet attempts to stab Claudius, he tries to defend himself. Ultimately, Laertes intervenes and stabs Hamlet despite the strange stage direction in which Hamlet is said to run into Laertes's sword and fall. Meanwhile, Gertrude rushes offstage and goes into a trance by her chamber door while insane Ophelia is left to her own devices, and the state of Demark is left in the hands of Horatio and Laertes (Dawson 40–41).

In spite of Garrick's butchered version, he continued to be extremely popular. so much so that on his 152nd and last performance on May 30, 1776, Hannah More recorded that she had been to a funeral. The tickets for this performance sold out within two hours, and when Garrick last appeared at the theatre on June 10, he drew tears from both the audience and himself. When he finally died three years later, his funeral was the finest one for any British subject other than for a deceased king, for the funeral procession was more than a mile long reaching from the Strand and Whitehall to Westminster. Even earls and dukes served as pallbearers. In as much as this was a funeral procession, it was very much a celebration of his life as a Shakespearean actor (Dawson 44).

Garrick's successor, Edmund Kean, was a Romantic who injected a bitterness into his role of Hamlet. Writers such as Goethe, Coleridge, and Hazlitt changed Hamlet into an extremely self-conscious individual who was incapable of action. At the same time, scenery came to function as an expression of the actor's character. Despite the artistry of Kean's acting, Fanny Kemble, who thought Kean's performances were mesmerizing, believed they were not always of the same quality (Dawson 45). Moreover, Kean was often compared to Garrick. Both of them were men of small stature even by the standards of the day as they were less than five feet four inches in height. Both of them placed a great deal of emphasis upon physical acting and strong emotions and changing their facial expressions. While Garrick tried to obtain a psychological integrity in his characterizations, Kean's acting ability was less developed and refined. Moreover, Kean had no comic ability, yet even as Hamlet he was less successful than Garrick because he failed to develop Hamlet's more intellectual qualities, and so he became more known for his "points," one of which was the final moment in the nunnery scene; for example, while Garrick was able to demonstrate tenderness for Ophelia, Kean appeared to have been indecisive in that he had almost rushed completely off the stage but then turned slowly around and returned to Ophelia whose hand he kissed with a sigh. Hazlitt recorded that this action had "an electric effect" upon the audience. Since the 1920s those who have played the role of Hamlet have been rougher with Ophelia in that they fought competing feelings of tender emotion or violent, erotic desire (Dawson 46–47).

Edwin Booth, brother of John Wilkes Booth, also performed the role of Hamlet. His scenes with Ophelia were filled with the love and tenderness that Kean had, but in general his interaction with Ophelia was not as emotionally violent. Moreover, in these performances Hamlet was aware of the presence of Claudius and Polonius hiding behind an arras, and therefore, he showed greater kindness to Ophelia. While Booth did not move from anger to tenderness as Kean did in this scene, he acted with restraint and courtesy. Booth insisted that Hamlet did not love Ophelia, but his audiences felt he communicated otherwise. Therefore, when Ophelia was to return the "tenders of his affection," she attempted to hand them to him, and he kissed the packet of letters, but he did not take them from her, which was to indicate that his romantic bond with her was still intact. After all, at the end of this scene, Booth held Ophelia with "infinite tenderness" and kissed her forehead, which perhaps demonstrated an appreciation for what late 19th-century America defined as its "vision of the beautiful" (Dawson 52–53).

Henry Irving, who performed in late 19th- and early 20th-century England, was a traditionalist concerning the incorporation of new plays into the repertoire; he was much like Booth in that he was more emotional than spiritual. He also combined some of the qualities of both Booth and Kean in his performance of Hamlet (Dawson 57–58 and 60). Above all else, his acting was more naturalistic than Booth's, which offended some audience members, causing some who attended the Lyceum to lament that he reminded them of feminine men who haunt drawing rooms in London (Taylor and Thompson 104). Not only was his acting naturalistic, unlike Garrick, Booth, or Kean's behavior, but also his hysteria, according to Dawson, was real (61). It is important to remember that Irving's behavior was more than merely moody, but rather in Irving's production his mental stability was at risk, and his emotional angst came from the intensity and ambiguity of his feelings toward characters to whom he was also very emotionally connected (Taylor and Thompson 105–6).

In the "Mousetrap" scene, Hamlet displayed control and emotional balance in which sexual matters are eschewed. To be sure, here as always, the sexually suggestive dialogue relating to Hamlet's laying his head in Ophelia's lap as well as the sexually provocative dialogue of her mad songs in addition to the reference to the erotically charged flower, "The long purples," in Gertrude's funeral elegy for Ophelia, were cut from the production in which Ellen Terry in the role of Ophelia cried and dropped her fan of peacock feathers, which Irving retrieved and used as a screen as it always had been by other actors playing Hamlet. Because of Hamlet's conflict regarding his erotic feelings for Ophelia and his anger at Claudius, he kept his emotional control, and therefore, he did not crawl across the stage as had been the custom. Irving believed that Hamlet loved Ophelia and that she was devastated by his refusal of her love, and so Irving perceived Ophelia's beauty as a trap for Hamlet. Irving felt that Hamlet came to Ophelia as a lover in the "nunnery" scene, but by the end of the scene, Hamlet's love for Ophelia has dissolved. Ophelia caused a conflict between Hamlet's erotic desire and his sense of duty to fulfill his father's command. Analogously, Gertrude's beauty was considered the cause of Claudius's erotic desires so that, ultimately, Gertrude is blamed for the murder of her husband because she caused Claudius to murder his brother in the garden (Dawson 62–63 and 65).

John Barrymore came to the fore as the Hamlet of his generation in the 1920s (Dawson 67). In addition to the scenic changes that arrived in the early 1920s came a new treatment of Gertrude. The 1925 production of *Hamlet* was an improvement in its treatment of both characters. Constance Collier, who played Gertrude, was praised by British newspapers, but more importantly, Barrymore lauded her for her acting because of its beauty and provocative qualities (Dawson 74). When Barrymore approached the closet scene with Gertrude, a number of critics noticed Freudian nuances in several of the emotionally charged embraces throughout the scene. Barrymore as Hamlet spoke his severest dialogue to Hamlet's mother immediately before the apparition of Hamlet's father appeared at which point Hamlet became immobile and fell onto his knees (Dawson 74–75).

Fay Compton, who played Ophelia opposite Barrymore's Hamlet, presented herself as charming and slightly sad. Barrymore thought she was the best actress to play Ophelia since Ellen Terry, and most of the theatre reviews vouchsafe his assertion. She impressed all of her critics as the epitome of innocence, and none of the critics thought of her as a "new woman"; moreover, one reviewer opined that there was no doubt that she was in love with Hamlet. Unlike Fay Compton, Rosalind Fuller exuded a patent eroticism, and this behavior was a significant quality of her performance. She sang the St. Valentine's song quite happily, brazenly accosted Claudius as she sang "Young men will do 't if they come to 't, / By cock they are to blame" (IV.v.60–61), and even leered at her own brother, Laertes. There was, however, a difference of opinion regarding Ophelia's speech and behavior. While some men playing Hamlet would evince a protective quality toward Ophelia, others such as Barrymore and Hopkins approved of her playing of the role, which was an indication of the mixed feelings that the general public felt toward female freedom and sexuality (Dawson 76–77).

To be sure, *Hamlet* had entered the modern age with the Kingsway Theatre production in 1925 directed by Barry Jackson and H.K. Ayliff in London. Finally, there was a production of Hamlet in modern dress in which the characters wore "morning coats, plus-fours, flapper dresses, bobbed hair, revolvers, and [drove] motor cars"! (Dawson 83). Besides the modern dress the alacrity with which the play was acted was little less than extraordinary. Although much more of the text was used than Barrymore's production, it lasted an hour less than in Barrymore's, ending after three hours with a 12-minute intermission. The dress of Ophelia and Gertrude very much indicated the modernity of the production. Ophelia wore a short, flimsy black dress in the mad scene, and at one point she sang her songs quite erotically and even added a few modern dance steps in order to make a contemporary connection with her audience, and Gertrude wore a luxe negligee in the closet scene, and so with the coming of the modern age, there was an anti-Romantic reaction to the play in which the importance of Hamlet was diminished, but Colin Keith-Johnston was quite rough with both Ophelia and Gertrude. He jerked Gertrude about the closet scene. In the case of Ophelia in the nunnery scene, he was rough and mean-spirited and then sexually interested in her the next, and finally, he cruelly dragged her down some stairs. In fact, a couple of critics noticed a heightened, sexualized performance on Muriel Hewitt's part. Edith Shackleton noticed a Freudian overtone in Ophelia's character while J.K. Prothero perceived a sexual quality in Hewitt's performance (Dawson 84, 87–89, 93–94).

Although there were many changes in the theatre in an effort to modernize it, a star system was still in place in the London theatre in 1930. John Gielgud was acutely aware of the play's theatrical tradition. He starred in six different productions of *Hamlet* from 1930 until 1945 and later directed the play in New York in 1964 with Richard Burton playing Hamlet (Taylor and Thompson 106). Over this period of 15 years, Gielgud performed Hamlet hundreds of times. He became more identified with Hamlet than any other actor in the 20th century. He was so aware of the history of the play that he wrote in 1937 an essay titled "The Hamlet Tradition" (Dawson 108). In his interaction with Ophelia in 1930 in the nunnery scene, their bodies almost touched, but this action was prevented by his ordering her to a nunnery at which point he ran after her, seized her, and when she told him that she did not know where her father was, he threw her off him, and then he threw down the set of pearls she had given him. Finally, he left the scene while she mourned his rejection of her. In this production Hamlet believed that if Claudius could use Ophelia to his own end, then he could as well. Once again, Hamlet chose duty over his love for Ophelia (Dawson 103–4).

Olivier's performance of Hamlet at the Old Vic, which was directed by Tyrone Guthrie in the 1937, literally set the stage for his film version in 1948. It was in the 1937 stage version that he used Freudian theory, which Ernest Jones advanced regarding the Oedipus complex. Strangely enough, few critics noticed the Freudian interpretation of the play; all the same, the Freudian paradigm provided Olivier with a means of gaining an understanding of the text. Once again Raymond Mortimer was quick to discern the Freudian overtones, and he made reference to Hamlet's "mother-fixation," and he argued that it was because of Hamlet's "mother-fixation" that he experienced the emotional shifts that he felt for Ophelia and his excessive feelings of admiration for his father. As far as Mortimer was concerned, Hamlet's mercurial emotional state was the most noticeable of his behaviors (Dawson 112–13). In sum, if Gielgud was regarded as the brightest star among British actors in the 1930s, then Olivier was a rapidly rising star, which would reach its apogee in his 1948 film version of *Hamlet* (Dawson 116).

In 1948 Laurence Olivier received the Academy Award for best actor for his portrayal of Hamlet, and the film itself won the award for best picture, which Anthony Dawson believes is the most widely viewed film version of *Hamlet* (171 and 176). This particular film version of *Hamlet*, one could argue, celebrated Freudian theory in its depiction of Hamlet's relationship with his mother. Peter Donaldson argues in his essay "Olivier, Hamlet, and Freud": "The Freud/Jones interpretation of *Hamlet* is a central, structuring presence the contours of which may be clearly discerned. At the same time, the Oedipus complex, so evident and even intentional in Olivier's *Hamlet*, serves as a mask or screen for other, perhaps even deeper issues. First, the Oedipal conflict, especially as it is manifested in Hamlet's interactions with the ghost of his father, often has a passive or submissive character in the film" (*Shakespeare Films/Shakespeare Directors* 34–35). Donaldson even goes so far as to argue quite strongly that the "visual design" of the film was influenced by Olivier's rape or near rape on the stairway at All Saints School at the age of nine. Donaldson detects a link in the depiction of Hamlet's passivity or submission to his father's ghost and its relation to the sexual assault that he suffered as a child on a stairway in that it caused Olivier to question his sexual orientation. In other words, Donaldson argues that Olivier interpreted *Hamlet* through the lens of his experience as a sexually violated youth (35). Neil Taylor in "The Films of *Hamlet*" astutely states the gist of Donaldson's argument in that the film articulates Olivier's psychological need to understand his Oedipal experience and the specific traumatic encounter during his childhood (183).

Olivier wanted to distance himself from the role of Hamlet because of his Freudian interpretation. Moreover, another example of the distancing may have been Olivier's choice of Eileen Herlie as his mother who was 27 years of age at the time; Olivier happened to be 40 years of age himself. While Gertrude's youth may have emphasized her sexuality, it may have undermined the credibility of the incestuous relationship or its subtext between Hamlet and Gertrude (Donaldson 37).

The interaction that occurs between Hamlet and his mother is fraught with Freudian overtones as shown in Gertrude's attempt to make Hamlet remain at Elsinore when she gives him a prolonged, erotic kiss. At this point, Claudius angrily pulls her away from Hamlet. Donaldson believes that the audience could understand how she was unaware of her husband's murder by Claudius because her response to a difficult decision that has moral implications is erotically charged, even with Hamlet. The eroticism seems to be reciprocated, if not intensified, in the closet scene with his mother when Polonius hides behind the arras. Hamlet tells her that she will sit down and not leave until he has made her cognizant of her wrongdoing. He continues to use the plural form of the pronoun "you." In the film, Hamlet throws his mother backward onto the bed, and shoves the dagger close to her throat. When Gertrude cries for help and Polonius responds, Hamlet, thinking the king is behind the arras, stabs Polonius, and continues to speak to his mother until he finally drops the dagger. Here the violence is blatantly erotic, and Hamlet convinces his mother to refrain from sexual intercourse with Claudius, and so the scene ends with a passionate hug and kiss as the camera circles around them as it would with lovers (Donaldson 47–49).

In the nunnery scene, Hamlet thinks that Ophelia has already gone against him and is in league with her father and Claudius. He remains seated in a chair and is unable to approach her, which is indicative of his Oedipal issue. Hamlet

Laurence Olivier as Hamlet kneels at the feet of Jean Simmons who plays Ophelia, in a scene from the film production of Shakespeare's *Hamlet*, in 1948. AP Photo.

is emotionally mercurial and anxious as he is aware of Polonius's and Claudius's presence behind the arras. When he asks her where her father is and she replies he is at home, Hamlet then becomes angry and pushes her away; his feelings shift from low self-esteem to disapproval of women. Even as she tries to embrace him, he flings her off him onto the stone steps (Donaldson 44–45). Overall, Donaldson provides a powerful Freudian critique of Olivier's film version of *Hamlet* in which the Oedipal issue is of great significance in relationships with both Gertrude and Ophelia.

In addition to the importance of *Hamlet* to American and British culture, it was also very significant to Russian intellectuals in the 19th century as they perceived it as a dramatic vehicle by which to articulate their political discontent with the rule of Alexander III, and later their dissatisfaction with the despotism of Joseph Stalin, and so it was in 1964 under the administration of Nikita Khrushchev that Grigori Kozintsev made his version of *Hamlet,* which derived from his 1954 stage production of it at the Pushkin Academic Theatre of Drama in Leningrad (Taylor, "Films" 184). This film version of *Hamlet* very much invites its audience to make comparisons between what happens in Elsinore and modern rulerships, especially Stalin's dictatorship (Kliman, *Hamlet* 88).

Despite the highly political nature of Kozintsev's film version of *Hamlet,* eroticism was inescapably present in many of the same scenes as in the other versions. In the scene in which Hamlet meets Ophelia after he has seen his father's ghost, he enters the room where she has worked with her easel with his cloak thrown over his arm. Then he grabs her arm and shades his eyes with his other hand. This section of the film indicates that they care deeply about each other, but they are separated by political forces beyond their control. Polonius has warned Ophelia to stay away from Hamlet whom she loves. Unlike Olivier's film version which mediates this scene through Ophelia's interpretation of events, Kozintsev provides an objective account of the encounter (Kliman, *Hamlet* 99–100). Later in the nunnery scene Hamlet watches Ophelia through a grille, which alludes to Elsinore as a prison house. She reaches out to him in an effort to return his "remembrances," but he knocks a jewel from her hand. In this scene Hamlet vacillates from ire and kindness as well as from erotic interest to doubt (Dawson 190). Finally, Gertrude and Claudius are no strangers to eroticism, for they, too, engage in revelry after their marriage. There is the sound of loud music, and inside a room one sees Gertrude and Claudius in the same room in which a satyr-like dance occurs; there are exposed legs and a dirt-covered figure with a bull's head, and a man carrying a girl. When Claudius looks at Gertrude, he signals his erotic desire. Through a doorway one can see satyrs and women dancing in a circle, and Claudius turns to Gertrude, once more clearly signaling his erotic desire (Kliman, *Hamlet* 99). Although one thinks of the political implications of this film for Russia, an unmistakable eroticism is present in spite of the image of oppression embodied in the portcullis under which Hamlet rides as he enters the castle at Elsinore (Taylor, "Films" 184).

Franco Zeffirelli's film version of *Hamlet* in 1990 offers yet another highly eroticized interpretation. Here Zeffirelli employed Mel Gibson and Glenn Close to play the roles of Hamlet and Gertrude respectively. In this film version of

Hamlet, Zeffirelli seems to have made a Freudian interpretation for the 1990s. Before meeting Hamlet, Gertrude gives Claudius a passionate kiss while he is atop horseback as Hamlet watches them. Here Gertrude and Claudius enter a darkened room in which Hamlet makes a feeble joke about being too much in the sun and agrees to remain in Elsinore rather than return to Wittenberg. Thus, the scene ends as it began with a kiss; this time Gertrude kisses Hamlet on his eyes and mouth, but this action also subtly suggests incestuous overtones in their mother-son relationship (Dawson 197 and 199).

In the scene involving "The Murder of Gonzago," as a change of routine, there are transposed lines from the nunnery scene in which Hamlet kisses Ophelia aggressively, for in this film version by Franco Zeffirelli, Ophelia now begins to show her madness, which becomes fully developed after the death of her father. She sexually accosts a guard with her hands that are like claws as she sings bawdy songs. Departing the scene, she kisses Gertrude's hands. After all, hands are very important in Zeffirelli's films as an indication of disintegration and reintegration of the self (Dawson 204–5).

In the closet scene, Gertrude and Hamlet meet in a highly erotic fashion. Gertrude is obviously very angry at Hamlet's upsetting Claudius with the "Mousetrap," and so she slaps him at the beginning of the scene. After Gertrude cries for help, Hamlet stabs Polonius behind the arras and shows effort in removing the sword from Polonius after which he weeps over his death. Then Hamlet pulls out the lockets with the pictures of his father and Claudius and shows them to her. In the most Freudian of interpretations, Hamlet climbs on top of her, epitomizing eros and anger by rocking and thrusting at her in a mockery of sexual intercourse. As always, Gertrude deals with any difficult situation with Hamlet as she always has: she kisses him. Suddenly, the ghost of Hamlet's father appears, and Hamlet quickly jumps off his mother. In much the same way that Olivier's experience as a child affected his interpretation of Hamlet, so too does Zeffirelli's experience of seeing his parents engaging in sexual relations when he was a child and being incapable of discerning whether pleasure or pain was experienced by his parents affects his interpretation of this erotic moment (Dawson 206 and 209).

The most significant recent film version of *Hamlet* is Kenneth Branagh's made in 1996. Set in what is 19th-century Russia with a palace that resembles a combination of Versailles's Mirror Gallery and Inigo Jones's Banqueting Hall with a blond-headed Hamlet, this film, too, has its share of eroticism with one imagined scene of Hamlet and Ophelia engaging in sexual relations. In the famous nunnery scene with its black-and-white marble floor, Hamlet speaks kindly to Ophelia until he notices that she lies to him about the whereabouts of her father. When Ophelia blushes guiltily, Hamlet angrily drags Ophelia behind him down the line of mirrored doors as he opens them and slams them shut (Crowl 135,137,140).

Unlike Zeffirelli's and Olivier's heavily Freudian interpretations, Branagh's is more in line with C.L. Barber and Richard Wheeler's interpretation that is dominated by fathers and brothers rather than mothers and sons. Consequently, Branagh does not make a great deal of the play's Oedipal undertones, and therefore, the play may have more in common with Kozintsev's politically motivated film version than Olivier's and Zeffirelli's Oedipal family romance. According to Crowl, this interpretation undermines how Branagh conflates both psychological and political concerns. Branagh possesses the ability to comprehend Hamlet's quandary: does he listen to his father or behave as a dutiful subject of Claudius? (Crowl 149,152–53). Ultimately, Hamlet learns the truth of the matter during the duel in which both he and Laertes are wounded and quickly die. Laertes's final admission of complicity with Claudius seals his fate.

While *Hamlet* is the most performed of Shakespeare's plays, *Othello* is perhaps the most contemporarily identified play in the canon because the issue of race is of such cultural significance in the 20th and 21st centuries. Just as *Othello* is one of Shakespeare's most popular plays today, so too was *Othello* immensely popular in the early modern English period; in fact, it was performed at the Banqueting House at Whitehall in 1604 for Princess Elizabeth's wedding and then later at Hampton Court in 1636. The King's Company in 1648 attempted to begin acting again. In fact, some of the younger actors were actually Royalists, and some of them fought Prince Rupert's men; later Thomas Killigrew became the manager of the King's Company, and consequently, *Othello* was included in its repertory (Vaughan, *Othello* 94–95).

Nicholas Burt happened to be the first Restoration Othello; moreover, *Othello* was performed at least three times in 1660, and again the play was revived in 1669 despite the fact that Samuel Pepys was disappointed in the performance of Michael Mohun as Iago. More importantly, Othello's nobility was emphasized given the documentation provided by the Smock Alley Promptbook. This particular promptbook dates between 1675 and 1685. The deletions that were made to *Othello* may reflect the decorum of the age to remove obsolete words and to make the text more in keeping with the language of polite society of the late 17th century (Vaughan, *Othello* 95 and 97–98).

One cannot underestimate the enormous cultural influence that *Othello* had on the production of other plays during the Restoration. The Duke's Players decided to perform Thomas Porter's *The Villain* in 1662 which imitated *Othello*. In many ways *The Villain* concerns two men having to choose between love and honor set within a military context. This play was actually performed by some former army officers who were in Charles II's army, and so there was a set of heroic behaviors that constituted a code of honor. Therefore, the importance given to the idealized hero occurred at the same time in the 1670s as audiences' interest in plays that focused upon the villain, which was manifested in Henry Nevil's *The Fatal Jealousie* in 1673. In this dramatic situation at least the villain has a credible reason for which to exact revenge against the hero because Don Sancho was once a man of nobility who was the vice admiral of Spain until he was disgraced, and then he became angry and wreaked havoc on the seas because of how the court had treated him (Vaughan, *Othello* 101, 103–4).

The Villain, unlike *The Fatal Jealousie*, is not about military concerns. Hume described it as a "pathetic tragedy" in which Caelia, like Desdemona, expires in bed after she has been stabbed to death by her jealous husband after he finds Antonio, a servant, in Caelia's chamber. In this play, Caelia dies innocently, having been a victim of trickery and jealousy. Caelia's death aroused the audience's feeling of pathos just as Desdemona's must have. This image of a young maiden's innocence destroyed is epitomized in Nicholas Rowe's frontispiece of his 1709 edition of *Othello* in which Desdemona lies in a four-poster bed with curtains opened to show her dead with her right breast exposed after an especially violent struggle with Othello, who still holds the pillow with which he smothered her in his right hand as he raises his left in a very dramatic gesture. This image represents a conflation of eros and thanatos or, in other words, an eroticized death (Vaughan, *Othello* 109–11).

The Delaval *Othello* in 1751 brought with it the flair that only an aristocratic amateur production could. Sir Francis Blake Delaval, the heir of Northumberland's Seaton Hall, put on a production of *Othello* in order to demonstrate his social position and wealth but also to evince his appreciation of Shakespeare's plays. Desdemona was to deliver the epilogue in which she alluded to the heroine's "chastity, unblemish'd and unbridl'd"; interestingly, Delaval's mistress played the role of Emilia, a role that was an ironic commentary on the concept of chastity. Finally, this production of *Othello* indicated that while Shakespeare's plays were highly prized, they were also used to represent the cultural values and beliefs of the time (Vaughan, *Othello* 125–27 and 133–34).

To be sure, every age interprets a Shakespearean play in the fashion that it wishes in order to reflect its own culture's concerns; for example, at the beginning of the 19th century, Othello no longer wore an army officer's uniform but a costume reflecting the customs of the country from whence he originated. At the same time at the beginning of the 19th century, a shift occurred in the importance of the role of Iago, for the actor playing Iago would switch roles with the actor playing the role of Othello. William Charles Macready, who was an actor–stage manager of the early 19th century in England, may have been the first to switch roles with Charles Young who was playing Iago. Macready may have once planned to have changed roles with Edmund Kean, but Kean enjoyed the role too much to alternate roles with him (Vaughan, *Othello* 135; Potter 77–78).

Interestingly enough, Macready was not an outstanding Othello, but he held a demanding rehearsal practice. Helen Faucit Martin, who played Desdemona, said that rehearsals began at 10:00 A.M. and did not end until 3:00 or 4:00 P.M. As far as Othello's relationship to Desdemona was concerned, John Foster wrote that Othello thought of his love for Desdemona "as that grand principle of virtue, tenderness, and affectionate admiration of beauty and good into which all the hopes and habits of an active life at length settled down, and which is to carry him happily and calmly and with a tranquil mind through the 'vale of years'" (Vaughan, *Othello* 136–37).

The eroticism of the early Victorian period was defined by imagery and the color of a character's clothing. The image of a scenic drawing in a promptbook of a performance at Covent Garden designed for William Macready in which the bedchamber is set at the back of the stage with curtains has an erotic significance not unlike those in the bedchamber of Gertrude in Olivier's *Hamlet*. In this scene there are three sets of colorful curtains that draw the viewer's gaze to the bed.

Ironically, the entire set is colored in yellow, blue, and pink despite the horrific nature of the crime that Othello commits in this room. In most instances the colors of one's clothes indicate one's social status. For example, in Macready's production in London in 1837, Desdemona's white lace signifies her innocence, and Emilia's black and red underskirt hints at her pragmatic qualities (Vaughan 142 and 145).

In terms of sexual language, Macready's version of the play also exercised the deletion of expressions deemed too risqué for the Victorian period. For example, in the scene outside Brabantio's window in which Iago and Roderigo shout insulting remarks about Desdemona, the allusion to the double-backed beast is expunged because of its graphic erotic nature as a vulgar expression for sexual intercourse. Iago also does not make the bawdy comment at the dock about wives' erotic practices in bed; moreover, references to "strumpet" and "whore" were deleted. In sum, all erotically charged language was removed from the play-text in order not to offend Victorian cultural sensibilities. Finally, one must remember that Othello's dignity was in keeping with the Victorians' sense of both masculinity and honor at the same time. Desdemona epitomized the age's notion of what became feminine innocence and beauty (Vaughan, *Othello* 146–47 and 157).

British actors did not reign supreme during the 19th century, for there was one Italian actor by the name of Tommaso Salvini who gained international celebrity as a performer of Othello and began his performances in Italy in 1856, later performing in the United States in 1874 and in Britain in 1875 (Potter 41). Salvini kissed and hugged Desdemona as this was the way that Italian men expressed affection for their wives, and it is also important to note Salvini depended upon gestures rather than speech to indicate his feelings for Desdemona. William Winter, a theatre critic of his time, of course, took such behavior as an expression of sensuality while Salvini, on the other hand, thought no such thing. Nonetheless, Salvini's expressions of affection for Desdemona must have been too demonstrative for a Victorian audience (Vaughan, *Othello* 170–71). Lastly, one must keep in mind that there were differing responses to Othello's expressions of affection. What one Shakespearean actor thought was an acceptable expression of marital love and affection within the cultural mores of the time was perceived by a newspaper critic as risqué behavior (Potter 41).

Just as there were deletions in Macready's 1839 text, so too were there deletions in Henry Irving's of 1881, which epitomized high Victorianism. Irving represented Othello as an honorable man undermined by a duplicitous villain rather than a solitary man who embodied the ideals of heroism and gallantry (Vaughan, *Othello* 173). In keeping with the decorum of the day, all of Iago's sexually suggestive comments were cut from the play-text; nonetheless, Iago's hostility toward women is quite apparent (Vaughan, *Othello* 176). Yet when Desdemona is overcome by Othello's denunciation of her, she seeks consolation from Iago who seems to have given it; Ellen Terry, who played Desdemona, was later criticized for throwing her head upon Iago's chest and being receptive to his embraces and comfort (Vaughan, *Othello* 178).

The disapproval that Ellen Terry garnered from her performance of Desdemona with Iago was inconsequential by comparison to the uproar that occasioned the performance of Peggy Ashcroft alongside Paul Robeson, an African American actor, when they performed at the Savoy Theatre in London in 1930. As provocative as this production was in casting an African American as Othello, the Savoy Theatre actually lost money despite the fact that the production made theatre history (Vaughan, *Othello* 182). Ashcroft was quite interested in the role because even then Robeson was an important cultural figure (Potter 119). To be sure, the actors felt uncertain about interracial casting even in sophisticated London. Later Ashcroft was taken aback by the angry letters she received for playing Desdemona opposite Robeson as she had never experienced racism, for both she and Sybil Thorndike received angry, hateful letters from people who were profoundly offended by the interracial casting (Vaughan, *Othello* 183).

The fact that Robeson kissed Ashcroft was considered scandalous; in fact, the theatre viewer with the initials H. S. writing for the *Express* actually counted the number of times that Robeson kissed Ashcroft before and after Othello killed her. While the theatregoing public may have been surprised and even shocked by the physical interaction between Othello and Desdemona, the reviewers were generally laudatory commending Ashcroft and Sybil Thorndike, but apparently, they had mixed feelings about Robeson and believed that the production had been poorly conceptualized. Ellen Van Volkenburg attempted to create an Expressionistic production. The sets, for example, were very heavy to move, and so the "willow scene" was made almost inaudible by the noise created behind it (Potter 120). Although the bed is very austere, it is extremely large, almost overwhelming in its magnitude with the valance towering over the occupants of the bed. In fact, the bed was placed at the back of the stage so that the audience would not see Othello smother Desdemona with a pillow. Ironically, while the production carefully tried to have the audience not see the murder of Desdemona, both the actors who played Iago, Maurice Browne and Van Volkenburg, were gay, and they argued that Iago behaves as he does because he has fallen in love with Othello, but Browne gave Robeson direction regarding this interpretation of the play, and the reviewers thought so too. Recent queer readings of *Othello* have suggested that Iago has a homosexual attraction to Othello; however, theatregoers would have considered that quite a radical interpretation of Iago's character in 1930 (Vaughan, *Othello* 185 and 190–91).

While the 1930 production was in many ways experimental because of the interracial casting as well as Browne and Volkenburg's homosexual identification of Iago, the 1942 and 1943 productions were successful, according to its director, Margaret Webster, partially because of their timing and its locations. Instead of a commercial venue such as the Savoy Theatre, *Othello* opened at Brattle Theatre near Harvard University and was overwhelmingly successful, and then later it opened in Princeton, New Jersey, where again it was extremely successful. Finally, *Othello* opened on Broadway on October 19, 1943, and it ran for 296 performances under the auspices of the Theatre Guild (Vaughan, *Othello* 193).

In many ways Paul Robeson was the consummate Othello of his age in the same way Orson Welles may well have been one of the finest film auteurs of his. Welles is best remembered for his eccentric and experimental interpretations. In his film version of *Othello*, most significantly, Welles focused on the relationship

Paul Robeson and actress Mary Ure as shown in their final rehearsal for *Othello* at Stratford-upon-Avon, England, April 5, 1959. AP Photo.

between Othello and Iago in which Desdemona functioned largely as a means of exchange between men. Desdemona is first seen as such in the scene in which Brabantio confronts Othello in the Duke's council chamber. Throughout the film Welles is fixated on the female body and makes a fetish of it through his patriarchal gaze, which dominates the film (Vaughan 199–200).

What is strange is that the male-dominated camaraderie extended into the real-life interactions among Welles, Micheál MacLiammoir, who played Iago, and Hilton Edwards, who played Brabantio, for MacLiammoir and Edwards were lovers. Welles thought highly of Edwards, and despite the fact that Welles was sexually attracted to women, MacLiammoir was jealous of their friendship. Moreover, Vaughan astutely suggests that in the meeting of human existence and artistic creation, MacLiammoir as Iago provided an additional edginess, focusing upon the same-sex dynamics of Iago's motivation for his behaving as he did, which many reviewers have perceived as integral to Shakespeare's play (202–3).

Welles suggested that MacLiammoir play the role of Iago as impotent. Vaughan refers to MacLiammoir's extraordinary diary, *Put Money in Thy Purse: The Filming of Orson Welles's Othello*, in which he records Welles's perceptions of Iago. Apparently, at dinner one evening, Welles, who enjoyed eating a great deal as shown by his girth, exclaimed that Iago should be impotent: " 'Impotent,' he roared in (surely somewhat forced) rich baritone, 'that's why he hates life so much—they always do,' continued he (voice by this time way down in boots). He then gobbled up some sturgeon, ordered some more and went on to talk about the costumes, which were to be made in Rome" (MacLiammoir 26). Potter suggests that Welles was calling his virility into question because he knew of his relationship with Edwards, but apparently MacLiammoir challenged that presumption by making a practice of seducing policemen in Mogador (143).

Male bonding that occurred among Welles, Edwards, and MacLiammoir while they drank late at night effectively excluded Suzanne Cloutier, who was chosen to play the role of Desdemona because of her appearance, from their masculine world in much the same way as did their interaction in the actual film. In fact, her voice was dubbed, and her body was even doubled at some points in the film by other women actors (Potter 142). All of this exchange of female voices and bodies reinforced Welles's and MacLiammoir's belief that the ideal Desdemona was a composite of many qualities that she needed to possess (Vaughan, *Othello* 205). Welles very much fixates on Desdemona's hair. In fact, Suzanne Cloutier's hair was dyed so that it would have a lustrous quality about it, on which the camera's eye focused a great deal; in fact, Othello eroticizes Desdemona's body throughout the film just as Iago directs his homoerotic gaze toward Othello (Vaughan, *Othello* 207–8). While Welles's production of *Othello* in the 1950s seemed idiosyncratic with his massive excisions and editing not to mention the sexual subtext, today almost every later film version of *Othello* depicts a flashback of Othello and Desdemona's wedding (Potter 146). To be sure, Welles's film version of *Othello* remains an auteur's masterpiece which both film and Shakespeare scholars will continue to view with amazement and awe because of its cinematography and provocative interpretation.

Olivier's 1964 film version of *Othello* arrived at an extremely interesting time politically speaking in terms of race relations in America and Africa, for in Africa, it was a time of decolonization, and in America it was the time of the great civil rights movement in which many rights were accorded blacks that had hitherto been denied; secondly, on artistic and political levels the negritude movement and the Black Power philosophies reflected the social strains and struggles of this era (Neill 62). Hence, this production of *Othello* produced by Stuart Burge raised questions about the appropriateness of Laurence Olivier playing Othello. On film the camera did not blink at the theatricality of Olivier's African/Caribbean gestures and the embarrassing smudge of blackface grease on Maggie Smith's cheek as Desdemona (Neill 59 and 62).

As the decades passed, productions of *Othello* became increasingly ideologically driven. Surely, Janet Suzman's production came at a time of great political upheaval in 1988 when she directed *Othello* at the Market Theatre in Johannesburg, South Africa, during the waning years of apartheid, which was the segregation of Africans from whites, very much like it was in the Deep South

American actor Orson Welles is shown with French actress Suzanne Cloutier in a scene from the film version of Shakespeare's *Othello*. He plays the title role; she plays Desdemona. AP Photo.

in America until integration occurred. Suzman's decision to stage *Othello* was particularly brave because apartheid would not end for another three years. At the same time, Martin Orkin published *Shakespeare against Apartheid*, and it was profoundly ironic that *Othello* was not taught in South African schools during this time. To be sure, the relevance would have been all too blatant. Interestingly, having a black man perform the role of Othello would not have been considered a politically charged decision in most countries, but in South Africa the decision to cast a black in this role would have carried an ideological valence that it would not otherwise have elsewhere (Potter 176).

Suzman decided to film the play within a six-day time frame. Since Suzman perceived all of the characters in terms of their outlook on ethnicity, Richard Haines's portrayal of Iago was based upon Eugene Terreblanche's vicious intensity (Potter 176–77). This particular Iago focuses upon the animalistic qualities of the Moor by placing his fingers in inappropriate orifices such as his nostrils, and Othello's sexuality is parodied as he compares Othello to an ass as he mimics the sounds that it would make and waves an imaginary phallus about him. Asses were supposedly known for the enormity of their phallic endowment just as African men were stereotypically perceived within white society as sharing the same quality. Within the cultural context of South Africa in the late 1980s, one must remember that interracial sexual relations were still a criminal offense (Potter 177–78).

The use of violence is extreme in this film version of *Othello*. In the aftermath of the scene in which Cassio has been injured in his fight with Roderigo, Iago's thugs circle about Bianca, grab her, viciously pull back the top of her dress to reveal her breasts, and ultimately, carry her off camera to be gang-raped. This is by far the most violent version of this scene on film. Bianca's horror at being carried off by these thugs and rapists is very palpable, and watching this scene is extremely chilling and discomforting for any remotely decent human being. Suzman believes Othello alternates between insanity and self-pity because of his sexual jealousy until he is finally compelled to murder Desdemona (Program note 10). Sexual violence also occurs after Othello has learned that Iago has lied to him, and so Othello does what would be most psychologically and physically disturbing to Iago: he stabs Iago in the groin. For Suzman, this act of violence is unmistakable, for "Othello castrates Iago and then kills himself in grief" (Program note 10). In many ways this is a very telling response on the part of Othello. Just as Othello will never be able to produce an heir no longer having his wife, neither will Iago as he is now a eunuch. It is the first time in the entire film that Iago shows any pain. This sexual attack on Iago is in keeping with the heightened level of sexuality and eroticism that occurs throughout the film. This film in many ways is such a timely interpretation of this play with the intertwining of racism and sexual violence.

The Trevor Nunn film version of *Othello* in1990 continues to stress gender relations. The women's dialogue is not cut, and all of the human relations are fraught with problems because of society's male-dominated power structure. Nunn does not hesitate to show men's fear of female sexuality (Vaughan, *Othello* 219). At the same time, Othello and Desdemona were not shy about showing their affection for each other when they met on the dock upon first reaching Cyprus. While on the dock, Othello places Desdemona on a box and moves around her, and then she leaps into his arms. She blatantly refuses to be the Petrarchan lady on the pedestal. Apparently, Emilia makes a disapproving expression on her face at this point in the conversation (Potter 190).

Sexuality runs to the homoerotic in this film version as it has in other productions of this play. For example, throughout the play the promptbook indicates that Iago should "cuddle" different male characters. Iago is directed to run his hands through Roderigo's hair at the end of the first act, and in the third scene of Act II, Iago holds Cassio's head when he vomits and later sees him to bed; he even "cuddles" Roderigo after he has been injured in his fight with Cassio. In a moment of heteroerotic pleasure, Iago even holds Desdemona's hands and "cuddles" her when she is upset after Othello denounces her as a prostitute (Vaughan, *Othello* 224). Potter suggests that these outward and visible signs of affection are insincere, but she also notes the intense male-male bonding that occurs when Iago vows his undying loyalty to Othello in a marriage-like exchange of devotion (Potter 192). Vaughan makes an extremely astute comment by recognizing the significance of male bonding in this film. This film asserts that male bonding is more intense than any other relationship. Because of women's roles in society, they are perforce kept out of the barracks and off the battlefield (Vaughan, *Othello* 226).

The final version of *Othello* to be considered is the 1995 Oliver Parker film version in which Laurence Fishburne played Othello, Irene Jacob played Desdemona, and Kenneth Branagh played Iago. Unlike other film versions of *Othello*, the voyeuristic eroticism of the camera's eye leaves no doubt as to whether Othello and Desdemona consummated their relationship. Kenneth Rothwell is convinced that the filming of Othello and Desdemona answers the question as to whether they engage in sexual relations as Othello takes off his leather belt, and Desdemona suggestively takes off her dress in a long shot (236–37).

To be sure, this film version of *Othello* abounds in heterosexist fantasies of Othello and Desdemona's erotic relationship in addition to those that Othello has of Cassio with Desdemona, for this film version provides visual representation of these fantasies. However, in this version, after Othello has experienced the purported illusion, he still sees them in bed. The camera's eye even lets us see assorted parts of Desdemona and Cassio's bodies, allowing viewers to concretize the physicality of their sexual congress (Potter 194).

In fact, as far as sexuality is concerned regarding Parker's interpretation of *Othello*, Rothwell believes that Parker is more concerned with interpreting *Othello* than in engaging in cinematic rhetoric. Parker has no interest in the trendy fashion of an erotic connection between Othello and Iago (237). This is an interesting assertion given the fact that as early as 1930 Maurice Browne and Ellen Van Volkenburg had encouraged Paul Robeson to insinuate that a homoerotic relationship existed between him and Iago (Vaughan, *Othello* 190). Potter seems to challenge Rothwell's perception of hegemonic heterosexuality in this film version of *Othello* as she argues that Iago and Roderigo's being together under a wagon appears to stir up questions about their relationship (Potter 195). Neither Potter nor Rothwell notices that as Iago speaks to Roderigo underneath the wagon explaining how Desdemona will eventually tire of Othello, Iago slowly but surely moves his hand ineluctably between Roderigo's legs until it presumably reaches Roderigo's genitals, for Roderigo would have no reason otherwise to jerk inexplicably away from Iago. Iago's homoerotic proclivity does not preclude his sexual interaction with Emilia. Potter asserts, "Anna Patrick leaves no doubt to the character's sexual frustration when she invades her husband's bed, bringing the handkerchief with her as a bribe. Iago seems to be about to give her what she wants, then brutally turns her over and mimes sodomizing her" (195). In other words, even Iago's sexual interaction with Emilia takes on a sodomitical eroticism in which he would otherwise engage Othello if he were of a homosexual orientation. Finally, whatever one wishes to make of this interpretation of *Othello*, it is fraught with sexual angst of both a hetero- and homoerotic nature.

Turning from *Othello* to *The Tempest*, Shakespeare's romance with its own Prince Charming in the figure of Ferdinand and heroine in the figure of Miranda, one realizes that this play engaged not only the masses but also the royalty of its day because the Revels Accounts record the play as having been performed at Whitehall, specifically the Banqueting Hall instead of the Cockpit in December 1611 for three days. In fact, sometimes literary scholars have perceived a link between James I and Prospero (Orgel 3–4).

If the topicality of actual historical events is to be perceived as playing a role in *The Tempest*, one needs to go no further than William Strachey's "True Reportory of the Wracke, and Redemption of Sir Thomas Gates" in Bermuda in July 1609. Strachey had actually been on board the *Sea Venture*, the fleet's flagship under the command of Admiral George Somers, when a hurricane separated the fleet, destroyed one vessel, and ran the *Sea Venture* aground on the rocky coast of Bermuda, to which Ariel refers in I.ii.229 as "the still-vexed Bermudas." Needless to say, those whose ship washed ashore apparently enjoyed themselves on the island, and finally, they constructed two other vessels by which they made their way to Virginia where Gates gained passage for England and arrived there in early September 1610 with Strachey's manuscript. Interestingly, this account of the shipwreck did not see print until 1625 in Samuel Purchas's *Hakluytus Posthumus; or, Purchas His Pilgrimes*, and it may well have been consumed by many of London's political and cultural elite. As luck would have, it, Shakespeare was acquainted with members of the Virginia Company of London, and so he may very well have read Strachey's manuscript while it was in circulation as this was a popular means of receiving responses from one's prospective audience during the late 16th and 17th centuries (Vaughan and Vaughan, *The Tempest* 41–42).

Sadly, when *The Tempest* did reappear on the London stage after the Restoration, it was quite different from its former incarnation by William Shakespeare. Just as Nahum Tate saw fit to rewrite *King Lear*, so too did William Davenant and John Dryden see fit to radically reconstruct *The Tempest* so much so that they even added characters. When their rendition of the play found its way into print in 1670, even its title had been changed to *The Enchanted Island* only to be made into an opera seven years later by Thomas Shadwell. In *The Enchanted Island*, Prospero has a second daughter, Dorinda, and an adopted son Hippolito, the duke of Mantua. Since there has been a prophecy that a woman will undermine Hippolito's success in life, Prospero hides him on the island where Miranda and Dorinda cannot have access to him. Analogously, Caliban has a twin sister by the name of Sycorax, and Trinculo, who is the boatswain, and Stephano, the ship's master, compete for Sycorax, and they quarrel about who will hold the positions of duke and viceroy. They, of course, are unfit to rule because of their inebriated states (Vaughan and Vaughan, *The Tempest* 76–77).

Shadwell decided to use Davenant and Dryden's version of *The Tempest* and add yet more songs and more extravagant scenery to it. The dramatic work took on operatic proportions with the storm at sea accompanied by music. In fact, the frontispiece of Nicholas Rowe's 1709 edition of the play provides a highly theatrical interpretation with waves crashing over the sides of the ship while winged demons fly above the vessel, and then on shore a small figure appears with what seems to be a wand. This figure is Prospero, who has conjured up the storm in order to affect the changes that he desires. Apparently, once the storm comes to an end, the characters appear on two quite different areas of the island. The location on which the members are situated is quite elegant with cypress trees while Caliban, Trinculo, and Stephano find themselves on a desolate part of the island where they have no such pleasant scenery. Again, the distinctions between members of the classes are maintained, which were surely violated in Thomas Durffett's version, *The Mock Tempest*. After Prospero has joined Dorinda and Hippolito and Miranda with Quakero, otherwise known as Ferdinand, there is a Chorus of a procurer and prostitutes, clearly an incongruous juxtaposition (Vaughan and Vaughan, *The Tempest* 80–82).

Finally, in 1746, James Lacy's production in Drury Lane attempted to present the play as it had been written despite the masque of Neptune and Amphitrite in the fifth act. Although *The Tempest* was largely intact, it ran for only six performances, which prompted Garrick to return the operatic version to the stage the next year. Almost ten years later, Garrick introduced yet another operatic version of the play. This time John Christopher Smith wrote the music for it. Although Smith deleted Davenant's changes, he retained only the barest elements of the play's plot. Happily, in 1757, Garrick presented *The Tempest* largely as Shakespeare wrote it despite the excisions of some 400 lines, half of which came from II.i., and so the play remained in this truncated state until Garrick finally retired from the stage in 1776 (Orgel 67).

With the arrival of Sheridan the following year, productions of *The Tempest* yet again contained the masque of Neptune and Amphitrite, and he was roundly chastised for doing so by critics who complained that the production was reminiscent of a Christmas pantomime because of the attention given to dancing and singing. Still in the way of spectacle, mechanical devices were popular, especially the storm, which occurred at the request of latecomers who would otherwise miss it, and at the same time Londoners could watch a competing operatic version at Covent Garden from 1776 until 1779 (Orgel 68).

The Victorian period was one in which the cult of womanhood was at its height with the idealization of the young, innocent unmarried woman who was wholly unaware of the dynamics of sexual relations, which in turned functioned to keep women in their subordinate social position. Representations of maiden purity were reified in the figure of Miranda. Mary Cowden Clarke did not include Miranda in her description of *The Girlhood of Shakespeare's Heroines* (1852), and Miranda's most aggressive lines in I.ii.352–63, in which she upbraids Caliban for his lack of civility, were customarily given to Prospero because middle- and upper-class British mores deemed such language on the part of young ladies inappropriate. In fact, John Foster approved of Helena Faucit's performance of Miranda in 1838 as she embodied a chaste affection or love for Ferdinand (Vaughan and Vaughan, *The Tempest* 93).

It was inevitable that with the rise of Sigmund Freud's influence in the late 19th century that by the mid-20th century *The Tempest* would be subject to a Freudian interpretation and, hence, the significance of sexuality in the play. The figures of Ariel and Caliban were interpreted as reified representations of the superego and libido, or id, respectively. Caliban was most powerfully represented as the libido in the 1956 science-fiction film *Forbidden Planet,* which was destined to become a cult classic of late-night television viewing; in this futuristic rendering of *The Tempest,* Ariel becomes Robby, the robot, and Miranda becomes Altaira while Prospero becomes Professor Morbius, whose name implies death. Morbius's own psyche, which is filled with repressed anger, is projected onto an electromagnetic field and consequently causes the destruction of his spaceship and the deaths of several of his crew members. Given Morbius's jealousy of his daughter, naturally a display of his pent-up anger was an eventuality. Finally, only through the destruction of Prospero is this barbaric force quelled (Vaughan and Vaughan, *The Tempest* 109–10).

Freudian readings were transferred to the stage as well. In 1981, Gerald Freedman asserted in the play's program notes that he considered Caliban and Ariel as aspects of Prospero's psyche. Caliban, of course, epitomized Prospero's libidinous impulses, and so the disparate qualities of Prospero's psyche were visually realized on the stage by the ethnicities and costumes of Ariel and Caliban whose roles were performed respectively by a white actor dressed in a silver costume and a black actor dressed in a brown costume (Vaughan and Vaughan, *The Tempest* 115).

A similar psychological model was at play in Ron Daniel's 1982 production in which Mark Rylance's interpretation of Ariel resulted in his having punk-styled hair and an iridescent-colored bodysuit while Caliban was attired in no more than a loin cloth with the dreadlocks of a Rastafarian, once again reinforcing the imagery of diametrically opposed forces. Finally, perhaps the most effective use of the Freudian psychoanalytic model was Peter Brook's 1968 version in London in which Sycorax was performed by a huge woman who was able to enlarge her face and body, and so at one point in the production, she gives a violent yell and so gives birth to Caliban who makes his way into the world with a black sweater over his head. In this production of the play, unlike traditional productions, Caliban is capable of seizing power and actually capturing Prospero and assaulting him in what appears to be homosexual rape. Fortunately, Ariel comes to the rescue and is able to distract the demonic beings with the same kind of frippery that distracts Stephano and Trinculo despite Caliban's warnings to leave the tawdry clothes alone (Vaughan and Vaughan, *The Tempest* 115–16).

Without a doubt Derek Jarman's 1979 queer punk version of *The Tempest* is one of the most radical interpretations to date, and it was *not* well received when Vincent Canby reviewed it in the *New York Times*. Kenneth Rothwell seems to hold the same opinion as Canby, for Rothwell vehemently asserts that Jarman did not let prescribed conventions of refinement keep him from looking for a new kind of cinema with a gay punk cultural sensibility to challenge the status quo. Rothwell also says that Jarman was like Oscar Wilde in that he was more concerned about aesthetics than with an occasional interest in leftist politics concerning the condition of mistreated workers (Rothwell 204). Happily, times have changed since Canby's review, and Jarman's films enjoy ever greater acclaim as demonstrated through discussion of them at academic conferences, articles about them in professional journals, and finally, in-depth analysis of them in often well-illustrated books of film criticism.

Most critics were offended by the overt eroticism and nudity of Jarman's film version, especially the homoeroticism that abounds in his version of this play. Two scholars note that Ferdinand emerges from the sea wearing nothing, holding his sword in his hand. Rothwell asserts that Jarman deliberately includes nudity in his films in order to affront or shock the Western European middle-class's sensibility, and he notes that Ferdinand, played by David Meyer, who had also performed the roles of Hamlet and Lysander in Celestino Coronando's films, is shown in a "modestly remote long shot" (206). David Hawkes suggests how the camera's gaze spends more time fixed upon Ferdinand's naked body than conventional cinematography would (108). Another critic describes Ferdinand's walk to the room in Prospero's manor as one during which he moves as quickly as he can while he is stooped over, finally locating a warm room with a blazing fire. The implication is that the element of fire draws Ferdinand to this room, not the magical music of the island (Buchanan 161). Later in the film when Prospero meets Ferdinand, Ferdinand is shown naked, sitting helpless in straw into which he has curled for warmth, as Prospero uses his sword to flick straw at him as he cowers, and Ariel stands there laughing at Ferdinand's plight. Rothwell goes so far as to suggest that this depiction of Ferdinand is representative of "Jarman's sado-masochistic fantasies of the martyrdom of St. Sebastian" (206), who incidentally is a gay icon.

Figures of gay males are quite prevalent in this film version of the play. Ariel is clearly a figure of a feminized gay male, who is shown naked in a flashback when Sycorax was in charge of the island as she pulls Ariel to her by means of a chain around his neck (Vaughan and Vaughan, *The Tempest* 118). In this flashback a full-grown Caliban appears nursing at Sycorax's breast, both figures of grotesquerie. Once again, Rothwell asserts that this disgusting scene has been rationalized as aesthetically legitimate (206). If this scene has any serious function, it reminds the audience of Sycorax's "earthy and abhorred commands" (I.ii.273) that Ariel refused to perform, and for that reason she confined him within a cloven pine from which Prospero was able to extricate him with his own most potent magic. Caliban is represented as an older effeminate gay male who intrudes upon Miranda while she is bathing, but he poses no sexual threat, for he is a parodic incarnation of a lecherous man (Vaughan and Vaughan, *The Tempest* 118). When he barges into the room while she is in a washtub, she throws a sponge at him, and he quickly leaves the room as she laughs at the ridiculousness of his intrusion. Here Caliban is an absurd annoyance rather than a sexual predator.

Even Caliban's interaction with Trinculo and Stephano takes on a campy quality, for Trinculo is shown riding Caliban's back through the halls of the manor while Stephano trails behind him histrionically exclaiming, "Monster, monster," because he is intoxicated. Later both Trinculo and Stephano find a room filled with frippery and wear it; Trinculo disrobes, dons a woman's clothes and hat, and even applies makeup. They appear as figures of fun rather than posing any serious conspiratorial threat to Prospero's well-being. The hilarity of Trinculo's cross-dressed state reaches its zenith when Caliban, Stephano, and he barge into the ballroom at the end of the play after Prospero has forgiven his evil brother

Antonio and Alonso, the King of Naples, and his brother Sebastian, who was easily convinced to kill Alonso. Trinculo appears in full drag, denying his sexual identity all the while wearing a transparent dress which leaves no doubt of his true sex. Perhaps the most amusing moment comes shortly before the transvestite appearance of Trinculo when sailors dance in a circle in increasing intensity to the sounds of a lute which culminates in their jumping into each other's arms at its conclusion. This is, by far, one of the campiest moments in the film, but the film ends in an abrupt fashion.

Given the emphasis of the homoerotic element in Jarman's film version of the play, it should come as little surprise that the romance of Ferdinand and Miranda is underplayed; they are shown decorously sitting on a couch or playing badminton indoors, and so they restrain themselves from sexual activity despite Miranda's free-spirited appearance and attitude. Their celebratory moment comes at the end of the play when Elisabeth Welch appears as a goddess instead of Juno, Iris, and Ceres, and sings "Stormy Weather," a meta-dramatically brilliant touch reflecting upon the title of the play as well as all of the trials and tribulations that this cast of characters had undergone before the play's felicitous end.

WORKS CITED

As You Like It. Dir. Kenneth Branagh. HBO Films, 2007. DVD.

Barnet, Sylvan. *Henry IV, Part One*. "*Henry IV, Part One* on Stage and Screen." Signet Shakespeare Classic. Ed. Maynard Mack. New York and London: Signet, 1998. 232–45. Print.

Bevington, David. *Henry IV, Part One*. By William Shakespeare. The Oxford Shakespeare. Oxford: Oxford UP, 1998. Print.

Brissenden, Alan, ed. *As You Like It*. By William Shakespeare. The Oxford Shakespeare. Oxford: Oxford UP, 1998. Print.

Buchanan, Judith. *Shakespeare on Film*. London and New York: Pearson Longman, 2005. Print.

Buhler, Stephen. "Textual and Sexual Anxieties in Michael Hoffman's Film of *A Midsummer Night's Dream*." *Shakespeare Bulletin* 22.3 (2009) : 49-64. Print.

Bulman, James C. "Bringing Cheek by Jowl's *As You Like It* out of the Closet: The Politics of Gay Theater." *Shakespeare Bulletin* 22.3 (2004): 31–46. Print.

Calarco, Joe. *Shakespeare's R &J*. New York: Dramatists Play Service, 1999. Print.

Cartmell, Deborah. *Interpreting Shakespeare on Screen*. New York: St. Martin's Press, 2000. Print.

Charlebois, Elizabeth. *The Taming of the Shrew*. *Shakespeare Bulletin* 22.2 (2004): 108–11. Print.

Collins, Jane. *A Midsummer Night's Dream*. *Shakespeare Bulletin* 22. (2004): 117–19.Print.

Cox, John F., ed. *Much Ado about Nothing*. By William Shakespeare. Shakespeare in Production. Cambridge: Cambridge UP, 1997. Print.

Crowl, Samuel. *Shakespeare and the Cineplex: The Kenneth Branagh Era*. Athens: Ohio UP, 2003. Print.

Davies, Anthony. *Filming Shakespeare's Plays: The Adaptations of Laurence Olivier, Orson Welles, Peter Brook, and Akira Kurosawa*. Cambridge: Cambridge UP, 1988. Print.

Dawson, Anthony. *Hamlet*. Shakespeare in Performance. Manchester and New York: Manchester UP, 2000. Print.

Donaldson, Peter S. *Shakespeare Films/Shakespeare Directors*. Boston: Unwin Hyman, 1990. Print.

Dusinberre, Juliet, ed. *As You Like It*. By William Shakespeare. The Arden Shakespeare New York: Thomson Publishing, 2006. Print.

Falstaff. Dir. Orson Welles. 1966. Internacionale/Peppercorn Continental/Brazil. Date unavailable. DVD.

Friedman, Michael D. "The Feminist as Shrew in *10 Things I Hate about You*." *Shakespeare Bulletin*. 22.2 (2004): 45–65. Print.

Garber, Marjorie B. *Shakespeare and Modern Culture*. New York: Pantheon, 2008. Print.

Gates, Anita. "In the 19th Century, Parting Is Still Sweet Sorrow." *New York Times* 5 Feb. 1998, sec. E6. Print.

Goldberg, Jonathan. "Hal's Desire, Shakespeare's Idaho." *Henry IV, Parts One and Two*. Ed. Nigel Wood. Buckingham, UK and Philadelphia: Open UP, 1990. 35–64. Print.

Halio, Jay L. A *Midsummer Night's Dream*. Shakespeare in Performance. Manchester, UK and New York: Manchester UP, 2003. Print.

Hamlet. Dir. Kenneth Branagh. 1996. Castle Rock Entertainment, 2007. Warner Bros. Entertainment, DVD.

Hamlet. Dir. Laurence Olivier. 1948. Two Cities Film Ltd., 2000. The Criterion Collection, DVD.

Haring-Smith, Tori. *From Farce to Metadrama: A Stage History of The Taming of the Shrew 1594–1983*. Westport, CT: Greenwood Press, 1985. Print.

Hawkes, David. "'The Shadow of This Time': The Renaissance Cinema of Derek Jarman." *By Angels Driven: The Films of Derek Jarman*. Ed. Chris Leppard. Westport, CT: Praeger, 1996. Print.

Hodgdon, Barbara. "Baz Luhrmann's *William Shakespeare's Romeo + Juliet*." *Romeo and Juliet*. Ed. R. S. White. Basingstoke, UK and New York: Palgrave Macmillan, 2006. Print.

Holland, Peter. A *Midsummer Night's Dream*. By William Shakespeare. The Oxford Shakespeare. Oxford: Oxford UP, 1998. Print.

Jones, Maria. *Shakespeare's Culture in Modern Performance*. New York and Basingstoke, UK: Palgrave Macmillan, 2003. Print.

Jones, Maria. *The Taming of the Shrew. Shakespeare Bulletin* 23.1 (2005): 149–51. Print.

Kastan, David Scott, ed. *Henry IV, Part One*. By William Shakespeare. Arden Shakespeare. Oxford: Thomson, 2002. Print.

Klett, Elizabeth. *The Taming of the Shrew. The Shakespeare Bulletin*. 23.1 (2005): 149–151. Print.

Kliman, Bernice. *Hamlet: Film, Television, and Audio Performance*. London and Toronto: Fairleigh Dickinson UP/Associated Presses, 1988. Print.

Kliman, Bernice. *Much Ado about Nothing. Shakespeare Bulletin* 25. 2 (2007): 55–58. Print.

Kott, Jan. *Shakespeare Our Contemporary*. Trans. Boleslaw Taborski. New York and London: W. W. Norton, 1974. Print.

Levenson, Jill, ed. *Romeo and Juliet*. By William Shakespeare. The Oxford Shakespeare. New York and Oxford: Oxford UP, 2000. Print.

Lynch, Stephen J. *As You Like It: A Guide to the Play*. Westport, CT: Greenwood, 2003. Print.

MacLiammoir, Micheál. *Put Money in Thy Purse*. Foreword. Orson Welles. London: Columbus, 1988. Print.
Marshall, Cynthia, ed. *As You Like It*. By William Shakespeare. Shakespeare in Performance. Cambridge: Cambridge UP, 2004. Print.
McMillin, Scott. *Henry IV, Part One*. *Shakespeare in Performance*. Manchester, UK and New York: Manchester UP, 1991. Print.
A Midsummer Night's Dream. Dir. Michael Hoffman. 1999. 20th Century Fox, 2003. DVD.
A Midsummer Night's Dream. Dir. Max Reinhardt and William Dieterle. 1935. Warner Bros., 2007. Warner Home Video, DVD.
Much Ado about Nothing. Dir. A.J. Antoon with Nick Havinga. 1973. Broadway Theatre Archive, 2002. Kultur Video, DVD.
Much Ado about Nothing. Dir. Kenneth Branagh. Sony Pictures, 1993. MGM, 2003. DVD.
Neill, Michael, ed. *Othello*. By William Shakespeare. The Oxford Shakespeare. Oxford: Oxford UP, 2006. Print.
Oliver, H.J. ed. *The Taming of the Shrew*. By William Shakespeare. The Oxford Shakespeare. Oxford: Oxford UP, 1998. Print.
Orgel, Stephen, ed. *The Tempest*. By William Shakespeare. The Oxford Shakespeare. Oxford: Oxford UP, 1998. Print.
Othello. Dir. Stuart Burge. 1965. BHE Productions Ltd., 2007. Warner Bros. Entertainment, DVD.
Othello. Dir. Oliver Parker. 1995. Turner Home Entertainment, Warner Bros., 2000. DVD.
Othello. Dir. Janet Suzman. 1988. Focus Films and Channel Four UK, 2005. Arthaus Musik, DVD.
Othello. Dir. Orson Welles. 1952. Mogador/Mercury, 2003. South Korea, DVD.
Pollard, Tanya. *Much Ado about Nothing*. *Shakespeare Bulletin* 22. 2 (2004): 15–18. Print.
Potter, Lois. *Othello*. Shakespeare in Performance. Manchester, UK and New York: Manchester UP, 2002. Print.
Romeo and Juliet. Dir. George Cukor. 1936. Warner Bros, 2007. Turner Entertainment, DVD.
Romeo and Juliet. Dir. Franco Zeffirelli. 1968. Paramount Pictures, 2000. DVD.
Rothwell, Kenneth. *A History of Shakespeare on Screen: A Century of Film and Television*. Cambridge: Cambridge UP, 2001. Print.
Schafer, Elizabeth. *The Taming of the Shrew*. By William Shakespeare. Shakespeare in Production. Cambridge: Cambridge UP, 2002.
Shaltz, Justin. *The Taming of the Shrew*. *Shakespeare Bulletin* 25.1 (2004): 62–65. Print.
Shewey, Don. "Star-Crossed Lovers." *The Advocate* Mar. 1998: 53. Print.
Shteir, Rachel. "Making Juliet One of the Guys in Macho Verona." *New York Times* 14 Jun. 1998, sec. 2: 6+. Print.
The Taming of the Shrew. Dir. William Ball and Kirk Browning 1976. Broadway Theatre Archive, 2002. Kultur Video, DVD.
The Taming of the Shrew. Dir. Franco Zeffirelli. 1967 Paramount, 1999. Sony Pictures, DVD.
Taylor, Neil. "The Films of Hamlet." *Shakespeare and the Moving Image on Film and Television*. Ed. Anthony Davies and Stanley Wells. Cambridge: Cambridge UP, 1994. 180–210. Print.
Taylor, Neil, and Ann Thompson. *Hamlet*. By William Shakespeare. The Arden Shakespeare. London and New York: Thomson, 2006. Print.
The Tempest. Dir. Derek Jarman. 1979. London Films, 2000. Kino Video, DVD.
Twelfth Night. Dir. Trevor Nunn. Fine Line Pictures, 1996. Image Entertainment, 2005. DVD.

Vaughan, Virginia Mason. *Othello: A Contextual History*. Cambridge: Cambridge UP, 1996. Print.

Vaughan, Virginia Mason, and Alden T. Vaughan, eds. *The Tempest*. The Arden Shakespeare. Oxford: Thomson, 1999. Print.

Wilson, Robert F., Jr. "Star-Crossed Generations: Three Film Versions of *Romeo and Juliet*." *Approaches to Teaching Shakespeare's Romeo and Juliet*. Ed. Maurice Hunt. New York: MLA, 2000. Print.

Zitner, Sheldon. *Much Ado about Nothing*. By William Shakespeare. The Oxford Shakespeare. Oxford UP,1994. Print.

5

SCHOLARSHIP AND CRITICISM

Shakespeare's plays have been interpreted from a multiplicity of critical and theoretical perspectives. This chapter will provide an overview of largely feminist and New Historicist interpretations of Shakespeare's plays as these more recent interpretative paradigms have been enormously successful in elucidating the power dynamics concerning gender issues. The essays included in this chapter were chosen because of their authors' significant contributions to early modern English literary studies; in many ways these essays have reconceptualized our understanding of early modern English texts, and their influence continues to make their presence known in graduate and upper-division English courses. This chapter will largely follow the chronological order of the plays as they were discussed in the previous chapters. Finally, one must not underestimate the extraordinary impact of feminist criticism not only upon Shakespeare's plays and poems and English and American literature but also upon disciplines as disparate as history and art history as well as the social sciences, including political science, anthropology, sociology, and psychology; moreover, Shakespeare's comedies in particular lend themselves to especially productive and insightful interpretations because of feminist and New Historicist criticism.

Before one may discuss a Shakespearean play from a New Historicist perspective, one must appreciate its intellectual origins and how New Historicists perceive Shakespearean texts. Lisa Hopkins does an admirable job of articulating the rudimentary principles of New Historicism in *Beginning Shakespeare*, for she states:

> For New Historicists, what matters is not whether Shakespeare is definitely known to have read some thing or not, which is a sine qua non of source study, but whether a given idea is 'circulating' in a particular culture at a particular time. So New Historicists study not just Shakespeare but other texts of the period—the more obscure and unusual the better—and read the two together without worrying about whether Shakespeare knew of them directly or not, or indeed without even worrying about whether they were actually written before or after the Shakespearean text on which they are being brought to bear. For New Historicism, Shakespeare is above all a

> product of his culture, and he is, moreover, merely one voice amongst many which we can hear speaking from it and showing us how it worked. (63–64)

Needless to say New Historicism came under critique by feminist scholars because of its "traditional inattention to women" in a most celebrated public debate at the 1986 World Shakespeare Congress in Berlin (Hopkins 82–83). Feminist readings of Shakespeare's plays have been justly celebrated because of the insights that they provide regarding power relations within the sphere of domesticity. Karen Newman in her brilliant essay, "Renaissance Family Politics and Shakespeare's *Taming of the Shrew*," in *Fashioning Femininity and English Renaissance Drama* combines the use of New Historicist, feminist, and psychoanalytic theory in her interpretation of *The Taming of the Shrew* in a truly virtuosic fashion.

Like New Historicists, Newman begins her discussion of *The Taming of the Shrew* with an anecdote from early modern England. It is important to note that Newman's use of anecdote is a hallmark of New Historicist critics. This anecdotal opening has its roots in Stephen Greenblatt's appropriation of Clifford Geertz's use of "thick description"; Greenblatt is regarded as the premier exponent of New Historicism because of his truly groundbreaking essay "Invisible Bullets." Geertz is a cultural anthropologist who used a great amount of detail concerning any event in order to "counterbalanc[e] the historiographical tendency to produce 'grand narratives'—sweeping, all-embracing accounts of historical change, in which local detail is subordinated to the bigger picture—of which Geertz, like so many other critics, has grown suspicious" (Hopkins 65–66). Needless to say, the use of the anecdote functions as a particularly effective rhetorical means of engaging one's audience at the outset of one's essay regardless of whether one believes it is representative of that particular society at that given time.

Newman opens her essay with an anecdote that presumably is representative of early modern marital conflict. The account of the altercation runs as follows:

> Wetherden, Suffolk. Plough Monday, 1604. A drunken tanner, Nicholas Rosyer, staggers home from the alehouse. On arriving at his door, he is greeted by his wife with "dronken dogg, pisspott and other unseemly names." When Royser tried to come to bed to her, she "still raged against him and badd him out drunken dog drunken pisspott." She struck him several times, clawed his face and arms, spit at him, and beat him out of bed. Royser retreated, returned to the alehouse, and drank until he could hardly stand up. (Newman 35)

This particular account is especially exacting in its details, for we have the name of a specific couple, place, time, and circumstance. This marital conflict ultimately functions as a reflection of domestic strife in early modern England. The neighbors react to the troubling situation by enacting a "skimmington," a shaming ritual which was to compel the offending couple into behaving in a socially acceptable fashion. The skimmington itself involved Thomas Quarry, who crossdressed, and the offending couple's neighbors who acted as the husband, and a procession accompanied by "rough music" past the home of the Roysers. Mr. Royser was not amused by this skimmington; in fact, he brought charges against his neighbors alleging that they caused him disgrace and scandal to him, his wife, and relatives in addition to "tumult and discention in the said towne" (35). As Newman astutely asserts, "The community's ritual action against the couple who transgress prevailing codes of gender behavior seeks to reestablish those conventional modes of behavior—it seeks to sanction a patriarchal order. . . . The skimmington [also] seeks 'in merriment' to assert traditional gender behaviors that are naturalized in Elizabethan culture as divinely ordained" (36). Overall, Newman uses this anecdote to contextualize domestic violence in early modern London in order to exemplify the dynamics of power relations within this marriage.

In addition, to this anecdote, Newman avails herself of two images involving domestic strife and how the community contained its subversive potential. In the first image a woman is shown in the foreground beating her older husband with a fan. As a consequence of this topsy-turvy husband-wife relationship, in the background a husband and wife are depicted on horseback with the wife facing the front of the horse while the husband rode backward, which was supposed to indicate the inappropriate inversion of orthodox gender relations. Here again there is a procession involving neighbors and a man beating a drum in order to provide the offending couple "rough music." In the second image, a series of interactions involving husbands and wives in domestic disorder are depicted. Beneath the images is an aphorism concerning how forward wives should be dealt with so that on Sunday a husband may eat his meat in peace. To be sure, the most frightening image is of a demonic figure with a pitchfork chasing an obviously hysterical wife. Both of these images function to contextualize domestic strife within visual terms.

After the initial introduction to the essay, Newman begins her discussion of the play itself. Here she transitions into a feminist interpretation of the play when she asserts that Sly is finally convinced of his aristocratic status only after being told that he has a wife. She goes on to assert that in this masculinist culture "men depended on women to authorize their sexual and social masculine identity" (38). Finally, she works up to her argument when she avers at the end of the second section of her essay, "Our task is to articulate the particular sexual/political fantasy, or in [Frederic] Jameson's Althusserian formulation, the 'libidinal apparartus' this play projects as an imaginary resolution of contradictions that are never resolved in the Wetherden case, but which the formal structures of dramatic plot and structure in Shakespeare's play present as seemingly reconciled" (39). This approach to *The Taming of the Shrew* is very much in keeping with "Greenblatt's theory of containment, which suggests that power licenses drama to appear to challenge it, because this functions as a 'letting off of steam' which prevents any real challenge from developing" (Hopkins 67). Ultimately, this is part and parcel of the subversion/containment argument in which the state allows certain festivals in order for the populace to vent their anger and to prevent real social and political upheaval from occurring.

In the latter half of her essay, Newman shifts to psychoanalysis in order to make sense of Kate's behavior. She suggests, "A feminist characterological rereading of Freud might suggest that Kate's ambitious fantasies, which the culture allows her to express only in erotic directions, motivate her shrewishness" (45). Freud has become a means to an end in Newman's interpretation of Kate's unruly attitude and actions. "It is clear, though, that Newman is using Freud less as a guide than as a figure whose ideas might themselves be critiqued and interrogated" (Hopkins 84). Newman, not finished with psychoanalytic critics, cites Luce Irigaray, who "argues that women are cut off from language by the patriarchal order in which they live, by their entry in to the Symbolic, which the Father represents in a Freudian-Lacanian model" (47). Newman argues that Kate subverts the patriarchal law of the Father by engaging in what Irigaray calls "mimeticism," in which she replaces "her earlier language of revolt and anger" (47). In the scene in which Kate and Petruchio engage in language games as to whether the sun or moon is shining so brightly, Kate mimics the language of the Father in order to survive or at least be able to return to Padua so that she may see her father, Baptista, or to put it more simply, Kate learns how to play the linguistic games that allow her to live with Petruchio peacefully.

In Newman's conclusion to the essay, she perceives the play's subversion as uncontained as opposed to the closure that theoretically occurs at the end of the drama, for she asks, "But can a staged transgression of the law of women's silence be subversive? It is, after all, a theoretical commonplace to argue that transgression presupposes norms or taboos. Anthropologists have claimed that such ritual transgression insures order and stability; and literary critics, influenced by anthropology and a fashionable cultural pessimism that skirts the reactionary, argue that such subversion is always already contained" (Newman 49). Hopkins certainly thinks that Newman believes this play to be subversive, for she states, "Most startling of all, however, is Newman's willingness to see the play as potentially subversive, which is a marked departure from New Historicism's traditional interpretative preference of finding that drama works ultimately to produce containment" (86).

In the last sentence of Newman's brilliant essay, she argues that the very construction of the sex/gender system demolishes naturalized categories by which society creates femininity and masculinity: "The very indeterminateness of the actor's sexuality, of the woman/man's body, the supplementarity of its titillating homoerotic play (Sly's desire for the page boy disguised as a woman, Petruchio's 'Come Kate, we'll to bed'), foregrounds its artifice and therefore subverts the play's patriarchal master narrative by exposing it as neither natural nor divinely ordained, but culturally constructed" (50). Ultimately, Newman argues very powerfully that the very categories of gender are nothing more than social conventions that society constructed so it can negotiate its daily acts of human interaction in an uncomplicated fashion.

Unlike Petruchio and Kate, who almost desire each other against their will, Romeo and Juliet are smitten by each other from the first glance. When one thinks of *Romeo and Juliet,* one usually thinks of erotic desire and the untimely deaths of the play's eponymous figures. In Lloyd Davis's essay. " 'Death-Marked Love': Desire and Presence in *Romeo and Juliet,*" the issue of "unfulfillable desire" is emphasized because the Petrarchan mode of erotic discourse is found to be lacking and ultimately, "tragically fatal" (29). Davis argues, "[T]heir love ends in reciprocal death with the Petrarchan images fatally embodied and materialized. The links between love and death unveil a dark skepticism about desire, despite bursts of romantic idealism" (29).

Davis articulates most powerfully that "desire remains 'predicated on lack and even its apparent fulfillment is a moment of loss.' In this view, desire and presence are forever intertwined" (30). Therefore, a conflict occurs between "ways of representing and interpreting desire" (30). Consequently, *Romeo and Juliet* become the means by which to "inform[] and illustrate[] a cultural history of desire" (30). In this particular text, like many early modern English texts, desire and eroticism are inextricably linked to death. The play's prologue creates this nexus for the audience. The link between sexuality and death is determined by "temporal shifts which define the characters' relations" (32).

Traditionally, literary critics have claimed that Shakespeare's characters transcend time and place because of the universality of their experiences; it is because of such transhistorical claims that materialist critics have scrutinized his plays. Nonetheless, the issue of personal erotic desire has always been part and parcel of humanity's existence, and because of it "universal images of the personal in *Romeo and Juliet* can be seen as helping to naturalise notions of desire which reinforce an 'ideology of romantic love' in terms of 'heterosexualising idealisation' and the 'canonisation of heterosexuality' " (34). Davis in this essay alludes to the historical construction of heterosexuality as a sexual category created by the medical community in the late 19th century.

Davis attempts to contextualize desire by referring to Socrates's *Symposium* in which love is conceptualized as "desire for what one lacks, either a specific quality or a lost or missing element of the self" (34), and Pietro Bembo reconstructs this model of love in Neoplatonic terms at the end of Castiglione's *The Courtier*, the seminal text which delineated how courtiers should woo their beloveds. In this scenario love is transformed into a divine quality, which transcends its sexual aspect, and Davis cites Edmund Spenser's *Foure Hymnes* in order to demonstrate this concept of divine love. Finally, images of Platonic desire and identity were used throughout Shakespeare's comedies during the 1590s; to be sure, all of the young lovers undergo various challenges before reaching marital bliss (36). Of course, Romeo, "a virtual stereotype of the romantic lover," briefly finds marital bliss, "whose role-playing brings a kind of egotistic reassurance. The lament of self-loss becomes proof of self-presence, a 'boastful positiveness,' with Romeo still to know the unsettling force of desire" (37). Sadly, the force of desire drives Romeo and Juliet ineluctably to their deaths.

Davis makes the assertion that desire ultimately overwhelms personal experience and "realizes an intersubjective union" (39). Romeo and Juliet's intersubjective union is made manifest at the time of their deaths in the Capulets' tomb. He further asserts, "[T]heir union will be ended by events that literalise poetic tropes of love and death" (39). Romeo literally expires with the kiss of Juliet on his lips while Juliet expresses an "eternal sexual embrace" (39) by stabbing herself with Romeo's dagger, becoming in psychoanalytic terms the phallic woman, metaphorically appropriating Romeo's phallus.

Jonathan Goldberg's "*Romeo and Juliet's* Open R's," an extraordinary queer reading of this canonical text of young Italian lovers, which has universalized the West's notion of romantic love, significantly reconceptualized how one could think about sexuality and desire regarding this play. Goldberg initiates his critique of traditional orthodox readings by scrutinizing Coppélia Kahn's essay, "Coming of Age in Verona" and quoting from her essay's opening commentary: "'*Romeo and Juliet* is about a pair of adolescents trying to grow up. Growing up requires that they separate themselves from their parents by forming with a member of the opposite sex an intimate bond which supersedes filial bonds'" (Qtd. in Goldberg 196). Goldberg's commentary is devastating to say the least, for he avers, "These blandly descriptive sentences reek of prescriptiveness, most notably when growing up is allowed, indeed required to have, a single heterosexual trajectory. How far this might be from *Romeo and Juliet* the term 'homosocial' has already begun to suggest, and Kahn's rewriting of the play to suit her normalizing plot couldn't be clearer" (196). In fairness to Kahn, this early feminist reading of *Romeo and Juliet* originally appeared in volume 8 of *Modern Language Studies* in 1977–1978, when writing even feminist readings of canonical texts was considered risky business by some members of a male-dominated academy. It is extremely important to remember that Kahn's interpretation was highly significant because of its groundbreaking nature in the late 1970s. Goldberg clearly takes issue with Kahn's belief that the pair of young opposite-sex lovers will eventually marry as their parents did before them. Therefore, Goldberg definitively asserts at the beginning of the essay proper, "I do not seek to enlist Shakespeare for the projects of a formalist and heterosexualist agenda, but rather, following Eve Kosofsky Sedgwick, to suggest that the homosocial order in the play cannot simply be reduced to a compulsive and prescriptive heterosexuality; that sexuality in the play cannot be found enshrined in an artifice of eternity because the social work that the play performs nor the play itself (a formalist phantasm) can be thought of in these terms" (197).

Rather than arguing that Juliet functions as an emblem of undying love, Goldberg suggests the interchangeability of Juliet with Rosaline; as Goldberg opines, "Seen in that light, Juliet as replacement object is inserted within a seriality rather than the locus of uniqueness and singularity" (197). When Benvolio asks Romeo to forget Rosaline, his request is equivalent to his asking Romeo to remember him and his friends. Goldberg even suggests that Benvolio's notion of Romeo selecting another more cooperative mate is similar to the young man's situation in the *Sonnets* in that he too needs to find an appropriate spouse in order to perpetuate his family's name. Therefore, the young man could meet the social needs of his family and community, and still maintain his friendship with the poet.

The possibility of future happiness in *Romeo and Juliet* was destroyed as soon as Romeo declared his effeminacy after killing Tybalt. According to Goldberg, Janet Adelman suggests that the tragedy begins when Romeo declares his effeminacy: "[B]ecause it signals the break-up of male-male relations in the play, solidified by their aggression toward and fear of women, this marks a tragedy that she regards as inevitable when comedy takes the form of male bonding or, worse, as it seems in Adelman's account, when male bonding can extend itself to the transvestite actor" (Goldberg 202). Adelman, according to Goldberg, refers to this state of relations as a "fantasy," which is counterproductive to mature male development that has to eventuate in heterosexuality (202). Of course, this developmental stance is problematic because it militates against the possibility of long-lasting male-male relations. Despite the misogyny that Adelman and Kahn's feminist interpretations reveal about a text, the main point that Goldberg wants to make is "their enforcement of heterosexuality and gender difference belies energies in the plays that cannot be reduced to the erasure of women" (202). Goldberg continues the trajectory of his argument to its logical conclusion concerning the substitution of one character for another in the chain of erotic desire.

Throughout the text, Mercutio makes highly suggestive sexual comments about Romeo's relationship with Rosaline. Goldberg makes some extraordinarily astute comments about Mercutio's "lines that a blind love that does and does not hit the mark [which] recall Benvolio's counsels earlier about the deflection of Romeo's desires from Rosaline" (206). Without a doubt Goldberg's most powerful and provocative insight culminates in the following statement: "The locus of anal penetration, of course, is available on any body, male or female. Mercutio's conjuring also conjures him into the magic circle, an O that is not, as some commentators would have it be, the vaginal opening, for this is how Mercutio voices—through Rosaline—his desire for Romeo, his version, that is, of Benvolio's most benign voicing of the place she can occupy between men" (206). The risqué open Rs are, in fact, the arse, which is to be penetrated in sodomitical fashion. In many ways, Goldberg's argument is at once shocking to many and at once dazzlingly brilliant, concluding at the point at which Mercutio had begun, "To return to the scene of conjuring, then, is to register Mercutio's rivalry for a place that anyone might occupy, and to recognize his projection into Rosaline's place as his own, as his way, that is, of occupying the magic circle or owning, to vary the metaphor slightly, the desires named by the open Rs in the text" (207). Finally, the argument that Mercutio may be harboring erotic feelings for Romeo is not especially revelatory, for critics have alluded to this possibility for years, but what is significant about Goldberg's argument is the fact that he makes his argument in such sexually explicit terms. In the final analysis, Goldberg's queer critique radically challenges any conventional interpretation or understanding of *Romeo and Juliet*.

Just as eroticism is highly significant to the action of the drama in *Romeo and Juliet* so too does it figure significantly in the action of the drama in *A Midsummer Night's Dream*. Traditionally, instructors have taught this play as a triumphant celebration of young love over the powers of inchoate chaos and its darkness. In "Rape, Repetition, and the Politics of Closure in *A Midsummer Night's Dream*," Laura Levine's feminist interpretation is a powerful corrective to this orthodox understanding of this play. She asserts her argument very clearly at the end of her first paragraph: "In the first part of the essay, I am going to be arguing that Shakespeare shows us Theseus turning to theatre to transform sexual violence in order to show the way that theatre exactly fails to accomplish such a transformation. In the second part, I am going to be examining the question that this claim logically raises" (Levine 210).

Levine begins her essay with a very provocative quotation made by Theseus to Hippolyta after he has brought her back to Athens following his battle with the Amazons, a triumph which clearly defines the dynamics of their erotic interaction:

> I woo'd thee with my sword,
> And won thy love doing thee injuries;
> But I will wed thee in another key,
> With pomp, with triumph, and with reveling. (I.i.16–19; qtd. from *Riverside Shakespeare*)

This passage has unmistakable overtones of phallic violence. Theseus says that he wants to transform erotic violence into celebratory marital bliss, but instead of doing so, he reinforces the patriarchal law of the father when Egeus insists that Hermia marry Demetrius against her will. As Levine so urgently articulates, "Rather than transforming the sexual coercion that he begins the play by promising to get rid of, Theseus immediately repeats it. Rather than undoing an act of sexual violence, he reenacts one. In fact, sexual violence is embodied in the principle of Athenian law itself" (211). Egeus's desire to force his daughter, Hermia, to marry against her will is an egregious act of brutality. The court of Athens is depicted as a place in which the patriarchy is reified in the law of the father.

The forest, instead of acting as an escape from the patriarchy, also functions as the locus of patriarchal power as reflected in Oberon, the King of the Fairyland. Oberon, too, is accustomed to having his way, and when Titania refuses to give up the changeling boy, whose mother died giving birth to him, Oberon becomes incensed; his parting comment to her is "Thou shalt not from this grove / Till I torment thee for this injury" (II.i.146). Oberon decides to humiliate his own wife by causing her to experience sexual congress with a wild animal, for Levine asserts, "But the means of torment (as well as the means of gaining the child) is the production in her of sexual appetites she will be powerless to resist" (212). He is not even concerned that she engages in bestiality so long as she is sufficiently humiliated to his satisfaction.

Later Oberon tells Puck to retrieve for him the flower called "love-in-idleness" so that he can sprinkle its love-juice on the eyes of Titania and the other young lovers' eyes. Interestingly, the flower itself has been metaphorically violated by Cupid's arrow: "It fell upon a little western flower, / Before milk-white, now purple with love's wound" (II.i.166–67). Therefore, as Levine points out, "[I]t is also the occasion of Cupid's attempted seduction of the vestal, and that seduction is at once both successfully resisted and the occasion of the manufacture of a new aphrodisiac—the love-in-idleness—that will engender the next coerced love" (215). Love's wound is often read metaphorically as hymenal bleeding, caused by a sexual violation.

On the other side of the woods, Helena pursues Demetrius to her own detriment. He disdainfully articulates his barely veiled sexual threat. Levine makes a significant connection between sexual violation and wild animals as there are allusions to wild beasts throughout the play: "Trying to get rid of her, he vacillates between threatening to leave her to 'wild beasts' and to his own impulses, as if the two were interchangeable" (218). Here Levine demonstrates the ability to discern and link seemingly disparate moments within the play, for she perceives a nexus between Helena's being left to feral animals and the artisans' concern that if they were to frighten the ladies of the court by having one of them appear disguised as a lion that their lives would be in jeopardy. Levine notes that Thisby is later to be supposedly "deflowered" by a lion in the playlet of "Pyramus and Thisby," which here again constitutes the eroticization of two classical figures.

Levine concludes her essay by suggesting that the very theatricality of the masque of Pyramus and Thisby embodies the play's "production of insistent and unmanageable sexual desire, a desire that is inherently animalistic" (222). This assertion is supported by the example of Stephen Gosson, an anti-theatricalist, who conceived of the theatre as a place that encouraged a "desire to inordinate lust," for Levine cites Stephen Gosson's *School of Abuse* and Anthony Munday's *A Second and Third Blast of Retrait from Plaies and Theatres* in order to show that these writers conceived of the theatre as a place where men's minds underwent a "ravishing" or overwhelming of the senses. Therefore, it came as no surprise to the Puritan ministers that the cross-dressing actors confused the visual and auditory senses of male theatergoers, and so Levine suggests that ultimately Theseus resorts to a form of sexual violation in order to conceal his own.

To be sure, the Puritans' fears were realized in *As You Like It* with Rosalind, the heroine of the play, cross-dressing as a male called Ganymede, a name synonymous with male same-sex eroticism in the early modern English period. In this instance one sees a male actor playing a female role playing a male role. Marjorie Garber, in a fairly early feminist essay titled "The Education of Orlando" (1986), critiques the psychological development that Orlando must undergo in order to be fully prepared to be involved in a complex romantic relationship and ultimately love Rosalind as he should so that they will have a successful marriage.

First of all, Garber asks why Rosalind remains in her male disguise, and she systematically explains why Viola and Portia wear them in *Twelfth Night* and *The Merchant of Venice* respectively. Stephen Lynch correctly states, "While Portia and Viola assume masculine disguise as a means to advance the plot of the play, Rosalind does not have any particular need to remain in the disguise once she arrives in Arden and meets Orlando" (114). Lynch quickly arrives at the reason which Garber provides as to why Rosalind remain incognito: "According to Garber, Rosalind remains disguised to 'educate Orlando about himself, about her, and about the nature of love'" (Lynch 114). Garber also explains why Orlando is successful in the education administered by Rosalind in the Forest of Arden, "The degree to which Orlando is successfully educated, and the limits of his final understanding, can be seen by examining their various encounters in the court and in the forest and by considering what happens as a result of those encounters" (104). Again, Garber astutely charts Orlando's psychological and emotional development and aptitude for a complex relationship with a woman of Rosalind's sophistication.

Lynch is right to see Garber dividing Orlando's stages of development into three parts. The first part occurs after Orlando defeated Charles in a wrestling bout and Orlando was almost inarticulate when Rosalind presented him a chain: "Can I not say, 'I thank you'? My better parts / Are all thrown down, and that which here stands up / Is but a quintain, a mere lifeless block" (I.ii.249–51). Garber refers to this as the first stage, "that of ineffability; for the match to succeed he must somehow learn to communicate his feelings" (106). Therefore, Orlando learns to communicate how he feels so that he can pursue a relationship with Rosalind.

Orlando's attempt at writing sonnets expressing his love and affection for Rosalind constitutes one ineffective way of articulating his erotic desire for her. Lynch suggests that this is the initial part of the second stage of Orlando's development, according to Garber's psychological schema. During this time Orlando must learn to engage with Rosalind other than by attaching sonnets onto the forest's trees, for Garber asserts, "Dialogue and interplay have already begun to replace the sterile and stereotypical intercourse between a man and his pen" (107). Sadly, even though Orlando is completely focused upon the character of Ganymede/Rosalind, he still is incapable of discerning his true love beneath the disguise. Unlike Bassanio who does not recognize Portia cross-dressed as Balthazar because he is concerned about Antonio's life, Orlando has no such excuse as Garber asserts, "Orlando, by contrast, has his mind wholly on Rosalind, yet he does not see her as she stands before him" (107).

The third and final stage as indicated by Lynch in Garber's analysis of Orlando's psychological maturity comes when he rescues his brother Oliver from the lioness and the subsequent "bloody napkin" which is a consequence of Orlando's fight with the beast. According to Garber, this encounter with the lioness is an "initiation ritual, both in marital terms and sexual terms" (109), and she asserts, "I see the gift of the bloody napkin as a curiously but appropriately displaced version of the ceremonial 'showing of the sheets' by which in some cultures a newly married woman demonstrates her virginity and fidelity to her husband" (109). This is, indeed, a very powerful symbolic statement, but certainly, according to Garber, the statement that best expresses Orlando's emotional maturity is "I can no longer live by thinking" (V.ii.49). Finally, Orlando begins to understand the complexities of love and the degree of commitment that he needs to provide Rosalind in order to have a legitimate romantic relationship.

Valerie Traub's brilliant essay, "The Homoerotics of Shakespearean Comedy" in *Desire and Anxiety: The Circulation of Sexuality in Shakespearean Drama* directs her focus on *As You Like It* and *Twelfth Night* in order to critique issues of gender and sexuality regarding the boy actors who played the roles of young girls and women on the early modern English stage. Traub makes her argument unequivocally: "I mean to demonstrate my earlier assertion that certain Shakespearean texts display a homoerotic circulation of desire, that homoerotic energy is elicited, exchanged, negotiated, and displaced as it confronts the pleasures and anxieties of its meanings in early modern culture" (118).

Traub uses the term "transvestism" rather than disguise or cross-dressing in order "to describe the consequences of Rosalind's and Viola's adoption of (what was then perceived to be) a masculine attire" (118). Inasmuch as transvestism is a fascinating topic of discussion for modern culture, it was, indeed, a most troubling one for the anti-theatricalists of the early modern period, such as Stephen Gosson, John Rainolds, Phillip Stubbes, and William Pyrnne, who were at once fearful and enraged by youth who dressed as women and girls, for they thought they transgressed not only gender and socioeconomic borders but also erotic ones. Sumptuary laws indicated one's social status as well as one's gender and one's sexual availability or lack thereof (118). To be sure, feminist readings are engaged with the issue of transvestism, and some feminist and New Historicist interpretations argued that subversion concerning sexual and gender boundaries "is contained by the comic form which mandates marriage in the final act" (119), but currently, discussions focus on how subversive or contained the "power of gender" is according to the degree to which women call into question and undermine through disruption or loss of their agency and are once again treated as a means of exchange in a male-dominated society (119–20).

Gender and eroticism become closely intertwined in plays such as *As You Like It* and *Twelfth Night*. Traub explains a great of deal of theoretical matter regarding sexuality and gender in the first section of her essay concerning both plays; for she argues, "If young boys are erotically compelling because of their 'femininity,' it is in part because they represent all of the attractions and none of the threats of female heterosexuality" (121). She believes that anxiety surrounding gender is a factor in the particular ways that homoerotic activity is shown and accorded meaning in Elizabethan culture. Moreover, anxiety concerning gender is not any more part and parcel of homoerotic desire than it is of heterosexual desire. Furthermore, Traub asserts that there are a plethora of desires accessible to people's erotic unconscious, and "ideological and institutional elicitations, enticements, and disciplines" (121) determine whether a particular expression of desire is demonstrated. Finally, Traub avers, "These plays are sites of struggle for the signification of homoeroticism: they demonstrate that within the early modern erotic economy the homoerotic relation to desire could be represented as both celebratory and strained" (122). In other words, these plays possess the capacity to show same-sex erotic affection and love in a positive light but these kind of relationships can also be problematic and difficult, especially those involving Rosalind/Ganymede and Phoebe in *As You Like It* and Viola/Cesario and Orsino and Olivia and Antonio and Sebastian in *Twelfth Night*, and finally, Bassanio and Antonio in *The Merchant of Venice*.

Traub makes the argument that the homoeroticism in *As You Like It* demonstrates the ability to breach the binary opposition of heterosexuality and homosexuality. The character of Rosalind/Ganymede is desired by both Orlando and Phoebe. Because of the disruption of the sexual binarism, despite the fact that homoeroticism may have confirmed certain male bonds, according to Traub, it "transgresses the erotic imperative of the Law of the Father" (Traub 123). By Rosalind's use of transvestism, she involves the play in both homosexual and heterosexual eroticism. Traub makes the provocative claim that while she expresses erotic desire for Orlando, she also likes being Phoebe's object of desire and more importantly, Orlando's. She undermines the sexual binarism of heterosexuality and homosexuality as it has been regulated and defined for the last 400 years (124).

As You Like It is fraught with homoerotic associations from the time that Rosalind decides to run away from Duke Frederick's court when she takes the name of Ganymede, who is the young lover of Zeus, and this figure would have been familiar to those with a knowledge of Greek and Roman literature in England and Europe during the early modern period. Art historian James Saslow, who has researched the history of Ganymede in Western culture from the 15th century to the 17th century, makes the case that the term "ganymede" had been used from the medieval period into the 17th century as a reference to a male who was the object of same-sex male desire (Traub 125).

The attraction that Phoebe has for Rosalind is one of heterosexual desire, yet ironically what attracts Phoebe to Ganymede are her/his feminine attributes. Traub points out the degree to which he/she is attractive. Phoebe begins her discussion of Ganymede concerning his complexion which was often part of the blazon, which was a catalogue of a woman's physical attributes. She believes that his complexion is his best quality, and she proceeds to describe his height, which she says is acceptable for his age while his leg is of mediocre quality. Then Phoebe decides to return to her description of his complexion, focusing on the beauty of his cheek, which was a stereotypical blandishment made by a young man about his beloved. Traub asserts, "In the last four lines, as she 'feminizes' Ganymede's lip and cheek, she capitulates to her desire altogether" (125). In many ways, this litany of items is characteristic of the list of attributes read by Olivia when Viola/Cesario visits her as Orsino's emissary for the first time.

Interestingly, it is Rosalind/Ganymede who first notices Phoebe's attraction to her, and she certainly seems to be intrigued and delighted by it. Traub goes so far as to suggest that Rosalind/Ganymede enjoys the effect that she has on Phoebe (126) so erotic desire then becomes a form of power. In fact, Rosalind/Ganymede even tells Phoebe that she should be grateful for the attention that Silvius gives her: "For I must tell you friendly in your eye, / Sell when you can, you are not for all markets" (III.v.57–60). Indeed, Rosalind/Ganymede appears quite in control as a male when s/he tells Silvius to inform Phoebe that she should love him (Traub126).

The homoeroticism between Rosalind/Ganymede as a shepherd and Orlando is even more outré than that between Rosalind/Ganymede and Phoebe. Orlando accepts Ganymede as his beloved despite the fact that he believes this person is male. Also of interest is the fact that Rosalind/Ganymede is the more aggressive partner in this relationship, which is ironic because in a same-sex relationship the figure of Ganymede would play the passive role because of his youth so Rosalind "not only inverts gender roles; s/he disrupts alleged homoerotic roles as well" (127). The figure of Rosalind/Ganymede may be one of Shakespeare's most subversive characters. One of the play's most transgressive moments occurs when Celia marries Rosalind still dressed as Ganymede and Orlando in a mock marriage. Traub makes a brilliant insight regarding the differences between homosexuality and heterosexuality: "The point is not that Orlando and Ganymede formalize a homosexual marriage, but rather that as the distance between Orlando and Ganymede collapses, distinctions between homoerotic and heterosexual collapse as well" (127).

At the epilogue when Rosalind comes forward to address the audience, she calls attention to the socially constructed quality of gender: "If I were a woman I would kiss as many of you as had beards that pleas'd me, complexions that lik'd me, and breaths that I defied not" (Epilogue 16–19). Traub summarizes and critiques multiple arguments very efficiently: "As Orgel, Howard, and Phyllis Rackin, and Catherine Belsey all intimate, the effect of this statement is to highlight the constructedness of gender and the flexibility of erotic attraction at precisely the point when the formal impulse of comedy would be to essentialize and fix both gender and eroticism" (128). Again, as Traub has argued earlier, the figure of Rosalind tends to conflate masculinity and femininity as well as heterosexuality and homosexuality in such a fashion that only she can untangle the complexity of their dualities.

Unlike *As You Like It, Twelfth Night* lacks the playfulness regarding its gender and sexual dynamics, for its homoeroticism, "on the other hand, is anxious and strained. . . . The homoerotic energies of Viola, Olivia, and Orsino are displaced onto Antonio, whose relation to Sebastian is finally sacrificed for the maintenance of institutionalized heterosexuality and general continuity" (123). Nonetheless, many characters are erotically interested in others in *Twelfth Night*: "Viola/Cesario's dual desire for Olivia and Orsino; Orsino's ambivalent interest in Viola/Cesario; Sebastian's responses to Olivia and Antonio; and finally, Antonio's exclusive erotic wish for Sebastian" (130). There is no question that eroticism is floating freely throughout this play. While Viola/Cesario may have wished to appear almost androgynously when she first appears at Orsino's court and to remain inconspicuous, she quickly distinguishes herself and becomes both an erotic object and a subject of desire (130). Viola/Cesario takes up a double-edged position of erotic desire.

Ironically, Viola/Cesario cannot express her affection for Orsino because s/he pretends to be a male in his entourage, and s/he cannot reciprocate Olivia's affection, for she is first Orsino's emissary whose charge is to woo Olivia in his stead, and s/he is actually female. Traub opines, "S/he 'fonds' on her master, while simultaneously finding erotic intrigue and excitement as the object of Olivia's desire. The flip side of her anxiety about Olivia's desire is her own desire to be the object of Olivia's desire" (131). In fact, Viola/Cesario's unique situation causes her to lament her absurd predicament, incapable of determining how she can extricate herself from it, as she sighs: "O time, thou must untangle this, not I; / It is too hard a knot for me t'untie" (II.ii. 40–41). Indeed, it is a nonce occasion that allows for the truth to become known.

Unlike Rosalind/Ganymede in *As You Like It,* Viola/Cesario thinks that she needs to maintain her disguise for her safety as she is afraid of the duel with Sir Andrew Aguecheek. Viola/Cesario is concerned about the biological specificity of his/her anatomy, and the "little thing" that she does not have. "The little thing" is literally the point of contention, for Viola/Cesario fears that her/his sex will be revealed through this duel because s/he will be incapable of demonstrating the masculinity to enact the duel appropriately. Traub makes a very good point when she asserts, "At this (phallic) point, Viola/Cesario's 'lack' is upheld as the signifier of gender difference. And yet, to the extent that masculinity is embodied in the sword, it depends upon a particular kind of performance rather than any biological equipment" (132). This statement returns us to Judith Butler's notion that gender is defined through the repetition of certain specific actions which delineate the categories of masculinity and femininity, and therefore, masculinity is not exclusively the attribute of men, but women may possess it as well (24).

At the same time, Antonio, who passionately loves Sebastian and clearly evinces homoerotic affection for him and follows him through the streets of Illyria, appears at just the moment to defend Viola/Cesario from Sir Andrew Aguecheek whom he mistakes for Sebastian. He even says, "But come what may, I do adore thee so / That danger shall seem sport, and I will go" (II.i.44–45). Traub is unequivocal in her interpretation of this relation between Sebastian and Antonio, which is definitely based on same-sex eroticism: "For Antonio's words allude to the perils in early modern culture of an exclusively homoerotic passion: in order to remain in the presence of one's beloved, 'danger' must be figuratively, if not literally, transformed into 'sport' " (132–33). Earlier in the scene Antonio importuned Sebastian, "If you will not murder me for my love, let me be your servant" (II.i.33–34). One can only imagine the kind of love that Antonio bears Sebastian. Is this the heretical love that dare not speak its name? As early modern court documents indicate, sodomitical interactions, however heartfelt, could sometimes result in the death penalty for both parties involved.

It is notable before the swordfight that Antonio avers in the most impassioned fashion: "I could not stay behind you. My desire, / More sharp than filed steel, did spur me forth" (III.iii.4–5). Traub argues that this assertion is the epitome of phallic imagery, asserting, "Male desire in Shakespearean drama is almost always figured in phallic images. . . . Antonio describes his desire in terms of sharp, filed steel, which spurs him on to pursuit, [and] homoerotic desire is figured as permanently erect, the desire of man for man that is coded as the more 'masculine' " (134). On the contrary, in the early modern period men's constant association with women and erotic desire for women functioned to call their masculinity into question and engender "fears of 'effeminancy' " in men (134).

Orsino, who is in constant pursuit, even through a proxy, of Olivia, has impressed more than one critic as overly concerned with the Petrarchan language of the court, and he appears more in love with the idea of love than really being in love with Olivia. Traub cites Jean Howard's assertion concerning Orsino's self-love and how destructive it is to the early modern sex-gender system, for she makes the point that Orsino's passivity causes problems as he should be an aggressive, masculine wooer, and instead of wooing Olivia himself, he sends Cesario/Viola. In this instance, Orsino's "narcissism and potential effeminacy are displaced, respectively, onto Malvolio and Andrew Aguecheek, who suffer fairly severe humiliations for their follies" (Howard qtd. in Traub 135). Unlike Howard, Traub does not perceive Orsino's narcissism and "effeminacy" as indicative of his erotic desire for men; rather she argues that his "effeminacy" is characteristic of both his "heterosexual desire for Olivia and his homoerotic desire for Cesario" (135). The fact of the matter is that in early modern English society male desire was by its very definition phallic regardless of whether it was of a homoerotic or heterosexual orientation; it was the means by which masculinity was defined and demonstrated.

Issues concerning sexuality and gender in *Much Ado about Nothing* may lack the subtlety and nuance of *As You Like It* and *Twelfth Night*, but it powerfully deals with the issue of power relations and eroticism between women and men. In " 'The Sign and Semblance of Her Honor': Reading Gender and Difference in *Much Ado about Nothing*," Carol Cook, in a still fairly early feminist interpretation, argues in a very cogent and compelling fashion, "The play masks, as well as exposes, the mechanisms of masculine power and that insofar as it avoids what is crucial to its conflicts, the explicitly offered comic resolution is something of an artful dodge" (186). She makes intriguing and engaging comments linking phallic imagery and language as the realm of "masculine privilege and masculine aggression" (186). Cook perceives jokes that concern cuckoldry, the practice of married women having illicit sexual relations with men not their husbands, constitute a form of masculine aggression; as Cook asserts, "[H]orns are not only signs of cuckoldry but also phallic symbols. What Benedick's metaphor of the invisible baldrick suggests is that marriage emasculates a man and flaunts the evidence of emasculation by displaying the displaced phallus in his forehead" (187). Throughout the play, literally from its opening scene to its last, men tell jokes concerning cuckoldry in which they express their fear and hostility toward women (188).

Cook argues that Freud's theories about "tendentious jokes" are helpful in interpreting the ideological significance of the cuckoldry jokes; for example, these jokes have three functions: the hostility of the joke expresses "masculine competition"; the "cynical joke" critiques marriage as an institution; and finally, the "obscene joke" is the third one (188). Although the cuckoldry joke articulates fear and hostility, it also offers compensation in terms of reinstituting "male prerogative: it returns the woman to silence and absence, her absence authorizing the male raconteur to represent her in accordance with particular male fantasies, and produces pleasure through male camaraderie" (189). In other words, the cuckoldry jokes function as a means of managing men's sexual anxiety concerning the power that women have over them.

When a man becomes a cuckold, he loses his place of power and authority as a male figure because he has become symbolically castrated. He takes up the subjected position of a woman in society who functions as the object of male desire. It is the place of the woman to be silent, chaste, and obedient in Elizabethan society. In Elizabethan society the "woman [is] to be the object, or referent, a sign to be read and interpreted; silent herself, she becomes a cipher, the target of unconscious fantasies and fears, and is dangerously vulnerable to the representations and misrepresentations of men as the plot of *Much Ado* bears out" (188). One of the ways to defend oneself is "To brandish phallic wit . . . against others' castrating 'swords' or to deny a castration already accomplished" (190). In *Much Ado about Nothing,* wit functions as a means of both aggression and defense by Beatrice and Benedick as they brilliantly demonstrate their verbal skills in the opening scene when Don Pedro first arrives with his entourage.

If verbal acuity is a masculine attribute, then Beatrice engages with it wholeheartedly. She completely appropriates masculine discourse with its "phallic wit, speaking poniards as an escape from feminine silence or inarticulate expression of emotion" (190); after all, Benedick tells Don Pedro at the masked ball that Beatrice's "words speak poniards; every word stabs" (II.i.216). On another occasion, when Benedick speaks with Margaret, he is taken aback by her aggressive use of language. Margaret asserts: "Give us your swords; we have bucklers of our own" (V.ii.18).

Benedick responds defensively: "If you use them, Margaret, you must put in the pikes with a vice; and they are dangerous weapons for maids" (V.ii.19–22). Benedick "claims swordlike phallic wit as a masculine prerogative that women only wield through language" (Cook 190). A verbal tug of war exists among them as Leonato told the messenger at the beginning of the play, "A merry war exists between Beatrice and Benedick" (I.i.49–50).

Despite the fact that Beatrice is verbally aggressive, she does not engender the sexual anxiety that Hero does after Claudio is told of her purported sexual infidelity with a ruffian at her chamber window. While Beatrice presents herself as quite a complex character, Hero, by contrast, is minimally delineated; she is a conventional woman from a wealthy family: "meek, self-effacing, vulnerable, obedient, seen and not heard, she is a face without a voice" (191). Cook goes so far as to suggest that Hero is the "nothing" of the play's title. Nothing also was sexual slang for female genitals. Emphasizing the importance of the act of interpreting female bodies in this play, Cook defines "noting" as the act of observing or reading or making note or writing; both of these actions involve the process of interpretation, which is a central concern of this play. The question of how one interprets the female body or imposes meaning upon it is constantly vetted by characters, for upon learning of Hero's sexual transgression, he perceives her in a much different fashion. Now "Claudio's references to Hero here take on sexual overtones wholly lacking in his earlier 'noting' of her modesty and sweetness. He perceives her as a sexual being only in her capacity to betray and then perceives her as a powerful threat, suggesting that in his imagination he has desexualized the Hero he wishes to marry" (Cook 193). Because of Claudio's idealized Petrarchan perceptions of women, his view of Hero will vacillate from exquisite virgin to degraded prostitute because he is incapable of conceptualizing a woman's identity in any other fashion than by means of this duality.

Many critics have remarked upon Claudio's overly chaste protest when Leonato asks him about the amorous nature of his relationship with Hero. Cook, too, notices that his denial of any sexual activity has a "priggish distaste" (194) about it, for she had commented earlier that "Claudio's desires seem a little too delicate" (192), and "his love [is] a little too bloodless" (192). After all, he refers to Hero as "a modest young lady" (165), and she is the "sweetest lady that ever I looked on" (187–88). One comes away from these conversations with the sense that Claudio knows little about erotic matters; in fact, his protestations make him appear as virginal as Hero, and more than likely he probably is. Later in the same scene, Claudio refers to Hero's body as an object to be interpreted, and he feels confident that he is capable of interpreting it correctly when he avers:

> She's but the sign and semblance of her honor.
> Behold how like a maid she blushes here!
> O, what authority and show of truth
> Can cunning sin cover itself withal! (33–36)

Here Claudio compares Hero's body to a book with a cover, and of course, the saying, "You can't judge a book by its cover," quickly comes to mind in this situation. In his hasty naïveté and anger Claudio is all too ready to pronounce judgment on Hero because of what he thinks he has seen in Hero's bedroom window on the previous night. Claudio goes on to denounce Hero claiming, "Comes not that blood as modest evidence / To witness simple virtue?" (37–38). Claudio believes that Hero is guilty of sexual infidelity because she blushes, for Cook argues, "[H]e asks with the ironic jubilance of a reader onto the meaning of a text, the truth that her 'blush is guiltiness, not modesty' " (194). Leonato picks up on the same textual imagery, and he uses it himself in describing Hero's guilt, "Could she here deny / The story that is printed in her blood?" (195). The female body in *Much Ado about Nothing* functions as a sexualized text to be analyzed by men.

No sooner does Claudio learn of Hero's innocence than he reverts back to his earlier image of her. He exclaims: "Sweet Hero, now thy image doth appear / In the rare semblance that I lov'd it first" (251–52). Note Claudio uses the same word "semblance" just as he did when he renounced her. Cook argues, "The image of the witch is dispelled—and replaced by its opposite—but the sexual dualism that governs Hero's 'image' is not displaced or questioned" (197). Cook, too, notices that Friar Francis also takes it upon himself to interpret Hero's body, for he states:

> Trust not my reading, nor my observations,
> Which with experimental seal doth warrant
> The tenure of my book. (IV.i.165–167)

Once again the imagery of a print text comes to the fore. For Friar Francis as for Claudio and Leonato, Hero's body functions as a book to be read. Cook finds this practice highly problematic politically.

Despite Claudio's public apology at the "tomb" of Hero at which he attempts to atone for slandering her, some critics are concerned about whether this highly public ritual "signifies a change in Claudio sufficient to warrant his good fortune in the next scene, where Hero is restored to him. The question cannot be answered" (Cook 198). The larger question is determining the significance of the ritual and Claudio's involvement in it (198). Cook remains convinced that the "dualistic nature of her identity" (200) remains firmly in place. In spite of the importance accorded Claudio's ritual at the tomb, the fact remains that men's fear of women's sexuality is demonstrated by Benedick's joke concerning cuckoldry to Don Pedro at the very end of the play after he promises to marry Beatrice. In spite of the fact that Beatrice is an extraordinarily powerful character, even her mouth is stopped by a kiss from Benedick just as she had suggested that Hero kiss Claudio after he had promised to marry her earlier in the play at the masked ball. Finally, one would be hard pressed to believe that Beatrice would become submissive after her marriage to Benedick.

In *Engendering a Nation: A Feminist Account of Shakespeare's Histories*, Jean E. Howard and Phyllis Rackin address the role of women in the world of early modern English realpolitik. They make very clear how Shakespeare's history plays depict the agonistic relationships between the monarchs of England and their foreign counterparts and also the internecine warfare that existed between English kings and very powerful English families who wished to play a significant role in the political life of England often at odds with the wishes of the reigning monarch. In spite of the significance that is attributed to male history in the governance of England in these history plays, Howard and Rackin in their feminist reading of the Henry IV plays demonstrate unmistakably the ideological import of women's presence in their relationships with men as they relate to affairs of state.

Interestingly, only the rebel leaders, Hotspur and Mortimer, have wives, as pointed out by Barbara Hodgdon in Howard and Rackin's book. Mortimer, with perhaps a stronger claim to the throne, is married to Glendower's daughter, and Hostpur, Northumberland's son, is married to Mortimer's sister. One could say that the affairs of state are a family affair (162). Howard and Rackin argue that Mortimer should be on the throne because he is the heir to Richard II. However, the rebellion is presented as devastating to the country "because it threatens to dismember the body of the land, a threat that is graphically illustrated when the rebel leaders haggle over the map of Britain and finally agree to have the river Trent turned from its natural course in the interest of their 'bargain' " (163). Needless to say, women become very involved in matters of national import as well as matters of local neighborhood politics in taverns and alehouses.

Eastcheap's London's theatres and taverns are eroticized realms of indolence and frivolity in the Henry IV plays. In *Henry IV, Part 2*, Mistress Quickly's tavern is located in Eastcheap, a site of all kinds of low-life comedic and sexual activity. Although the Boar's Head Tavern is not identified as such in the play, there were no less than six actual taverns by that name, one of which was used as a theatre (Howard and Rackin 164). The clientele that frequented these taverns included unsavory characters including thieves and prostitutes. Here again the risks and temptations about which Puritan ministers inveighed concerning the theatre involved eroticism and women (165).

At the national level women are also perceived as a sexual, literally castrating threat. In the opening scene of *Henry IV, Part 1*, the Earl of Westmorland arrives at the English court in order to inform Henry IV that after the defeat of Mortimer in Wales, Owen Glendower captured him; to add insult to injury, the Welsh women mutilated the soldiers' bodies sexually by castrating them, an act to which Westmorland referred as a "beastly shameless transformation" (Howard and Rackin 169). Shakespeare does not describe in detail what the women have done to the soldiers' bodies, but apparently, he had consulted the 1587 edition of Holinshed's *Chronicles*.

Howard describes Wales as a site of female power and emasculation. Mortimer's wife, who remains nameless, invites him to place his head in her lap as she sings seductively. As Howard and Rackin suggest, "In Shakespeare's play, however, Mortimer is motivated—and emasculated by sexual passion for his wife. Although Shakespeare emphasizes Mortimer's lineal claim to the English throne, we see him agreeing to a treaty that will divide the land, and we hear him identify that division as 'gelding' the portion that will be left for him" (III.i.109) (170). If not literally, then metaphorically, Mortimer is emasculated by his wife's feminine wiles. Interestingly, on another occasion, Hotspur's wife, Kate, jokingly says that she will break his "little finger" (II.iii.87), a fairly obvious phallic reference. References to emotional emasculation, if not literal castration, are plentiful within this play, indicative of men's fear of women as seen in *Much Ado about Nothing* when men were anxious about being cuckolded by their wives.

While the tavern scenes in Eastcheap in *Henry IV, Part 1* depict dissolute ways of living, those in *Part 2* amplify the "sense of lawlessness, anarchy, and disease not only in Henry IV's kingdom but also in Nell Quickly's tavern" (Howard and Rackin 170). Quickly is now joined by her partner in crime, Doll Tearsheet, a prostitute. This play's representation of the prostitute is a potent figure, and she metaphorically functions to signal an overall collapse of hierarchy and distinctions of social status (177). The marital status of Quickly becomes increasingly ambiguous as she becomes more and more an integral part of this world of prostitution as the husband is less and less available, and she wishes to marry Falstaff as he has expressed a desire to marry her (178).

Howard and Rackin, stressing the economic aspect of these women's entrepreneurship, focus on the money and servants that Quickly has in her employ. She owns a going concern at which she can earn a living through the sale of alcoholic beverages and the availability of prostitutes' sexuality. Taverns such as these more than likely had upper rooms in which sexual favors might be rendered in exchange for money. Both Doll Tearsheet and Mistress Quickly comprise a menace to the English early modern status quo, for they, according to Howard and Rackin, "challenge both gender and ideology and the system of social stratification distinguishing man from man" (179). Tearsheet and Mistress Quickly, of course, are punished for their transgressive behavior by being whipped and imprisoned while Falstaff is only banished by his one-time jubilant friend, Prince Hal, later King Henry V (179).

Finally, in *Henry V*, Mistress Quickly finds many kind words for Falstaff despite their checkered relationship. Rather than thinking that Falstaff's soul has been lost, she firmly believes that he is in Arthur's bosom and affirms his lifestyle of eating, drinking, and engaging in sexual relations with women. Quickly conflates spiritual and sexual elements and by so doing inverts the social and sacred hierarchies (184).

Howard and Rackin conclude their chapter by arguing that Owen Glendower's daughter functions as an "exotic, eroticized object of desire and anxiety [that] is a projection of male fantasies, but it is tempting to imagine real-life counterparts for Doll and Quickly in the audience to the Henry IV plays" (185). Both of these widely disparate groups of women act to undermine men's control of the kingdom whether it is in courtly circles in which they emasculate their warrior husbands or deplete the middling or working class of its monetary or sexual worth or power in London taverns. Appropriately, Howard and Rackin cite Thomas Heywood in *Apology for Actors* who asserts that the theatre, because of its inclusive and communal qualities, "bears more resemblances to Quickly's tavern than to the king's court" (185). Given the level of erotic energy and ideological subversion in London theatres, it is no wonder that theatres attracted such a wide variety of theatergoers, including aristocrats as well as prostitutes and thieves.

Dympna Callaghan's essay, "Looking Well to Linens: Women and Cultural Production in *Othello* and Shakespeare's England," addresses the ideological significance of textiles as they relate to women's work and texts to be interpreted in terms of domestic, erotic, and economic import. While the essay has a clear feminist orientation, Callaghan also takes into consideration the socioeconomic value of the textiles that women produced in early modern England. Throughout this essay Callaghan constantly makes comparisons between writing and textile production by women and notes their similarities, for she very strongly states, "I will argue that, even as the play anticipates the gender-coded taxonomies of private and public, work and leisure, art and artifact, which constitute the framework of full-blown capitalism, women's labor in *Othello* was far more visible to Shakespeare's audience than it is to us" (55). Therefore, Callaghan concentrates her attention on significant textile items such as the sheets and, especially, Desdemona's handkerchief in which Othello invests a great deal of ideological significance; after all, this handkerchief functions as a "miniature of the nuptial linens, bearing berries as the blood stains of marital defloration. Indeed, the terms 'sheet' and 'napkin' were sometimes used interchangeably" (57). Consequently, the importance of Desdemona's handkerchief cannot be underestimated in relation to Desdemona's marital relationship with Othello.

The production of linens and other goods made from textiles were certainly the domain of women in early modern England, and for this reason Othello prefers the battlefield to luxuriously appointed chambers which he associates with women and effeminate men, who are unaccustomed to warfare, for he is disdainful of that kind of opulent existence. In fact, textiles, including bed linens and other cloth products pertaining to the house, were principally the possessions of women. These linens could be used again and again, and so they were sold; moreover, linens and such almost had the liquidity of money. Callaghan cites the example of a widow from Manchester who bequeathed 34 pairs of sheets, which were considered to be an expression of a great deal of wealth (59).

In *Othello*, of course, Desdemona's handkerchief has not only economic value, but it also carries much ideological import, which is "freighted with socio-cultural value as a love token" (Callaghan 60). The case is made that the handkerchief acquires economic value in an increasingly capitalistic society. Callaghan cites the passage in which Desdemona avers that she would prefer to lose her "purse / Full of crusadoes" (III.iv.25–26) than this handkerchief, but the larger point is that Desdemona values this gift from Othello over and above the purse filled with Portuguese gold coins which had the image of the Cross (Neill 314). Callaghan argues that an Elizabethan audience would have been aware of the monetary as well as the symbolic value of linens. Apparently, because of the value of linens, they were susceptible to theft; in *Othello* Iago obviously has Emilia steal Desdemona's handkerchief because of its emotional impact on Othello and Desdemona's marriage. The theft of linen was especially linked to female criminality, for the women who stole linen were not those industrious ones depicted in marriage manuals (Callaghan 60–61).

Linens and handkerchiefs are perceived as necessities today, while in early modern England, handkerchiefs were thought of as luxury goods, for in a time devoid of tissues, it was not uncommon for the populace to wipe their noses on the sleeves of their shirts. Emilia perceives handkerchiefs as luxury goods that were emblematic of female consumption. She links female consumption to feminine infidelity, and she does not wish for anyone to perceive any similarity between her and Bianca, the courtesan to whom Cassio gives Desdemona's handkerchief which he found in his room having been placed there by Iago (61).

A compelling case is made for the perceived link between feminine consumption, indolence, and sexuality in the popular consciousness, or in at least the consciousness of the Puritan Phillip Stubbes, in *The Anatomy of Abuses* (1597), in which he delivers a devastating indictment against women and the attendant self-indulgence that accompanies laziness and the display of luxury goods. Stubbes laments female self-indulgence, sexuality, and conspicuous consumption, concerns with which all Puritans were familiar.

It would come as no surprise then that women were to be kept busy with housework in order to stay out of trouble, especially in the area of sexual transgression. Hence, women and girls of the middling sort and of higher social status were to be kept busy, and one way that they could productively use their time was through the creation of embroidery; they were to refrain from indulging in trifles such as handkerchiefs. Therefore, the reading of morally improving books was encouraged by male authority figures. The great early modern humanist, Erasmus, wrote in a letter to Bude, another humanist, that in the home of Sir Thomas More women are not involved with frivolous trifles, but on the contrary, they read Livy's texts to keep their minds usefully occupied (Callaghan 64).

Bianca, the courtesan, who probably does not have time or the ability to read Livy's texts, becomes involved with Desdemona's handkerchief when Cassio gives it to her in order for her to duplicate it; Callaghan intriguingly suggests that prostitution may not be her main line of employment, but rather she may engage in prostitution in order to increase her income. Callaghan cites the example of a very large number of spinsters and women who worked in needlework and had been accused of prostitution in Augsburg in the 16th century (65).

Unlike Bianca in *Othello*, Bianca in *The Taming of the Shrew* is instructed by Baptista to "Go ply thy needle" (II.i.25), as any good woman would do. Here Callaghan makes a compelling case for the needle as a displacement for the masculine pen. Moreover, Callaghan argues, "The lexical parallel between the prick of the needle and the male member had its counterpart in social reality all over Europe" (66). The frontispiece of John Taylor's *The Needles Excellency* (1634) is a brilliant example of three representations of women as allegorical figures. These three allegorical female figures stand outside in an enclosed garden, long recognized as a *hortus conclusus*, which emblematized female sexuality in early modern England and Europe. Standing under a tree, the female figures of Wisdom, Industrie, and Folly appear in various modes of action. The dignified figure of Wisdom stands upright reading a book with her hands judiciously crossed on her chest while Industrie sits on the ground sewing on what appears to be a sampler, as she is turned toward Folly. Folly gestures extravagantly while her gown is open displaying her elegantly sewn petticoat, a sign of conspicuous consumption. Callaghan describes Folly as "a fascinating figure of the woman who neither stands nor reads—the very epitome of Stubbes's female consumer" (66). The full title of this text is *The Needles Excellency: A New Booke wherin are diuers Admirable Werkes wrought with the Needle. Newly inuented and cut in Copper for the pleasure and profit of the Industrious*. While the figure of Industrie does not enjoy the elevated status of Wisdom, she remains actively engaged in the act of sewing even as she interacts with Folly. In many ways Industrie is the middle ground between Wisdom and Folly. Wisdom represents the contemplative life while Industrie represents the active life. These women must have functioned as at once cautionary and exemplary figures within the Puritan vision of the world.

Callaghan argues that regardless of whether women were reading or weaving, men constantly scrutinized women's intellect and eroticism so that they could contain these disparate energies. The humanist Richard Hyrde asserted that even as literacy compelled women to focus their intellectual energy on the ideas presented to them, reading also allowed women the chance to think independently of them (Callaghan 71). While women should be focused upon the text that they are reading, the act of reading allows women to fantasize about that which they should not. Once again the text's central concern entails not only control of women's actions but also their very thoughts.

Desdemona's handkerchief, not unlike the textiles that women wove in the early modern period, is not only a textile, but it also becomes a text to be read and interpreted. As Callaghan asserts, the handkerchief "is treated liked a printed book—as we have seen [it] is repeatedly described with the scribal term 'copy' which renders needlework as especially analogous to writing as the physical activity that produces a manuscript" (72). Moreover, in *Othello* not only is the handkerchief textualized, so too is Desdemona's body; after all, "she herself becomes an object—a sheet—when she is literally positioned as a text," according to Callaghan (72). Desdemona textualizes herself when she exclaims, "Was this fair paper, this most goodly book / Made to write 'whore' upon?" (IV.ii.72–73). Desdemona's body becomes, in effect, a text on which Othello inscribes his sexuality. (Analogously, in *Much Ado about Nothing*, Hero, the slandered heroine, not unlike Desdemona, finds her body textualized after Claudio renounced her at the altar alleging that she had engaged in sexual relations with a "ruffian" at her chamber window.)

Ultimately, there is a conflation of the body of Desdemona as text and textile as text; the handkerchief is all-important to the stability of Othello and Desdemona's marriage, for "the charmer knows the power of the handkerchief as an object because she partakes of not only the physical but, crucially, also the psychic energy which has produced it—an energy that is palpable in Othello's history of the object" (77). Finally, the passage concerning the handkerchief is highly significant as an example of needlework, but much more importantly it functions as one of the most "compelling accounts of creative inspiration in the canon of English literature" (78). The most renowned handkerchief in English literature attests to the enduring aesthetic and ideological influence that is accorded textiles not only by Western Europeans but also by Africans and Jews (57).

One of the finest essays in Janet Adelman's book, *Suffocating Mothers: Fantasies of Maternal Origin in Shakespeare's Plays, Hamlet to The Tempest*, is "Man and Woman Is One Flesh: Hamlet and the Confrontation with the Maternal Body" in which the figure of the woman's body comes to the fore, again, here in Gertrude's body. Interpreting Hamlet, both the play and the character, is possible without the use of psychoanalysis, and to be sure, this play has more than its share of such interpretations. In Adelman's psychoanalytic interpretation, she employs object-relations theory. As Ross Murfin states, "Whereas Freud saw the mother-son relationship in terms of the son and his repressed oedipal complex (and saw the analyst-patient relationship in terms of the patient and the repressed truth that the analyst could scientifically extract), object-relations analysts see both relationships as *dyadic*—that is, as being dynamic in both directions" (249). Freud stressed the early relationship between the mother and her child, but object-relations theorists stress the significance of the relationship as early as the first days of the mother with her child, and so according to Murfin, Adelman "stresses the overriding importance of Gertrude and the centrality of fantasies and anxieties about the sexualized body of the mother" (249). Hamlet becomes obsessed with the erotized body of his mother after the marriage to his uncle within two months of his father's murder. Adelman asserts quite cogently, "For the ghost, as for Hamlet, her chief crime is her uncontrolled sexuality; that is the object of their moral revulsion, a revulsion as intense as anything directed toward the murderer Claudius" (15). Again characters' perceptions of Gertrude are much different from those of theatregoers. Critics tend to believe Gertrude is a woman who is far more confused as to how she feels about her deceased spouse, Old Hamlet, Hamlet and her new husband, Claudius than a deliberately malicious wife who is interested in her spouse's demise (15).

Many literary critics have thought Hamlet's response to his mother's remarriage is incommensurate to how he should actually react. T. S. Eliot, most famous as the author of the first modernist poem, "The Love Song of J. Alfred Prufrock," asserted that *Hamlet* lacked an "objective correlative" which would function as an emotional equivalence to Hamlet's sense of moral outrage. Adelman argues Hamlet's anger results in "fantasies of maternal malevolence, of maternal spoiling, that are compelling as they are out of proportion to the character we know, exactly as they seem therefore to reiterate infantile fears and desires rather than an adult apprehension of the mother as a separate person" (16). In fact, Hamlet's maternal fantasies occur almost immediately when he delivers his first soliloquy as he makes reference to his "sullied flesh" (I.i.129) in which he expresses how he feels dirtied and morally tainted and wishes that he could slough off his body through death (16). (Adelman quotes from the Arden edition of *Hamlet*, edited by Harold Jenkins.)

Renaissance scholars have emphasized the significance of the garden imagery throughout *Hamlet*. In *Romeo and Juliet* the Capulet garden, also known as a *hortus conclusus*, is a metaphor for the sexuality of Juliet; here again in *Hamlet*, the metaphor of the garden figures significantly. According to Adelman, if the world and more particularly the state of Denmark is like an "unweeded garden," and the garden has traditionally represented the Virgin Mary, then the figure of the garden functions as tainted and corrupted (16). Sexuality and mortality are conflated in a powerfully compressed psychoanalytic fashion; the upshot of this conflation of sexuality and death results in a "maternal sexuality [which] turns the enclosed garden into the fallen world and brings death into that world by making flesh loathsome" (17). In this complex feminist psychoanalytic essay, Adelman spends a great deal of time providing background information before stating her thesis: "the sexualized maternal body as the initial premise of tragedy [is] the fall that brings death into the world: Hamlet in effect rewrites Richard III's sense that he has been spoiled in his mother's womb as the condition of mortality itself. The structure of *Hamlet* —and I will argue, of the plays that follow from *Hamlet*—is marked by the struggle to escape from the condition, to free the masculine identity of both father and son from its origin in the contaminated maternal body" (17). Adelman's argument focuses inexorably and ineluctably upon the maternal body as the site of contaminated contestation. In other words, all of the problems of Denmark ultimately lead back to female sexuality as its cause.

First, Hamlet must distance his father, Old Hamlet, from his stepfather, Claudius. The only way that he can accomplish this task is by deifying him into an almost asexual god when he states in an almost histrionic fashion: "So excellent a king, that was to this / Hyperion to a satyr" (I.ii.139–40). Hamlet compares his father to Hyperion in order to distance him from Claudius whom he compares to a satyr.

Adelman goes a bit far when she asserts that his "sexual power [is] analogous to God's power to impregnate the Virgin Mother" (19). Her comment, "Ordinary genital sexuality then becomes the province of Claudius the satyr: below the human, immersed in the body, he becomes everything Hyperion/Old Hamlet is not, and the agent of all ill" (19), makes considerably more sense than the previous one. Hamlet must somehow make sure that Old Hamlet is not involved in maternal violation. Hamlet is obsessed with determining that his mother can tell the difference between his father and Claudius, for he presents her with images of both his father and Claudius; then Hamlet verbalizes the differences between them; once again, Hamlet refers to his father as having "Hyperion's curls, the front of Jove himself, / An eye like Mars" (III.iv.56–57) while Claudius is transformed into a "mildew'd ear / Blasting his wholesome brother" (II.iv.64–65), but here again the discourse cannot render a difference between them because "the most significantly contaminated ear in the play belongs to Old Hamlet" (22), and Adelman reiterates this point of maternal contamination throughout this text.

Apparently, this image of poisoning Old Hamlet comes of a biblical origin in which the narrative of Cain and Abel is the model. Adelman is absolutely convinced that the Cain and Abel narrative is only a diversion from the main issue: the fact is that the murderer does not receive the father's blessing, but rather it has to do with a woman's body; taking a strong feminist approach, Adelman argues that Hamlet's father's death is not so much about the sibling rivalry of brothers as it may appear in a cursory reading of the text, but rather this murder of Old Hamlet has much more to do with how Old Hamlet was subjected to the feminine wiles of this crafty woman. In true patriarchal fashion, according to Adelman, the significant narrative concerns how women lead men to their deaths through subjection to their seductive trickery (24).

In keeping the focus on the maternal body which leaves destruction in its wake, Adelman alludes to the scene in which Hamlet queries Guildenstern and Rosencrantz as to the nature of their relations with Fortune. This is a highly suggestive dialogue, for Hamlet asks Guildenstern whether he lives "about her waist, or in the middle of her favours?" (II.ii.230). He replies that they live in "her privates" (231), and at this point, Hamlet avers, "She is a strumpet" (232). Therefore, Fortune is a prostitute. Adelman is convinced that this passage presages the scene in which King Lear spews out a great deal of vitriol about female sexuality (26), for he exclaims, "There's hell, there's darkness, / There is the sulphurous pit" (IV.vi.129–30). Female sexuality becomes tantamount to hell in Lear's mind because two of his daughters, Goneril and Regan, expelled him from his home once he abdicated his throne.

Hamlet increasingly becomes fixated upon the erotic relations of Claudius and Gertrude, for he perceives the father's body becoming contaminated by its interaction with the female body, and so the boundary between male and female becomes blurred at this juncture. Hamlet utters the famous words which become the title of this essay, "Father and mother is man and wife, man and wife is one flesh" (IV.iii.55). At this point in the deterioration of Hamlet's psyche, it is inconsequential as to whether Hamlet is referring to this own father or his stepfather because Hamlet perceives any sexual relations between men and women as "an adulterating mixture" (28).

Any sexual act for Hamlet is one of corruption and destruction as Adelman states, "The royal bed of Denmark is always already corrupted, already a couch for luxury, as Hamlet's own presence testifies" (32), and it is for this reason that Hamlet also wishes to separate his mother from sexual activity. After Hamlet tells his mother to refrain from sexual relations with Claudius, he tells her good night and that when she wishes to be blessed, he will bless her. Adelman argues that this moment functions as the turning point at which he "mark[s] his progression from rage at his mother's sexuality to repossession of the good mother he had lost" (33). Of course, both scholars and playgoers will never know if she turned away from Claudius's bed.

Traditionally, directors have represented her as a lascivious woman, but sadly, as Adelman remarks, "[S]he remains opaque, more a screen for Hamlet's fantasies about her than a fully developed character in her own right: whatever individuality she might have had is sacrificed to her status as mother" (34). Whether on the stage or page, Gertrude will always be one of Shakespeare's characters about whom we will never know as much as we would like to know. Characters, as Adelman astutely suggests, respond to her more than allow her to act, and so she becomes in effect a sounding board for what others in the drama have to say about her; nonetheless, that will not stop crowds or critics from attempting to ferret out her identity or Hamlet's for that matter.

Moving from *Hamlet*, a play whose characters exude an almost maddening self-consciousness, to *The Tempest*, a play defined as a romance by genre but which seems more like a fairy tale, can seem an extraordinary transition, but the issues of gender and sexuality in *The Tempest* are extremely significant vis-à-vis that of colonialism and postcolonialism. In "Caliban versus Miranda: Race and Gender Conflicts in Postcolonial Rewritings of *The Tempest*," Jyotsna G. Singh begins her essay by providing background information regarding the critical reception of this play by Latin American and Caribbean writers who perceive their situation in the 1960s as similar to Caliban's. Singh refers to Roberto Fernandez Retamar as a Latin American writer who cites a number of responses from other Latin American writers who perceived Ariel as an intellectual. Others such as Retamar thought of Caliban as their symbol instead of Ariel. In 1971 Retamar wrote: "Prospero invaded the islands, killed our ancestors, enslaved Caliban, and taught him his language to make himself understood" (Qtd. in Singh 207). Ten years earlier George Lamming, a writer from Barbados, who also thought that his nationality identified with Caliban, continues to examine the colonizer's language in which he asserted, "Prospero lives in the absolute certainty that Language, which is his gift to Caliban, is the very prison in which Caliban's achievements must be realized and restricted" (Qtd. in Singh 207). Finally, Aimé Césaire, a writer from Martinique and the founder of the Negritude movement, writes with greater ambiguity in his play, *A Tempest*, in which Caliban is presented as an adept revolutionary, and therefore, he constantly rejected Europe's version of world history (Singh 207). Singh asserts that Césaire represents the relationship between Caliban and Prospero as one of slave to master in which there is this ineluctable struggle between them.

Having presented African and Latin American writers' perceptions of Caliban and Prospero's relationship, Singh asserts, "I wish to look afresh at the relationship between Miranda and Caliban, especially at the way in which Shakespeare's play intersects with postcolonial reappraisals of it, which I believe, do not adequately address the interactions between race, sexuality, and political struggle. At the centre of my concerns lies the gendering of these postcolonial discourses of revolution in which Caliban as the prototype of a male revolutionary becomes a convenient, homogenising symbol for decolonization" (208).

Singh critiques the colonialist readings of Césaire, Lamming, and Fanon because they fail to take into consideration the category of gender in power relations, who in her words are "oddly oblivious to dissonances between race and gender struggles" (209). For example, Singh quickly points out that Fanon and other writers represent Caliban as a creature who wishes to rapaciously grasp the beautiful white body of Miranda as a product of Western civilization, yet he and others fail to question the ethics of that action (210). Before going into greater depth in her discussion of Césaire's *A Tempest*, Singh wants to "examine the discourse of sexuality in Shakespeare's *The Tempest* and explore how it offers the crucial nexus for Prospero's colonial authority" (210–11). Therefore, Singh discusses the issue of how women function as an exchange of gifts in primitive cultures, which provided a structure or system of competition and kinship among men in a patriarchal society.

When Miranda first sees Ferdinand, she expresses her erotic desire for him, for she says, "This / Is the first man that er'er I saw; the first I sighed for" (I.ii.445–46). Miranda articulately expresses her desire for Ferdinand over and above Caliban and her father, Prospero; as Singh points out, Ferdinand's concern is not one of the heart. Rather he immediately thinks of the right of patriarchal succession and erotic desire; after all, he does say, "O, if a virgin / And your affection not gone forth, I'll make you the / Queen of Naples" (I.ii.448–49). Miranda's virginal state is an extremely significant quality in Ferdinand's wife, perhaps her most important asset. Of course, one must remember that Prospero is the ultimate stage manager of the wooing that takes place between Ferdinand and Miranda. Prospero decides which man will have sexual access to his daughter. Singh makes an astute comment when she asserts that despite the fact that Miranda has "cultural superiority over Caliban, she nonetheless has a marginal role within a *kinship* system in which all the three males are bonded through their competing claims on her" (213). Citing Claude Lévi-Strauss and Marcel Mauss, both cultural anthropologists, Singh stresses the importance of women as exchanges of gifts among men. This exchange of women as gifts was extremely significant because it "enacted a relationship of kinship" (213). Ferdinand makes it clear that his marriage to Miranda is dependent upon her virginity, for Singh notes that when Ferdinand finally speaks with his father Alonso at the end of the play, he tells him, "I chose her when I could not ask my father, / For his advice" (V.i.190–91). To be sure, women as a means of exchange are the most basic kind of gift (214).

Miranda is not the only woman who functions as a mean of exchange in this play, for Claribel, Ferdinand's sister, married the King of Tunis in North Africa. This was not the usual marriage between two European families. Sebastian mentions this fact when he opines, "That would not bless our Europe with your daughter / But rather loose her to an African" (II.i.129–30). Singh cites Peter Hulme, who thinks that Claribel could possibly "have been a gift to fend off a dangerous new power in the central Mediterranean" (Qtd. in Singh 216). Singh herself perceives the reference to North Africa as ambiguous and multiple. Finally, she suggests that the marriage of Claribel to the king of Tunis in spite of its interracial nature was ultimately one of political convenience (217).

Some feminists attempt to demonstrate a connection between Caliban and Miranda in relation to the power that Prospero has over both of them. Singh cites Lorrie Leininger's article, "The Miranda Trap: Sexism and Racism in Shakespeare's *The Tempest*" as a critical example of a feminist reading in which Miranda responds to Prospero. In an imagined reply to her father, Miranda asserts, "I will not be used as the excuse of [Caliban's] enslavement . . . I need to join forces with Caliban—with all who are exploited" (Qtd. in Singh 217). Singh argues that feminist concerns are seldom represented in postcolonial versions of the play, and while Césaire may call for decolonization, race and gender issues are not necessarily mutual but may be diametrically opposed to each other.

In Césaire's *A Tempest* there should be no question that Caliban is the hero of the play, not Ferdinand. Singh notes that Caliban shrugs off Prospero's charges of attempting to rape Miranda. In Césaire's version of the play, Caliban accuses Prospero of putting those sexual thoughts in his head, but Miranda speaks up for herself in Act II, scene 1 in which she demolishes Caliban's argument that he is not sexually interested in her, describing him as that "awful Caliban who keeps pursuing me and calling out my name in his stupid dreams" (Qtd. in Singh 218).

Singh finds Césaire's lack of discussion regarding the issue of sexuality and its relation to power highly problematic as it concerns Caliban, Miranda, and Prospero, for Caliban's refusal to accept responsibility for his actions toward Miranda is actually a "convenient structural device for mobilizing an all-male revolution—one which recapitulates the kinship structure in its most basic form, giving a minimal presence to Miranda" (220). Prospero's plans for an alliance between Naples and Milan are affected through the marriage of Miranda to Ferdinand. Ultimately, despite Césaire's pleas for decolonization, the play fails to negotiate the relationship between representations of sexual difference and liberation movements in such a way that both women and the enslaved natives achieve the independence which they seek (221–22). In the final analysis, Singh persuasively argues that postcolonial theory simply does not take into account the category of gender in relations of power, especially in relation to women, who have traditionally held a subordinate position to men in all cultures around the world.

WORKS CITED

Adelman, Janet. *Suffocating Mothers: Fantasies of Maternal Origin in Shakespeare's Plays, Hamlet to The Tempest*. New York and London: Routledge, 1992. Print.

Butler, Judith. *Gender Trouble: Feminism and the Subversion of Female Identity*. London and New York: Routledge, 1990. Print.

Callaghan, Dympna. "Looking Well to Linens: Women and Cultural Production in *Othello* and Shakespeare's England." *Marxist Shakespeares*. Ed. Jean E. Howard and Scott Cutler Shershow. London and New York: Routledge, 2001. 53–81. Print.

Cook, Carol. "'The Sign and Semblance of Her Honor': Reading Gender Difference in *Much Ado about Nothing*." *PMLA* 101.2 (1986): 186–202. Print.

Davis, Lloyd. "'Death-Marked Love': Desire and Presence in *Romeo and Juliet*." *Romeo and Juliet*. Ed. R. S. White. Basingstoke, UK and New York: Palgrave Macmillan, 2001. 28–46. Print.

Garber, Marjorie. "The Education of Orlando." *Comedy from Shakespeare to Sheridan: Change and Continuity in the English and European Dramatic Tradition*. Ed. with an intro. by A. R. Braunmuller and J. C. Bulman. Newark: U of Delaware P and London and Toronto: Associated Press, 1986.102–12. Print.

Goldberg, Jonathan. "Romeo and Juliet's Open R's." *Romeo and Juliet*. Ed. R. S. White. Basingstoke, UK and New York: Palgrave Macmillan, 2001. 194–212. Print.

Hopkins, Lisa. *Beginning Shakespeare*. Manchester and New York: Manchester UP, 2005. Print.

Howard, Jean, and Phyllis Rackin. *Engendering a Nation: A Feminist Account of Shakespeare's Histories*. London and New York: Routledge, 1997. Print.

Levine, Laura. "Rape, Repetition, and the Politics of Closure in *A Midsummer Night's Dream*." *Feminist Readings of Early Modern Culture: Emerging Subjects*. Ed. Valerie Traub, M. Lindsay Kaplan, and Dympna Callaghan. Cambridge: Cambridge UP, 1996. 210–28. Print.

Lynch, Stephen. *As You Like It: A Guide to the Play*. Westport, CT: Greenwood, 2003. Print.

Murfin, Ross C. "Psychoanalytic Criticism and *Hamlet*." *William Shakespeare, Hamlet*. Ed. Susanne L. Wofford. Boston and New York: Bedford/St. Martin's Press, 1994. Print.

Newman, Karen. *Fashioning Femininity and English Renaissance Drama*. Chicago: U of Chicago P, 1991. Print.

Neill, Michael. Ed. *Othello*. By William Shakespeare. The Oxford Shakespeare. Oxford: Oxford UP, 2006. Print.

Singh. Jyotsna. "Caliban versus Miranda: Race and Gender Conflicts in Postcolonial Rewritings of *The Tempest*." *Shakespeare's Romances*. Ed. Alison Thorne. New York: Palgrave Macmillan, 2003. 205–25. Print.

Traub, Valerie. "The Homoerotics of Shakespearean Comedy." *Desire and Anxiety: The Circulations of Sexuality in Shakespearean Drama*. New York and London: Routledge, 1992. 117–144. Print.

PRIMARY DOCUMENTS

The following excerpt is from William Whately's *A Bride-bush or a Wedding Sermon: Compendiously Describing the Duties of Married Persons: By persons whereof, Marriage shall be to them a greate Help, which now finde it a little Hell.* This text, which was printed in London by William Jaggard for Nicholas Bourne and sold at his shop at the entrance of the Royal Exchange in 1617, acts as a marriage manual prescribing the appropriate behavior and attitudes of husbands and wives in order to fulfill their responsibilities to their spouses. Whately's *A Bride-bush or a Wedding Sermon* concerns the responsibilities that husbands and wives owe each other in marriage. This excerpt begins on page 1 and continues through page 11.

This text would be especially relevant to *The Taming of the Shrew* as there is an engaging discussion of how wives are to behave toward their husbands and how husbands are to behave toward their wives (Courtesy of the Folger Shakespeare Library).

DOCUMENT 1: EXCERPT FROM WILLIAM WHATELY'S *A BRIDE-BUSH OR A WEDDING SERMON*, PAGES 1–11

If it were not growne out of custome to preach without text, I should think that the fittest course for meetings of this nature. Not one place of Scripture doth either directly containe, or plainly express the full dutie of the married couple: which yet from many places may well bee collected into the body of one discoverie. But lest I should seeme to affect novelty, in recalling the long disused practise of antiquity, I will make the ground of all my speech, those words of the Apostle Paul, *Ephes*. 5.23 where hee saith,

The Husband is the Wives head.

The comparison which the Holy Ghost heere useth, affords this generall point, That there is a mutuall bond of duty standing betwixt man and wife. They are indebted each to other in a reciprocall debt. The parcels and specials of which debt, I am this time to declare unto you for the direction of all such as either are or shall be entered into this estate.

2. Now that we may proceed in some order for the help of our owne and your memories, these duties are all of two kinds. Some be principall, some lesse principall. Principal terme those by the breach whereof this knot is dissolved and quite undone: and which being observed (other smaller infirmities notwithstanding) the bond remaines entire on both sides.

3. These main duties are two. The first is, the chaste keeping of each ones body each for the other. The Husband must not dare to give himself to the any woman in this world but to his wife; not the wife to company with any under heaven besides her owne husband. Against which duty if either of them shall offend, the party so transgressing, hath committed adultery, broken the covenant of God,
Lev. 20,40 remooved the yoke from the yokefellowes neck and laide himselfe open (if the
Deut. 21,22 Magistrate did as God's law commands) to the bloody stroke of a violent death.

But if it be demanded, whether the party may lawfully admit the other party againe, after the offense knowne: I answer, that in case the man or woman have offended once or so, through infamy, and yet being convicted, shall manifest outward tokens, testify his or her repentance, and sure desire of amendment, then it is meet and convenient that this offense bee by the yoke- fellows passed by; for the love of the married couple should be very fervent and abundant, and therefore able to pass by great, yea the greatest wrongs, so farre as it may with safe conscience be done. And we reade not of any expresse commandment which enjoins final separation. But againe I say, that in case the party transgressing, shall continue in the begunne fault, and declare himself irreformable, the party thus injured is bound in conscience both to complaine of the sinne, and separate himself utterly: for no man must make himself a member of a harlot, nor woman of a whore-master. The chiefe things therefore that married people must take heed of, is this, left by any means they should so far offend God, neglect their publick covenant, wrong their yoke-fellow, scandalize the Church, pollute their bodies, and advenure their soules to damnation, as to follow strange flesh, and receive unto the use of their bodies any besides themselves, whom God hath coupled together, and sanctified one for another. Yet not alone the grosse act of adultery, but all such over-familiar and light behaviours, as may give occasion or suspicion of an evill meaning, must be by them forborne and sundered; always bearing in minde the grave speech of wise and Salamon, [*Whosoever toucheth her (speaking of his neighbor's wife) shall not be innocent*.] Let no man
Prov. 6.23 therfore, let no woman take this burning fire into their bosomes, or walk upon these scorching coales. And for the principall dutie so much.

4. The next is cohabitation or dwelling together, enjoined in expresse termes
1 *Peter* 3.7 to the husband by the Apostle *Peter* (who bids him, *Dwell with his Wife*) and therefore by good consequent extending to her also: for who can dwel with a
1 *Cor.* 7.3,5 woman that will runne from him ? And the Apostle Paul commands the husband to give unto his wife due benevolence, and the wife to give the same to the husband; which cannot be without this cohabitation: yea, he especially forbids them to *defraud each the other, unlesse it be by consent, and afterwards to come*

together againe. Which doth necessarily import the abode in one home. So that the married man or woman may not dwell where each of them pleaseth, but they must have the same habitation as one bodie. I deny not, that the service of the countrey, and needefull private affaires, may cause a just departure for (even) a long time: but a willfull and angry separation of beds or houses must not be tollerated. And if it so fall out, that either partie doe forwardly and pervertly withdraw him or herselfe from this matrimoniall society (which fault is tearmed desertion) the man or woman thus offending, doth so far violate the covenant of marriage, (the thing being found incureable, through the obstinancie of that party, after just care had to redresse it) the other is loosed from the former band, and may lawfully (after an orderly proceeding with the Church or Magistrate in that behalfe) joine him or herselfe to another. Of which there is very great reason. First, because such a separation is a willful frustrating of the proper purpose & end of marriage, annihilating the same through this default and sinfullnesse (even presumptuous) which is found guilty, and for this cause deserveth (yea constraineth) that hee should be rejected, as no longer a yoke-fellow. Secondly, because such unfaithfull desertion is almost never separated
from adultery, as the Apostle intimateth in the forenamed place, saying, *Lest* 1 *Cor.* 7,5
Satan tempt you for your inconstinency. He doth unavoidably cast himselfe upon uncleannesse that so lewdly casts off marriage, which he might avoide. And for this matter, wee have received cleare direction from the Holy Ghost by the Apostle, who saith, *If the unbeleever depart, let him depart: a brother or a sister is not bound* 1 *Cor.* 7,15
in such thing. In which words, he permits not to the unbeleever such separations as lawfull, but casts the fault upon him alone, and after frees the other party from the band which he or shee was formerly tied: as if hee has saide; If he will needes be gone, let him; and trouble not yourselves about it, the sin lies wholly upon his owne soule. A Christian man or woman, when cases of this nature fall out, is no longer tied to his former covenant, nor to the former partie, which hath himselfe first broken it. Neither is this any whit contrary to that of our Saviour, who forbids a man to put away his wife & marry another, unlesse it be for adultery. For *Matt.* 12,8
we allow not to him or her, any such liberty of putting away, but upon that only cause. Yet if he or she be wrongly put away (the yoke-fellow withdrawing him or herselfe out of the way, so that there be no hope to recall them, or else not returning upon good perswasion or meanes used) we yeelde with the Apostle, a freedome to the party so wronged. And these things you may well see stand together. No man may lawfully forsake his wife, nor the wife the husband (but in the case of adultery) to marry another; and yet any man or woman, being wrongfully forsaken by his or her yolk-fellow, may lawfully then marry another, without any sinne, on their parts, in that thing, procuring it. Only we professe, that in cases of this nature, a just and orderly course must bee taken. Every one may not be headdily, and upon a sudden, carve to themselves: but seeke direction, and crave helpe from the Church and Magistrate, whose dutie bindes them to provide remedy for such inconveniences. So that this thing also must bee diligently avoided by married people, that they doe never upon occasion of discontentment, or the like, absent themselves, or runne away from each other; which to

doe, were to untie that knot, which God before had knit betwixt them, and to separate things which God (and man by Gods allowance) had conjoined. Yea, they must not alone beware of making an utter rent and total breach in their society, but avoid also those smaller jarres and cracks, that make way thereunto. They must not through passionate fal[l]ings out, and proud distasting of each other's behaviour, separate house, bed or table, no not for a short space. They must not seeke occasions of long and needlesse absence, through carelesnesse or slight respect each of other, or following vaine pleasures and company-keeping abroad. For it is not madness to procure a strangenesse betwixt themselves, which ought to bee most familiar ? And were it not better, not to depart, than to make an open jarre of that which might have beene privately reconciled ?

5. And for the maine and principal duties required in matrimony; viz. chastity and cohabitation, so much. The lesse principall follow, to which, men and women are indeed bound by their promise and vow, but yet not with so much strictnes, than any offense in them should make the former bargain voide: wants in these matters; doe stretch the cord of matrimony, and give (as I may say) a sore gird unto it, but breake it not; only they breake Gods Commaundement exceedingly, that have not in these things also great care to confirme that union, which should be made indissoluble, by their diligence. Now these also are of two sorts, whereof the first respecteth their ordinary society; the second looketh to the society of the marriage-bed. Again, those which concern their ordinary society, are of two sorts: Some bee mutuall, pertaining to both: others speciall pertaining to either of them.

6. The mutuall therefore (that wee may speake of them in order) are required both of man and wife, though not in equall measure of both. For in all these common duties, the husband should bee most abundant, knowing that more of every grace is looked for from him, then from the weaker vessell. Wee call them not therefore common or mutuall, because both of them should have a like quantity of them; but because both must have some of all, and the husband most of all. And for these common duties, you must know in generall, that whatsoever is required of all men and women, generally towards other, by the Law of Christianity and Charity, as they bee men and neighbors; the same is in an higher degree and larger measure required from the husband toward the wife, and from her to him. So that looke from the Law of Love or Religion bids thee performe to any such person, as a man or a Christian, that it bindes thee much more diligently and carefully to performe to thy yoke-fellow. The neerer band of matrimony weakens not, but confirmes the more common of humanity. But it shalbe needfull more particularly to describe these common duties.

7. They bee of two kindes: The former respectfing themselves: the latter their families. Unto themselves they owe in common; first love; secondly, faithfulnesse and helpfulnesse; joined together, a faithfull helpfulnesse, and an helpefull faithfulnesse. As for love, it is the life, the soule of marriage, without which it is not more it selfe, than a carcase is a man; yea, it is uncomfortable, miserable, and a living death. For this, all must labour, as all will yeeld, that take marriage upon

them. The want of this, causeth defectivenesse in all other duties: the abundance of it, supplieth what is wanting in the rest. Love seasons and sweetens all estates: Love breakes off, and composeth all controversies: Love over-ruleth all affections, it squareth all actions; in a word, it the King of the heart, which, where it prevaileth, marriage is it selfe indeede, viz. a pleasing combination of two persons, into one home, one purse, one heart, and one flesh. But to commend it, and the good effects of it, (which all doe confesse) were needlesse paynes. Let us rather shewe what a kinde of love it must bee, and how it may bee gotten.

8. This love therefore which wee speake of, must bee first spirituall, then matrimoniall. Spirituall I say, that is, grounded principally upon the Commaundement of God that requires it, (for I speake of Christians) not upon the face, favour, proportion, beauty, dowrie, nobility, gifts or good parts of him or her, to whom it is due: for that naturall love which builds it selfe upon such sandy considerations, as the fore-named, will either bee blown downe by some storme or tempest of displeasure, or full of it selfe, or else degenerate into jealousy, the most devouring and fretting canker that can harbour in a married persons brest: but spirituall love, that lookes upon God, rests upon his will, yeeldes to his Commaundement, and resolves to obey it, cannot change it selfe, because the cause is unchangeable. Thou lovest thy Wife, for that shee is faire, well-spoken, courteous, of good feature, brings much, and is huswifely. It is well. But what will become of thy love, when all those things faile, as all may, the most must faile ? Thou lovest thine husband, because hee is a proper man, and hath an active and able body, is of good health, wit, carriage; because hee is kind, loving, of faire condition, useth thee well. But where shall we finde thy love, if an altercation come to these things, as to all earthly things it may come ? Loe then how is there no constancy or firmitude in other causes. But he which loves his wife, and shee which loves, her husband, because God hath so bidden, the maker of all things hath enjoyned it, the Lord and Maker of the heart, who alone may command the very affections, appoints it so; shall finde his or her love lasting and durable, as God alters not, and his Law continues alwayes the same. This right foundation of love, is God's Commandement, and then it is spirituall when built upon this rocke.

9. It must be also matrimoniall: Wee are to love our friends, our kindred, our neighbors, yea forreiners, and our utter enemies, even all men every-where: but the nuptial love of yoke-fellowes, is a speciall and peculiar love, forre more deare and inward than all, or any of all these. It is the fixing of their hearts in the good liking each of other, as the onely fit and good match that could bee found under the Sunne for them. The husband must rest his heart in his wife, as the best wife that the world could have yeelded him. The wife must settle her very soule upon her husband, as the best husband that might have beene had amongst men for her. Thus doing, they should love perfectly; thus striving to doe, they love intirely. They may lawfully thinke others better men or women, but none a better husband or wife for them than their yoke-fellow: for this were to admit the desire of changing, which cannot stand with true love. Who would change his Childe with any man ? Every mans owne son pleaseth him best, though perhaps

his qualities displease; so should the husband, so the wife. They therefore that are still upbraiding each other with the by-path matches, which they might, or should have had, love not soundly, though they may smile upon each other. Marriage-love admits of no equall, but placeth the yoke-fellow next of all to the soule of the party loving; it will know none dearer, none so deare. And of this quality is the love we require.

10. But how shall one that wants this love, attaine it, and he which hath some portion thereof, gaine a larger increase ? I answere, there bee two things, which will even cement and glew the soules of man and wife together; the first is, that take speciall notice of Gods gracious providence, for good in the match. They which look to God as the match-maker, and that in favour take each other as love-tokens from Heaven, and therefore cannot but love well, which comes as a signe of his favour, whom they strive to love above all. But they which see not his hand mercifully coupling them in this friendship, must needs fall out speedily, seeing they want this third thing, as it were the ligament and juncture of their affections. A matter of finall value is not smally respected, when it comes in good-will, from a great friend and a deare withal. Hee that loves the giver, will lose his gift also, although not so pretious: So the husband or the wife, though not of the best parts, shall be deare to the yoke-fellow that loves God, if he or she resolve in their hearts, God in great goodnesse hath bestowed this man or woman upon mee. Yea, say he or she be somewhat froward an sullied (as I may say) with ill conditions, the dearenesse of the giver wil countervaile some blemishes in the gift. Say the Lord did correct thee, in giving thee this husband, this wife: It was in favour, and for thy good. Cant thou chuse but kisse and love the rod that comes from thy father's hand ? But to this meanes add a second (which will also further unto this) and love shall grow without faile: Let married couples joine together in privat prayer, good conference, singing of Psalmes, and other like religious exercises betwixt themselves alone. S. *Peter* would not have the prayers of the married interrupted: for hee knew full well, that these were the best means of nourishment to their loves. In these things, the bright beames of Gods Image will shine forth, which have power to make them amiable each to other. Heere they shall bring forth so much profite and good to each others soule, even to their owne feelings, as will effectively provoke their feelings to bee mutually fervent. Heere they shall see themselves to bee children of the same father. Heere they shall see themselves as servants of one Master, strangers of one Countrey, & Pilgrims travailing both to one & the same home. So when the sudden land-floud of youthfull & violent affections are quite dried up, these fountains of spirituall love, which prayer, and other exercises of Religion shall have digged, will still runne with a more moderate and sober, but yet more lasting and constant streame. Let them season their naturall society with this spirituall communion, in the secret serving of God, and they shall avoide the surfet of satiety, which cloaketh love. Religion will knit the hearts of strangers fast in one, making them deare to each other ever after, that for the space but of one moneth or weeke, shall converse and joine together in the same; how much more effectuall will it bee to fasten their soules that are tied with so many and perpetuall bandes besides ? Therefore to you all that are, to

you that shall bee husbands and wives, bee this delivered as a direction; which if you faile to observe, you heare without profite. Pray together one with and for another in secret; conferre, reade the Word of God together, and sing Psalmes alone; this will so rivet your hearts, that no contention shall dissever them. For if you doe fall to some actions of unkindnesse, when you meete together againe in prayer, instead of assaulting each other, the husband shall blame himselfe and the the wife herself: she communing in Gods presence, wil see the greatnesse of her owne sinnes, hee of his, and then the offences one of another shall appeare but small. Thus they shall bee ashamed after to jarre, considering they must shame themselves before God for jarring: so that if any grudge arise, prayer wil heale and compose the same, that it doe not fester, rankle, or grow to a continued hard conceite. And let every man aske counsel of his owne heart, if the little praying together of husbands and wives, the seldome joining together in any good exercises, be not the true cause of their little love. Fond hee or shee may bee, that pray not betweene themelves, loving they cannot be.

A Discourse, of Marriage and Wiving and of the Greatest Mystery Contained: How to Choose a Good Wife from a Bad by Alexander Niccholes in London in 1615. This excerpt is from page A3 and pages 8 through 11 (Courtesy of the Huntington Library). This particular excerpt would be particularly appropriate regarding *Othello* because of Othello's obsessive concern with Desdemona's fidelity after his suspicions are raised because of Iago's nefarious insinuations and lies concerning it.

Document 2: Excerpt from *A Discourse, of Marriage and Wiving and of the Greatest Mystery Contained: How to Choose a Good Wife from a Bad*, page A3 and pages 8–11

To the Youth and Batchelary of *England, hote bloods at high Revels*, which forethought of this action, and all other, that hereafter intend this adventure

Since that the meanest blessing in mans life,
Is not the Dowry of a vertuous wife;
No otherwise then is the adverse crosse,
To him that beares it the most easy losse.
Therefore to you, whose weary bonds yet keepe,
Severing the Armes in which you long to sleepe;
Wisht that approaching minute in your power,
Which when arriv'd, most slowly brought to passe,
Cancels but Parchment to inroule in Brasse:
What not so short a terme of yeares shall end,
Unlesse one show himselfe the kinder friend:
Wherein, lest your to forward hast should stray,
Here is beforehand chalked out a way:
(As conscience craveth, for so large connexion

Should not be entred in without direction.)
Which who so walkes in to the true intent,
Shall not commit that action to repent.
The ignorant by this have sharper eyes,
More deeper insight to these miseries,
And more their understanding darke or blinde,
To passe this Laborinth 'tis here refinde:
Here are the characters insculpt and read,
That make a happy or a loathed bed.
What woman is on whom all these depend,
Her Use, Creation, Excellence, and End
In making choice how much to be confin'd,
To Beauty, Riches, Parentage, or Kinde:
What are the chiefe disturbers of this state,
That soonest point a man that sorest fate.
Here are the Rockes discovered to the eye,
That he that would not shipwracke may saile by.
And these the rather being aforehand laid,
Unballanst pleasures to each youth and maid,
That when experience shall they sweetnesse tell,
Instead of heaven then purchase not a hell.
And that the joy their forward youth hath sought,
Uncrosly match'd may come more neere their thought.
But you whose lust this limit shall not tie,
To those that For large inlargement to variety,
forebear mar- That will not any your owne proper call,
raige for The better interessed to commerce with all.
more liberty As when your Lord and Lady downe are laid,
of sin Behind the dore to woe the Chamber-maid:
Or amongst neighbours, where you lead your lives,
To be the more familiar with ther wives,
Or any place where you do espye,
A pretty morsell pleasing to your eye,
To seize it more suspectlesse, being knowne
Then hee that both at home a wife of's owne.
Well take that blessing, but with all this curse,
To walke on weake legges with an empty purse.

Chap. IIII

How to Choose a Good Wife from a Bad

This undertaking is a matter of some difficulty, for good wives are many times so like unto bad, that they are hardly discerned betwirt, they could not otherwise deceive so many as they do, for the devil can transform himselfe into an Angel of Light, the better to draw others into the chaines of darknesse, so these, his creatures, themselves into the shape of honesty, the better to entangle others in the bonds of his repentance:

If therefore the poke of marriage be of such perpetuity, and lasting even Usque ad naecem, and the joyes or grievance thereon depending equall continuance therwith, either to make as host heaven or hell in this world, is not therefore to be undergone but upon the [sic] regard and most advised consideration that may be, and because it is such a sea wherein so many shipwracke for want of better knowledge and advise upon a Rock, that took not better counsel in the haven; I have therefore in some sort, to prevent this danger, erected (as it were) certaine Land-markes and directions in the way, to give aime to such passangers as shall hereafter expose themselves to the mercy of this fury, and the rather because our age is so adventurous, whether boldnes or blindnes be their guid, the mere children dare undertake with vessels scarce capable to house up saile, the adventure of those passengers, the former tunes in their nonage, nere president as in the like, would have thought scarce navigable, but many times this calme that leads them forth in a sunshine with pleasure, brings them home in a tempest with sorrow; and therefore (as I said) he that would not repent him afterwards let him be advised before, for wise foresight for the most part is crowned with happy successe, therefore, say not hereafter (for it is weake remedy) Utinam saperem, would God I had bene better advised but be so.

The first aime that I would give to him, that would adventure this voyage (for marriage is an adventure, for whosoever marries adventures, hee adventures his peace, his freedom, his liberty, his body; yea, and sometimes his soule too) is, that in his election, after hee hath made choice of his wife, which ever I would have grounded upon some of these promising likelihoods, vid. That she be of sober and milde aspect, courteous behaviour, decent carriage, of a fired eye, and of an unaffected gate, the contrary being oftentimes signes of ill portent and consequence; for as the common saying is, an honest woman dwels at the signe of an honest countenance, and wilde lookes (for the most part) accompany wilde conditions; a revolving eye is not fired, but would fire upon objects it likes, it lookes for, and affected nicety is ever a signe of lascvious petulancy.

Next regard, according as thine estate and condition shall best intrust thee, the education, and quality, of her thou hast so related; her personage not being unrespected, for, so love lookes sometimes as well with the eye of the body, as with the minde, and beauty in some begets affection, and affection augmenteth love, whereas the contrary would decrease, and diminish it, and so bring thee to a death bed, which must be bitterly taken heed of, for the dangerous consequences that follow; so therefore, let thy wisdome so governe thine affection, that as it seize not up deformity to thine owne proper use, for some sinister respect to be mostly after repented of, so likewise (for the meane is ever best) that if levell not at so high and absolute involvement and perfection that every carnall eye shall bethinke thee injury, that every Gotish disposition shall levell to throw open thy inclosures, that thy wife shall bee harder to be kept then the Garden of Hesperides, for the Italian proverbe is,

Whose horse is white, and wife is faire,
His head is never voide of care.

Next after thou hast thus elected thy choice, and considered her in herselfe, with the aforesaid circumstances, this one more (not being of his minde that merrily said (speaking of his wife) since he was to make choice out of things that were evill, he thought it most wisdome to choose the least) to regard that shee be not of too dwarfish a size, and kindred, to store the with a generation of Pigmies, halfe men, that want the maiegty and power of heigth and strength, and the comelinesse and good stature is for the most part wedded unto: After this, a little look back to the stock from whence she sprung, for as Ezekiell saith, Like mother, like daughter; and experience and nature approves it, that the fruite will relish of the Tree from whence it sprang, as the Rose is not gathered from the Hawthorne, and as his Maiegty well observed, if men be so carefull to have their horses and dogs of a good breed, which are only for externall and superficial uses and pleasures, how much more should they then wives of their own bosomes, from whom they expect to raise and continue their owne generations and posterities upon earth, to represent and preserve alive their owne image and virtues behind them, from generation to generation, usq; ad longuinqum, & c.

A *Preparative to Mariage: The Summe whereof was spoken at a contract, and inlarged after.* Whereunto is annexed a Treastise of the Lords Supper: and another of Usurie by Henrie Smith newly corrected, and augmented by the Author. Imprinted at London by R. Field for Thomas Man, dwelling in Posternoster Row, at the signe of the Talbot. 1591. This excerpt begins on page B1and continues through page 57 (Courtesy of the British Library). This text is very much in keeping with the kind of prescriptive discourse that Prospero delivers to Ferdinand after Miranda has accepted his marriage proposal in *The Tempest,* and it would be very useful in contextualizing the kind of discussions that fathers and mothers would have with their daughters and even their sons concerning marriage.

DOCUMENT 3: EXCERPT FROM *A PREPARATIVE TO MARIAGE: THE SUMME WHEREOF WAS SPOKEN AT A CONTRACT, AND INLARGED AFTER,* PAGES B1 THROUGH 57

You are come hither to be contracted in the Lord, that is, of two to be made one for God: for God hath knit the bones and sinews together for the strengthening of mens bodies, so he hath knit man and woman together for the strengthening
Eccles. 9.9 of their life, because two are firmer then one and therefore when God made the
Gen. 2.18 woman for man, he said, *I will make him a helpe*: shewing that man is strongest by his wife. Every marriage, before it be knit should be contracted, as it is shewed in
Exod. 22.16 *Exod* 22.16 and *Deut*.22.28: which stray betweene the contract and the marriage,
Deut. 22.28 was the time of longing for their affections to settle in, because the deferring of that which we love, doth kindle the desire, which if it came easily & speedily unto us,

would make us set lesse by it. Therefore we read how Joseph and Marie were contracted before they were married. *Matt.* 1.18 In the contract Christ was borne, that he might honor both estates, *Luke* 1.27 virginitie with his conception, & marriage with his birth. You are contracted but to be married before, therefore I passe from contractes to speake of marriage, which is nothing but a communion of the life betweene man and woman, joined together according to the ordinance of God.

First I will shewe the excellencie of marriage: then the institution of it: then the causes of it: then the choice of it: then the duties of it: and lastly the divorcement of it.

Well might Paule say, marriage is honorable, for God hath honored it himselfe. It is honorable for the author, honorable for the time, and honorable for the place. Whereas all other ordinances were appointed of God by the hands of *Act.* 7.53 men, or the hands of Angels,marriage was ordained by God himselfe, which cannot errre. No man nor Angel brought the wife to the husband but God himselfe: *Heb.* 2.2 so marriage hath more of God in this, then all other ordinances of God beside, *Gen.* 2.22 because he solemnized it himselfe.

Then it is honorable for the time, for it was the first ordinance that instituted, ever the first thing which he did after man and woman were created, and that in the state of innocencie before either had sinned, like the finest flower, which will not thrive but in a cleane ground. Before man had any other calling he was called to be a husband: therefore it hath the honour or antiquities above all other ordinances, because it was ordained first, and is the ancientest calling of men.

Then it is honorable for the place, for whereas all other ordinances were instituted out of *Paradise*, marriage was instituted in *Paradise*, in the happiest place, to signify, how happy they are that marrie in the Lord, they do not onlie marrie one another, but Christ is married unto them, & so marriage hath the honor of the place above all other ordinances to, because it was ordained in *Paradise*.

As God the Father honoured marriage, so did God the Sonne, which is called, *Gen.* 3.15 *the seede of woman*: and therefore marriage was so honoured amongst woman *Luke* 1.25 because of this seede, that when Elizabeth brought forth a sonne, she said, that God has taken away her rebuke: counting it the honor of women to beare children, and by consequence, the honour of women to be married; for the children which are borne out of marriage are the dishonour of women called by the shameful name of bastardes. *Deut.* 32.2

As Christ honoured marriage with his birth, so he honored it with his miracles: For the first miracle which Christ did, he wrought at a marriage in *Chanaan*, where he turned their water into wine: so, if Christ be at your marriage, that is, if *John* 2.8 you marrie, that is, if you marrie in Christ, your water shall be turned into wine, that is, your peace, and your rest, & your joy, and your happiness shal begin with your marriage: but if you marrie not in Christ, then your wine shall be turned into water, that is, you shall live worse hereafter then you did before.

As he honoured it with miracles, so he honoured it with praises for he compa- *Matt.* 22.2 reth the kingdome of God to a wedding, and he compareth holinesse to a wedding garment. And in the fifth *Canticles* he is wedded himselfe. *Cant.* 5.9

We read in Scripture of three marriages of Christ. The first was, when Christ
and our nature met together. The second is, when Christ and our soule joine
together. The third is, the union of Christ and his Church. These are Christes
*Rev.*19.7 three wives. As Christ honouredmarriage, so do Christes Disciplines: for *John* cal-
*Rev.*17.1 leth the conjunction of Christ and the faithfull, *a Marriage*. And in *Revel.* 21.9.
the Church hath the name of a Bride, whereas Heresie is called a harlot. Further
for the honour of marriage, *Paule* sheweth how by it the curse of the woman was
Gene. 3.16 turned into a blessing; for the womans curse was the paines which she should
Gene. 1.28 suffer in her travaile. Now by marriage this curse is turned into a blessing: for the
children are the first blessing in all the Scripture. And therefore Christ saith, that
John 16.21 so soone as the mother seeth a man child borne into the world, she forgetteth all
her sorrowes, as though her curse were turned into a blessing. And further. *Paule*
saith that by bearing children, if she continue in faith and patience, she shall be
1 *Tim*. 2.15 saved: as though one curse were turned into two blessings. For the first she shall
have children, and after she shall have salvation. What merciful God have we,
whose curses are blessings ? who would have thought that God had hid a blessing
in a curse ? So he loved our Parentes when he punished them, that he could scarce
punish them for love and therefore a comfort was folded in his judgement.

Gene. 2.22 To honour marriage more, it is said that God tooke a rib out of *Adams* side,
and thereof built the woman. He is not said to make a man and a wife, but to build
him a wife, signifying, that man and wife make as it were one house together, &
that the building was not perfect, until the woman was made as well as the man,
therefore if the building be not perfect now, it must be destroyed againe.

Before God made woman, it is said, that he cast the man into a sleepe, and in
his sleepe he tooke a rib out of his side, and as he made the man of earth, so he
made the woman of bone, while *Adam* was asleepe.

1 *Cor*. 15.22 This doth teach us two things: as the first *Adam* was a figure of the second
& 45 *Adam*, so he first *Adams* sleepe, was a figure of the second *Adams* sleepe, and
the first *Adams* spouse, was a figure of the second *Adams* spouse. That is, as in
the sleepe of *Adam*, *Eve* was borne, so in the sleepe of Christ the Church was
borne; as a bone came out of the first Adams side, so blood came out of the
second Adams side. As Adams spouse received life in his sleepe, so Christes
spouse received in life his sleepe: that is, the death of Christ is the life of the
E. 5.14 Church, for the Apostle calleth death a sleepe but Christ which died is called
John 14.6 life, shewing that in his death we live. Secondly, this sleepe which was created,
doth teach us, that out affections, our lustes, and conscupiscences, should sleepe
while we go about this action. As the man slept while his wife was making,
Gene. 27.3 so our flesh should sleepe while our wife is choosing, least as the love of the
venison was *Issack* to bless one for another, so the love of gentrie, or riches, or
beautie, make us take one an other.

To honor marriage more yet, or rather to teach the married how to honor one
another, it is said, that the wife was made of the

Gene. 2.22 husbandes rib: not of his head, for Paul calleth the husband the wives head:
Ephe. 5.23 nor the foote, for he must not set her at his foote: the servaunt is appointed to
serve, & the wife to helpe. If she must not match with the head, not stoope at

the foote, where shall he set her then ? He muste set her at his heart, and therefore she which should lie in his bosome, was made in his bosome, and should be close to him as his rib of which she was fashioned.

Lastly, in all nations the day of marriage was reputed the joyfullest day in their life, and is reputed still of all, as though the Sunne of happiness began that day to shine upon us, when a good wife is brought unto us. Therefore one saith, that marriage, doth signifie merriage, because a play-fellow is come to make our age merrie, as *Isaak Rebeccah* sported together.

Salomon considering all these excellencies, as though we were more indebted to God for this than other temporall giftes, faith: *House and riches are the inheritance of the fathers, but a prudent wife commeth of the Lord.* *Prov.* 14.14

House and riches are given of God, and all things else, & yet he saith, house and riches are given of Parents, but a good wife is given of God: as though a good wife were such a gift as we shold account from God alone, and accept it as if he should send us a present from heaven, with his name written on it, *The gift of God.* *Gene.* 2

Beasts are ordained for food, & cloths for warmth, and flowers for pleasure, *Gene.* 19.20 but the wife is ordained for man, like little Zoar, a Citie of refuge to flie to in all his troubles, and there is no peace comparable unto her, but the peace of conscience.

Now it must needs be, that marriage, which was ordained of such an excellent Author, and in such a happy place, and of such an ancient time, and after such a notable order, must likewise have speciall causes for the ordinance of it. Therefore the holy Ghost doth shew us the causes of this union. One is, the propagation of children, signified in that when *Moses* saith, *He created them male and female,* *Gen.* 27 not both female, but one male, and the other female, as if he created them fit to propagate other. And therefore when he had created them so, to shew that propagation of children is one end of marriage, he said unto them, *Increase and* *Gene.* 1.28 *multiplie,* that is, bring forth children, as other creatures bring forth their kinde. For this cause marriage is called Matrimonie, which signifieth because it makes them Mothers, which were Virgins before: and in the seminarie of the world, without which all things should be in vaine, for want of men to use them, for God reserveth the great Cittie to himselfe, & this suburbs he hath set out to us, which are regents by sea and by land. If children be such a chiefe end of marriage, then it seemes, that where there can be no hope for children, for age and other causes, there marriage is not lawfull, because it is maimed of one of his ends, and seemes *Deut.* 23.1 rather to be sought for wealth, or for lust, then for this blessing of children. It is not good grafting of an old head upon young shoulders, for they will never beare it willingly but grudginglie.

Twise the wife is called, *the wife of thy youth,* as though, as when men are old, *Mala.* 8.18 the time of marrying is past. Therefore God makes such unequall matches so *Prov.* 5.18 ridiculous every where, that they please none but the parties themselves.

The second cause is to avoid fornication: this *Paule* signifieth, when he saith: *1 Cor.* 7.8 *For the avoiding of fornication, let every man have his owne wife.* He saith not for avoiding of adulterie, but for avoiding fornication, shewing, that fornication is unlawfull to, which the Papists make lawfull, in mainteyning their Stewes, as a

2 *Sam*. 16.22 stage for fornicators to play upon, & a Sanctuarie to defend them, like *Absoloms*
Tent, which was spread upon the top of the house, that *Israell* might see how he
Mala. 2.15 defiled his fathers concubines. For the cause, *Malachi* saith, that God did create
but one woman for the man, he had power to create mo, but to shew that he
would have him sticke to one, therefore he created of one rib, but one wife for
1 *Pet*. 3.20 one husband: and in the Arke, there were no more women then men. But foure
wives for foure husbandes, al though it was in the beginning of the world, when
many wives might seeme necessarie to multiplie mankind.

If any might have a dispensation herein, it seemes the Kings might be
privileged before any other, because of their sucession to the Crowne, if his
Deut. 17.17 wife should happen to be barren. And yet the King is forbidden to take many
1 *Tim*. 3.2 wives in *Deut*. 17.17 as well as the Minister in 1 *Tim*. 3.2. shewing, that the
danger of the State, doth not countervaile the danger of fornication. For this
Gene. 4.23 cause we read of none but wicked *Lamech* before the Flood, that had mo wives
then one, whom *Jovinian* calleth a monster, because he made two ribs of one.
And an other saith, that the name of his second wife doth signifiy a shadow,
because she was not a wife but the shadowe of a wife: for this cause the Scrip-
Mat. 9.5 ture never biddeth man to love his wives, but to love his wife, & saith, *They*
Prov. 2.16 *shall be two in one flesh*, not three, nor foure, but onlie two. For this cause, *Salomon*, calleth the whorish woman a strange woman, to shew that she should
be a stranger to us, and we should be strange to her. For this cause, children
which are borne in marriage, are called Liberi, which signifieth free borne: and
they which are borne out of marriage, are called Bastards, that is, baseborn,
Gen. 36.24 like the Mule which is engenderd of an Asse and a Mare. Therfore adulterers
Mat. 13.25 are likened to the devil, which sowed another mans ground, other sow for a Har-
Psal. 128.4 vest, but they sowe that which they dare not reape. Therefore children borne
Gene. 1.28 in wedlocke are counted Gods blessing, because they come by vertue of that
blessing, *Increase and multiplie*. But before *Adam & Eve* were married, God never
said, *Increase*, shewing, that he did curse & not blesse such increase. Therefore
Judg. 11.1 we read not in all of the Scripture of one Bastard that came to any good, but
only *Iphtah*, and to shew that no inheritance did belong to them in heaven,
they had no inheritance in earth, neither were counted of the congregation, as
Deut. 23.2 other were.

Now, because marriage was appointed for a remedie against fornication, ther-
Levit. 20.10 fore the Law of God inflicted a sorer punishment upon them which did commit
Deut. 22.22 uncleanness after marriage, then upon him which was not married, because he
sinned although he had the remedie of sinne, like a rich theefe which stealeth,
and had no neede.

Now if marriage be a remedy against the sinne of fornication, then unlesse
Ministers may commit the sinne of fornication, it seemes that they may use the
1 *Cor*. 7.9 remdeie as well as other: for as it is better for one man to marry then to burne,
Heb. 13.4 so it is better for all men to marrie then to burne: & therfore Paule saith, *Marriage is honorable amongst all men*. And agayne, *for the avoiding of fornication, let
every man have his wife*. And as though he did fore-see, that some would except
the Minister in time to come, in the first of *Tim*. 3.2. he speaketh more precisely

of the Ministers wife, then of any other, saying, *Let him be the husband of one* 1 *Tim*. 3.2
wife, and least ye should say that by one wife, he meaneth one Benefice like the
Papistes: He expoundeth himselfe in the fourth verse, and saith, that he must be
one that can rule his house well, and his children. Sure God would not have these
children to be Bastards, and therefore it is like that he alloweth the Minister a 1 *Cor*. 7.6
wife. Therefore Paule said well, that he had no commandement for virginitie, for
virginity cannot be commanded because it is a special gife, but not a special gift
to Ministers, & therfore they are not to be bound man than other. A peculiar gift
may not be made a genrall rule, because none can use it, but they which have it. 1 *Cor*. 7.17
And therfore in 1 *Cor*. 7.17 he saith *As God hath distributed to every man, so let*
him walke. That is, if he have not the gift of continencie, he is bound to marrie,
and therfore *Paul* commandeth in the seventh verse, whether he be Minister or
other, *If they can not abstaine, let them marrie*, as though they tempted God if they
married not.

The Law was generall, *It is not good for man to be alone*, exempting one order *Gene*. 2.18
of men no more than other. And again, Christ speaking of chastity, saith, *All men* *Mat*. 19.11
cannot receive this thing. Therefore unlesse we know that this order of men can
receive this thing: Christ forbids to binde them more than other, and therefore
as the Priestes were married that taught the Law, so Christ chose Apostles which
were married to preach the Gospell. Therefore the doctrine of Papists, is the doctrine of devils, for *Paule* calleth the forbidding of marriage, the doctrine of devils, 1 *Tim*. 4.3
a fit title for all their bookes.

Lastly, if marriage be a remedie against sinne, then marriage itselfe is no sinne:
for if marriage itselfe were a sinne, we might not marry for any cause, because *Rom*. 3.8
we must not doe the least evill that the greatest good may come of it: and if marriage be not a sinne that is, the secret of marriage is not evill, and therefore Paule *Heb*. 13.4
saith, not onely *Marriage is honourable*, but the bed is honourable, that is, the
action of marriage is as lawfull as marriage. Besides, *Paule* saith, *Let the husband* 1 *Cor*. 7.8
give unto the wife, due benevolence, here is a commaundement to yeeld this duetie:
that which is commaunded, is lawfull; and not to do it, is breach of the commaundement. Therefore marriage was instituted before any sinne was, to shewe
that there is no sinne in it if it be not abused: but because this is rare, therefore *Levit*. 12.4.5
after women were delivered, God appointed them to be purified, shewing some
staine or other doth creepe into this action, which had neede to be repented, & 1 *Cor*. 7.5
therfore when they prayed, *Paule* would not have them come together, least their
prayers should be hindered.

The third cause is, to avoid the inconvenience of solitarines, signified in these *Gene*. 2
wordes, *It is not good for man to be alone*, as though he had said, this life would be
miserable & irksome and unpleasant to man, if the Lord had not given him a wife
to companie his troubles. If it be not good for man to be alone, then it is good for
man to have a fellow: therefore as God created a paire of all other kinds, so he
created a paire of this kinde.

We say that one is none, because he cannot be fewer than one, he cannot be
lesser than one, he cannot be weaker than one, and therfore the wiseman said, *Eccles*. 4.10
Woe to him which is alone, that is, he which is alone, shall have woe. Thoughtes

and cares, and fears, will come to him, because he hath none to comfort him,
as theeves steale in when the house is emptie; like a Turtle, which hath lost his
mate, like one legge when the other is cut off, like one wing when the other is
clipt, so had the man been, if the woman had been joined to him: therefore for
mutuall societie, God coupled two together, that the infinit troubles which lie
Prov. 19.7 upon us in this world, might be eased, with the comfort and helpe one of another,
and that the poore in the world, might have som comfort as well as the rich,
Prov. 27.10 *for the poore man* (saith *Salomon*) *is forsaken of his owne brethren*, yet God hath
1 *Sam*. 14.7 provided one comforter for him, like *Jonathans* Armour- bearer, that shall never
forsake him that is another selfe, which is the onely commoditie as I may terme
it, wherein the poore doe match the rich, without which, some persons should
have no helper, no comforter, no friend at all.

Psal. 21.9 But as it is not good to be alone, so *Salomon* sheweth, *That it is better to be*
alone, then to dwell with a froward wife, which is like a quotidian ague, to keepe
1 *Sam*. 16.14 his patience in ire. Such furies do haunt some men, like Sauls spirit, as though
the devill had put a sword into their handes to kill themselves, therefore choose
whom thou maist enjoy, or live alone still, and thou shalt not repent thy
bargaine.

That thou maist take and keepe without repentence, now we will speake of
the choice, which some call the way to good wives dwelling, for these flowers
grow not on every ground; therefore, they say, that in wiving and striving a man
Deut. 1.23.4 should take counsel of theworld, least he light upon a curse while he seekes a
blessing. As Moses considered what spies he sent into *Chanaan*, so thou must
regard whom thou spendest to spye out a wife for thee. Discretion is a warie spye,
but fancie is a rash spye, and liketh whom she will mislike agayne.

Zach. 5.7 In the Revelation, Antichrist is described by a woman, & in *Zacharie*, sinne
is called a woman, which sheweth, that women have many faultes, therefore he
which chuseth of them, had neede have judgement, and make an Anatomie of
their hearts and mindes, before he say, This shall be mine. For the wisest man
Eccles. 7.30 saith, *I have found one man of a thousand, but a woman among them all have I not*
found. Although this may be understood of his concubines, yet it implieth that
there is a greater infirmitie in women then in men, because he compareth them
together, as though there were a dearth of good women over the world

For helpe hereof, in 1 *Cor*. 7.39, we are taught to marrie in the Lord, then we
1 *Reg*. 3.9 must chuse in the Lord to: therefore we must begin our Marriage where *Salomon*
began his wisedome. *Give unto thy servaunt an understanding heart*: so give unto
Gene. 24.12 thy servuant an understanding wife, If *Abrahams* servaunt prayed unto the Lord
to prosper his businesse, when he went about to chuse a wife for an other, how
should thou pray when thou goest about a wife for thyselfe, that thou mayst say
after. My *lot is fallen in a pleasaunt grounde*. To direct thee to a right choice herein
the Holie Ghost gives thee two rules in the choice of a wife *Godlinesse* and *Fit-*
nesse: Godlinesse, because our Spouse must be like Christe's Soule, that is, graced
with giftes, and imbrodered with vertues, as if we married *Holinesse herselfe*. For
Ephes. 5.29 the marriage of man and woman, is resembled of the Apostle to the marriage of
Cant. 6.8 Christ and the Church. Now the Church is called *Holie*, because she is holy. In

the 6 *Cantic* she is called *Undefiled*, because she is undefiled. In the 45 *Psal*. She is called *faire within*, because her beautie is inward: so our Spouse should be holy, undefiled, & faire within. As God respecteth the heart, so we must love, & not the face. Covetousnes hath ever been a Sutor to the richest, & pride to the highest, and lightnes to the fairest, & for the revenge hereof, his joy hath ever ended with his wives youth, which tooke her beauty with it. The goods of the world are good, & the goods of the body are good, but the goods of the minde are better. As *Paule* commendeth faith, hope, & charity, but faith the greatest of these is charitie: so may I commend beauty, and riches, and godlines, but the best of these is godlines, because it hath the things which it wants and makes every state alike with her gift of contentation.

Psal. 45.9

1 *Sam*. 16.7

1 *Cor*. 13.13

Secondly, the mate must be fit: it is not enough to be to be vertuous, but to be sutable; for divers women have many vertues, & yet do not fit with some men; & divers men have many vertues, & yet do not fit to some women: and therfore we see many times, even the godly couples to jarre when they are married, because there is some unfitnes betweene them, which makes oddes. What is oddes but the contrarie to even ? therefore make them even (saith one) and there will be no oddes. From hence came the first use of the Ring in weddings, to represent this evennesse: for if it be straighter then the finger it will pinch, and if it be wider then the finger it will fall of; but if it be fit, it neither pinchest nor slippeth: So they which are like, strive not, but they which are unlike, as fire and water. Therfore one observeth, that concord is nothing but likensse,& all that strife is unfititnesse: as in things when they fit not together, and in persons when they sute not one another.

How was God pleased when he had found a king according to his owne heart ? So shall that man be pleased that finds a wife according to his own hart, whether he be rich or poore, his peace shall afford him a chearful lfe, & teach him to sing, *In love is no lacke*. Therfore a godly man in our time, thanked the Lord that he had not only given him a godly wife, but a fit wife: for he said not that she was the wisest, not the holiest, nor the humblest, nor the modestest wife in the world, but the fittest wife for him in the world, which every man should thinke when that knot is tied, or else so often he seeth a better, he will wish that his choice were to make againe. As he did thanke God for sending him a fit wife, so the unmarried should pray God to send them a fit wife: for if they be not like, they will not like.

1 *Sam*. 2.35

The fitnesse is commended by the holy Ghost in two words: one is in the 2 of *Gen*. and the other is in the 2 *Cor*.6.14. That in *Gen*. she is *Meete*. God saith, *I will make man a helpemeete* for him. Shewing that a wife cannot help well unless she be meete. Further, it sheweth that man is such an excellent creature, that no creature was like unto him or meet for him, till the woman was made. This meetnesse God shewest againe in the 22 *verse* where *Moses* saith, that of the rib which was taken out of man, God built the woman: signifying, that as one part of the building doth meete & fit with another; so the wife should meete & fit with the husband, that as they are called couples, so they maye be called paires, that is, as a paire of gloves, or a pair of hose are like: so man and woman should be

Gen. 2.18

2 *Cor*. 6.14

like, because they are a paire of friends. If thou be leanred, chuse one that loveth knowledge: if thou be Martiall, chuse one that loveth prowesse: if thou must live by thy labour, chuse one that loveth husbandrie: for unlesse her mind stand with thy vocation, thou shalt neither enjoy thy wife, nor thy calling.

That other word in the 2 *Cor.* 6.14 is *Yoke*, there Marriage is called a Yoke.
Paule saith, *Be not unequally yoked*. If Marriage be a Yoke, then they which draw
in it must be fit, like two Oxen which draw together, or else all the burthen
Phil. 4.3 will lie upon one. Therfore theyare called yoke fellowes too, to shew that they
which draw this yoke must be fellowes. As he which soweth seede, chuseth a fit
ground, because they say it is good grafting uppon a good stocke: so he which
Ezek. 16.44 wil have godly children, must chuse a godly wife: for like mother (saith *Ezekiel*)
like daughter. Now, as the traveller hath marks in his way, that he may proceede
aright: so the suter hath marks in his way, that he may chuse aright.

There be certaine signes of this fitnesse, and godlinesse, both in the man
and in the woman. If thou wilt know a godly man or godly woman, thou must
mark five things: the report, the lookes, the speech, the apparel, & the companions, which ar like the pulses that show whether that shew whether we be
wel or ill. The report, because as the market goeth, so they say the market men
Psal. 11.26 wil talke. A good man commonly hath a good name, because a good name is
Prov. 10.7 one of the blessings which God promiseth to good men, but a good name is
Mar. 14.9 not to be praised from the wicked: & therefore Christ saith, *Cursed are you*
Luke 6.26 *when all men speake well of you*: that is when evill men speake well of you, because
John 15.19 this is a signe that you are of the world, *for the world liketh and prayseth her owne*.
Luke 11.6 Yet as Christ said, *Who can accuse me of sinne* ? So it should be said of those of us,
not who can accuse me of sinne ? but who can accuse me of this sinne, or who
can accuse me of that sinne ? That is, who can accuse me of swearing ? who can
accuse me of dissembling ? who can accuse me of fornication ? No man can say
this of his thought, but everie man should say it of the acte, like *Zachariah* and
Elizabeth, which are called unblameable before men, because none could call
accuse them of open sinnes.

Eccles. 8.7 The next signe is the looke, for *Salomon* saith, *Wisedome is in the face of a man*:
so godlinessse is in the face of a man, and so follie is in the face of man, and so
Esay. 3.9 wickednesse is in the face of a man. And therefore it is said in *Esay*. *The triall*
of their countenance testifieth against them. As though their lookes could speake,
and therefore we read of proud lookes, and angrie lookes, and wanton looks:
because they bewray pride, and add anger and wantonnesse. I have heard one
say, that a modest man dwels at the signe of a modest countenace, and an honest
Act. 3.2 woman dwelleth at the signe of an honest face, which is likethe gate of the Tem-
ple that was called *Beautifull*: shewing, that if the entry be so beautifull, within is
great beautie.

To shew how a modest countenance, and womanlie shamefastnes, doe commend a chast wife, it is observed that the word *Nuptia*, which signifieth the marriage of the woman, doth declare the manner of her marriage: for it importeth a
covering, because the Virgins which should be married, when they came to their
Gene. 24.65 husbands, for modestie & shamefastnesse did cover their faces: as we read of

Rebeccah, which so soone as she saw *Isaak*, and knew that he should be her husband, she cast a vaile before her face, shewing that modestie should be learned
before marriage, which is the dowrie that God addeth to her portion.

The third signe is her speach, or rather her silence: for the ornament of a
woman is silence; and therfore the Law was given to the man rather than to
the woman, to shewe that he should be the teacher, & she the hearer. As the
Eccho answereth but one for many which are spoken to her; so a maides answere
should be in a word, for she which is full of talke, is not likelie to proove a quiet *Matt*. 12.34
wife. The eye and speach are the mindes Glasses; *for out of abundance of the heart*
(saith Christ) the mouth speaketh: as though by the speach we might know what *Matt*. 12.36
aboundeth in the heart: and therefore he saith, *By thy wordes thou shalt be justified,*
and by thy wordes thou shalt be condemned. That is, thou shalt be justified to be wise,
or thou shalt be condemned to be foolish: thou shall be justified to be sober, or
thou shalt be condemned to be rash; thou shalt be justified to be humble, or thou
shalt be condemned to be proud, thou shalt be justified to be loving, or thou shalt *Prov*. 18.7
be condemned to be envious. Therfore *Salomon* saith, *A fooles lips are a snare to*
his soule. Snares are made for other, but this snare catcheth a mans selfe, because
it bewrayeth his folly, & causeth his trouble, and bringeth him into dicredite. *Prov*. 17.23
Contrariewise, *The heart of the wife* (saith *Salomon*) *guideth his mouth wisely, and* *Ecles*. 12.10
the wordes of his mouth have grace. Now, to shewe that this should be one marke
in the choice of thy wife. *Salomon* describing a right wife, saith, *She opened her* *Prov*. 19.15
mouth with wisedome,& the law of grace is in her tongue. A wife that can speak this
language, is better then she which hath all the tongues. But as the open vessels *Num*. 19.15
were counted uncleane, so account that the open hath much uncleannesse.

The fourth signe is the apparell: for as in the pride of the Glutton is noted, *Luke* 16.19
in that he went in purple every day, so the humilities of *John* is noted, in that he *Mar*. 1.6
went in haire-cloth every day. A modest woman is knowne by her sober attire, as *2 Kin*. 1.8
the Prophet *Eliah* was knowne by his rough garment. Look not for better within,
that thou seest without; for every one seemeth, better than she is, if the face be
vanity, the heart is pride. He which biddeth the abstaine from the *shew of evill*, 1 *Thes*. 5.22
would have thee to abstaine from those Wives which have the shewes of evill: for
it is hard to come in the fashion, and not to be in the abuse. And therefore *Paule* *Rom*. 12.2
saith, *Fashion not yourselves like unto this world*, as though the fashions of men did
declare of what side they are.

The fifth signe is the companie: for birds of a feather will flie together, and 1 *Reg*. 12.8
fellowes in sinne will be fellowes in league, even as young Rehoboam chose
young companions.

The tame beasts will not keepe with the wild, nor the cleane dwell with the leprous. If a man can be knowne by no thing els, then he may be knowne by his companions: for like will unto like, as *Salomon* saith, theeves call one another. Therefore when *David* left iniquitie, he said, *Away from me all ye that worke iniquite*. Shewing that a man never abandoneth evill, untill he abandoneth evill, until he abandon evil companie: for no good is concluded in this parliament. Therefore chuse such a companion of thy life, as hath chosen company like thee before: for they which did chuse such as loved prophane companions before, in a while were drawne to be prophane to, that their wives might love them. All these properties are not spied at three or foure comings, for hypocrisie is spunne with a fine thred, and none so often deceived as lovers. He which will know all his wives qualities before he be married to them, must see her eating and walking, and working, and playing, and talking, and laughing, & chiding, or else he shall have lesse with her then he looked for, or more then he wished for.

Gen. 24.50 When these rules are warily observed, they may joine together and say, as
Laban and *Bethuel* said, *This cometh of the Lord, therefore we will not speake against it*. How happie are those in whose Faith and Love, and Godlinesse are married together, before they marrie themselves ? For none of these Martiall, & cloudie & whining marriages, can say that godlines was invited to their bridall; & therfore the blessings which are promised to godlines, do flie from them.

Now in this choice are two questions. First, whether children may marrie without their Parentes consent: and the second, whether they may marrie with Papists,
Exod. 20 or Atheistes, & c. Touching the first, God saith, *Honour thy father and thy mother*.
Now, wherein canst thou honour them more, then in this honorable action, to
which they have preserved thee, and brought thee up, which concerneth the
state of the whole life ? Agayne, in the first institution of marriage, when there
Gene. 2.22 was no father to give consent, then our heavenlie Father gave his consent: God
supplied the place of the father, and brought his daughter unto her husband, and
ever since the father after the same manner, hath offered his daughter unto the
husband.

Exod. 22 Beside, there is a law, that if a man deflower a virgine, he shall marrie her. But
if the father of the virgine doe not like of the marriage, then he shall pay unto her the dowrie of virgins, that is, so much as her virginitie is esteemed, so that the father might allowe the marriage or forbid it.

Num. 30.6 Agayne, there is a Law, that if any free man, or free woman make a vow,It
must be kept. But if a virgin make avowe, it should not be kept, unlesse her
father approve it, because she is not free: therefore if he did vowe to marrie, yet
the Father hath power by his law to break it. Agayne, our Saviour saith, that in
heaven there is no marrying, nor giving to marriage, shewing that in earth there
Deut. 7.3 should be a giving to marriage, as well as marrying. Therfore, the law speaketh
unto the father, saying, *Thou shalt not take a wife for thy sonne of strangers*. Ther-
1 *Cor*. 7.38 fore, *Paul* speaketh to the father, *If thou give thy daughter to marriage, thou doest*
Job 1.3 & 10 *well*. Therfore *Job's* children are counted part of the *Jobs* substance, shewing, that
as a man hath the disposition of his owne substance, so he hath the disposition
of his owne children. Therefore in *Math*. 22.30. the wife is said to be bestowed
Gene. 29.18 in marriage, which signifieth, that some did give her besides herselfe: therefore it
1 *Sam*. 18.17 is said that Jacob served *Laban*, that *Laban* might give him his daughter to wife.
Gen. 28.6 Therefore *Saule* saith to *David*, I will give thee mine eldest daughter to wife:
Gen. 34.9 therfore it is said, that Judah took a wife to *Er* his sonne. Therefore *Sichem* saith
Gene. 24.51 to his father, get me this maide to wife. Therefore in the marriage of *Isaake*, we
52.53 see *Abrahams* servaunt in the place of *Isaake*, and *Rebeccah* the maide and her
Judg. 14.2 parents, sitting in parliament together: therefore *Sampson*, though he had found
a maid to his liking, yet he would not take her to wife, before he had told his

parents, and craved their assent. It is a sweet wedding, when the father and the mother bring a blessing to the feast, and a heavie union which is cursed the first day that it is knit.

The parents commit their children to Tutors, but themselves are more then Tutors. If children maye not make other contracts without their good will, shall they contract marriage, which have nothing to maintaine it after, unlese they returne to beg of them whom they scorned before ?

Will you take your fathers money, and will you not take his instruction ? Marriage hath neede of many counselers, and doest thou count thy Father too many ? which is like the foreman of thy instructers. If you marke what kind of youthes they be, which have such hast, that they dare not stay for their parents advise, they are such as hunte for nothing but beauty, and for punishment hereof they marry to beggerie, & lose their Father and Mother for their wife: therefore honour thy parents in this, as thou wouldest that thy children should honour thee.

The second question is answered of Paule, when he saith, *Be not unequellie yoked with Infidels*. As we should not be yoked with Infidels, so we should not be
yoked with Papists, & so we would not be yoked with Atheists, for that also is to Gene. 24.3
be unequallie yoked, unlesse we be Atheists to. As the *Jewes* might not marrie Exod. 34.16
with *Chananites* so we may not marrie with them which are like Chananites, but Gene. 28.1
the sonnes of *Jacob* said into *Emor*, which would marrie their sister, *We may not* Mala. 2.11 Ezra. 9.12
give our sister to a man uncircumcised, but if you will be circumcised like us, then we Gene. 34.14
will merrie with you.

So parents should say to suters, I may not give my daughter to a man unsanctified, but if you will be sanctified, then will I give my daughter unto you. Though heresie and irreligion be not a cause of divorce, as *Paule* teacheth, yet it is a cause of restraint, for we may not marrie all, with whom we may live being married. If adultery may separate marriage, shal not idolatry hinder marriage, which is
worse than it ? Christ saith, *Let no man separate whom God hath joined*, so I may Mar. 10.9
say, Let no man joine whom God doth separate. For if our Father must be pleased with our marriage, much more should we please that Father which ordained marriage.

Shall I say, *Be my wife*, to whom I may not say, *Be my companion* ? Or, *Come* Esay. 52.12
to my bed, to whom I may not say, *Come to my table ?* How should my marriage
speede well, when I marrie one to who I may not say *Godspeede*, because she is 2 Jolm 10
none of Gods friends ?

If a man long for a bad wife, he were best to go to hell a wooing, that he may have choice. If there is no friend but the enemie ? no tree but the forbidden tree
? He marrieth with the devill, which marrieth with the tempter: for *Tempter* is Mat. 4.3
his name, and to tempt is his nature. When a man may chuse, he should chuse the best, but this man chuseth the worst, like them which call good evill, and evill good.

He prayeth *Not to be led in to temptation*, and leadeth himselfe into temptation. Luke 11.4
Surely he doth not feare sinne, which doth not shunne occasions, and he is wor-
thy to be snared, which maketh a trappe for him selfe. When *Salomon*, the mir- 1 Reg. 11.1
rour of wisedome, the wonder of the world, the figure of our Lord, by Idolatrous

Concubines is turned into an Idolater, let no man say, I shall not be seduced, but say, how shall I stand, where such a Cedar fell ? The wife must be meete, as God said, *Gene*.2.18. But how is she meete, if thou be a Christian, and she be a
1 *Cor*. 7.39 Papist ? We must marrie in the Lord, as Paule saith, but how doe we marrie in the Lord, when we marrie the Lordes enemies ? our Spouse must be like Christes spouse, but Christes spouse is neither harlot nor Hereticke, nor Atheist. If she be poore, the Lord reproveth not for that: if she be weake, the Lord reproveth not for that: if she be hard-favoured, the Lord reproveth not for that: all these wants
Gene. 3.4 may be dispensed with: but none giveth any dispensation for godlinesse but the devill. Therefore they which take that privilege, are like them which seeke to witches, and are guiltie of preferring evill before good. This unequall marriage,
Gene. 6.2 was the chief cause that brought the flood, and the first beginning of Giants, and monstrous birthes, shewing by their monstrous children, what a monstrous thing it is, for beleevers and unbelleevers to match together.

The following excerpt is from Robert Cleaver's celebrated marriage manual, *A Godly Forme of Household Government: for the ordering of private Families, according to the direction of Gods word*, which was published in 1603 in London.

This excerpt begins on page 13 and ends on page 24 of the original text. This particular document would be especially appropriate for an understanding of *Romeo and Juliet*, for Old Capulet insists that Juliet marry Paris just as Egeus in *A Midsummer Night's Dream* insists that his daughter Hermia marry Demetrius against her will despite the fact that she wants to marry Lysander, who loves her (Courtesy of the Folger Shakespeare Library).

DOCUMENT 4: EXCERPT FROM *A GODLY FORME OF HOUSEHOLD GOVERNMENT: FOR THE ORDERING OF PRIVATE FAMILIES, ACCORDING TO THE DIRECTION OF GODS WORD*, PAGES 13–24

A Household is as it were a little Common-wealth, by the good Government whereof, Gods glorie may be advanced, the Commonwealth which standeth of severall families, benefited, and all that live in that familie receive much comfort and commoditie.

But this government of a family is not very common in the world, for it is not
Pro. 24.3.4 a thing that men can stumble on by chance, but *wisedom* must leade us unto it *Through wisedome (saith Salomon) is an house builded, and with understanding it is established: and by knowledge shall the Chambers thereof bee filled with all precious pleasant riches*: that is, shall obtaine all kind of blessings. See also *Pro*. 28.2 by which two places it manifest, that such families as are not ordered by haphazard, or as it falles, but by Wisedome, Discretion, and Counsell, do prosper in inward and outward goods, and indure long. When we speake of wisedome, we do not meane that this government can be in all points excused by naturall reason and Wisedome: for mans wisedome teacheth but unto one point, and that the least of that, which family-government tendeth unto.

But the Wisedome that wee speake of is not naturall, but fetched from the fountaine of all wisedom, God himselfe, who by his word shineth unto us pure light to walke by, not in the Church alone, nor in publicke societie of men onely, but even within the secret of our owne walles, and toward such as bee abiding *Gen.* 5.24
under the same roofe. And if we desire to walk with GOD, as *Enoch* did, wee *Psal.* 119.3
must set up this light for ourselves to live by at home: *For then we doe no iniquitie, when we walk in his way.* Where no wisedome is used in governing families, there all goeth to wracke, & there many enormities are to be found, as wofull breaches betweene man and wife, gracelessnesse and unthriftinesse of children, lewdnesse of servants, and foule escapes. And where carnall policie ruleth, and not the wisedome which is from above, there all that is done tend to be the case, pleasure, and profit of this life, which is the ende and felicitie of a brute beast, and not of a man.

Now that there is a good kind of governing of a family, which they who follow wisely, may be said to governe well, appeareth out of the first Epistle to *Timothie* *Psal.* 101.2
3 verse 4.5. *One that guideth his house well, &c.* And after, *He that knowth not to gouverne his owne house, &c.* Wherby it is evident, that there is a way of ordering the family aright, and there is a misgoverning of it.

To set downe this Government exactly, is a hard matter. Here only we will note some things which doo appertaine unto that government which we speake of. And to do it more orderly to the better understanding, wee must consider, that (as may also be gathered out of that place of *Timothie*) there are two sorts in everie perfect family.

{1. The Governours.
{2. Those that must be ruled.

And these two sorts have special duties belonging to them, the one sort towards the other. In the carefull performance whereof, from the one to the other, consisted the *good government of a family.*

The Governours of a family, be such as have authoritie in the family by Gods ordinance, as the father and mother, maister and mistresse.

To whom, as God hath given authoritie over their children and servants, so he would have them to use it to the wise government of them not onely for their owne private profit, credit, or pleasure, but also for the good of those whom they are to governe: for by a wise government, much good commeth to the parties governed. If maisters then or parents doo not governe, but let servants and children do as they list, they not onely disobey God, and disadvantage themselves, but also hurt those whom they should rule: for when any have such libertie to do as they list, it maketh them grow out of order, to the provoking of Gods dis- *Gen.* 24.2
pleasure, and curse against themselves; whereas if they had beene held in by the *Gen.* 59.4
bridle of the Government, they might be brought to walke, so as the blessing of God should follow them in their courses.

All government of a family must bee in a comelinesse or decencie, that is, *1 Tim.* 3.4
it must bee such as is meete and convenient both for the governour, and for the

person governed. And therefore it is impossible for a man to understand how to governe the Common- wealth, that does not know how to govern his own house, or order his owne person, so that he that knoweth not to governe, deserveth not to raigne.

Lordlinesse is unmeete in a household government, and yet familiaritie with such as are under government, breedeth contempt. Againe for the persons governed, all in the family are not to be governed alike.

There is the one rule to govern the wife by, an other for children, another for servants. One rule for young ones, another for olde folkes.

The government of a family tendeth unto two things especially. First, Christian holinesse, and secondly the things of this life. By the first God is glorified; by the second this present life is sustained, in such sort as God seeth for us.

Howsoever, where humane pollicie is the rule of household Government, there men only have an eye to the things of this life: yet they which fetch their wisedome to rule by out of the word, shall understand, that their government must not onely be civill, but righteous also: that is, they must seeke to have Holinesse found in their habitation, whereby God may be glorified, as well as riches, whereby they may be comforted. This hath bene the course of holy men in former ages.

Gen. 12.78 *Abraham* flitted often from place to place yet hee built an Altar wheresoever
Gen. 13.18 hee became yea, and trained up his family in the feare of God. Hee did not
Gen. 11.13 seeke excuse in his unsetled estate, to let passe the care of holinesse. Holy *Job*
Gen. 11.19 was not contented to worship God himeselfe alone, but sanctified his sonnes,
Job. 1.5 that is, prepared them to worshippe God with him. *Jacob* at his returne from
Josu. 24.15 *Padam Aram* purged his family, and set up Gods worship there. *Joshua* saith,
Hest. 4.16 though others should forsake the Lorde, yet hee and his family would cleave
Prov. 31.26 unto him, and serve him. *The vertuous woman openeth & c her mouth in wisedom, and teacheth mercie unto her servants.* Many of the faithful, when they themselves beleeved in Christ,

Act. 10 & laboured to bring their families to the faith, also. Parentes also are com-
16.14.15 maunded to bring up their children in the *instruction and information of the Lord.* By
Ephes. 6. 4 all which places it is evident, that Religion must be stirring in Christian families, and that good government looketh to bring godly behaviour into families, as well as thrift and good husbandrie.

For want of this care, many parentes leave their children faire faces, and foule mindes; proper bodies, and deformed soules; full coffers, and emptie hearts: for want of this, God may dwell in Churches if he will, but hee hath no abode allowed him in private families. For will God be where hee may not rule, but must
1 *Joh.* 3.24 & be an underling and stand and looke on, when profit and pleasure shall be served,
4.12.13 and set aloft ? yet the spirit of God saith, that God will come and dwell with them that they love him, and keepe his commaundments. Where therefore holinesse is not sought for in families, their God hath no friends, nor lovers, nor walkers with him; howsoever they will sometime come visit him in the Church.

Besides, the ill success that such walkers have, who make their houses temples to Mammon, and riches, should teach us to have a principall respect to God in

Christianitie, ruling our houses. Many thrive not, but put that which they get Mat. 6.24
in a bottomelesse bagge. For God who hath none, or the lowest regard in their courses, and household affaires, withholdeth his blessings from them: and then in vaine doo men rise early, and goe late to bed, and eat the bread of carefulnesse. Others thrive, but it is a wofull thrift, that serveth to harden the heart, and to bewitch the soule with love & liking of this world. Yet is Gods just judgement upon many this, because they will needes serve their owne commoditie chiefly at home, the Lorde giving them up to themselves, they never serve him but coldly and for custome sake at the Church and God accepteth no more of their worship they doo there, then they doo love and like of his government in their houses. *Haggi.* 1.6 *Psal.* 127.2

The governours of families, if (as it is in marriage) there be more then one upon whom the charge of government lieth, though unequally, are; first, the *Chiefe governour,* which is the *Husband*; secondly, *a fellow-helper,* which is the Wife.

These both do owe duties to their family, and dutie one to another.

These duties they owe to their familie, both concerning godlinesse, and the things of this life, belong either to the husband especially, or to the wife especially. The duties that belong to the husband touching, holinesse, are such as either.

He must {1. Performe to them of his familie
{2. Or require of them

The duties which he must performe to them, are, first touching the publicke ministerie of the word, to provide that they may live under an ordinarie ministerie of the word, or else to take order, that alwaies upon the Sabbath, and at other times when it may be, they resort to such places, where they may have the word ministered unto them: for else how they how shal they be brought into the sheepefold of God, (from which naturally they go astray) but by hearing the voice of the chiefe shepheard, speaking unto them by those whom he sendeth ? how shal they beleeve, and so be begotten againe by the seede of the word; except they hear such as God sendeth for the egetting of men unto men; but by hearing his messengers, into whose mouthes he hath put the word of reconciliation: how shall they growe in faith, and increase in grace, but by receiving with meeknesse the ingrafted word, which is able to save their soules ? *Amo.* 8.11 *Math.* 9.36.37 *Esa.* 32.1 & 2.3.4 *Rom.* 10.14 *Jam.* 1.86 19.21 1 *Pe.* 2.2 *Haba.* 21 *Ephe.* 4.11.12

Seeing then the word preached, is the meanes to beget men to a new life, and to nourish them in it as great duties lieth upon the governours of families, to provide by some meanes that they may have it. For where the word is not preached, there the Lorde Sabbath cannot be hallowed as it ought.

Now the Lord would not only have Masters of families to keep holy the Sabbath themselves in all the parts of his worship publike and private, but also that every one should, in his severall place and roome, carefully take order; that, so many as be committed to his charge, should sanctifie the Lords day as well as himselfe: which though it be true all other commandements, (namely that whatsoever we are bound to doe ourselves, we must be meanes to further other in

doing the same, because the love of God and of neighbor, spreadeth itselfe over all the commaundments: and therefore though be not expressed, it is necessarily understood) yet in the fourth commaundment, it is so much the more required, because besides the analogie and proportion betweene it and the other commandements which doth inforce it, the very words themselves do bind us there unto. For when it is said, *Thou and thy sonne and thy daughter, thy manservant and thy master,* though it speaketh by name, onely of resting upon the Sabbath, yet because the ende of that is, that they day might be sanctified, looke how many reasons there be to binde the inferours to the rest, and the superiour to provide that they do so indeed, so many are to compell them to sanctifie the day in their owne persons; and in so many as belong unto them. Therefore when first of all
Deut. 12.14.15 it is generally saide in this fourth commaundement, *Remember the Sabbath day that thou keep it holy*: and afterwards *The seventh day is the Sabbath day of the Lord by God,* that is, which must be dedicated unto his service and in the ende you must therefore rest; that you might serve him serve him in it as hee requireth: and then nameth the eternall parties that should rest: his meaning is to declare the right ende of their resting, and so speaking by name to the governours, saith: *Thou and thy sonne and thy daughter, thy manservant and the maide, the stranger that is within thy gates,* to shewe unto them. That it is not sufficient for them to looke that they under the government should rest, unlesse they sanctifie the day of rest also,which they must be carefull of, by how much the sanctification of the day is greater, then the ceasing to work upon it, as the end wherunto this is but referred; and therefore if it be a sinne in them at any time not to have a sufficient regard unto them that they worke, then it must needs be a greater sin, if that through their negligence they do not sanctifie and keep holy this day of rest.

So that here the Lorde God requireth, that in all places there should be such good lawes publikely in the Common-wealth, and privately in mens houses established, and diligently executed, as whereby not onely the rulers, but also all in subjection should be compelled to sanctifie the Lords day, and that they should be sure they do it indeede. And as hee must not leave it indifferent to them, to choose whether they will work or rest, and so thinke it sufficient that they doo not lay any worke upon them, so it is not inough that they hinder them not from serving God upon that day, unlesse they procure all the meanes unto them, whereby God might bee worshipped of them, and see that they worshippe God in them, as well themselves. Therefore the maisters of families must provide as much as lieth in them, that the word bee publickely preached where they dwell not for themselves alone, but for their children and servants sake that they might keepe holy the day together with them: and they must not only come themselves to the place of common praise and divine service, but bring these also with them and so spend the rest of the day in all private godly exercises themselves, and cause others to do so also.

And here, least this might seem too heavie unto us, and that it might be too grievous to take so great a charge upon us, wee must remember that as we have great helpe by our inferiours in many things, so the Lord would have us to helpe them in the chiefe and principall and as he hath made them our servants, so we should make them his servants and when they have served us six times, we might cause them to serve him upon the seventh: and as the Lord hath preferred us above them with their service, so hee would humble us with this charge and care over them, or rather exalt us, in that hee would have us to be as it were the overseers of his worke, and not only seve him ourselves, but alos fee his service done by others, committed to our charge which if yee doo not, wherein shall the Christian governours of householdes, differ from the Infidels and Heathen, and what greater thing that we shall doo for our servants then they; what shall we doe more for them then for the bruit beasts and can tell that worke under us to whom we give rest and ease from labor upon whom the Sabbath, if we cause them not to sanctifie these beasts of rest, in which they shall differ from the other, not only beastes but men.

GLOSSARY

agela—adolescent youth organization whose members entered at 17 years of age and where they participated in athletic events, hunting, and simulated combat

agoge—age-based educational system

apeleutheroi—slaves who have been freed

Archaic Age—700–525 B.C.E.

aulos—a kind of double flute

brephos—a newborn baby

Classic Period—490–335 B.C.E.

enkrateia—self-mastery

epheboi—trainees

ephebos—a youth who has reached the age of 18

erastes—lover

eromenos—beloved for the youth

eros—a form of sexual passion or obsession

gynaikes—women

Hellenistic Period—306 B.C.E.–30 C.E.

hetairai—female companions

hetaireia—private drinking club

hetaireukotes—male prostitutes

kalos k'agathos—an enthusiast of beauty

kleos—immortal fame

krater—a bowl for mixing wine with water

kylix—drinking cup

kyrios—male citizen who is the head of a household

lechos—marital bed

leukopygoi—homosexuals

menos—liquid force

metics—individuals who were women, slaves, and nonresidents

moichagria—adultery

neaniskos—approximately the age of 25 or older when males took on the active role in sexual relations

nothoi—children born out of wedlock

oikos—household

oinochoe—water-pitcher

paidagogos—slave attendant

paideia—boys at the age of seven, which is the first stage of their development into manhood

partheneia—maiden songs

peplos—a woman's dress

pharmaka—drugs

philia—affection

philotes—friendship, love, affection

pornai—prostitutes

pornos—the male prostitute whose status was recognized by the government

symposia—all-male banquets

thiasoi—associations of young women

tondo—circular painting

tribas—a homosexual woman

BIBLIOGRAPHY

PRINT SOURCES

Literary Approaches

Adelman, Janet. "Bed Tricks: On Marriage as the End of Comedy in *All's Well That Ends Well* and *Measure for Measure*." *Shakespeare's Personality*. Ed. Norman H. Holland, Sidney Horman, and Bernard J. Paris. Berkeley: U of California P, 1989. 151–74. Print.

Adelman, Janet. "Male Bonding in Shakespeare's Comedies." *Shakespeare's "Rough Magic."* Ed. Peter Erickson and Coppélia Kahn. Newark, NJ: U of Delaware P, 1985. Print.

Adelman, Janet. *Suffocating Mothers: Fantasies of Maternal Origin in Shakespeare's Plays*. New York: Routledge, 1992. Print.

Adelman, Janet. "'This Is and Is Not Cressid': The Characterization of Cressida." *The (M) other Tongue*. Ed. Shirley Nelson Garner, Claire Kehane, and Madelon Sprengnether. Ithaca, NY: Cornell UP, 1985: 119–41. Print.

Austern, Linda Phyllis, ed. *Renaissance Women: Constructions of Femininity in England*. London and New York: Routledge, 1995. Print.

Baines, Barbara. "Assaying the Power of Chastity in *Measure for Measure*." *Studies in English Literature* 30 (1990): 284–98. Print.

Barbour, Reid. "'When I Acted Young Antinous': Boy Actors and the Erotics of Jonsonian Theatre." *PMLA* 110.5 (1995): 1006–22. Print.

Barker, Deborah, and Ivo Kamps, eds. *Shakespeare and Gender: A History*. London and New York: Verso, 1995. Print.

Bate, Jonathan. "Sexual Perversity in *Venus and Adonis*." *Yearbook of English Studies* 23 (1993): 80–92. Print.

Bates, Catherine. "Love and Courtship." *The Cambridge Guide to Shakespearean Comedy*. Ed. Alexander Leggatt. Cambridge: Cambridge UP, 2002. 102–22. Print.

Bates, Catherine. *The Rhetoric of Courtship in Elizabethan Language and Literature*. Cambridge: Cambridge UP, 1992. Print.

Belsey, Catherine. "Disrupting Sexual Difference: Meaning and Gender in the Comedies." *Alternative Shakespeares*. Ed. David Drakakis. London and New York: Methuen, 1995. 166–90. Print.

Belsey, Catherine. *The Subject of Tragedy: Identity and Difference in Renaissance Drama.* London: Methuen, 1985. Print.

Berger, Harry, Jr. "Against the Sink-a-Pace: Sexual and Family Politics in *Much Ado about Nothing.*" *Shakespeare Quarterly* 33 (1982): 302–13. Print.

Berger, Harry, Jr. "Marriage and Mercifixion in *The Merchant of Venice*: The Casket Scene Revisited." *Shakespeare Quarterly* 32 (1981): 155–62. Print.

Binns, J. W. "Women or Transvestites on the Elizabethan Stage? An Oxford Controversy." *Sixteenth Century Journal* 5 (1974): 95–120. Print.

Bly, Mary. *Queer Virgins and Virgin Queens on the Early Modern Stage.* Oxford: Oxford UP, 2000. Print.

Boose, Lynda. "Scolding Brides and Bridling Scolds: Taming the Woman's Unruly Member." *Shakespeare Quarterly* 42 (1991): 179–213. Print.

Breitenberg, Mark. *Anxious Masculinity in Early Modern England.* Cambridge: Cambridge UP, 1996. Print.

Brink, Jean, ed. *Privileging Gender in Early Modern England.* Tempe, AZ: Sixteenth-Century Studies Conference, 1992. Print.

Brown, John Russell. "Recreating Sexuality in Shakespeare's Plays." *Shakespeare and Sexuality.* Ed. Catherine Alexander and Stanley Wells. Cambridge: Cambridge UP, 2001. 168–82. Print.

Brown, Steve. "The Boyhood of Shakespeare's Heroines: Notes on Gender Ambiguity in the Sixteenth Century." *Studies in English Literature 1500–1900* 30: 243–63. 1990. Print.

Callaghan, Dympna, ed. *A Feminist Companion to Shakespeare.* Oxford: Blackwell, 2000. Print.

Callaghan, Dympna, ed. *Shakespeare without Women: Representing Gender and Race on the Renaissance Stage.* New York and London: Routledge, 2000. Print.

Callaghan, Dympna, ed. *Women and Gender in Renaissance Tragedy: A Study of "King Lear," "Othello," "The Duchess of Malfi," and "The White Devil."* Atlantic Highlands, NJ: Humanities Press International, 1989. Print.

Callaghan, Dympna, Lorraine Helms, and Jyotsna Singh, eds. *The Wayward Sisters: Shakespeare and Feminist Politics.* Oxford: Blackwell, 1994. Print.

Carroll, William C. *The Metamorphoses of Shakespearean Comedy.* Princeton, NJ: Princeton UP, 1985. Print.

Coleman, E.A.M. *The Dramatic Use of Bawdry in Shakespeare.* London: Longman, 1974. Print.

Comensoli, Viviana, and Anne Russell, eds. *Enacting Gender on the English Renaissance Stage.* Urbana: U of Illinois P, 1998. Print.

Cook, Carol. "'The Sign and Semblance of Her Honor': Reading Gender Difference in *Much Ado.*" *PMLA* 101 (1986): 186–202. Print.

Cook, Carol. "Unbodied Figures of Desire." *Theatre Journal* 38 (1986): 34–52. Print.

Crosman, Robert. "Making Love Out of Nothing at All: The Issue of Story in Shakespeare's Procreation Sonnets." *Shakespeare Quarterly* 41(1990): 470–88. Print.

Dash, Irene. *Wooing, Wedding, and Power: Women in Shakespeare's Plays.* New York: Columbia UP, 1981. Print.

Dekker, Rudolf, and C. Lotte Van de Pol. *The Traditions of Female Transvestism in Early Modern Europe.* New York: St. Martin's Press, 1989. Print.

diGangi, Mario. *The Homoeroticism of Early Modern Drama.* Cambridge: Cambridge UP, 1997. Print.

Dollimore, Jonathan. "Transgression and Surveillance in *Measure for Measure*." *Political Shakespeare: New Essays in Material Culturalism*. Manchester, UK: Manchester UP, 1985. 72–87. Print.

Dusinberre, Juliet. *Shakespeare and the Nature of Women*. 2nd ed. Houndmills, Basingstoke, UK: Palgrave Macmillan, 1996. Print.

Dusinberre, Juliet. "Women and Boys Playing Shakespeare." *"As You Like It": Essais Critiques*. Toulouse, France: PU du Mirail, 1998: 11–26. Print.

Erickson, Peter, *Patriarchal Structures in Shakespeare's Drama*. Berkeley and Los Angeles: U of California P, 1985. Print.

Felperin, Howard. *Shakespearean Romances*. Princeton, NJ: Princeton UP, 1972. Print.

Findlay, Alison. *A Feminist Approach to Renaissance Drama*. Oxford: Blackwell, 1999. Print.

Fineman, Joel. *Shakespeare's Perjured Eye: The Invention of Poetic Subjectivity in the Sonnets*. Berkeley: U of California P, 1986. Print.

Frye, Susan, and Karen Robertson, eds. *Maids and Mistresses, Cousins and Queens: Women's Alliances in Early Modern England*. Oxford: Oxford UP, 1999. Print.

Garber, Marjorie. *Coming of Age in Shakespeare*. London: Methuen, 1981. Print.

Garber, Marjorie. *Dream in Shakespeare: From Metaphor to Metamorphosis*. New Haven, CT, and London: Yale UP, 1974. Print.

Garber, Marjorie. "The Education of Orlando." *Comedy from Shakespeare to Sheridan*. Ed. A. R. Braunmuller and J. C. Bulman. Newark: U of Delaware P, 1986: 102–12. Print.

Garner, Shirley Nelson. "*A Midsummer Night's Dream*: 'Jack Shall Have Jill; / Nought Shall Go Ill.'" *Women's Studies* 9 (1981): 47–63. Print.

Geary, Keith. "The Nature of Turning to Men in *The Merchant of Venice*." *Shakespeare Survey* 37 (1984): 55–68. Print.

Girard, Rene. "The Politics of Desire in *Troilus and Cressida*." *Shakespeare and the Question of Theory*. Ed. Patricia Parker and Geoffrey Hartman. New York and London: Methuen, 1985. 188–210. Print.

Goldberg, Jonathan. *Sodometries: Renaissance Texts, Modern Sexualities*. Stanford, CA: Stanford UP, 1992. Print.

Grantham, James Turner, ed. *Sexuality and Gender in Early Modern Europe: Institutions, Texts, Images*. Cambridge: Cambridge UP, 1993. Print.

Green, Douglas E. "Preposterous Pleasures: Queer Theories and *A Midsummer Night's Dream*." *A Midsummer Night's Dream: Critical Essays*. Ed. Dorothea Kehler. New York and London: Routledge, 2001. 369–97. Print.

Greenblatt, Stephen Jay. *Shakespearean Negotiations: The Circulation of Social Energy in Renaissance England*. Berkeley and Los Angeles: U of California P, 1988. Print.

Hall, Kim F. *Things of Darkness: Economies of Race and Gender in Early Modern England*. Ithaca, NY: Cornell UP, 1995. Print.

Hammond, Paul. *Figuring Sex Between Men from Shakespeare to Rochester*. Oxford: Clarendon Press, 2002. Print.

Hayles, Nancy K. "Sexual Disguise in *As You Like It* and *Twelfth Night*." *Shakespeare Survey* 32 (1979): 63–72. Print.

Hopkins, Lisa. *The Shakespearean Marriage: Merry Wives and Heavy Husbands*. Basingstoke Houndmills, UK: Palgrave Macmillan, 1998. Print.

Howard, Jean E. *The Stage and Social Struggle in Early Modern England*. New York: Routledge, 1994. Print.

Howard, Jean E., and Marion O'Connor, eds. *Shakespeare Reproduced: The Text in History and Ideology*. London: Routledge, 1987. Print.

Howard, Jean E., and Phyllis Rackin. *Engendering a Nation: A Feminist Account of Shakespeare's English History Plays*. London and New York: Routledge, 1997. Print.

Hutson, Lorna. *The Usurer's Daughter: Male Friendship and Fictions of Women in Sixteenth-Century England*. London: Routledge, 1994. Print.

Jankowski, Theodora. *Women in Power in the Early Modern Drama*. Urbana: U of Illinois P, 1992. Print.

Jardine, Lisa. *Reading Shakespeare Historically*. London: Routledge, 1996. Print.

Jardine, Lisa. *Still Harping on Daughters*. 2nd ed. New York: Columbia UP, 1989. Print.

Jordan, Constance. *Renaissance Feminism*. Ithaca, NY: Cornell UP, 1990. Print.

Kahn, Coppélia. *Man's Estate: Masculine Identity in Shakespeare*. Berkeley and Los Angeles: U of California P, 1981. Print.

Kahn, Coppélia. *Roman Shakespeare: Warriors, Wounds and Women*. London: Routledge, 1997. Print.

Keach, William. "Venus and Adonis." *Elizabethan Erotic Narratives: Irony and Pathos in the Ovidian Poetry of Shakespeare, Marlowe, and Their Contemporaries*. New Brunswick, NJ: Rutgers UP, 1977. 52–84. Print.

Kimbrough, Robert. "Androgyny Seen through Shakespeare's Disguise." *Shakespeare Quarterly* 32 (1982): 17–33. Print.

Kirch, Arthur. *Shakespeare and the Experience of Love*. Cambridge: Cambridge UP, 1981. Print.

Leggatt, Alexander. "Comedy and Love." *The Cambridge Companion to Shakespearean Comedy*. Ed. Alexander Leggatt. Cambridge: Cambridge UP, 2002. 139–55. Print.

Leggatt, Alexander. *Shakespeare's Comedy of Love*. New York: Methuen, 1974. Print.

Lenz, Carolyn Ruth Swift, Gayle Greene, and Carol Thomas Nelly, eds. *The Woman's Part: Feminist Criticism of Shakespeare*. Urbana: U of Illinois P, 1980. Print.

Levin, Carol, and Karen Robertson, eds. *Sexuality and Politics in Renaissance Drama*. Lewiston, NY: Edwin Mellen Press, 1991. Print.

Levine, Laura. *Men in Women's Clothing: Anti-theatricality and Effeminization, 1579–1642*. Cambridge Studies in Renaissance Literature and Culture. New York: Cambridge UP, 1994. Print.

Lewalski, Barbara K. "Love, Appearance, and Reality: Much Ado about Something." *Studies in English Literature* 8 (1968): 235–51. Print.

Loomba, Ania. *Gender, Race, Renaissance Drama*. Manchester, UK: Manchester UP, 1989. Print.

MacCary, W. Thomas. *Friends and Lovers: The Phenomenology of Desire in Shakespearean Comedy*. New York: Columbia UP, 1985. Print.

Marotti, Arthur. "'Love Is Not Love': Elizabethan Sonnet Sequences and the Social Order." *ELH* 49 (1982): 396–428. Print.

Masten, Jeffrey. *Textual Intercourse: Collaboration, Authorship, and Sexualities in Renaissance Drama*. Cambridge, Cambridge UP, 1997. Print.

Maus, Katherine Eisaman. "Sexual Secrecy in *Measure for Measure*." *Inwardness and Theater in the English Renaissance*. Chicago: U of Chicago P, 1995. 157–81. Print.

Mikalachki, Jodi. *The Legacy of Boadicea: Gender and Nation in Early Modern England*. London: Routledge, 1998. Print.

Montrose, Louis Adrian. "'Shaping Fantasies': Figurations of Gender and Power in Elizabethan Culture." *Representations* 2 (1983): 61–94. Rpt. in *The Purpose of Playing: Shakespeare and the Cultural Politics of the Elizabethan Theatre*. Chicago: U of Chicago P, 1996. Print.

Neely, Carol Thomas. *Broken Nuptials in Shakespeare's Plays*. New Haven, CT: Yale UP, 1985. Print.

Neill, Michael. "Unproper Beds: Race, Adultery, and the Hideous in *Othello*." *Shakespeare Quarterly* 40 (1989): 383–412. Print.

Nelson, Shirley, and Madelon Sprengnether, eds. *Shakespearean Tragedy and Gender*. Bloomington: Indiana UP, 1996. Print.

Nevo, Ruth. *Comic Transformations in Shakespeare*. London and New York: Methuen, 1980. Print.

Newman, Karen. *Fashioning Femininity in English Renaissance Drama*. Chicago: U of Chicago P, 1991. Print.

Newman, Karen. "Portia's Ring: Unruly Women and the Structure of Exchange in *The Merchant of Venice*." *Shakespeare Quarterly* 38 (1987): 19–33. Print.

Novy, Marianne. *Love's Argument: Gender Relations in Shakespeare*. Chapel Hill: U of North Carolina P, 1984. Print.

Orgel, Stephen. *Impersonations: The Performance of Gender in Shakespeare's England*. Cambridge: Cambridge UP, 1996. Print.

Osborne, Laurie E. "Cutting up Characters: The Erotic Politics of Trevor Nunn's *Twelfth Night*." *Spectacular Shakespeare: Critical Theory and Popular Cinema*. Ed. Courtney Lehmann and Lisa S. Starks. Madison, NJ: Fairleigh Dickinson UP, 2002. 89–109. Print.

Osborne, Laurie E. *The Trick of Singularity: Twelfth Night and the Performance Editions*. Studies in Theatre History and Culture. Iowa City: U of Iowa P, 1996. Print.

Parker, Barbara L. *A Precious Seeing: Love and Reason in Shakespeare's Plays*. New York: New York UP, 1987. Print.

Parker, Patricia. "Fantasies of 'Race,' and 'Gender': Africa, Othello, and Bringing to Light." *Women, "Race," and Writing in the Early Modern Period*. Ed. Margo Hendricks and Patricia Parker. London: Routledge, 1994. 84–100. Print.

Parker, Patricia. *Literary Fat Ladies: Rhetoric, Gender, and Property*. London: Methuen, 1987. Print.

Parker, Patricia. "*Othello* and *Hamlet*: Dilation, Spying, and the 'Secret Place' of Woman." *Representations* 44 (1993): 60–95. Print.

Parker, Patricia. *Shakespeare from the Margins: Language, Culture, Context*. Chicago: U of Chicago, 1996. Print.

Partridge, Eric. *Shakespeare's Bawdry: A Literary and Psychological Essay and a Comprehensive Glossary*. 3rd ed. New York: Routledge, 1991. Print.

Paster, Gail Kern. *The Body Embarrassed: Drama and the Disciplines of Shame in Early Modern England*. Ithaca, NY: Cornell UP, 1993. Print.

Pequigney, Joseph. "The Two Antonios and Same-Sex Love in *Twelfth Night* and *The Merchant of Venice*." *Shakespeare and Gender: A History*. Ed. Deborah E. Barker and Ivo Kamps. New York: Verso, 1995. 178–95. Print.

Poisson, Rodney. "Unequal Friendship: Shakespeare's Sonnets 18–126." *New Essays on Shakespeare's Sonnets*. Ed. Hilton Landry. New York: AMS, 1976. Print.

Porter, Joseph. *Shakespeare's Mercutio: His History and Drama*. Chapel Hill: U of North Carolina P, 1988. Print.

Rackin, Phyllis. *Shakespeare and Women*. Oxford: Oxford UP, 2002. Print.

Roberts, Jeanne. "Horses and Hermaphrodites: Metamorphoses in *The Taming of the Shrew*." *Shakespeare Quarterly* 34 (1983): 159–71. Print.

Roche, Michael. *Forbidden Friendships*. New York: Oxford UP, 1996. Print.

Rose, Jacqueline. "Sexuality in the Reading of Shakespeare's *Hamlet* and *Measure for Measure*." *Alternative Shakespeares*. Ed. John Drakakis. London and New York: Methuen, 1985. 95–118. Print.

Rose, Mary Beth. *The Expense of Spirit: Love and Sexuality in English Renaissance Drama*. Ithaca, NY: Cornell UP, 1988. Print.

Rose, Mary Beth, ed. *Women in the Middle Ages and the Renaissance: Literary and Historical Perspectives*. Syracuse, NY: Syracuse UP, 1986. Print.

Saslow, James M. *Ganymede in the Renaissance*. New Haven, CT: Yale UP, 1986. Print.

Schiesari, Juliana. *The Gendering of Melancholia: Feminism, Psychoanalysis, and the Symbolics of Loss in Renaissance Literature*. Ithaca, NY: Cornell UP, 1992. Print.

Schwarz, Kathryn. *Tough Love: Amazon Encounters in the Renaissance*. Durham, NC: Duke UP, 2000. Print.

Scoufos, Alice-Lyle. "The *Paradiso Terrestre* and the Testing of Love in *As You Like It*." *Shakespeare Studies* 14 (1981): 215–27. Print.

Shannon, Laurie. *Sovereign Amity*. Chicago: U of Chicago P, 2002. Print.

Shapiro, Michael. *Gender in Play on the Shakespearean Stage: Boy Heroines and Female Pages*. Ann Arbor: U of Michigan P, 1994. Print.

Shell, Marc. *The End of Kinship: "Measure for Measure," Incest, and the Ideal of Universal Siblinghood*. Baltimore, MD, and London: Johns Hopkins UP, 1995. Print.

Shepherd, Simon. *Amazons and Warrior Women: Varieties of Feminism in Seventeenth Century Drama*. NY: St. Martin's Press, 1991. Print.

Sinfield, Alan. *Shakespeare, Authority, Sexuality: Unfinished Business in Cultural Materialism*. London and New York: Routledge, 2006. Print.

Smith, Bruce R. *Homosexual Desire in Shakespeare's England: A Cultural Poetics*. Chicago: U of Chicago, 1991. Print.

Smith, Bruce R. *Shakespeare and Masculinity*. Oxford: Oxford UP, 2000. Print.

Snow, Edward. "Language and Sexual Difference in *Romeo and Juliet*." *Shakespeare's "Rough Magic": Renaissance Essays in Honor of C. L. Barber*. Ed. Peter Erickson and Coppélia Kahn. Newark: U of Delaware P, 1985. Print.

Snow, Edward. "Sexual Anxiety and the Male Order of Things in *Othello*." *English Literary Renaissance* 10 (1980): 384–412. Print.

Spear, Gary. "Shakespeare's 'Manly' Parts: Masculinity and Effeminacy in *Troilus and Cressida*," *Shakespeare Quarterly* 44 (1993): 409–22. Print.

Sprengnether, Madelon, and Shirley Nelson Garner, eds. *Shakespearean Tragedy and Gender*. Bloomington: Indiana UP, 1996. Print.

Stallybrass, Peter. "Patriachal Territories: The Body Enclosed." *Rewriting the Renaissance: The Discourses of Sexual Difference in Early Modern Europe*. Ed. Margaret W. Ferguson, Maureen Quilligan, and Nancy Vickers. Chicago: U of Chicago P, 1986. 123–42. Print.

Stockholder, Kay. *Dream Works: Lovers and Families in Shakespeare's Plays*. Toronto: U of Toronto P, 1987. Print.

Summers, Joseph H. *Dreams of Love and Power: On Shakespeare's Plays*. Oxford: Clarendon Press, 1984. Print.

Traub, Valerie. *Desire and Anxiety: Circulations of Sexuality in Shakespearean Drama*. London: Routledge, 1992. Print.

Traub, Valerie, Lindsay M. Kaplan, and Dympna Callaghan, eds. *Feminist Readings of Early Modern Culture*. Cambridge: Cambridge UP, 1996. Print.

Von Koppenfels, Werner. "Dis-Covering the Female Body: Erotic Exploration in Elizabethan Poetry." *Shakespearean Survey* 47 (1994): 127–37. Print.

Wayne, Valerie, ed. *The Matter of Difference: Materialist Feminist Criticism of Shakespeare*. Ithaca, NY: Cornell UP, 1991. Print.

Wilcox, Helen, ed. *Women and Literature in Britain, 1500–1700*. Cambridge: Cambridge UP, 1996. Print.

Williams, Gordon. *A Dictionary of Sexual Language and Imagery in Shakespearean and Stuart Literature*. 3 vols. London: Athlone, 1994. Print.

Williams, Gordon. *A Glossary of Shakespeare's Sexual Language*. London and Atlantic Highlands, NJ: Athlone, 1997. Print.

Williamson, Marilyn L. *The Patriarchy of Shakespeare's Comedies*. Detroit, MI: Wayne State UP, 1986. Print.

Willis, Deborah. *Malevolent Nurture: Witch-Hunting and Maternal Power in Early Modern England*. Ithaca, NY: Cornell UP, 1995. Print.

Wofford, Susanne L. "'To You I Give Myself, For I Am Yours': Erotic Performance and Theatrical Performatives in *As You Like It*." *Shakespeare Reread: The Texts in New Contexts*. Ed. Russ McDonald. Ithaca, NY: Cornell UP, 1994: 147–69. Print.

Woodbridge, Linda. *Women and the English Renaissance: Literature and the Nature of Womankind, 1540–1620*. Urbana: U of Illinois P, 1984. Print.

Young, David. *The Heart's Forest: A Study of Shakespeare's Pastoral Plays*. New Haven, CT, and London: Yale UP, 1972. Print.

Zimmerman, Susan, ed. *Erotic Politics: Desire on the Renaissance Stage*. New York: Routledge, 1992. Print.

Early Modern Sexuality

Archer, Ian W. *The Pursuit of Stability: Social Relations in Elizabethan London*. Cambridge: Cambridge UP, 1991. Print

Aries, Philippe, and George Duby, eds. *A History of Private Life: Passions of the Renaissance*. Vol. 3. Ed. Roger Chartier. Trans. Arthur Goldhammer. Cambridge, MA: Belknap Press of Harvard UP, 1989. Print.

Ben-Amos, Ilana Krausman. *Adolesence and Youth in Early Modern England*. New Haven, CT: Yale UP, 1994. Print.

Cohn, S.K., Jr. *Women in the Streets: Essays on Sex and Power in Renaissance Italy*. Baltimore, MD: Johns Hopkins UP, 1996. Print.

Cox, V. "The Single Self: Feminist Thought and the Marriage Market in Early Modern Venice." *Renaissance Quarterly* 48 (1995): 513–81. Print.

Ferraro, J.M. "The Power to Decide: Battered Wives in Early Modern Venice." *Renaissance Quarterly* 48 (1995): 492–512. Print.

Fletcher, Anthony. *Gender, Sex, and Subordination in England, 1500–1800*. New Haven, CT: Yale UP, 1995. Print.

Fletcher, Anthony, and John Stevenson, eds. *Order and Disorder in Early Modern England*. Cambridge: Cambridge UP, 1985. Print.

Ingram, Martin. *Church Courts, Sex, and Marriage in England, 1570–1640*. Cambridge: Cambridge UP, 1987. Print.

Kirshner, J., and A. Molho, "The Dowry Fund and the Marriage Market in Early Quattrocento Florence." *Journal of Modern History* 50 (1978): 403–38. Print.

Klapisch-Zuber, C. *Women, Family, and Ritual in Renaissance Italy*. Chicago: U of Chicago, 1985. Print.

Klein, Joan Larsen. *Daughters, Wives, and Widows: Writings by Men about Women and Marriage in England, 1500–1640*. Urbana: U of Illinois P, 1992. Print.

Labalme, Patricia, and L. S. White, "How to (and How Not to) Get Married in Sixteenth-Century Venice. (Selections from the Diaries of Marin Sanudo)." *Renaissance Quarterly* 52 (1999): 43–72. Print.

Pearson, Emily Lu. *Elizabethans at Home*. Stanford, CA: Stanford UP, 1957. Print.

Stone, Lawrence. *The Family, Sex, and Marriage in England, 1500–1800*. New York: Harper & Row, 1977. Print.

Medieval Sexuality

Aers, David. *Community, Gender, and Individual Identity: English Writing, 1360–1430*. London: Routledge, 1988. Print.

Baldwin, John W. *The Language of Sex: Fives Voices from Northern France around 1200*. Chicago: U of Chicago P, 1994. Print.

Barron, Caroline. "The 'Golden Age' of Women in Medieval London." *Reading Medieval Studies*. 15 (1990): 35–58. Print.

Bennett, Judith. *Women in the Medieval Countryside: Gender and Household in Brigstock before the Plague*. New York: Oxford UP, 1987. Print.

Brown, Peter. *The Body and Society: Men, Women, and Sexual Renunciation in Early Christianity*. New York: Columbia UP, 1988. Print.

Bullough, Vern, and James A. Brundage., ed. *Sexual Practices and the Medieval Church*. Buffalo, NY: Prometheus Books, 1982. Print.

Bullough, Vern, and Bonnie Bullough. *Cross Dressing, Sex and Gender*. Philadelphia: U of Pennsylvania P, 1993. Print.

Cadden, Joan. *Meanings of Sex Difference in the Middle Ages: Medicine, Science, and Culture*. Cambridge: Cambridge UP, 1993. Print.

Elliott, Dyan. *Spiritual Marriage: Sexual Abstinence in Medieval Wedlock*. Princeton, NJ: Princeton UP, 1993. Print.

Erler, Mary, et al., *Women and Power in the Middle Ages*. Athens: U of Georgia P, 1988. Print.

Ferrante, Joan. *Woman as Image in Medieval Literature*. New York: Columbia UP, 1975. Print.

Fuchs, Eric. *Sexual Desire and Love: Origins and History of the Christian Ethic of Sexuality and Marriage*. Trans. Marsha Daigle. Cambridge: James Clarke; New York: Seabury Press, 1983. Print.

Goldberg, P.J.P., ed. *Woman Is a Mighty Wight: Woman in English Society, c. 1200–500*. Wolfeboro Falls, NH: Alan Sutton, 1992. Print.

Goodich, Michael. *The Unmentionable Vice: Homosexuality in the Later Medieval Period*. Santa Barbara, CA: American Bibliographical Center–Clio Press, 1979. Print.

Gravdal, Kathryn. *Ravishing Maidens: Writing Rape in Medieval French Literature and Law*. Philadelphia: U of Pennsylvania P, 1991. Print.

Green, Monica. "Female Sexuality in the Medieval West." *Trends in History* 4 (1990): 127–58. Print.

Helmholz, Richard H. *Marriage Litigation in Medieval England*. Cambridge: Cambridge UP, 1974. Print.

Jacquart, Danielle, and Claude Thomasset. *Sexuality and Medicine in the Middle Ages*. Trans. Matthew Adamson. Princeton, NJ: Princeton UP, 1988. Print.

Karras, Ruth Mazo. "Friendship and Love in the Lives of Two Twelfth-Century English Saints." *Journal Medieval History* 14 (1988): 305–20. Print.

Kelly, Henry Ansgar. *Love and Marriage in the Age of Chaucer*. Ithaca, NY: Cornell UP, 1975. Print.

Laqueur, Thomas. *Making Sex: Body and Gender from the Greeks to Freud*. Cambridge, MA: Harvard UP, 1990. Print.

Lees, Clare A., ed. *Medieval Masculinities: Regarding Men in the Middle Ages*. Medieval Cultures, 7. Minneapolis: U of Minnesota P, 1994. Print.

Leclerq, Jacques. *Monks on Marriage: A Twelfth-Century View*. New York: Seabury Press, 1982. Print.

Levin, Eve. *Sex and Society in the World of the Orthodox Slavs, 900–1700*. Ithaca, NY: Cornell UP, 1989. Print.

Macfarlane, Alan. *Marriage and Love in England: Modes of Reproduction, 1300–1840*. Oxford: Blackwell, 1986. Print.

Mertes, Kate. *The English Noble Household, 1250–1600: Good Governance and Politic Rule*. Oxford: Blackwell, 1988. Print.

Moore, R. I. *The Formation of a Persecuting Society: Power and Deviance in Western Europe, 950–1250*. Oxford: Blackwell, 1987. Print.

Otis, Leah Lydia. *Prostitution in Medieval Society: The History of an Urban Institution in Languedoc*. Chicago: U of Chicago P, 1985. Print.

Payer, Pierre J. *The Bridling of Desire: Views of Sex in the Later Middle Ages*. Toronto: U of Toronto P, 1993. Print.

Payer, Pierre J. *Sex and the Penitentials: The Development of a Sexual Code, 550–1150*. Toronto: U of Toronto P, 1984. Print.

Rossiaud, Jacques. *Medieval Prostitution*. Trans. Lydia G. Cochrane. Oxford: Blackwell, 1988. Print.

Ruggiero, Guido. *The Boundaries of Eros: Sex Crime and Sexuality in Renaissance Venice*. New York: Oxford UP, 1985. Print.

Ruggiero, Guido. "Sexual Criminality in Early Renaissance Venice 1338–1358." *Journal of Social History* 8 (1975): 18–37. Print.

Salisbury, Joyce. *Medieval Sexuality: A Research Guide*. New York: Garland, 1990. Print.

Salisbury, Joyce, ed. *Sex in the Middle Ages: A Book of Essays*. New York: Garland, 1991. Print.

Greek and Roman Sexuality

Beard, Mary. "The Sexual Status of the Vestal Virgins." *Journal of Roman Studies* 70 (1980): 12–27. Print.

Blundell, Sue. *Women in Ancient Greece*. Cambridge, MA: Harvard UP and London: British Museum, 1997. Print.

Boswell, John. *Christianity, Social Tolerance, and Homosexuality: Gay People in Western Europe from the Beginning of the Christian Era to the Fourteenth Century*. Chicago: U of Chicago P, 1980. Print.

Bradley, Keith. R. *Discovering the Roman Family: Studies in Roman Social History*. New York and Oxford: Oxford UP, 1991. Print.

Brisson, Luc. *Androgyny and Hermaphroditicism in Greco-Roman Antiquity*. Trans. Janet Lloyd. Berkeley: U of California P, 2002. Print.

Brooten, Bernadette J. *Love between Women: Early Christian Responses to Female Homoeroticism*. Chicago: U of Chicago P, 1996.

Calame, Claude. *The Poetics of Eros in Ancient Greece*. Trans. Janet Lloyd. Princeton, NJ: Princeton UP, 1999. Print.

Cantarella, E. *Bisexuality in the Ancient World*. Trans. C. O'Cuilleanain. New Haven, CT, and London: Yale UP, 1992. Print.

Carson, Anne. "Putting Her in Her Place: Women, Dirt, and Desire." *Before Sexuality: The Construction of Erotic Experience in the Ancient Greek World*. Ed. David Halperin, John J. Winkler, and Froma I. Zeitlin. Princeton, NJ: Princeton UP, 1990. 135–69. Print.

Clarke, J.R. *Looking at Lovemaking: Constructions of Sexuality in Roman Art*. Berkeley: U of California P, 1998. Print.

Clarke, W.M. "Achilles and Patroclus in Love." *Hermes* 106 (1978): 381–96. Print.

Cohen, B. ed. *"The Distaff Side: Representing the Female in Homer's Odyssey."* Oxford: Oxford UP, 1995. Print.

Cohen, David. *Law, Sexuality, and Society: The Enforcement of Morals in Classical Athens*. Cambridge: Cambridge UP, 1991. Print.

Cooper, K. *The Virgin and the Bride: Idealized Womanhood in Late Antiquity*. Cambridge, MA: Harvard UP, 1996. Print.

Craik, E.M. "Language of Sexuality and Sexual Inversion in Euripides' *Hippolytos*." *Acta Classica* 41 (1998): 29–44. Print.

Davidson, James. *Courtesans and Fishcakes: The Consuming Passions of Classical Athens*. New York: St. Martin's Press, 1998. Print.

Davis, Nathalie Zemon. *Society and Culture in Early Modern France*. Stanford, CA: Stanford UP, 1975. Print.

Dixon, Suzanne, *The Roman Family*. Baltimore, MD: Johns Hopkins UP, 1992. Print.

Dover, Kenneth. *Greek Homosexuality*. Cambridge, MA: Harvard UP, 1978. Print.

Dynes, Wayne R., and Stephen Donaldson, eds. *Homosexuality in the Ancient World*. New York: Garland, 1992. Print.

Edwards, C. *The Politics of Immorality in Ancient Rome*. Cambridge: Cambridge UP, 1993. Print.

Fantham, Elaine. "Sex, Status, and Survival in Hellenistic Athens: A Study of Women in New Comedy." *Phoenix* 29 (1975): 44–74. Print.

Fantham, Elaine, et al. *Women in the Classical World*. New York: Oxford UP, 1994.

Gardner, J.F. *Women in Roman Law and Society*. Bloomington and Indianapolis: Indiana UP, 1986. Print.

Greenberg, D.F. *The Construction of Homosexuality*. Chicago: U of Chicago, 1988. Print

Hallett, J.P. *Fathers and Daughters in Roman Society*. Princeton, NJ: Princeton UP, 1984. Print.

Hallett, J.P. "Woman as *Same* and *Other* in Classical Roman Elite." *Helios* 16 (1989): 59–78. Print.

Halperin, David M. *One Hundred Years of Homosexuality and Other Essays on Greek Love*. New York: Routledge, 1990. Print.

Hawley, R. and B. Levick, eds. *Women in Antiquity: New Assessments*. London and New York: Routledge,1995. Print.

Humphries, Sarah C. *The Family, Women, and Death*. 2nd ed. Ann Arbor: U of Michigan P, 1993. Print.

Johns, Catherine. *Sex and Symbol: Erotic Images of Greece and Rome*. Austin: U of Texas, 1982. Print.

Kampen, Nathalie B. "Between Public and Private: Women as Historical Subjects in Roman Art." *Women's History and Ancient History*. Ed. S.B. Pomeroy. Chapel Hill and London: U of North Carolina P, 1991. 218–48. Print.

Kampen, Nathalie B., with Bettina Bergmann, et al., eds. *Sexuality in Ancient Art: Near East, Egypt, Greece, and Italy*. Cambridge: Cambridge UP, 1996. Print.

Katz, A. M. "Sexuality and the Body in Ancient Greece." *Metis* 4.1 (1989): 155–79.

Kennedy, D. F. *The Arts of Love: Five Studies in the Discourse of Roman Love Elegy*. Cambridge: Cambridge UP, 1993. Print.

Keuls, Eva C. *The Reign of the Phallus: Sexual Politics in Ancient Athens*. 2nd ed. Berkeley: U of California P, 1993. Print.

Koloski-Ostrow, Ann, and Claire Lyons, eds. *Naked Truths: Women, Sexuality, and Gender in Classical Art and Archaeology*. New York: Routledge, 1997. Print.

Konstan, David. *Sexual Symmetry: Love in the Ancient Novel and Related Genres*. Princeton, NJ: Princeton UP, 1994. Print.

Konstan, David, and Martha Nussbaum, eds. *Sexuality in Greek and Roman Society*. Special Issue, *differences* 2.1. (1990). Print.

Lefkowitz, Mary, and Maureen B. Fant. *Women's Life in Greece and Rome*. 2nd ed. Baltimore, MD: Johns Hopkins UP and London: Duckworth, 1982. Print.

McGinn, T.A.J. "The Taxation of Roman Prostitutes." *Helios* 16 (1989): 79–111. Print.

Nussbaum, Martha C., and Julia Sihvola, eds. *The Sleep of Reason: Erotic Experience and Sexual Ethics in Ancient Greece and Rome*. Chicago: U of Chicago, 2002. Print.

Rabinowitz, Nancy Sorkin, and Amy Richlin, eds. *Among Women: From the Homosocial to the Homoerotic in the Ancient World*. Austin: U of Texas P, 2002. Print.

Rawson, B., ed. *Marriage, Divorce, and Children in Ancient Rome*. Oxford: Oxford UP, 1991. Print.

Rist, J. M. *Eros and Psyche: Studies in Plato, Plotinus, and Origin*. Toronto: U of Toronto P, 1964. Print.

Rouselle, Aline. *Porneia: On Desire and the Body in Antiquity*. Trans. Felicia Pheasant. London: Blackwell, 1988. Print.

Sealey, Richard. "On Lawful Concubinage in Athens." *Classical Antiquity* 3 (1984): 111–33. Print.

Sergent, Bernard. *Homosexuality in Greek Myth*. Trans. A. Goldhammer. Boston: Beacon Press, 1986. Print.

Sissa, Giulia. *Greek Virginity*. Trans. A. Goldhammer. Cambridge, MA: Harvard UP, 1990. Print.

Stehe, E. *Performance and Gender in Ancient Greece: Nondramatic Poetry in Its Setting*. Princeton, NJ: Princeton UP, 1997. Print.

Stehe, E. "Venus, Cybele, and Sabine Women: The Roman Construction of Female Sexuality." *Helios* 16.2 (1989): 143–64. Print.

Stewart, Andrew. *Art, Desire, and the Body in Ancient Greece*. Cambridge: Cambridge UP, 1997. Print.

Sussman, L. S. "The Birth of the Gods: Sexuality, Conflict and Cosmic Structure in Hesiod's *Theogony*." *Ramus* 7 (1978): 61–77. Print.

Williams, C. A. *Roman Homosexuality: Ideologies of Masculinity in Classical Antiquity*. Oxford: Oxford UP, 1999. Print.

Williams, Gordon. "Some Aspects of Roman Marriage Ceremonies and Ideals." *Journal of Roman Studies* 48 (1958): 16–32. Print.

Winkler, John J. *The Constraints of Desire: The Anthropology of Sex and Gender in Ancient Greece*. New York: Routledge, 1990. Print.

Veyne, P. *Roman Erotic Elegy: Love, Poetry, and the West.* Trans. D. Pellauer. Chicago: U of Chicago P, 1988. Print.

Zeitlin, F. I. *Playing the Other: Gender and Society in Classical Greek Literature.* Chicago: U of Chicago P, 1995. Print.

Electronic Sources

www.absoluteshakespeare.com
www.improvised.shakespeare.com
www.internetshakespeare.uvic
www.orshakes.org
www.shakespeare.com
www.shakespeareabout.com
www.shakespearedc.org
www.shakespeare-globe.org
www.shakespeareglobeusa.org
www.shakespeare.mit.edu
www.shakespeare-online.com
www.shakespeare.org
www.shakespeare.palomar.edu
www.shakespeare.santacruz.org

INDEX

About the Author

W. REGINALD RAMPONE, JR., received his undergraduate education at Washington and Lee University in Lexington, Virginia, his master's degrees at Boston College and Brown University, and his doctorate at the University of Rhode Island. He has also attended the University of Connecticut and Harvard University. Professor Rampone is very interested in early modern English drama, poetry, prose romances, feminist criticism and theory, gender criticism and theory, and New Historicism.

Recent Titles in
The Age of Shakespeare

Religion in the Age of Shakespeare
Christopher Baker

Family Life in the Age of Shakespeare
Bruce W. Young

Women in the Age of Shakespeare
Theresa D. Kemp